Serverless Computing
The Future of Cloud Infrastructure

Serverless Computing

The Future of Cloud Infrastructure

Dr. Satya Prakash Upadhyay

ARCLER
PRESS

www.arclerpress.com

Serverless Computing: The Future of Cloud Infrastructure

Dr. Satya Prakash Upadhyay

Arcler Press
4164 Lakeshore Road
Burlington, ON L7L 1A4
Canada
www.arclerpress.com
Email: orders@arclereducation.com

ISBN: 978-1-77956-419-1 (Hardcover)

ABOUT THE AUTHOR

Dr. Satya Prakash Upadhyay holds Ph.D. in Computer Science from DDU Gorakhpur University, Gorakhpur (U.P.), 2013. He has Technical/Teaching Experience (15 Years 08 Months) in DDU Gorakhpur University, Gorakhpur(UP). He has been the member of Academic/Administrative Committees. He has also participated in a large number on seminars/workshops/conferences, presented papers/keynote address and chaired technical sessions. He has authored several books. His areas of interest are Integrating University Administration with IT, Research on Pattern Recognition/Optimization of Algorithms/Big data analysis, and Innovation in Examination System.

TABLE OF CONTENTS

LIST OF FIGURES

LIST OF TABLES

PREFACE

Serverless computing has emerged as a transformative field in the IT industry over the past decade, fundamentally altering how applications are developed and deployed. By abstracting away the underlying server infrastructure, serverless computing allows developers to focus solely on writing code while the cloud provider manages the server provisioning, scaling, and maintenance. This shift has led to significant cost reductions, as users only pay for the actual compute time their code consumes, eliminating the need for pre-provisioned server capacity. Furthermore, serverless computing enhances scalability by automatically adjusting resources in response to demand, ensuring applications can handle varying workloads without manual intervention. Reduced latency is another critical advantage, as serverless platforms often deploy code closer to end-users, resulting in faster response times. The elimination of server-side management frees up developers to concentrate on innovation and feature development, rather than infrastructure concerns.

The potential of serverless computing extends beyond infrastructure optimization. Its flexibility allows for diverse applications across multiple domains, including serverless messaging, neural network training, video processing, and big data analytics. For instance, serverless messaging facilitates real-time communication without the overhead of managing messaging servers, while serverless frameworks for neural network training enable scalable machine learning workloads with minimal setup. In video processing, serverless architectures can handle the intensive computational tasks required for encoding and streaming, ensuring efficient resource use. Big data processing also benefits from serverless models, as they can dynamically allocate resources to manage large datasets and complex queries efficiently. These varied applications underscore the broad applicability and transformative potential of serverless computing, making it a valuable tool for both industry and academia.

This book aims to address these gaps by presenting state-of-the-art contributions to serverless computing. It examines into the foundational concepts, explores different platforms, and examines practical use cases, offering a holistic view of the field. By providing detailed analyses and real-world examples, this book seeks to equip developers, researchers, and IT professionals with the knowledge necessary to leverage serverless computing effectively. Through a balanced discussion of both the benefits and drawbacks, it highlights the progress made thus far and outlines the work that remains to be done.

Serverless Computing: The Future of Cloud Infrastructure is designed for a diverse audience encompassing professionals, researchers, and students in the fields of cloud computing and software development. This book is particularly valuable for IT professionals and developers who are seeking to understand and implement serverless architectures in their projects, aiming to optimize resource management, reduce operational costs, and enhance scalability. It also targets researchers and academics into the theoretical underpinnings and practical applications of serverless computing, providing insights into emerging trends and future directions in this rapidly evolving field. Additionally, technology managers and decision-makers will find the book beneficial for evaluating the strategic benefits of serverless computing and integrating these technologies into their organizational frameworks.

–Author

CHAPTER 1

SERVERLESS COMPUTING

Contents

INTRODUCTION

A cloud computing execution model known as "serverless computing" allows the cloud provider to manage the servers for their clients by allocating machine resources as needed. The term "serverless" is misleading since cloud service providers continue to use servers to run code for developers. Developers of serverless applications, on the other hand, are not concerned with virtual machines, physical servers, capacity planning, configuration, management, maintenance, fault tolerance, or scaling of containers. An application does not have any computing resources assigned to it when it is not in use. Pricing is determined by how many resources an application actually uses. It might be categorized as utility computing.

The process of putting code into production can be made simpler by serverless computing. The complexity is primarily transferred from the operations team to the development team, though it is not completely eliminated. Furthermore, managing an application becomes more difficult the more intricate it is. Code deployed in conventional ways, like microservices or monoliths, can be combined with serverless code. On the other hand, programs can be designed to be completely serverless, requiring no provisioned servers at all. This is not to be confused with networking or computer models like peer-to-peer (P2P) that operate without the need for a physical server.

According to one definition that takes these concepts into account, serverless computing is a cloud computing paradigm that includes a class of cloud computing platforms that enable the development, deployment, and operation of applications (or parts thereof) in the cloud without the need to allocate and manage virtualized servers and resources or worry about other operational details. The cloud provider assumes responsibility for operational elements like fault tolerance and the elastic scaling of computing, storage, and communication resources to meet changing application demands. Utilization-based billing is used by providers to charge cloud users at a fine granularity based on the resources (like computing time, memory, and storage space) that apps really use from the cloud infrastructure.

1.1. BASIC CONCEPT OF SERVERLESS COMPUTING

Developers can create and execute application code using the serverless computing paradigm without having to worry about setting up or maintaining back-end infrastructure or servers. No servers does not imply serverlessness. Despite the name, a cloud service provider (CSP) is in charge of managing the servers in serverless computing. The term "serverless" refers to how developers work with those servers; they are hidden from view, and they are not subject to any management or interaction. With serverless computing, developers can concentrate on creating the best front-end application code and business logic. Their application code only needs to be written, and it can be deployed to containers that are controlled by a CSP (Figure 1.1).

Figure 1.1. *Serverless computing.*

*Source: https://miro.medium.com/v2/resize:fit:2000/1*gnJscTW1yVwQ501j__ rlNg.jpeg.*

The cloud provider takes care of the rest, including all regular infrastructure management and maintenance, including operating system updates and patches, security management, capacity planning, system monitoring, and more. They also provide the cloud infrastructure needed to run the code and scale it up and down as needed. Additionally, with serverless, developers never have to pay for unused capacity.

When the code runs, the cloud provider spins up and provisions the necessary computing resources on demand. When the code stops running, it spins them back down, a process known as "scaling to zero.." Pricing is usually determined by the amount of resources needed and the duration of the execution; billing begins when the execution begins and ends when it concludes.

1.1.1. What is Serverless Computing?

A technique for delivering backend services on an as-needed basis is serverless computing. Users can write and run code without having to worry about the underlying infrastructure thanks to serverless providers. When a business uses a serverless vendor for backend services, the cost is determined by the vendor's computation; no fixed bandwidth or server count needs to be reserved or paid for because the service is auto-scaling.

Though they go by a different name, physical servers are still in use; developers do not necessarily need to be aware of this. In the early days of the internet, developing a web application required owning the expensive and clumsy physical hardware needed to run a server.

Then came cloud computing, which allowed for the remote rental of predetermined quantities of server space or numbers of servers. In order to make sure that an increase in traffic or activity won't cause their monthly allotment to be exceeded and cause their applications to malfunction, developers and businesses that rent these fixed units of server space typically overbuy. This implies that a large portion of the paid server space may be unused. In order to address this problem, cloud vendors have introduced auto-scaling models. However, even with auto-scaling, an unintentional spike in activity, like a DDoS Attack, could prove to be highly costly (Figure 1.2).

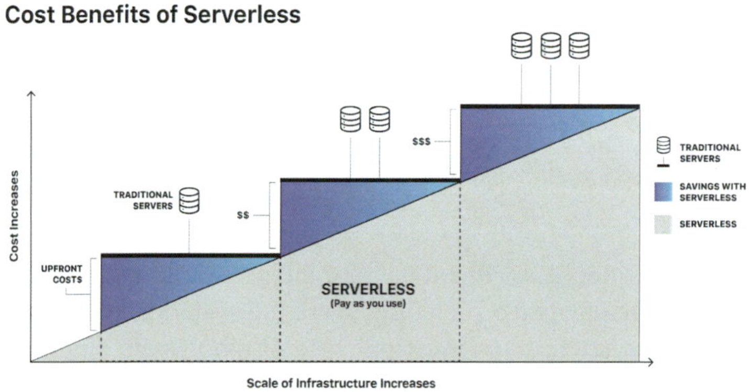

Figure 1.2. *Serverless computing is a method of providing backend services on an as-used basis.*

Source: https://cf-assets.www.cloudflare.com/slt3lc6tev37/7nyIgiecrfe9W6TfmJRpNh/dfc5434659e31300d1918d4163dfb263/benefits-of-serverless.svg.

Developers can buy backend services using serverless computing on a flexible "pay as you go" basis, which means they only have to pay for the services they really use. This is analogous to moving from a data plan for your cell phone that has a set monthly limit to one that only charges for the actual amount of data used.

Although these backend services are still provided by servers, the term "serverless" is a little misleading because the vendor manages all aspects of infrastructure and server space. Developers don't have to worry about servers at all when their work is serverless.

1.1.2. What are Backend Services? What's the Difference Between Frontend and Backend?

The two domains of application development are typically separated into the frontend and the backend. The portion of the program that users view and interact with, such as the visual design, is called the frontend. The portion of the application that is hidden from view by the user is called the backend, and it consists of the database and server hosting the user's data and business logic.

Consider, for illustration, a website that offers concert tickets. The browser sends a request to the backend server, which provides the website data in response, when a user types the address of the website into the browser window. After that, the user will see the website's front end, which may contain form fields for the user to fill out as well as text and image content. After that, the user can use one of the frontend form fields to look up their preferred musical act. The user's click of "submit" will cause the backend to receive another request. In order to determine whether a performer with this name exists, when they will play next, and how many tickets are available, the backend code queries its database. The frontend will then present the outcomes in a way that makes sense to the user after receiving the data from the backend. Similar to this, there will be additional back-and-forth communication between the frontend and backend when the user registers and provides payment details to purchase the tickets (Figure 1.3).

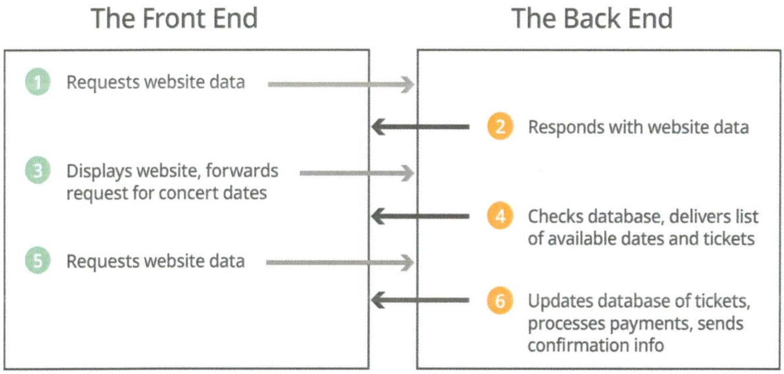

Figure 1.3. *The difference between frontend and backend.*

Source: https://www.cloudflare.com/img/learning/serverless/what-is-serverless/frontend-vs-backend.svg.

1.1.2.1. How Does Serverless Compare to Other Cloud Backend Models?

A couple of technologies that are often conflated with serverless computing are Backend-as-a-Service and Platform-as-a-Service. Although they share similarities, these models do not necessarily meet the requirements of serverless.

- **Backend-as-a-service (BaaS)** is a service model where a cloud provider offers backend services such as data storage, so that developers can focus on writing front-end code. But while serverless applications are event-driven and run on the edge, BaaS applications may not meet either of these requirements.

- **Platform-as-a-service (PaaS)** is a model where developers essentially rent all the necessary tools to develop and deploy applications from a cloud provider, including things like operating systems and middleware. However, PaaS applications are not as easily scalable as serverless applications. PaaS also don't necessarily run on the edge and often have a noticeable startup delay that isn't present in serverless applications.
- **Infrastructure-as-a-service (IaaS)** is a catchall term for cloud vendors hosting infrastructure on behalf of their customers. IaaS providers may offer serverless functionality, but the terms are not synonymous.

1.1.2.2. What is Next for Serverless?

As serverless providers find ways to get around some of the problems with serverless computing, the technology continues to advance. Cold starts are one of these disadvantages. In order to conserve energy and prevent over-provisioning, the provider usually turns off a serverless function that hasn't been used in a long. The serverless provider will have to spin it up again and begin hosting that function the next time a user runs an application that calls it. The term "cold start" refers to the substantial latency that this startup period adds. Once the function is operational, subsequent requests will be fulfilled much more quickly (warm starts).

However, the function will revert to dormant state after an extended period of inactivity. This implies that the subsequent user who makes that function request will encounter a cold start. Cold starts were thought to be an inevitable trade-off when utilizing serverless functions until quite recently.

1.1.3. How Does Serverless Computing Work?

When creating applications, developers typically have a number of additional server management responsibilities to complete before their code can be deployed. These responsibilities include specifying processing and storage resources, load balancing, patching, and more. Development teams become slower as a result of all of these extra items, which also increase operational overhead and lengthen provisioning times. The goal of serverless computing is to give developers an invisible "serverless" experience, freeing them from having to worry about servers or anything else that an application might require to function. Rather, the service provider takes care of everything in the background to guarantee that you have enough resources to run your code and fulfill requirements without having to pay for unused capacity. Developers can avoid managing cloud machine instances by utilizing serverless computing. Rather than requiring them to configure or maintain the servers, they can run code on cloud servers.

Instead of using pre-purchased capacity units, pricing is determined by the actual amount of resources used by an application. When developers host their apps on cloud-based virtual servers, they usually have to install operating systems on those servers, maintain them, keep an eye on them, and update their software all the time.

Developers can write a function in their preferred programming language and upload it to a serverless platform using a serverless model. The function is mapped to an application programming interface (API) endpoint by the cloud service provider, who also handles the software and infrastructure management. Function instances are transparently scaled on demand.

1.1.3.1. Here's a Simple Analogy to Make it Easier to Understand How Serverless Computing Works

Compare serverless computing to delivering water to your house. Digging a well for yourself, testing the water quality, installing and maintaining all the external plumbing required to run it into the house are all doable tasks. You can also connect to the main water supply in your city. Simply turn on the water faucet to get as much water as you need when you need it. The city bills you each month based on how much water you actually use. In a similar vein, cloud providers automatically spin up the runtime environments and infrastructure resources required to run your serverless apps, and when the execution is finished, they automatically scale back down to zero. Usually, the resources used during the execution period determine how much you are charged. But this can change based on the vendor and the service.

1.1.4. The Serverless Ecosystem

1.1.4.1. Serverless and FaaS

Function as a service (FaaS), a cloud computing service that lets developers run code or containers in response to particular events or requests without having to specify or manage the infrastructure needed to run the code, is just one aspect of serverless computing. The compute model at the heart of serverless computing is FaaS, and the two terms are frequently used synonymously.

In contrast to FaaS, serverless refers to a full stack of services whose provisioning, management, and billing are taken care of by the cloud provider and are hidden from developers. These services can react to specific events or requests and scale to zero when not in use. These services include databases and storage, event-driven architecture, and application programming interface (API) gateways in addition to FaaS.

1.1.4.2. Serverless Databases and Storage

The data layer is built on databases (both SQL and NoSQL) and storage, especially object storage. Moving away from provisioning instances with defined capacity, connection, and query limits and toward pricing and infrastructure models that scale linearly with demand is a key component of a serverless approach to these technologies.

In the past few years, a number of serverless databases have been developed. By extending the serverless execution model to the RDBMS, these systems do away with the requirement to scale or provision physical or virtualized database hardware. An existing RDBMS like Oracle, MariaDB, PostgreSQL, or Microsoft SQL Server can be converted into a serverless service with Nutanix's Era solution. Based on MySQL and PostgreSQL, Amazon Aurora provides a serverless version of its databases with auto-scaling configurations that are available on demand. Azure Data Lake is an analytics and data storage solution that is extremely scalable.

Microsoft's public cloud, Azure, is where the service is housed. Customers can pay for only the services they use with Azure Data Lake Analytics because it offers a distributed infrastructure that can dynamically allocate or de-allocate resources.

The Autonomous Transaction Processing service, a serverless variant of Oracle Autonomous Database, is provided by Oracle Cloud. There is a JSON version of the serverless service as well. Google also owns Firebase, which comes with fixed and pay-as-you-go plans and a hierarchical database.

1.1.4.3. API Gateways

API gateways act as proxies to web application actions and provide HTTP method routing, client ID and secrets, rate limits, CORS, viewing API usage, viewing response logs and API sharing policies.

1.1.4.4. Serverless and Event-Driven Architecture

For event-driven and stream-processing workloads, such as the open-source Apache Kafka event streaming platform, serverless architectures are well suited.

Stateless in nature, automated serverless functions are made to manage discrete events. These features are now fundamental to event-driven architecture (EDA), a software design paradigm centered on the recording, storing, processing, and publication of events. Within an EDA framework, event consumers receive real-time event notifications from event producers (such as microservices, APIs, and Internet of Things devices), which trigger particular processing routines. For instance, when a new Netflix original series is released, a number of EDA services wait for word of the release before informing users through a series of updates. Event-driven architecture is used by numerous other businesses that are centered around user-facing online and mobile applications (such as Uber, DoorDash, and Instacart).

1.1.4.5. Serverless Versus Paas, Containers and VMs

Because serverless, platform as a service (PaaS), containers and virtual machines (VMs) all play a critical role in the cloud application development and compute ecosystem, it's helpful to measure how serverless compares to the others across some key attributes.

- **Provisioning time:** Measured in milliseconds for serverless versus minutes to hours for the other models.
- **Administrative burden:** None for serverless, compared to a continuum from light to medium to heavy for PaaS, containers and VMs, respectively.
- **Maintenance:** Serverless architectures are managed 100% by CSPs. The same is true for PaaS, but containers and VMs require significant maintenance, including updating and managing operating systems, container images, connections and so on.
- **Scaling:** Autoscaling, including autoscaling to zero, is instant and inherent for serverless. The other models offer automatic but slow scaling that requires careful tuning of autoscaling rules and no scaling to zero.
- **Capacity planning:** None is needed for serverless. The other models require a mix of automatic scalability and capacity planning.
- **Statelessness:** Inherent for serverless, which means scalability is never a problem; state is maintained in an external service or resource. PaaS, containers and VMs can use HTTP, keep an open socket or connection for long periods and store state in memory between calls.
- **High availability (HA) and disaster recovery (DR):** Serverless offers both high availability and disaster recovery with no extra effort

or extra cost. The other models require extra cost and management effort. Infrastructure can be restarted automatically with VMs and containers.

- **Resource utilization:** Serverless is 100% efficient because there is no idle capacity—it is invoked only upon request. All other models feature at least some degree of idle capacity.
- **Billing and savings:** Serverless is metered in units of 100 milliseconds. PaaS, containers and VMs are typically metered by the hour or the minute.

1.1.4.6. Serverless, Kubernetes and Knative

An open-source platform for container orchestration called Kubernetes automates the deployment, scaling, and management of containers. The creation of containerized apps is made incredibly easier by this automation. Containers are a common way to deploy serverless applications.

But Kubernetes can only run serverless apps on its own when combined with specialized software that links Kubernetes to the serverless platform of a particular cloud provider. An open-source serverless framework for Kubernetes is offered by Knative.

It allows any container, built around a serverless function or some other application code (like microservices), to run as a serverless workload on any cloud platform running Kubernetes. In order to enable serverless execution, native abstracts away the code and manages event triggers, network routing, and autoscaling. Knative offers developers transparency. Kubernetes is used to build the container, and Knative handles the rest, executing the container as a serverless workload.

1.1.5. Pros and Cons of Serverless

1.1.5.1. Pros

Serverless computing offers individual developers and enterprise development teams many technical and business benefits:

- **Improved developer productivity:** As noted, serverless enables development teams to focus on writing code, not managing infrastructure. It gives developers more time to innovate and optimize their front-end application functions and business logic.
- **Pay for execution only:** The meter starts when the request is made and ends when execution finishes. Compare this to the IaaS compute

model, where customers pay for the physical servers, VMs and other resources required to run applications, from when they provision those resources until they explicitly decommission them.

- **Develop in any language:** Serverless is a polyglot environment that enables developers to code in any language or framework—Java, Python, JavaScript, node.js—that they're comfortable with.
- **Streamlined development or DevOps cycles:** Serverless simplifies deployment and, in a larger sense, simplifies DevOps because developers don't spend time defining the infrastructure required to integrate, test, deliver and deploy code builds into production.
- **Cost-effective performance:** For specific workloads (e.g., embarrassingly parallel processing, stream processing, specific data processing tasks), serverless computing can be both faster and more cost-effective than other forms of compute.
- **Reduce latency:** In a serverless environment, code can run closer to the end user, decreasing latency.
- **Usage visibility:** Serverless platforms provide near-total visibility into system and user times and can aggregate usage information systematically.

1.1.5.2. Cons

While serverless has many advantages, it's essential to consider some disadvantages:

- **Less control:** In a serverless setting, an organization hands server control over to a third-party CSP, thus relinquishing the management of hardware and execution environments.
- **Vendor lock-in:** Each service provider offers unique serverless capabilities and features that are incompatible with other vendors.
- **Slow startup:** Also known as "cold start," slow startup can affect the performance and responsiveness of serverless applications, particularly in real-time demand environments.
- **Complex testing and debugging:** Debugging can be more complicated with a serverless computing model as developers lack visibility into back-end processes.
- **Higher cost for running long applications:** Serverless execution models are not designed to execute code for extended periods. Therefore, long-running processes can cost more than traditional dedicated server or VM environments.

1.1.5.3. Serverless and security

According to a shared responsibility model, the client is also in charge of protecting the application code and data, even though CSPs offer security controls to manage serverless applications. Serverless cloud security measures encompass automated security policies and solutions such as identity and access management (IAM), threat detection and response, and security information and event management (SIEM). Development teams can improve serverless technology security by adhering to DevSecOps procedures. The term "DevSecOps" refers to the practice of developing applications by automating the integration of security and security procedures at each stage of the software development lifecycle, including initial design, integration, testing, delivery, and deployment.

1.1.6. Advantages

1.1.6.1. Cost

Serverless computing has the potential to be more economical than buying or leasing a set number of servers, which typically entails large stretches of idle or underutilized time. Because of the more effective bin-packing of the underlying machine resources, it may even prove to be more economical than setting up an autoscaling group. This is also known as "bare-code" or pay-as-you-go computing because there are no additional costs for idle time—instead, charges are made only for the time and memory used to execute code. Here, a useful comparison is made between ride-sharing services like Uber and Lyft (serverless computing) and rental cars (traditional cloud virtual machines). The absence of running costs, such as licensing, installation, dependencies, and labor costs for patching, maintenance, and support, is what results in immediate cost benefits.

1.1.6.2. Elasticity Versus Scalability

Furthermore, because the cloud provider handles scaling the capacity in response to demand, developers and operators can avoid spending time configuring and fine-tuning autoscaling policies or systems when using a serverless architecture. From prototype to production to planet-scale, as Google puts it. Cloud native systems are not scalable; instead, they are referred to as elastic because they can scale up and down on their own. The boundaries between software development and hardware engineering are becoming less clear, and small teams of developers can now run code independently without relying on teams of infrastructure and support engineers. More developers are also becoming proficient in DevOps.

1.1.6.3. Productivity

The code segments that are visible to the outside world when using function as a service are straightforward event-driven functions. This makes writing back-end software development easier because the programmer usually does not have to worry about multithreading or directly handling HTTP requests in their code.

1.1.7. Disadvantages

Serverless applications are prone to fallacies of distributed computing. In addition, they are prone to following fallacies:

- Versioning is simple
- Compensating transactions always work
- Observability is optional

1.1.7.1. Performance

Code that is deployed as serverless and used infrequently could experience higher response latency than code that runs constantly on a virtual machine, dedicated server, or container. This is because the cloud provider usually spins down the serverless code completely when it's not in use, unlike with autoscaling. This indicates that there will be extra latency if the runtime (such as the Java runtime) takes a long time to start up. In serverless computing, this is known as cold start.

1.1.7.2. Resource Limits

Because of the resource restrictions placed by cloud providers, serverless computing is not appropriate for all computing workloads, including high-performance computing. Moreover, it is probably less expensive to bulk-provision the number of servers that are thought to be needed at any given time. Because of this, implementing sophisticated applications (like those with a directed acyclic graph of functions) is difficult; serverless computing is best suited for the execution of single stateless functions out of the box. This difficulty is intended to be lessened by certain commercial products, such as Microsoft's Azure Durable Functions and Amazon's AWS Step Functions.

1.1.7.3. Monitoring and Debugging

Since functions can be timed in their entirety, diagnosing issues related to performance or excessive resource usage with serverless code may be more challenging than with traditional server code because more information cannot usually be obtained by attaching profilers, debuggers, or APM tools. Additionally, the code's execution environment is usually not open source, making it impossible to precisely duplicate its performance in a local setting.

1.1.7.4. Security

Serverless applications are susceptible to insecure code, some serverless-specific attacks (such as Denial of Wallet), and variations on classic attacks, according to OWASP. Thus, the threats have evolved, and preventing attacks now necessitates a mental adjustment. It's a common misconception that serverless architectures are less secure than traditional ones. While this is partially true—the cloud provider handles OS vulnerabilities—the overall attack surface is much greater because, in contrast to traditional architectures, the application consists of many more components, each of which serves as a point of entry for the serverless application. Additionally, because customers are unable to install and control security solutions like intrusion detection/prevention systems (IDS/IPS) at the endpoint and network level, they lose all relevance in protecting their cloud workloads. The mono-culture characteristics of the entire server network exacerbate this. (One weakness can be applied worldwide. Protego asserts that a close collaboration between developers, DevOps, and AppSec—also referred to as DevSecOps—is the key to securing serverless apps. Strike a balance so that developers are not exempt from responsibility but also do not own security. Make it everyone's problem by taking action. Form cross-functional teams and strive for close coordination between development teams and security experts. Work together to enable your company to quickly address security threats with serverless technology.

1.1.7.5. Privacy

Public cloud environments that are proprietary are the foundation of many serverless function environments. Some privacy implications, like shared resources and access by outside employees, need to be taken into account in this situation. However, serverless computing can also be carried out on-site or in a private cloud environment using the Kubernetes platform, for example. Like hosting on conventional servers, this grants businesses complete control over privacy measures.

1.1.7.6. Standards

The International Data Center Authority (IDCA) addresses serverless computing in their Framework AE360. But when transferring business logic from one public cloud to another, portability concerns may arise. This is why the Docker solution was developed. Along with Oracle, the Cloud Native Computing Foundation (CNCF) is creating a specification.

1.1.7.7. Vendor Lock-In

The service of serverless computing is offered by a third party. Software and apps that operate in a serverless environment are by nature restricted to a single cloud provider. Because serverless computing involves a higher degree of abstraction, public vendors only permit users to upload code to a FaaS platform; they do not have the ability to modify the underlying environments, which exacerbates this problem. More importantly, a Backend-as-a-Service (BaaS) offering can usually only natively trigger a FaaS offering from the same provider in a more complex workflow. Because of this, serverless computing workload migration is practically impossible.

1.2. ROLE OF SERVERLESS COMPUTING IN DIGITAL TRANSFORMATION

A significant component of the digital transformation is serverless computing. First of all, it makes developers more productive by allowing them to concentrate on creating code with business value rather than worrying about the infrastructure that will support it. By removing management overhead, a serverless computing approach can help boost developer productivity regardless of vertical industry or company size (Figure 1.4).

Features of a serverless computing software development environment include the following:

- zero server management;
- autoscaling to meet changing traffic demands; and
- managed integrated security.

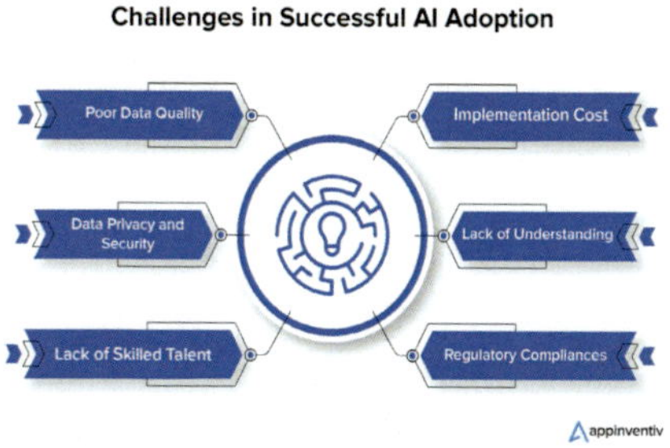

Figure 1.4. *The role of cloud in digital transformation.*

Source: https://appinventiv.com/wp-content/uploads/2022/09/Info_3-2.webp.

1.2.1. What to Look for in a Serverless Architecture

Businesses should search for serverless platforms that enable them to create applications from start to finish, utilizing services from messaging, databases, storage, machine learning, data analytics, and smart assistants. While selecting a serverless architecture, it's crucial to take into account the potential additional complications that some serverless cloud services may bring, such as limited runtimes or vendor lock-in. Some serverless cloud services do offer scalability and cost savings.

Developers frequently have to choose between the portability and flexibility of containers and the simplicity and speed of serverless computing. Because of this, most businesses find that a full-stack strategy works better than restricting serverless to compute tasks.

1.2.2. Serverless Computing Vendors and Languages

The major serverless computing vendors include the following:

- **Google Cloud Functions.** Released by Google in 2017, it supports Node.js, JavaScript, Python and Go, but allows for unlimited execution time for functions. Google Cloud Functions can also interact with many other Google services, enabling developers to quickly create and manage complex enterprise-class applications with almost no consideration of the underlying servers.
- **IBM Cloud Functions.** Based on Apache OpenWhisk, it supports JavaScript (Node.js), Swift and Cloudflare Workers, which runs functions written in JavaScript and any language that can be compiled to WebAssembly.
- **Amazon Web Services (AWS) Lambda.** Introduced in 2014, it's a function as a service (FaaS) offering from AWS. AWS Lambda functions can be written in Java, Go, PowerShell, Node.js, JavaScript, C#, Python and Ruby.
- **Microsoft Azure Functions.** Microsoft rolled out Azure Functions in 2016 to compete with AWS Lambda. It supports Bash, Batch, C#, F#, Java, JavaScript (Node.js), PHP, PowerShell, Python and TypeScript.
- **Cloudflare Workers.** Released in 2018, Cloudflare Workers combines edge computing with the FaaS model. It supports JavaScript and WebAssembly-compatible languages.
- **Netlify Functions.** Rolled out in 2018, Netlify Functions, which is built on top of AWS Lambda, lets developers deploy server-side

code as API endpoints. Developers can write functions in JavaScript, TypeScript and Go.

- **Vercel Serverless Functions.** Vercel Serverless Functions aims to simplify the serverless experience for web app developers. It supports Node.js, Go, Python and Ruby.
- **Oracle Functions.** Released in 2019, Oracle Functions integrates with Oracle Cloud Infrastructure, platform services and SaaS applications. Oracle Functions is based on the open source Fn Project. It supports Java, Python, Node.js, Go, Ruby and C#; for advanced use cases, developers can bring their own Dockerfiles and GraalVM.

1.2.3. Development Tools

There are numerous third-party vendor tools developers can use when they're working with serverless computing, including the following:

- **LambCI.** A package that can be uploaded to AWS Lambda to bring CI to serverless.
- **Dashbird.** A monitoring, debugging and intelligence platform to help developers build, operate, improve and scale apps on AWS.
- **Sls-dev-tools.** A set of open source tools that make it easy for developers to interact with their serverless functions.
- **Serverless-iam-roles-per-function.** An open source tool that lets developers easily and quickly define access roles for different serverless functions.
- **Thundra.** A platform that enables developers to monitor, debug and test their serverless applications.

1.2.3.1. Future of Serverless Computing

According to a report by Mordor Intelligence, the global serverless computing market is predicted to grow by more than 23.17 percent between 2021 and 2026.

According to the report, the market is growing as a result of companies being able to integrate a serverless environment thanks to advancements in computing technology.

The advantages of serverless computing, including its inherent scalability and ease of development and deployment, are contributing significantly to the technology's quick uptake and market expansion.

1.3. SERVERLESS FRAMEWORKS

The development, deployment, and management of serverless applications on a variety of cloud platforms are made much easier by serverless frameworks. With the help of these frameworks, developers can concentrate on developing application logic rather than managing infrastructure by abstracting away the difficulties involved in handling deployment workflows and configuring serverless resources.

The Serverless Framework, an open-source program that works with several cloud providers like AWS, Azure, Google Cloud, and others, is one of the most well-known serverless frameworks. Using a configuration file (serverless), it provides a declarative method for defining serverless functions, APIs, event sources, and infrastructure resources. yml). Developers can easily and succinctly specify functions, events, environment variables, and other settings with this YAML-based configuration.

The provisioning of required cloud resources is automated by the Serverless Framework, which streamlines the deployment process. Common serverless use cases that are supported by it include scheduled functions, background processing tasks, RESTful APIs, and more intricate workflows that involve several services. Furthermore, by integrating with CI/CD pipelines, it facilitates continuous integration workflows and automated deployments, which optimize the development lifecycle (Figure 1.5).

Figure 1.5. *Best serverless frameworks.*

Source: https://media.geeksforgeeks.org/wp-content/uploads/20240428004529/Serverless-Frameworks-You-Must-Now.png.

AWS SAM (Serverless Application Model), a specialized framework made for AWS Lambda and other AWS services, is another noteworthy serverless framework. AWS's infrastructure-as-code service, CloudFormation, is enhanced by SAM, which adds serverless application-specific shorthand notation and streamlined syntax. Using SAM templates, it facilitates the definition of serverless functions, API endpoints, event sources, permissions, and resource dependencies. yaml). For the purpose of creating and implementing serverless apps on Azure, Azure Functions offers its own serverless framework. With its seamless integration with other Azure services and support for multiple programming languages, developers can use triggers and bindings to create event-driven applications. The Azure Functions Core Tools can be used to develop and test Azure Functions locally. The Azure portal, Azure CLI, or CI/CD pipelines can be used to deploy Azure Functions to Azure. A framework for developing serverless apps on Google Cloud Platform is also provided by Google Cloud Functions. With its support for numerous programming languages and integrations with other Google Cloud services, developers can create scalable apps that react to HTTP requests and cloud events. Cloud Build or other CI/CD tools can help with automated deployments, and Google Cloud Console can be used to manage and monitor Google Cloud Functions.

The serverless frameworks abstract away the complexity of managing cloud infrastructure, making it easier to develop and implement serverless applications. In order to promote quicker development cycles, lower operational overhead, and better scalability, they give developers the tools and abstractions they need to define, deploy, and manage serverless functions and applications across various cloud platforms. These frameworks are essential to helping developers take advantage of serverless architecture and effectively create contemporary, event-driven applications as serverless computing develops.

1.3.1. Tools like Serverless Framework, AWS SAM (Serverless Application Model), and Others.

The development and deployment of serverless applications across various cloud platforms, especially AWS, are made easier by tools like the Serverless Framework and AWS SAM (Serverless Application Model). An open-source framework called the Serverless Framework supports a number of cloud service providers, such as Google Cloud Platform, AWS, and Azure. It frees developers from the burden of managing deployments and configuring serverless resources, enabling them to concentrate on developing application logic.

Key features include:

- **Declarative Configuration:** Applications are defined using a serverless.yml file, which specifies functions, events (e.g., HTTP requests, timers), environment variables, and other resources.
- **Multi-Provider Support:** Supports deployment to AWS Lambda, Azure Functions, Google Cloud Functions, and other providers, enabling developers to use a single framework across different environments.

- **Plugin Ecosystem:** Extensible through plugins that enhance functionality, such as additional deployment targets, monitoring tools integration, and custom workflows.
- **Integration with CI/CD:** Integrates seamlessly with CI/CD pipelines, enabling automated deployments and continuous integration workflows.

1.3.1.1. AWS SAM (Serverless Application Model)

AWS SAM is a framework specifically designed for building serverless applications on AWS. It extends AWS CloudFormation with simplified syntax and shorthand notation tailored for serverless resources. Key features include:

- **CloudFormation Integration:** Uses CloudFormation templates (template.yaml) to define serverless resources such as Lambda functions, API Gateway endpoints, DynamoDB tables, and more.
- **Local Development:** Supports local development and testing of Lambda functions using the AWS SAM CLI, which provides a local environment similar to AWS.
- **Resource Management:** Simplifies resource management and dependencies, allowing developers to define application architecture and resources in a structured way.
- **Deployment:** Facilitates deployment to AWS using the AWS CLI or directly from AWS CloudFormation, ensuring consistency and reproducibility in deployments.

1.3.1.2. Other Serverless Tools

Apart from Serverless Framework and AWS SAM, there are other notable tools and frameworks in the serverless ecosystem:

- **Azure Functions:** Microsoft's serverless framework for building and deploying functions on Azure, supporting multiple programming languages and integrations with other Azure services.
- **Google Cloud Functions:** Google's serverless framework for building functions that respond to cloud events, integrating with Google Cloud services and supporting multiple programming languages.
- **Terraform:** While not exclusively for serverless, Terraform is an infrastructure-as-code tool that supports serverless resources across different cloud providers, providing flexibility and automation in managing cloud infrastructure.

Together, these tools help to standardize and simplify the process of developing serverless applications, giving developers the confidence to adopt serverless architectures, increase productivity, and take advantage of cloud-native features in a variety of settings. These tools are essential for boosting the uptake and scalability of serverless apps in contemporary cloud environments as serverless computing develops further.

1.3.2. How these Frameworks Simplify Deployment and Management of Serverless Applications

Serverless frameworks such as Serverless Framework and AWS SAM (Serverless Application Model) simplify the deployment and management of serverless applications in several key ways:

- **Declarative Configuration:** Both frameworks utilize declarative configuration files (serverless.yml for Serverless Framework and template.yaml for AWS SAM) to define the resources and services required by the application. Developers specify functions, event sources, permissions, environment variables, and other configurations in a structured format. This approach abstracts away the complexities of manually configuring and managing individual resources, providing a clear and consistent definition of the application architecture.
- **Abstraction of Infrastructure Complexity:** Serverless frameworks abstract the underlying infrastructure management tasks, such as provisioning servers, networking, and scaling. Developers do not need to concern themselves with server provisioning or capacity planning, as these tasks are handled automatically by the cloud provider based on the defined configurations.
- **Cross-Platform Compatibility:** Both Serverless Framework and AWS SAM support deployment across multiple cloud providers (AWS, Azure, Google Cloud, etc.), offering a consistent development and deployment experience. Developers can write their serverless applications using a single framework and deploy them to different cloud environments without rewriting code or adapting configurations extensively.
- **Automation of Deployment Workflows:** These frameworks integrate seamlessly with continuous integration and continuous deployment (CI/CD) pipelines. They provide plugins and command-line tools that enable automated deployment workflows, including testing, building, packaging, and deploying serverless

applications. This automation reduces manual effort and ensures consistent deployments across development, testing, and production environments.

- **Local Development and Testing:** Both Serverless Framework and AWS SAM support local development and testing of serverless functions. Developers can emulate cloud environments locally using tools like the AWS SAM CLI, which simulates AWS Lambda and API Gateway locally. This capability accelerates the development cycle by enabling rapid iteration and debugging without the need for frequent deployments to the cloud.
- **Resource Orchestration and Dependency Management:** AWS SAM extends AWS CloudFormation, providing simplified syntax and constructs specifically tailored for serverless applications. This integration facilitates resource orchestration and dependency management within the application stack. Developers can define and manage dependencies between different resources (e.g., Lambda functions, DynamoDB tables, S3 buckets) using CloudFormation templates, ensuring consistent and reliable deployments.
- **Monitoring and Logging Integration:** Serverless frameworks often include integrations with monitoring and logging services, such as AWS CloudWatch, Azure Monitor, or Google Cloud Logging. Developers can monitor function execution, track performance metrics, and analyze logs directly from the framework's interface or through integrations with third-party tools. This visibility into application behavior helps in debugging issues, optimizing performance, and ensuring operational efficiency.

By abstracting infrastructure complexities, offering automated deployment workflows, supporting cross-platform compatibility, facilitating local development and testing, orchestrating resources, and integrating with monitoring and logging services, these frameworks essentially make it easier to deploy and manage serverless applications. By utilizing these frameworks, developers can concentrate more on business requirements and application logic, as the frameworks take care of the complex management and deployment of cloud infrastructure.

1.3.3. Serverless Application Design Patterns

Developers can optimize performance, scalability, and cost-effectiveness in serverless architectures by following serverless application design patterns, which are strategies and best practices. These patterns make use of the special features of serverless computing, like auto-scaling, event-driven processing, and pay-per-execution pricing, to create applications that are reliable and effective.

The Function-as-a-Service (FaaS) pattern is a popular design pattern in which separate functions carry out particular tasks in response to events that are triggered by external sources. By dividing applications into tiny, loosely coupled functions that communicate via lightweight messaging or event triggers, this pattern supports microservices architecture. It allows developers to optimize resource utilization and minimize overhead by allowing each function to scale independently based on demand.

Serverless application design patterns are strategies or templates for structuring serverless applications to leverage the benefits of serverless computing effectively. Here are some common serverless design patterns:

1. **Event-driven processing**: This pattern involves triggering functions (or serverless services) in response to events from various sources such as HTTP requests, message queues, or database changes. Examples include processing image uploads, handling API requests, or responding to IoT device data.
2. **Microservices**: Serverless architectures are well-suited for implementing microservices. Each microservice is encapsulated in a function that handles a specific task, promoting modularity and scalability.
3. **Backend-as-a-Service (BaaS)**: Using third-party services (e.g., authentication, database, storage) to handle backend functionalities, allowing developers to focus on business logic. Examples include AWS Cognito for authentication and DynamoDB for NoSQL database needs.
4. **Data processing pipelines**: Build pipelines for processing and transforming data. Functions are triggered sequentially or in parallel to handle data from sources like logs, IoT devices, or data streams.
5. **Static website hosting**: Use serverless services to host static websites, leveraging services like AWS S3 for storage and AWS CloudFront for content delivery. Functions can handle dynamic aspects like form submissions or user authentication.
6. **Scheduled tasks**: Implement functions triggered by time-based events (e.g., cron jobs) to automate tasks such as data backups, report generation, or system maintenance.
7. **IoT backends**: Manage IoT device data streams using serverless services. Functions process incoming data, store it in databases, and trigger alerts or notifications based on predefined rules.

8. **File and data processing**: Functions can handle file uploads, process data from different sources, and store results in databases or cloud storage.
9. **RESTful APIs**: Create scalable APIs using serverless functions, integrating with API Gateway to manage endpoints and route requests to appropriate functions. This pattern is commonly used for building web services and backend systems.
10. **State machine workflows**: Implement complex workflows using serverless state machines (e.g., AWS Step Functions), coordinating the execution of multiple functions and managing state transitions based on outcomes.

These patterns leverage the elasticity, cost-efficiency, and scalability benefits of serverless computing while addressing various application requirements and use cases. Each pattern can be combined or customized based on specific application needs and cloud provider capabilities.

1.3.4. Serverless and Microservices

Despite their differences, serverless computing and microservices architectures are two contemporary paradigms that frequently come together to produce extremely scalable and effective cloud applications. The goal of serverless computing is to completely abstract away infrastructure management, as demonstrated by services like AWS Lambda and Azure Functions. Programmers create functions that are called in response to various events, like file uploads, database updates, and HTTP requests.

In order to maximize cost efficiency, this model offers auto-scaling and pay-per-use pricing, in which resources are dynamically allocated and scaled down to zero when idle. For microservices and event-driven apps that need fast development cycles and can benefit from granular scaling based on demand, serverless computing is perfect.

Conversely, microservices break down applications into discrete, standalone services that exchange data through APIs. Every microservice can be developed, deployed, and scaled independently, with an emphasis on particular business capabilities. Teams can innovate and iterate more quickly thanks to this architecture's promotion of modularity, agility, and resilience. Microservices work well in complex applications where various system components have distinct resource requirements and need to be managed separately.

Microservices and serverless technologies work best together when combined. In a microservices architecture, serverless functions can be used to manage particular workflows or tasks, like data processing or external integrations. They enable quick development cycles and lower operational overhead by offering a lightweight execution model for transient tasks inside microservices.

Using serverless functions, event-driven communication between microservices can effectively manage asynchronous processing while preserving loose coupling and scalability. But there are some issues that must be carefully considered, like handling cold starts, or the initial latency when calling serverless functions, and state management.

Furthermore, combining several microservices and serverless services may result in greater complexity and possible vendor lock-in. In conclusion, utilizing serverless computing in a microservices architecture is a compelling way to create contemporary cloud-native apps that can satisfy a variety of business needs because it provides flexibility, scalability, and cost-effectiveness.

1.4. FUTURE TRENDS IN SERVERLESS COMPUTING

With regard to the future, serverless computing is expected to develop further due to both changing business requirements and technology breakthroughs. A few major themes will probably influence how serverless computing develops in the future. The spread of serverless beyond conventional cloud environments is one noteworthy trend. Edge computing is becoming more popular. It involves placing computing power closer to the end user or the source of data.

Because serverless architectures can easily scale in response to demand and can handle spikes in workloads with efficiency, they are a great fit for edge computing. For applications that need to process data in real-time, like mobile and Internet of Things applications, this trend offers quicker response times and lower latency. Furthermore, another significant trend is the fusion of container and serverless technologies. Serverless computing removes the need for managing infrastructure, while containers provide a consistent method for deploying and packaging apps.

Serverless capabilities are already being integrated with container orchestration by platforms such as AWS Fargate and Azure Container Instances, giving developers more freedom to run more complex workloads serverless. By utilizing a hybrid approach, organizations can optimize resource utilization and deployment efficiency by utilizing the advantages of both serverless and containers (Figure 1.6).

Furthermore, serverless AI and machine learning (ML) are becoming interesting use cases. Serverless platforms simplify operations and shorten time-to-market for AI-driven applications by allowing developers to deploy machine learning models and AI inference tasks without having to manage underlying infrastructure. Applications like fraud detection, customized recommendations, and autonomous systems that need real-time data processing and predictive analytics will find great potential in this trend. Moreover, stateful and event-driven applications are using serverless architectures more and more.

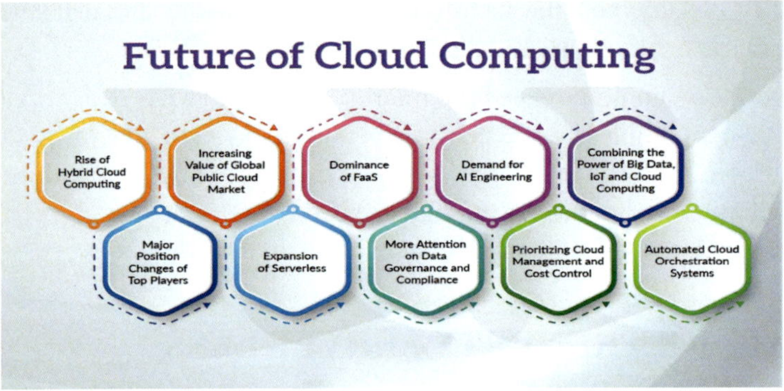

Figure 1.6. *Serverless computing: key advantages and future trends.*

Source: https://www.codewithfaraz.com/thumbnails/future-trends-in-serverless-computing.webp.

The difficulties of maintaining state and guaranteeing data consistency in serverless environments are being addressed by advancements in serverless databases and state management services. With the advantages of serverless scalability and cost-efficiency, these developments allow developers to create more complex applications, like real-time collaborative tools and event-driven workflows.

Finally, one important trend in the serverless space is the continuous focus on enhancing the developer experience and tooling. Improved monitoring and debugging capabilities, better workflow integration (e.g., Key areas of development include CI/CD pipelines, management interface simplification, and more. With these developments, developers will be able to concentrate more on application logic and less on infrastructure management, thereby lowering the learning curve associated with the adoption of serverless computing.

With advancements in edge computing, containerization, AI/ML integration, stateful applications, and developer tools, serverless computing has a bright and diverse future ahead of it. With serverless architectures becoming more and more popular among enterprises due to their affordability, scalability, and agility, these trends will influence the direction of serverless development and open up new avenues for contemporary application development and implementation.

1.4.1. Edge Computing and Serverless

The paradigms of edge computing and serverless computing are complementary and are transforming the way applications are developed, implemented, and overseen in contemporary computing settings. Edge computing lowers latency and speeds up response times for applications that need to process data in real-time by locating computing resources closer to the source of data. This strategy is essential for autonomous systems, Internet of Things devices, and applications that require quick decision-making.

Conversely, serverless computing relieves developers of the burden of managing infrastructure. Small, event-triggered functions that run in response to things like HTTP requests or database updates make up an application. Serverless platforms charge users only for the resources used when executing functions; they automatically handle scaling and provisioning. This model is perfect for microservices architectures and applications with erratic workloads because it provides scalability, cost-efficiency, and decreased operational overhead.

Combining serverless and edge computing allows for the effective use of each technology's advantages in solving difficult problems in distributed, latency-sensitive settings. Organizations can maximize resource utilization and attain extremely low latency responses by implementing serverless functions at the edge.

This integration facilitates event-driven architectures, in which events generated by edge devices cause serverless functions to carry out local calculations or actions. Additionally, by putting lightweight AI/ML inference functions directly on edge devices, the combination opens the door for intelligent edge applications. With the help of this capability, use cases like predictive maintenance, real-time analytics, and customized user experiences can be supported without depending entirely on centralized cloud resources.

However, overcoming obstacles like network connectivity, security worries, and efficiently managing distributed deployments are necessary when integrating edge computing with serverless architectures. By overcoming these obstacles, businesses can fully utilize serverless and edge computing, fostering efficiency and innovation in today's distributed computing environments.

1.4.2. Serverless Machine Learning and AI Applications

Because serverless computing provides a scalable and affordable platform for deploying and operating models without having to manage underlying infrastructure, it is completely changing the field of machine learning (ML) and artificial intelligence (AI) applications. This paradigm shift frees developers and data scientists from worrying about infrastructure provisioning and management so they can concentrate more on creating and implementing models. The ability of serverless computing to handle computational bursts and scale automatically on demand is one of its main advantages in machine learning and artificial intelligence applications.

When serverless platforms like AWS Lambda, Azure Functions, and Google Cloud Functions are used, ML inference tasks can be executed effortlessly in response to events like scheduled triggers, API requests, and data changes. By ensuring that compute resources are only allocated when necessary, this event-driven architecture maximizes resource efficiency and cost-effectiveness. Additionally, a variety of ML and AI workloads, such as real-time prediction, image and video analysis, natural language processing (NLP), and more, are supported by serverless environments.

Organizations can deploy lightweight inference models directly into production environments without the hassle of managing servers or containers by utilizing serverless functions. This flexibility helps with quick iteration and experimentation during the model-building process, which in turn speeds up the time-to-market for AI-driven applications.

Integration with additional cloud services and data sources is a major advantage of serverless for machine learning and artificial intelligence. Storage services can be easily integrated with serverless functions (e.g., for data intake and model training, Amazon S3, Azure Blob Storage), databases (e.g., Azure Cosmos DB, DynamoDB) for processing data in real time, and event streams (e.g., Kafka, and AWS Kinesis) to manage data streams. This smooth integration facilitates complex workflows including data preprocessing, model training, inference, and result visualization while making the development of end-to-end AI pipelines easier. Moreover, serverless architectures encourage the use of serverless microservices patterns in AI applications, allowing programmers to create modular, disassemble able parts that carry out particular functions. By separating functionality into separate functions that can be independently deployed, scaled, and updated, this method improves scalability and maintainability.

Notwithstanding these advantages, managing stateful computations, resolving cold starts—the initial latency experienced when a function is called—and guaranteeing compliance with data privacy laws are some of the difficulties that serverless ML and AI applications must overcome. But as serverless platforms continue to improve and the ecosystem of tools and libraries expands, these issues are being addressed, which makes serverless computing a more alluring choice for implementing and growing AI and ML applications in real-world settings.

1.4.3. Serverless in the Context of Serverless Databases and Stateful Applications

A major development in cloud-native architecture, serverless computing is moving beyond stateless functions to include stateful applications and databases. In the past, serverless computing has been associated with transient computing environments, in which programs run in response to events without maintaining state or storing data between calls. But by combining serverless databases and managed state storage options, developments in serverless platforms and services now enable stateful applications.

Without requiring users to provision or manage database instances, serverless databases—like AWS Aurora Serverless, Google Cloud Firestore, and Azure Cosmos DB—offer scalable and fully managed storage capabilities. These services complement the scalability and cost-effectiveness of serverless computing by automatically scaling capacity up or down in response to workload demands and charging only for actual usage. Because of this, database administration overhead is removed, freeing up developers to concentrate on application logic rather than infrastructure management.

Additionally, serverless architectures allow stateful computations to be easily orchestrated using services like Azure Durable Functions and AWS Step Functions, enabling event-driven workflows. Workflow orchestration services ensure consistent and dependable processing of intricate business workflows by managing state persistence across multiple function invocations and coordinating the execution of serverless functions. Applications needing transactional integrity, like order processing, finance, and batch processing, depend on this capability.

Building reliable, scalable, and resilient applications in serverless environments is becoming more prevalent with the combination of serverless databases and stateful application patterns. With the help of these features, developers can create architectures that combine the dependability and data persistence needed by contemporary applications with the advantages of serverless computing, like automatic scaling, lower operating overhead, and pay-per-use pricing. Organizations can anticipate a rise in the use of serverless architectures for a wider range of use cases, such as enterprise applications, real-time analytics, and IoT data processing, as serverless platforms enhance and broaden their offerings for stateful applications.

REFERENCES

1. Anderson, D. (2022). *Power the Future and Accelerate Your Organization to The Modern Cloud and Serverless With 'The Value Flywheel Effect'*. The Serverless Edge.
2. Aske, A., & Zhao, X. (2018). Supporting multi-provider serverless computing on the edge. In *Proceedings of the 47th International Conference on Parallel Processing Companion (ICPP Workshops '18)* (pp. 1–6). Association for Computing Machinery. https://doi.org/10.1145/3229710.3229711.
3. Hellerstein, J., Faleiro, J., Gonzalez, J., Schleier-Smith, J., Screekanti, V., Tumanov, A., & Wu, C. (2019). *Serverless Computing: One Step Forward, Two Steps Back* (arXiv:1812.03651). https://arxiv.org/abs/1812.03651 (accessed on 1 August 2024).
4. Jamieson, F. (2017). *Losing the Server? Everybody is Talking About Serverless Architecture*. BCS, the Chartered Institute for IT.
5. Kounev, S. (2023). *Serverless Computing: What it is, and What it is not?* Communications of ACM.
6. Miller, R. (2016). *Microsoft Answers Aws Lambda's Event-Triggered Serverless Apps with Azure Functions*. TechCrunch.
7. Roberts, M. (2016). *Serverless Architectures*. MartinFowler.com.
8. Zhao, H., Benomar, Z., Pfandzelter, T., & Georgantas, N. (2022). Supporting multi-cloud in serverless computing. In *2022 IEEE/ACM 15th International Conference on Utility and Cloud Computing (UCC)* (pp. 285–290). IEEE. https://doi.org/10.1109/UCC57221.2022.00040.

CHAPTER 2

PUNCHING HOLES IN THE CLOUD: DIRECT COMMUNICATION BETWEEN SERVERLESS FUNCTIONS

Contents

INTRODUCTION

A service called serverless computing enables programmers to run applications directly without needing to handle servers. Major cloud platforms, such as Amazon Web Services (AWS) Lambda, offer serverless computing, also referred to as Functions as a Service (FaaS). There's a growing trend in serverless computing to run large distributed workloads without provisioning a cluster of machines because of its rapid scalability. Serverless computing has been used recently in linear algebra, data analytics, machine learning, and video processing. But since serverless programs, also known as functions, operate in separate, isolated environments, data transfer between multiple instances of a function poses a significant challenge for large-scale computing applications. Many applications require inter-function communication because individual serverless functions have limited memory, computational power, and execution time. Prior research has employed object storage and in-memory databases to facilitate communication; however, these methods come with trade-offs concerning cost, scalability, and performance. Since it would be quick, cost-free, and scalable with the number of functions, using direct network connections between functions is appealing; however, serverless providers use network firewalls to block inbound connections.

In contrast to traditional server-based computing, where users provision virtual machine servers, serverless computing has the advantage of scaling quickly. While server-based machines may require up to a minute for initialization, serverless functions can be launched hundreds of times at once and typically take much less than a second. The maximum execution time for each serverless function, in the case of AWS Lambda, is 15 minutes. With AWS Lambda, users can also customize the memory and CPU power allotted to each function, with a range of 128 to 10,240 MB. With serverless computing, users pay according to the number of function invocations and the total execution time of their functions, which is proportionate to the configured memory size. Because users do not need to provision resources in advance, serverless is perfect for uneven or bursty workloads due to its rapid scalability and usage-based billing.

One of the primary features of serverless functions, aside from scalability, is that they operate in a stateless, isolated environment known as a container. Functions running in containers must use external storage mechanisms because, while they have some storage space available to them during execution (512 MB for AWS Lambda), this space is not persistent. Additionally, because containers prevent incoming network connections, it is not possible to access running function code in a remote shell for debugging purposes or to run web servers directly within functions. A FaaS provider may, at its discretion, repurpose a container from an earlier execution of the same function, even though distinct functions are guaranteed to run in separate containers. In contrast to running a function in a fresh, uninitialized container, which is known as a cold start, this shortens startup time because the function does not need to reinitialize and is referred to as a warm start. All things considered, serverless computing offers a number of unique characteristics, such as low management requirements, quick scalability, and isolated execution environments.

Applications that are serverless must find solutions for issues with data transfer and short function lifetimes that do not arise in server-based computing. Since functions are ephemeral by nature, one challenge in serverless architecture is how to persist data and move it between various functions. Functions can access a limited amount of storage during runtime, but this access is not persistent. Additionally, functions can be called with very little metadata, but data processing applications require more. For serverless functions to function, data must be input and output through one or more external data stores, like object storage or database servers. For heavy computing workloads, employing external data storage enables communication between functions as well because they are isolated from one another. This is not the case with conventional server-based computing frameworks, where data exchange between nodes is effortless across the network. Furthermore, serverless functions have a shorter lifespan than traditional server-based computing nodes. When scheduling functions, serverless computations need to take into consideration their limited lifespan and make sure that the functions complete writing their output before they time out.

Serverless functions can send and receive data using a variety of external cloud computing services, including proxied network connections, memory- and disk-backed databases, and object storage. AWS Simple Storage Service (S3), which offers persistent object storage, can store massive volumes of data for pennies on the gigabyte per month. Its lack of high throughput support and rate-limiting of requests to a few thousand per second is a drawback. Although object storage is inexpensive, memory-backed key-value stores—like those offered by AWS ElastiCache, which offers managed Memcached or Redis instances—are the fastest storage option currently available. Although these memory-backed databases are effective for small objects and can handle a very high request rate (over 100,000 requests per second), they are far more costly than S3. For example, ElastiCache costs hundreds of times more than S3 for the same amount of data that it stores. Servers that support memory-backed stores also need to be provisioned. Naturally, any other kind of database can also be used in conjunction with serverless to offer various performance and cost trade-offs. However, the majority of databases still require provisioned servers, which restricts scalability. Theoretically, another option for enabling network communication between serverless functions is to leverage external proxy servers. Nevertheless, this would only be feasible if each function's bandwidth requirements were lower than a server's, as setting up numerous servers merely to serve as proxies would negate the whole point of utilizing serverless computing. All things considered, object storage, databases, and proxied connections are among the external storage options available for large computing serverless workloads; however, each of these options requires trade-offs between performance and cost.

2.1. FAAS PLATFORMS

Function as a Service (FaaS), a model where developers concentrate only on coding without managing the underlying infrastructure, is introduced by the evolution of cloud computing. FaaS stands out from the crowd by responding to event-driven triggers and dynamically scaling resources in response to demand. It is a component of the serverless computing paradigm. FaaS, a subset of Serverless, is essential for microservice deployment, which enables functions to carry out particular tasks inside an application. The FaaS market is predicted to grow at a rapid rate, from $301.01 billion in 2018 to $24 billion by 2026. This expansion demonstrates the influence of fault tolerance, scalability, and availability (FaaS) in cloud computing. This article explores FaaS, emphasizing its importance in the current cloud computing landscape as well as its role in cloud service models like IaaS, PaaS, and SaaS. ."

Some Popular Examples of FaaS Platforms Include

- IBM Cloud Functions
- Amazon's AWS Lambda
- Google Cloud Functions
- Microsoft Azure Functions (Open Source)
- OpenFaaS (Open Source)

2.1.1. FaaS and Serverless

Serverless computing focuses on any kind of service, including computing, databases, storage, and API gateways. where the end user is not aware of server configuration, messaging, or billing. While the event-driven computing paradigm—in which functions only execute in response to events or requests—is the main focus of FaaS, serverless computing is also implemented using this method. Any action, such as clicking a button or pressing a key, can be considered the event. , capable of calling the function (Figure 2.1).

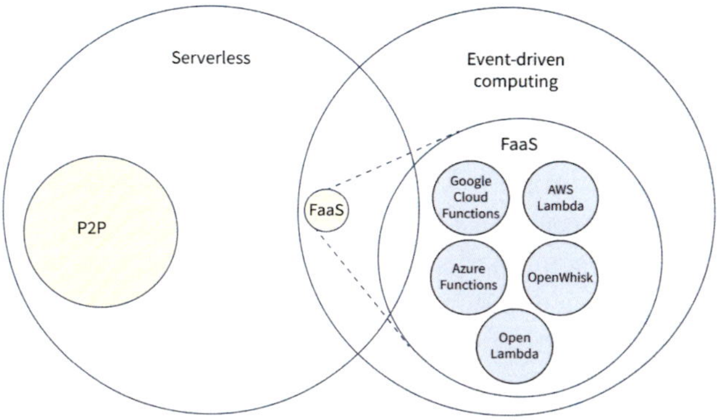

Figure 2.1. *Focused on the event-driven computing paradigm.*

Source: https://www.scaler.com/topics/cloud-computing/faas/.

In other models, even when a server is idle, it is always running to provide services. The users paid more as a result of this. With FaaS, you can run a single function, a single logic block, or a single application, and you only pay when the code runs. Faas only operates when a function is called, which prompts the distant servers to carry out the desired action before shutting down. This way, when the server is idle, nothing is paid for it.

2.1.2. How does Function-as-a-Service Work?

Applications were created in the early stages of development using monolithic architecture. This indicates that the application was created as a single execution that required a single trigger. This architecture required more time and money to develop. Developers have started utilizing microservices more and more over time. An application is divided into independently deployable functions in a microservice architecture. A function is a piece of software that an operating system can use to execute a single business logic in response to an event. Numerous functions can make up an application.

When an event triggers the function in FaaS, the service provider initiates the server. After carrying out the function to complete the intended task, the server will be shut down. After the server is shut down, the same computer power can be used in another way. By using the development platform made available by FaaS, developers can run the code for their apps. A single action should be performed by each function in order to optimize FaaS efficiency. During runtime, the system automatically scales up and down based on server requirements and workload. This is a crucial component of cloud computing's Function-as-a-Service.

2.1.3. Dynamic Scaling with FaaS

An application programming interface (API) is used by a service provider to make a function available, and the provider handles resource allocation independently. Because FaaS functions are event-driven rather than resource-driven, they can be easily scaled, which boosts effectiveness and value. For a function to start and run quickly, its execution time should be as short as possible. In milliseconds, a function begins processing each request. A function adheres to shared-nothing architecture and is stateless. This indicates that only one request will be handled at a time by each active function, which is isolated. The system will make as many copies of a function as necessary to satisfy demand if there are several simultaneous requests for the same function. The system scales down automatically when demand declines. This is how FaaS works dynamically.

Dynamic Scaling is cost-efficient as users only have to pay for the resources utilized and not for the idle time.

2.1.4. Benefits of FaaS

Function-as-a-Service model is widely used in a development environment that requires a high level of agility. Similarly, the following benefits of FaaS make it shine in rapid application development (Figure 2.2).

- The ability to focus solely on coding and development of the application.
- Increased developer productivity and faster development time.
- Easy to scale and horizontal scaling is managed by the platform.
- Cost-efficient, since you pay only for what you use.
- Faster time to market due to ease of development and testing.
- Platforms are polyglot, meaning functions can be written in any language.

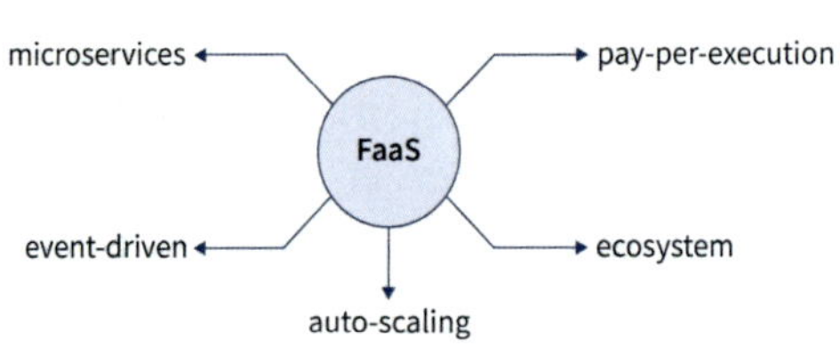

Figure 2.2. *Benefits of FaaS.*

Source: https://www.scaler.com/topics/cloud-computing/faas/.

2.1.5. Principles and Best Practices

Function-as-a-service is well-known due to the system's scalability and ease of development. It is possible to implement FaaS more effectively and more easily by adhering to certain practices.

- **Each function should perform only one action** – A FaaS function is a single piece of code that is intended to carry out a particular task or piece of business logic. As a result, a function should only have one task assigned to it. To ensure that the function loads and runs quickly, the function code should have a small, effective, and light scope.
- **Do not call other functions from one function** – The isolation of functions is necessary for FaaS. More function calls from a single function will increase the execution time and therefore the cost.
- **Use as few libraries as possible** – Using too many libraries in function will slow down the execution time and will make scaling of application a difficult task.

Following these practices will make the FaaS application more efficient in terms of complexity, deployment, cost, and scalability.

2.1.6. How do FaaS and Serverless Differ?

There is a very thin line that separates serverless computing and fail-safe architectures when discussing them. One technique for delivering backend services only when needed is serverless computing. Numerous areas are included in the term "serverless," including computing, storage, DevOps pipelines, Kubernetes, and serverless databases. In a serverless architecture, the cloud service provider manages the servers and underlying infrastructure behind the user's back. A subset of serverless that concentrates on the computing paradigm is called function-as-a-service. With FaaS, the user doesn't have to worry about other infrastructure management because they have a platform to write code and develop business logic. The cloud provider manages the stateless compute instances, or containers, where the code is run. FaaS uses an event-driven methodology to call functions in order to complete the given task. Serverless is much more flexible than FaaS and isn't just for building functions. It works well when the primary objective is to keep control over application configurations while reducing the amount of infrastructure management duties.

2.1.7. Use Cases of FaaS

Function-as-a-Service is a rapidly growing service model because of its simplicity, cost-efficiency, fault tolerance, availability, and high scalability.

FaaS can be used in a variety of ways; some of the most popular use cases of FaaS are:

- APIs for mobile and web applications
  - FaaS is a great option for event-driven applications like RESTful. Sites that load dynamic content use functions to call an API and then populate the appropriate information. Moreover, websites that require user input, use functions to call API for verification of input data.
  - Serverless APIs are easy to build and maintain and get scaled up or down on-demand basis. This saves a lot of costs for organizations during peak times and heavy traffic.
- Multimedia and Data Processing
  - Faas is frequently used to process the input data, such as multimedia. One common use case is using FaaS to trigger a response based on the type of multimedia input.
  - FaaS is very efficient in handling large amounts of input data for the processing which allows developers to make robust data pipelines with little or no maintenance of infrastructure. FaaS allows developers to write single function for different processing components which save a lot of development time and ultimately cost.
- Internet of Things
  - Internet of Things(IoT) refers to devices that use the internet to perform functions. IoT has seen immense growth and these devices can easily be found in our homes. These devices are increasingly using FaaS to execute their task by sending and receiving data when triggered by an event. Since they are not using any computing power, the user does not need to pay for the same. At the same time, due to auto-scaling, the developer need not to worry about the unpredictable usage pattern of the devices.

2.1.8. FaaS vs PaaS, Containers and VMs

Function-as-a-Service, Platform-as-a-Service, Containers, and Virtual Machines all play a significant role in serverless computing. But, FaaS is the most central element of the Serverless stack. Let's understand how FaaS differs from other models.

- **Provisioning Time** – Milliseconds for FaaS and minutes to hour for other models.
- **Administration** – No administration is required for Faas while it is easy to hard for PaaS, containers, and VMs respectively.

- **Scalability** – Each action is instantly scaled based on the functional needs while other model offers automatic but slow scaling that requires careful tuning of auto-scaling tools.
- **Availability** – FaaS is highly available with no extra cost or effort. Other models require additional cost and management for high availability.
- **Capacity Planning** – No planning is required due to dynamic scaling while other models require the provision of some auto-scaling and capacity planning.
- **Persistent Connection and State** – FaaS functions run in stateless containers which means they have limited ability to persist connections and the state must be stored in an external resource. On the other hand, the other models can leverage http methods to keep an open socket or connection for long durations and can store the state in memory between calls.
- **Resource Utilization** – Maximum resource utilization in FaaS due to event-driven architecture, the resources are allocated only when the function is triggered by an event. All other models require at least one server to continuously run to provide service, even when it is idle.
- **Resource Limits** – Only FaaS model set boundaries on code size, memory, execution time, etc.
- **Maintenance** – In FaaS and PaaS, the underlying infrastructure is maintained by the Cloud Service Provider. Containers and Virtual Machines require significant maintenance which includes updating the operating systems, connections, container images, etc.

2.2. SERVERLESS FUNCTIONS

In serverless architecture, the infrastructure is managed by the backend (server-side) provider, leaving the developer free to concentrate only on writing code. Cloud computing companies host serverless functions, which are programmatic, single-purpose functions on managed infrastructure.

These online functions are intended to automate processes, lower latency, and offer on-demand computing capabilities. Serverless architectures offer near-perfect uptime (operational level), redundant instances globally, and scalability to accommodate any volume of incoming network requests when properly maintained by engineering teams.

2.2.1. Examples of a Serverless Functions Providers

All major cloud providers offer serverless functions:

- PubNub Functions – Check full server-less technical documentation
- Vercel (formerly ZEIT Now) Functions
- Netlify Functions
- AWS Lambda
- Google Cloud Functions
- Kubeless
- Cloudflare Workers

2.2.2. Serverless Infrastructure: Monolithic Architecture vs. Microservice Architecture

Microservices, a well-liked idea in the serverless environment, can be thought of as serverless functions. Within the software development community, the move from encapsulated microservices to monolithic platforms is generating a lot of excitement.

2.2.2.1. Why Using Serverless Functions and Architectures?

Traditionally, monoliths have had sizable, cohesive codebases that necessitate a complete platform deploy for every commit, or shipment or deployment, of new code. Along with simple bug fixes, this also includes new features. Monoliths have their uses, but some tasks become difficult when a platform's codebase grows to the point where there is a large development team.

Software development teams benefit from better maintainability of code bases and an enhanced developer experience when using a microservices architecture. A large engineering organization can divide itself into autonomous, loosely-coupled teams thanks to microservices. A small number of microservices that operate separately from the rest of the platform can be the focus of each team's efforts. Keep in mind that even though microservices can be managed relatively independently, they are still members of a single team.

Microservice architecture makes it possible for new developers to quickly become productive contributors to engineering projects without requiring them to have a thorough understanding of the entire monolith. The fact that customers experience little to no downtime when minor code updates are deployed to individual services is another benefit of microservices. When a monolith requires code updates, it may result in a serverless deploy function that is unavailable to all customers during that time (Figure 2.3).

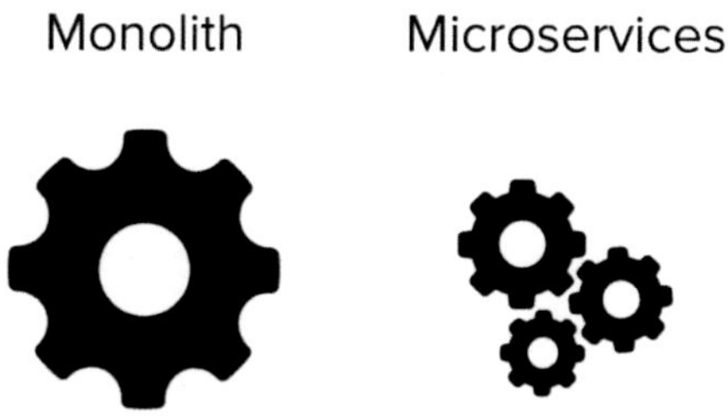

Figure 2.3. *Monolithic architecture vs. microservice architecture.*

Source: https://www.pubnub.com/blog/what-is-a-serverless-function/.

2.3. NETWORK ADDRESS TRANSLATION

Through the use of Network Address Translation (NAT), a single IP address can now serve as the representative for a whole network of computers. A network device, frequently a router or NAT firewall, assigns a public address to a computer or computers inside a private network through network address translation. Network address translation enables a single device to function as an agent or mediator between a local private network and the public internet network. The primary objective of NAT is to preserve the quantity of public IP addresses in use for both security and financial reasons (Figure 2.4).

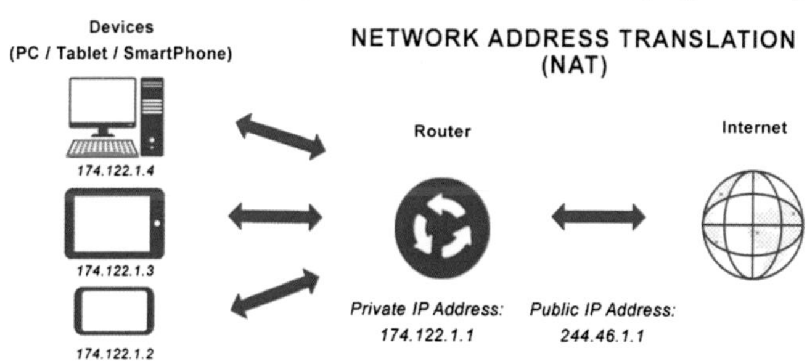

Figure 2.4. *Network address translation (NAT).*

Source: https://avinetworks.com/glossary/network-address-translation/.

2.3.1. NAT Traversal

Network Address Translation Traversal is referred to as NAT Traversal. When data is being transferred over an IPSec tunnel, web technologies use this kind of traversal method to handle and process all of the IP addresses in order to resolve any translation-related problems that may have arisen during data transmission. It facilitates overcoming the difficulties in data transfer brought on by data transmission through an IPSec tunnel. Another name for the NAT traversal is UDP Encapsulation. It works in the following ways:

1. It detects the number of devices that are connected to the IPSec tunnel in the network. It senses the devices in data path connection of the devices using the User Datagram Protocol (UDP) encapsulation to IPsec data packets.
2. The User datagram protocol network helps to produce large-scale data translations so that they can communicate between their peer nodes of the computer by disabling the IKE and the ESP traffic by using the User datagram protocol network.

2.3.1.1. Purpose of NAT-Traversal

Network Address Translation Traversal (NAT) is primarily used to save IP addresses by enabling several devices connected to a small Local Area Network (LAN) or network on the Internet to map to a single IP address. To make it easier to identify the network that these devices are connected to and to prevent IP addresses from being wasted by assigning different IP addresses to different networked devices, it associates a large number of four to five devices that are connected to the same network on the Internet and assigns them all the same IP addresses.

2.3.1.2. Types of NAT

There are basically two broad criteria of classification of Network Address Translation Traversal (NAT). They are as follows:-

- **Static NAT:** Static Network Address Translation Traversal is a kind of network traversal where the public and private IP addresses have a necessary relationship in order to support the IPsec tunnel's inbound and outgoing connections.
- **Dynamic NAT:** Unlike the single layer of relationship between the networking nodes in the static NAT, the relationship between the networking nodes in the IPsec tunnel can exist across multiple layers thanks to the use of dynamic network address translation traversal. The primary drawback of dynamic network address translation (NAT) is that it only facilitates outgoing IPSec tunnel connections; inbound IPSec connections are not supported.

2.3.1.3. Working of NAT

Using the User Datagram Protocol (UDP) encapsulation, the Network Address Translation Traversal (NAT) encrypts the file's headers and payloads. It keeps the data transmission in the IPSec tunnel authentic and intact. It carries out the operation by encapsulating the IPsec tunnel ESP header file after first encapsulating the Network Address Translation Traversal (NAT) header file using the User Datagram Protocol (UDP).

The encapsulation of data being transferred between two computers connected to a VPN (virtual private network) is essentially processed by the Network Address Translation Traversal (NAT). It uses VPNs to generate the hashing function on the payload and header file of the data in the IPSec tunnel in order to perform hashing. The data packets are then transferred via the tunnel or the transport mode of data transfer within the IPSec, contingent upon the circumstances.

Only devices with robust firewall security for users can support Network Address Translation Traversal (NAT). It controls all data coming into and going out of the computer and routinely scans every data packet to prevent any issues. It uses dynamic destination NAT to effectively handle every challenge. It is most frequently utilized in settings where users are required to connect to a minimum number of IP addresses. To prevent network traffic, it maps and links a sizable number of IPSec-connected devices to the same IP address (Figure 2.5).

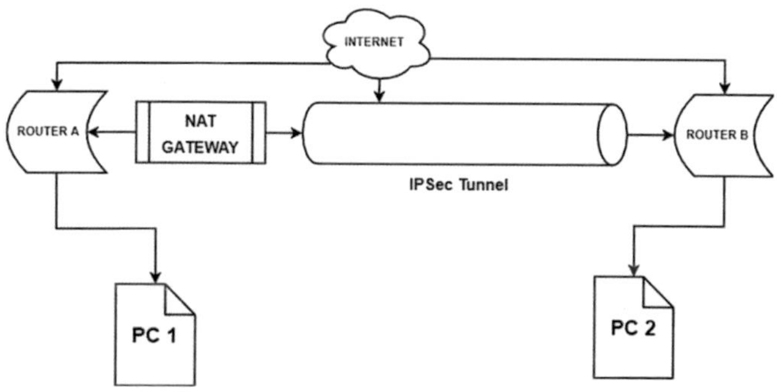

Figure 2.5. *Nat gateway.*

Source: https://www.geeksforgeeks.org/how-nat-traversal-in-vpns/.

2.3.2. AWS Lambda NAT Behavior

Every function container that is created by AWS Lambda has a private IP address that is protected from inbound connections by a NAT firewall. In order for the function to access the public internet, the NAT firewall converts its private IP address into a public one. However, this means that Lambda cannot be used to run externally-accessible servers and that two functions cannot directly communicate with each other over the network without NAT traversal because the firewall prevents functions from receiving connections. The way that AWS's NAT firewall handles Lambda function containers is not made clear. On the other hand, the observed behavior is that it keeps the function's TCP port open while rewriting the function's private IP address to a public IP for outgoing connections. Additionally, a container's public IP address is fixed for the duration of the container, meaning that an outgoing connection's public IP address and port are predictable—both of which are necessary for TCP hole punching. NAT implementations are categorized by RFC 3489 as either symmetric or cone NAT depending on whether or not the mappings they assign are consistent across different connections. Cone NAT reliably maps outgoing connections made by a client from the same private IP address and port to the same public IP address and port; symmetric NAT, on the other hand, assigns a different public IP address or port to subsequent connections. Since the public IP address and port number cannot be known in advance, hole punching with symmetric NAT is generally not feasible (unless symmetric NAT uses a sequential or other predictable assignment). However, hole punching is possible because AWS Lambda makes use of cone NAT. This work incorporates this capability into the proposed communication library and shows that NAT traversal can be used to establish a TCP connection between two Lambda functions that are running concurrently.

2.4. DESIGN OF AN EPHEMERAL COMMUNICATION LIBRARY

2.4.1. Communication Library Functionality

There is some setup required to use serverless functions to run a distributed application. After being started, each function needs to be given instructions on which input sources and output destinations to use. Functions must also exchange the network address information for the peer functions they intend to communicate with in order to have direct network communication. In order to carry out this setup and create network connections between functions, this paper presents a communication framework. The implemented communications library is made up of two main components: worker functions that execute application code for data processing and perform NAT traversal, and an orchestrator that calls functions and controls communication between them. Because NAT traversal requires a machine that accepts inbound network connections, the orchestrator must be hosted on one of these machines. Prior to initiating an application run, the orchestrator creates a communication graph of all the functions that need to be deployed. This graph indicates which function pairs need to connect directly to the network and includes a list of all the inputs and outputs for every function. After invoking the required functions with the help of the data in this graph, the orchestrator launches a listening server. Every worker function connects to this server through a WebSocket connection as soon as it launches in order to register with the orchestrator and obtain a list of peer functions to connect to.

Following the receipt of its peers' addresses, a function uses NAT traversal to create direct TCP connections with them. To ensure dependable data transfer between functions, the suggested library employs TCP rather than UDP. The worker starts executing the actual application code after this setup is finished. Figure 2.6. illustrates the initialization procedure for the first TCP connection made between two functions. Worker applications using the communication library have to implement interface methods in order to process input data into output data, create and consume input and output data, and move data between functions.

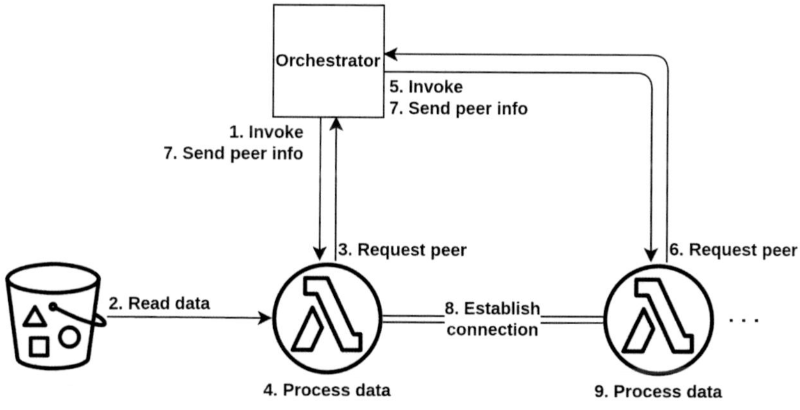

Figure 2.6. *Communication library initialization procedure for the first two worker functions. The first worker starts reading and processing data while establishing a connection to the second in parallel. If the second worker has any other peers, it will repeat this setup with them once it starts reading data from the first worker.*

Source: https://vtechworks.lib.vt.edu/server/api/core/bitstreams/75f6f77c-7f68-416b-919b-8008c7a6a922/content.

2.4.2. Client-Server Design

Because Lambda functions do not permit inbound connections, our framework gets around this limitation by using a different server for communication. It is not feasible for one function to directly connect to another since Lambda functions are protected by AWS firewalls. Nonetheless, it is feasible to facilitate

NAT traversal so that functions can establish a direct connection or to relay traffic between functions using a server that is external to Lambda. We chose to use the server as an orchestrator to call functions and send control messages between them because using NAT traversal in our communication library requires a server. Upon invocation, the server adds this data to the function event data and launches a service on a publicly accessible host and port via the WebSocket protocol. Next, in order to exchange brief control-plane messages, each function establishes a persistent connection with the orchestrator server upon startup. At this stage, for every pair of functions that require NAT traversal, the orchestrator transmits peer network information.

Scalability may be impacted by implementing the orchestrator on a single server, but given the low per-function resource requirements in our design, we think this is a fair trade-off. The only design variable is whether to have that server support additional functionality because NAT traversal requires an external server in order for functions to exchange network address information. Using that server, the communication library implements a function orchestrator that sends and receives control messages by keeping a persistent connection with each function over the course of its lifetime. An alternative approach, though, would be to implement the orchestrator as part of the serverless functions themselves, with the central server serving only as a NAT traversal relay. One advantage of putting the orchestrator on a conventional server is that it can enable recurring connections to a single location. By doing this, there is no longer a need for a more involved peer-to-peer control method or for the orchestrator to be run in a separate function and deal with the situation where it needs to run longer than the function's maximum lifetime of 15 minutes and employ a replacement scheme. Relocating more features to the server could have the primary disadvantage of reducing the design's scalability. The server needs to keep a single persistent connection and a few data structures in memory for each function. The distinction is that in our design, the server must hold these resources until the function exits, but in the NAT-traversal-only case, the server can release them for a function after NAT traversal is finished. However, since the resources allocated to each function are relatively small, a single server should be able to support thousands of concurrently running functions. Nevertheless, executing jobs at that scale would likely necessitate further design improvements.

2.4.3. NAT Traversal Protocol

We chose to use a custom implementation of TCP hole punching because we wanted to use TCP for data reliability and to use the same system for both exchanging control messages and NAT traversal, even though there are multiple protocols that can be used to perform NAT traversal. A network address translator can be configured in a variety of ways in general, but our design only needs to function in the AWS Lambda environment. Our primary design choice was to employ TCP rather than UDP. TCP is used in the suggested communication library because it automatically recognizes and fixes transmission errors. It's possible that TCP hole punching is less common than UDP hole punching, but both are equally "fast and reliable.." On the other hand, because the application needs to listen on and establish outgoing connections from the same socket, TCP hole punching is a little more difficult to implement from an application standpoint. Since we are in charge of the implementation and can set it up to permit socket reuse in this way, this does not present a challenge for our communication library.

Another possible issue with TCP is that, shortly after establishing a connection, its slow-start behavior and handshake may cause data rates to drop below those of UDP. We leave the study of UDP for future work, but these startup costs should not significantly affect large-scale data transfers. Nevertheless, applications concerned with fine-grained performance optimizations should not overlook this. We also decided against using TURN or STUN, two established protocols, to aid in NAT traversal. In order to assist a client in determining its public IP address, whether it is behind NAT, and the type of NAT if it is, the STUN protocol makes use of a public server.

However, it was simpler for us to use our orchestrator server to find the public IP address than it was to set up a separate STUN server specifically for that purpose, as we already knew the NAT behavior for AWS Lambda. Additionally, in situations where NAT traversal is not feasible, the TURN protocol offers a method to implement relaying; however, this is not relevant to our situation and would be extremely inefficient anyhow. The TCP hole punching technique works for most NAT configurations, such as cone NAT and nested NAT when the outer NAT supports hairpin translation, but it does not work with symmetric NAT. Our hole punching implementation is tailored specifically for AWS Lambda. Our testing indicates that AWS Lambda does not support IPv6, which, if implemented to assign a public IP address to each function directly, could remove the need for NAT. A stateful firewall would probably still be in place, though, and it would continue to deny incoming IPv6 connections. A similar procedure to get around this by creating simultaneous outbound connections might still be required if AWS Lambda deployed IPv6 but prohibited functions from communicating directly. We chose to use TCP hole punching because, while there are many possible NAT behaviors, our communication library only needs to support the one utilized by AWS Lambda.

2.5. IMPLEMENTATION OF EPHEMERAL COMMUNICATION LIBRARY

2.5.1. NAT Traversal Technique

The suggested communication library circumvents Lambda's inability to permit incoming connections to functions by using TCP hole punching, a well-known NAT traversal technique, to establish a direct connection between Lambda functions. The function component of the library establishes a connection with the orchestrator server upon startup to obtain control data. The orchestrator server is not a part of Lambda, so the firewall allows this outgoing connection. The public IP address and TCP port number of each function are sent to the other once the orchestrator has accepted connections from both functions that intend to create a mutual TCP connection. As a result, both functions are equipped with the IP address and port number needed to establish an outgoing TCP connection and keep attempting to establish a connection with the other function. Each function opens a socket to listen on a fixed port number while attempting to establish an outbound connection, just in case the connection from its peer is successful before it does. The Lambda NAT firewall will eventually permit traffic from the other function through as it interprets this as return traffic from the outbound connection after both functions have attempted outbound connections. At this point, the listening socket either accepts a connection from the other function or the outgoing function's attempt to connect is successful. The function has a legitimate TCP connection open to its peer function and is ready to start sending and receiving data, regardless of which event occurs first in a non-deterministic manner.

See an example sequence diagram of TCP hole punching between two AWS Lambda functions in Figure 2.7. In this example, Function 1 has public IP 3.0.1.1 and Function 2 has public IP 3.0.2.2 Also, both functions start listening for incoming connections on their corresponding private IP addresses and ports: address 172.16.1.1 port 10001 for Function 1 and address 172.16.2.2 port 20002 for Function 2. At this point, both functions have exchanged public IP addresses and listening port numbers via the orchestrator server. Once they receive this information, both functions try to open an outbound TCP connection to the other. In the diagram, the first connection attempt is made by Function 1 to the public IP address of Function 2. Note that Function 1 sets the source port of the TCP SYN connection request packet to be the same as the port number it is listening on. The NAT firewall for Function 1 rewrites the private source port of this packet to the public IP of Function 1, namely 3.0.1.1, but it keeps the source port number the same. The fact that the AWS Lambda firewall preserves port numbers makes TCP hole punching possible. However, at this point the

NAT firewall for Function 2 sees the incoming packet as unsolicited and drops it. Independently, Function 2 now sends a connection request to Function 1, and its NAT firewall rewrites the source IP address to the public IP address of Function 2. When the connection request reaches the firewall for Function 1, the source and destination addresses and ports are exactly switched compared to the connection previously initiated by Function 1. Thus, the Function 1 firewall treats the second connection request as a response to the first, and allows it. Now, Function 1 receives the connection SYN request from Function 2 on its listening port, and sends a SYN-ACK acknowledgment packet back to continue the TCP connection setup. The firewall for Function 2 will also accept the acknowledgment because it is a valid response to the SYN packet Function 2 sent. Thus, both firewalls will allow traffic through, so the functions can finish the handshake to establish a valid TCP connection between them.

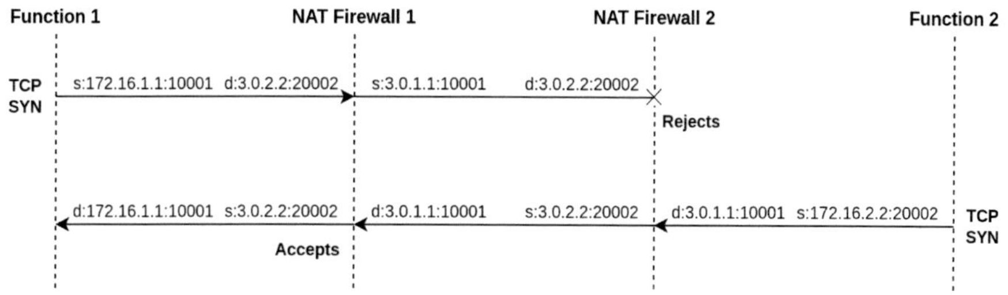

Figure 2.7. *TCP hole punching example.*

Source: https://vtechworks.lib.vt.edu/server/api/core/bitstreams/75f6f77c-7f68-416b-919b-8008c7a6a922/content.

2.5.2. Server-Function Communication

The suggested communications library makes use of Python Socket-implemented persistent WebSocket connections. IO library to allow worker functions and the orchestrator server to communicate control messages. The orchestrator server is in charge of transmitting and receiving commands and status updates between functions in this work's client-server communication library.

These control messages notify when a function has completed, when its output is available so that the orchestrator can call functions that rely on it, and the initial data required for NAT traversal. Every time a function is called, the server launches a WebSocket service that is listening and connects to it at startup. Only when the function exits does it close this connection, which it maintains the entire time. Pushing messages to functions is one of the requirements of this design for the orchestrator. Because functions cannot accept incoming connections, they need to either create a persistent full-duplex communication channel or poll the server frequently for updates. The library chooses to use one persistent connection instead of polling, which uses multiple connections and inevitably introduces more overhead and latency. Because WebSocket is lightweight for short messages and allows full-duplex communication over a single TCP connection, the library uses it. Using an existing message protocol with an available Python library has the advantage of making implementation simpler than writing a custom protocol directly on top of TCP. The Python Socket is used by the library as a result. IO library that implements WebSocket as a client and server for message sending.

2.5.3. Communication Library API Overview

A high-level Application Programming Interface (API) that facilitates the creation of serverless apps with inter-function communication over TCP is provided by the serverless communications library that is the subject of this work. Applications that use the library have to define two things: the data processing implementation itself and a topology graph of worker functions that specifies how they should talk to one another. All of the functions and NAT traversals required to create every

TCP connection for data transfer specified by the application topology must be carried out by the communication library. Applications must specify the inputs and outputs for each worker function in the topology, with two options available for each: an external application-implemented subroutine or an internal TCP connection. The communication library itself controls inputs and outputs with internal TCP types, whereby the output data from one function is sent over TCP to become the input data for another. The topology graph's directed edges are formed by these internal TCP connections between functions. In order to prevent circular dependencies between functions, the application must ensure that the function graph is acyclic.

Although data can be sent between functions via TCP connections, serverless functions are transient, so applications need to be able to read the initial data and write their results to an external source. As a result, applications can define unique input and output subroutines using the communication library, and then indicate in the graph which functions should call these subroutines and with what parameters. As an example, Figure 2.8 defines a topology with three functions. The application's custom input and output subroutines could respectively read from and write to the S3 object specified in the path metadata field. Then, the first two functions, worker-0 and worker-1, download data from S3, process it, and send their immediate results over TCP to worker-2, which combines them and writes the final output to S3.

```
[ { "name": "worker-0",
    "inputs":  [ {"type": "s3", "path": "s3://example-bucket/input-0.csv"},
                 {"type": "s3", "path": "s3://example-bucket/input-1.csv"} ],
    "outputs": [ {"type": "tcp", "name": "worker-2"} ] },
  { "name": "worker-1",
    "inputs":  [ {"type": "s3", "path": "s3://example-bucket/input-2.csv"} ],
    "outputs": [ {"type": "tcp", "name": "worker-2"} ] },
  { "name": "worker-2",
    "inputs":  [ {"type": "tcp", "name": "worker-0"},
                 {"type": "tcp", "name": "worker-1"} ],
    "outputs": [ {"type": "s3", "path": "s3://example-bucket/result.csv"} ] } ]
```

Figure 2.8. *Example function topology definition.*

Source: https://vtechworks.lib.vt.edu/server/api/core/bitstreams/75f6f77c-7f68-416b-919b-8008c7a6a922/content.

Applications using the proposed communications library need to implement the data processing logic that powers the serverless functions in addition to the function topology. Applications are expected to write a Python class that implements a list of necessary methods in order to use the communications library. Each of these techniques runs concurrently in its own thread and makes efficient use of Python generators to create and/or consume a stream of data objects. As was previously mentioned, the communication library anticipates that the application will implement two ways to manage the function topology's specified external inputs and outputs. The application's primary data processing method, which converts objects received as inputs into objects that can be sent as outputs, must also be written. In order to serialize and deserialize the data objects it uses into a binary format for transmission over TCP, the application must lastly implement two methods.

2.5.4. Function Program Design

The suggested communication library executes network communication and application data processing subroutines using a multi-threaded architecture. The ability to use pipelining to increase throughput for multiple functions operating in parallel is a significant benefit of using TCP for communication. Therefore, once a function has completed processing a block of data, it can move straight on to the next function in the pipeline and process the next block of data. Therefore, for pipelining to be implemented effectively, each function needs to be reading, processing, and writing output data at the same time. The communication library implements parallelism within a function by using separate threads for each of these tasks, allowing data pipelining across a sequence of functions. The library uses one thread per function to run the data processing subroutine of the application and one thread per source or destination of input or output, be it a custom application subroutine or a TCP connection. An alternate design would be to use Python coroutines for event-based programming, but this would require non-blocking input/output, which is challenging to implement. Additionally, the library's implementation of NAT traversal needs to simultaneously make outbound connections and listen on a socket; the easiest way to do this is to use a different thread for each. Each application's input and output subroutine can block to read or write without affecting data processing if it is placed in its own thread. The Python interpreter employs a global lock, so threads do not benefit from running on a multi-core CPU. This is one drawback of using Python threads. This doesn't matter for small function sizes because AWS Lambda will only assign one virtual CPU to the function; however, for larger function sizes, it does prevent the communication library from making full use of all available cores. Nevertheless, because the communication library can process data while executing blocking input and output, its use of multiple threads enables it to still support pipelining with other functions.

2.6. EVALUATION OF COMMUNICATION LIBRARY IN AWS LAMBDA

One of the most popular serverless computing environments, AWS Lambda, is used to test the performance of the suggested communication library. This section assesses the Lambda latency and throughput of the suggested library, compares it with communication via S3 cloud storage, and shows how these factors scale with data transfer sizes and the number of communicating functions. The performance analysis comprises templates of data-intensive applications written in MapReduce, a popular programming paradigm for creating pipelines for data processing, as well as microbenchmarks.

2.6.1. TCP Performance in Lambda

2.6.1.1. Throughput

This work conducted multiple experiments to measure the performance of TCP connections between Lambda functions, with the goal of setting some expectations for the network communications performance. The raw throughput for a single connection between two functions was the first metric to be measured. This work used the suggested communication library, which makes use of Python TCP sockets with default settings, to implement a basic benchmark application. The benchmark comprised of two distinct components, namely a producer and a consumer, each operating independently. The consumer read data from its connection and counted the total amount of data received, while the producer continuously transmitted a fixed block of data as quickly as possible.

To calculate throughput, the consumer also recorded the time between the first and last block of data received. Each of the tests sent 1 GB total and used functions with 3072 MB of memory. The orchestrator server used for the tests was hosted on an Ubuntu 18.04 virtual machine with 4 CPU cores and 8 GB of memory. This work tried different buffer sizes from 1 kB to 1 MB for reading and writing from the network socket and measured each with 5 runs. For each buffer size, Run 1 was a cold start due to the fact that the function code was modified and Lambda was thus forced to provision a new container for execution. The remaining Runs 2–5 were warm starts, but since the experiment only measured time while sending data after both functions had already initialized and established a TCP connection between them; this should not affect the results. The results are graphed in Figure 2.9 with the full data listed in Table 2.1. The maximum throughput of about 680 Mbps is achieved when using buffers of 8 kB or larger. It makes sense that smaller buffer sizes would increase overhead, and the data show that the performance drops off with 4 kB buffers and smaller. While there was some variability in the results; this is understandable because AWS Lambda makes no guarantees on the performance or bandwidth available to functions. An additional comment is that Fouladi et al. report observing speeds of 600 Mbps for direct network communications between functions in their future work discussion, which is similar if not quite as fast as the results in this work.

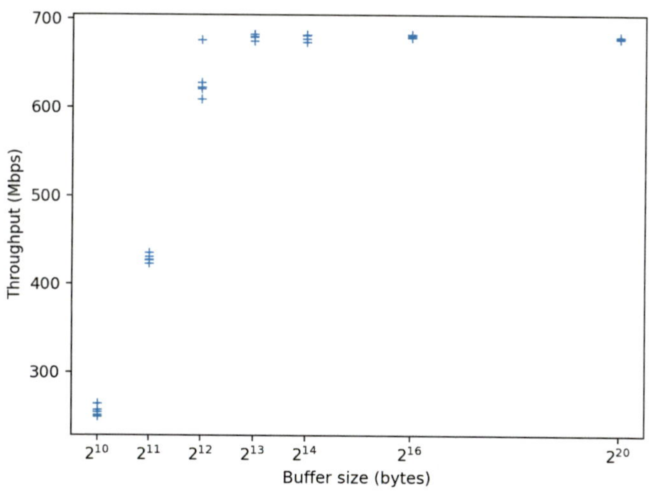

Figure 2.9. *Throughput (Mbps) between two Lambda functions based on buffer size.*

Source: https://vtechworks.lib.vt.edu/server/api/core/bitstreams/75f6f77c-7f68-416b-919b-8008c7a6a922/content.

Table 2.1. *Throughput (Mbps) Between Two Lambda Functions Based on Buffer Size*

Buffer	1 kB	2 kB	4 kB	8 kB	16 kB	64 kB	1 MB
Run 1	264.965	435.219	676.116	682.517	673.219	678.374	679.434
Run 2	250.180	427.054	621.060	674.673	681.465	679.088	679.643
Run 3	257.868	423.257	609.191	680.248	677.673	682.674	680.327
Run 4	254.905	430.758	627.690	680.236	681.192	681.604	679.864
Run 5	252.256	427.881	622.661	679.362	681.917	680.902	677.918
Average	256.035	428.834	631.344	679.407	679.093	680.528	679.437

Source: https://vtechworks.lib.vt.edu/server/api/core/bitstreams/75f6f77c-7f68-416b-919b-8008c7a6a922/content.

In order to determine whether a different function topology would result in a higher throughput, this work also experimented with two producers and two consumers. Every experiment had two functions and the same methodology, with the exception of the addition of a producer or consumer.

To ensure that every consumer received precisely 1 GB of data as before, it either doubled or halved the data sent by each producer. Based on the results of the previous experiment, the buffer size was fixed at 8 kB because increasing the size further did not affect the measured throughput. Table 2.2 lists the outcomes of the first test, which involved sending two producer functions to a single consumer function.

Similarly, Table 2.3 displays the outcomes for a single producer function sending to a pair of consumers.

Both the aggregate throughput and the throughput for each individual customer are displayed here. Since the maximum throughput in both experiments was roughly 680 Mbps, the authors speculate that Lambda places a bandwidth cap on each function, thereby limiting the speed that is observed in each scenario.

Table 2.2. *Throughput (Mbps) with Two Producer and One Consumer Functions*

	Throughput
Run 1	679.197
Run 2	682.057
Run 3	677.897
Run 4	680.409
Run 5	681.373
Average	680.187

Source: https://vtechworks.lib.vt.edu/server/api/core/bitstreams/75f6f77c-7f68-416b-919b-8008c7a6a922/content.

Table 2.3. *Throughput (Mbps) with One Producer and Two Consumer Functions*

	Consumer 1	Consumer 2	Total
Run 1	309.753	372.020	681.773
Run 2	369.452	307.845	677.297
Run 3	313.596	311.577	625.173
Run 4	306.886	354.791	661.677
Run 5	367.429	318.463	685.892
Average	333.423	332.939	666.362

Source: https://vtechworks.lib.vt.edu/server/api/core/bitstreams/75f6f77c-7f68-416b-919b-8008c7a6a922/content.

The experiment was expanded to see if the throughput would drop when employing a longer chain of functions after the network throughput for direct connections was measured. Implementing a data pipeline with a chain of functions where each function receives data over TCP, processes it, and then transmits its results to be processed by the next function would be one use case for the suggested communication library. The benchmark application's function count was increased in order to observe the impact of network speed on the communication library's performance. In order to measure throughput for an execution with a chain of n functions, there would be a single producer, n − 2 forwarders, and finally a single consumer because this work used a simple copy operation for the data processing stage. This graph of functions is displayed in Figure 2.10. Without performing any additional processing, each forwarder in the chain merely copied the data it received on its input connection and wrote it to its output connection as quickly as it could. Keep in mind that the configuration for the previous throughput test between two functions is the same as the case n = 2 with no forwarders. The present study employed the identical methodology as its predecessors, utilizing identical function memory (3072 MB), read buffers (8 kB), and data sent (1 GB) sizes. For every value n = 3, 4, 5, 10, 50, it conducted five trials. Table 2.4 presents the findings. For comparison, the results of the previous throughput test for n = 2 are also included in this table. Notably, even for a very basic application that performs no real computation, the performance varies greatly between runs. Even though there is a lot of variation between runs and none of the larger cases are as consistent as n = 2, you should still be able to use TCP communication at the end of a long function pipeline to obtain data throughput that is significantly higher than 600 Mbps. Another finding is that a trial with 50 functions took roughly 28 seconds to complete in real time, while a trial with just two functions took about 12 seconds. This discrepancy can be attributed to the time required for function initialization and

NAT traversal to establish connections, as well as the fact that there are more functions for the data to pass through. This experiment was designed to measure potential throughput rather than latency. The outcomes show that, under certain conditions, a workload where CPU processing is not a bottleneck, a multi-stage data processing pipeline with high throughput can be implemented using the suggested communication library. This demonstrates the inherent variability in its performance as well as the maximum throughput that can be achieved with AWS Lambda using the communication library (Figure 2.10).

Table 2.4. *Throughput (Mbps) for n-Function Chain*

n	2	3	4	5	10	50
Run 1	682.517	613.047	679.856	604.428	679.200	629.934
Run 2	674.673	679.712	636.615	673.883	652.200	610.505
Run 3	680.248	681.710	667.813	620.689	647.970	631.217
Run 4	680.236	677.091	643.818	519.874	672.744	608.416
Run 5	679.362	679.981	665.965	646.269	677.361	618.527
Average	679.407	666.308	658.813	613.029	665.895	619.720

Source: https://vtechworks.lib.vt.edu/server/api/core/bitstreams/75f6f77c-7f68-416b-919b-8008c7a6a922/content.

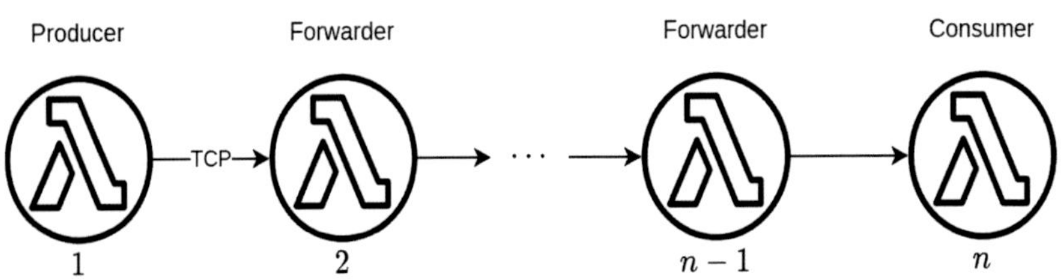

Figure 2.10. *n-function chain for throughput experiment.*

Source: https://vtechworks.lib.vt.edu/server/api/core/bitstreams/75f6f77c-7f68-416b-919b-8008c7a6a922/content.

2.6.1.2. Latency

While the throughput between Lambda functions is more important for data processing, this work also tried to measure the network latency. There is variance to where Lambda provisions containers for different instances of a function—they could possibly be on the same machine or separate machines either close together or far apart. The latency experiment started two instances of a function where one sent a small message over a TCP connection, and the other waited to receive it and then responded immediately. The first function measured the total round-trip time between when it sent the original message and received a response. A small message size of 16 bytes was chosen so it would be guaranteed to fit in a single packet and because using other sizes made no appreciable difference. Each trial with two functions sent 500 round trip messages at 50 ms intervals. There were ten trials and each of which was a cold start so that Lambda used new containers for every function to get a broader sample. The round-trip times varied from 0.38 to 22.34 ms with an average across trials of 0.98 ms. See box plots for each trial in Figure 2.11. A notable finding is high variability between trials. Since using cold starts for each trial forced Lambda to provision new containers each time, this shows that the latency between functions depends on AWS Lambda's internal placement of containers. The results also had a high number of outliers; note that Figure 2.11 only shows outliers up to 3 ms, but the maximum overall time was 22.34 ms. Even though the round-trip time for TCP connections between functions has variability, the average latency of around 1 ms will be more than sufficient for most data processing applications, as throughput is more important.

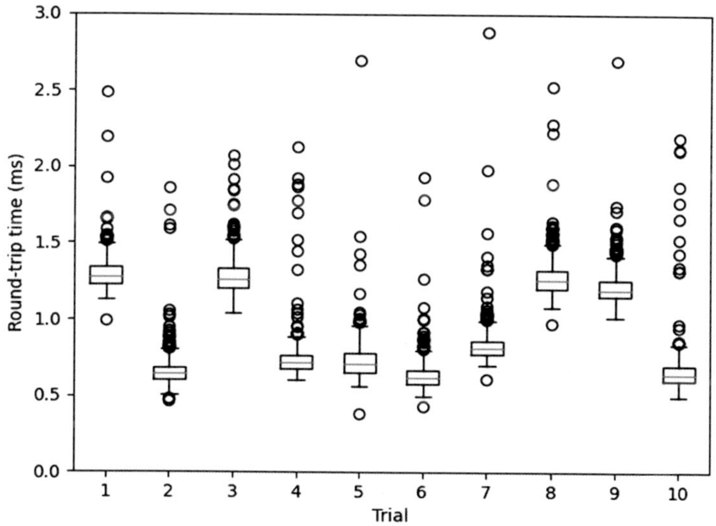

Figure 2.11. *Round-trip time between pairs of function instances.*

Source: https://vtechworks.lib.vt.edu/server/api/core/bitstreams/75f6f77c-7f68-416b-919b-8008c7a6a922/content.

2.6.2. TCP Versus S3 Comparison

In order to compare the performance of using TCP networking for communication versus S3 object storage, this work developed a distributed serverless application using the suggested communications library. Based on a map-reduce computation paradigm, it implemented a large-scale reduce-by-key application using several stages of functions for merging. String keys and floating point values made up the input data set, which was combined by adding the values for each unique key. As seen in Figure 2.12, the application employed a binary tree topology. Two sources provide data to each function: TCP connections for later stages or S3 objects for the first. After processing its input, it sends it to a function in the next stage via a TCP connection, except in the case of the final function, which writes the completely reduced output to S3. The experiments used 101 input files with a total of 44.5 million key-value pairs that were reduced to 1.9 million unique keys. Each run used 104 Lambda functions configured with 3072 MB of memory each. The experiment consisted of 6 executions, but the first was discarded so that all runs used warm starts for consistency. It measured the total billed duration of all functions as well as the real time elapsed from when the communication library orchestrator started the first function to when the last function exited.

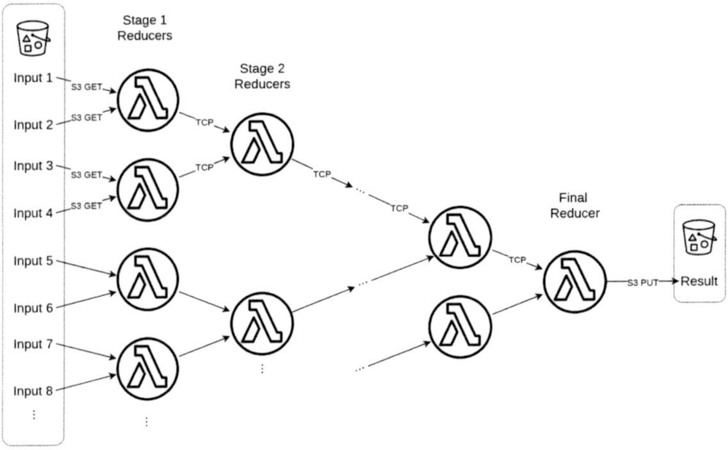

Figure 2.12. *Function graph for reduce-by-key application.*

Source: https://vtechworks.lib.vt.edu/server/api/core/bitstreams/75f6f77c-7f68-416b-919b-8008c7a6a922/content.

Table 2.5. *Communication Method Performance for Reduce-by-Key Application*

For comparison, this work ran an experiment using the same data and methodology but using S3 for inter-function communication instead of TCP. Instead of using TCP connections between pairs of functions to send data, the first function wrote all the data to an S3 object, and the receiving function read that object once it was completely written. Table 2.5 compares the real-time and cost measurement results for the TCP and S3 implementations. Using TCP connections is 4.7 times faster and costs only 52% as much based on Lambda execution time.

Trial	S3		TCP	
	Billed duration (s)	Real time (s)	Billed duration (s)	Real time (s)
Run 1	821.158	156.972	434.830	33.310
Run 2	758.467	157.013	420.921	33.631
Run 3	808.216	154.258	430.776	32.629
Run 4	837.696	153.305	419.542	32.907
Run 5	810.812	155.919	405.974	32.412
Average	807.270	155.493	422.409	32.978

Source: https://vtechworks.lib.vt.edu/server/api/core/bitstreams/75f6f77c-7f68-416b-919b-8008c7a6a922/content.

One reason the proposed communication library achieves a large improvement using network connections is that functions send data incrementally so later stages can start processing data in parallel to previous ones. However, when using S3, an entire object must be created before it could be read, so the implementation with S3 does not achieve this same parallelism. This could be somewhat optimized by writing multiple smaller S3 objects, but this would require significant implementation effort and is not done by Amazon Web Service's sample Lambda map-reduce implementation either. Compared to am S3-only implementation, the proposed communication library achieves significant time and cost savings by using direct TCP connections for inter-function communication.

REFERENCES

1. Cadden, J., Unger, T., Awad, Y., Dong, H., Krieger, O., & Appavoo, J. (2020). SEUSS: Skip redundant paths to make serverless fast. In *Proceedings of EuroSys 2020*. ACM. https://doi.org/10.1145/3342195.3387518.
2. Carver, B., et al. (2020). Wukong: A scalable and locality-enhanced framework for serverless parallel computing. In *Proceedings of the 11th ACM Symposium on Cloud Computing (SoCC'20)* (pp. 1–15). Association for Computing Machinery. https://doi.org/10.1145/3458805.3476033.
3. Chard, R., et al. (2020). FuncX: A federated function serving fabric for science. In *Proceedings of the 29th International Symposium on High-Performance Parallel and Distributed Computing (HPDC'20)* (pp. 65–76). Association for Computing Machinery. https://doi.org/10.1145/3367682.3398158.
4. Deese, A. S. (2018). Implementation of unsupervised K-means clustering algorithm within Amazon Web Services Lambda. In *Proceedings of the 18th IEEE/ACM International Symposium on Cluster, Cloud and Grid Computing (CCGrid'18)* (pp. 626–632). IEEE Press. https://doi.org/10.1109/CCGrid.2018.00087.
5. Dukic, V., Bruno, R., Singla, A., & Alonso, G. (2020). Photons: Lambdas on a diet. In *Proceedings of the 11th ACM Symposium on Cloud Computing (SoCC'20)*. Association for Computing Machinery. https://doi.org/10.1145/3456726.3456738.
6. Dukic, V., et al. (2020). Photons: Lambdas on a diet. In *Proceedings of the 11th ACM Symposium on Cloud Computing (SoCC'20)* (pp. 45–59). Association for Computing Machinery. https://doi.org/10.1145/3456726.3456738.
7. Eppinger, J. L. (2005). *Tcp Connections for P2p Apps: A Software Approach to Solving the Nat Problem* (Tech. Rep. ISRI-05-104). Carnegie Mellon University. https://www.isri.cmu.edu/techreports/ISRI-05-104.pdf (accessed on 1 August 2024).
8. Fouladi, S., et al. (2017). Encoding, fast and slow: Low-latency video processing using thousands of tiny threads. In *14th USENIX Symposium on Networked Systems Design and Implementation (NSDI 17)* (pp. 363–376). USENIX Association. https://doi.org/10.5555/3027476.3027505.
9. Fouladi, S., et al. (2019). From laptop to lambda: Outsourcing everyday jobs to thousands of transient functional containers. In *2019 USENIX Annual Technical Conference (USENIX ATC 19)* (pp. 475–488). USENIX Association. https://doi.org/10.5555/3320073.3320125.

10. Jonas, E., et al. (2017). Occupy the cloud: Distributed computing for the 99%. In *Proceedings of the 2017 Symposium on Cloud Computing (SoCC'17)* (pp. 445–451). Association for Computing Machinery. https://doi.org/10.1145/3132595.3132618.
11. Klimovic, A., et al. (2018). Pocket: Elastic ephemeral storage for serverless analytics. In *13th USENIX Symposium on Operating Systems Design and Implementation (OSDI 18)* (pp. 427–444). USENIX Association. https://doi.org/10.5555/3293061.3293090
12. Klimovic, A., et al. (2018). Understanding ephemeral storage for serverless analytics. In *2018 USENIX Annual Technical Conference (USENIX ATC 18)* (pp. 789–794). USENIX Association. https://doi.org/10.5555/3321217.3321296.
13. Perez, A., et al. (2019). A programming model and middleware for high throughput serverless computing applications. In *Proceedings of the 34th ACM/SIGAPP Symposium on Applied Computing (SAC'19)* (pp. 106–113). Association for Computing Machinery. https://doi.org/10.1145/3293663.3293712.
14. Pu, Q., Venkataraman, S., & Stoica, I. (2019). Shuffling, fast and slow: Scalable analytics on serverless infrastructure. In *16th USENIX Symposium on Networked Systems Design and Implementation (NSDI 19)* (pp. 193–206). USENIX Association. https://doi.org/10.5555/3318216.3318236.
15. Sampe, J., et al. (2018). Serverless data analytics in the IBM cloud. In *Proceedings of the 19th International Middleware Conference Industry (Middleware'18)* (pp. 1–8). Association for Computing Machinery.
16. Shankar, V., et al. (2020). Serverless linear algebra. In *Proceedings of the 11th ACM Symposium on Cloud Computing (SoCC'20)* (pp. 281–295). Association for Computing Machinery. https://doi.org/10.1145/3458805.3476034.
17. Singhvi, A., et al. (2020). SNF: Serverless network functions. In *Proceedings of the 11th ACM Symposium on Cloud Computing (SoCC'20)* (pp. 296–310). Association for Computing Machinery. https://doi.org/10.1145/3456726.3456735.
18. Tariq, A., et al. (2020). Sequoia: Enabling quality-of-service in serverless computing. In *Proceedings of the 11th ACM Symposium on Cloud Computing (SoCC'20)* (pp. 311–327). Association for Computing Machinery. https://doi.org/10.1145/3456726.3456739.
19. Thomas, S., et al. (2020). Particle: Ephemeral endpoints for serverless networking. In *Proceedings of the 11th ACM Symposium on Cloud*

Computing (SoCC'20) (pp. 16–29). Association for Computing Machinery. https://doi.org/10.1145/3456726.3456737.

20. Wang, A., et al. (2020). InfiniCache: Exploiting ephemeral serverless functions to build a cost-effective memory cache. In *18th USENIX Conference on File and Storage Technologies (FAST 20)* (pp. 267–281). USENIX Association. https://www.usenix.org/conference/fast20/presentation/wang
21. Zhang, M., et al. (2019). Seneca: Fast and low cost hyperparameter search for machine learning models. In *2019 IEEE 12th International Conference on Cloud Computing (CLOUD)* (pp. 404–408). IEEE. https://doi.org/10.1109/CLOUD.2019.00068.
22. Zhang, M., et al. (2019). Video processing with serverless computing: A measurement study. In *Proceedings of the 29th ACM Workshop on Network and Operating Systems Support for Digital Audio and Video (NOSSDAV'19)* (pp. 61–66). Association for Computing Machinery. https://doi.org/10.1145/3314140.3314149.
23. Zhang, T., et al. (2019). Narrowing the gap between serverless and its state with storage functions. In *Proceedings of the ACM Symposium on Cloud Computing (SoCC'19)* (pp. 1–12). Association for Computing Machinery. https://doi.org/10.1145/3357223.3362718.
24. Zhang, W., et al. (2020). Kappa: A programming framework for serverless computing. In *Proceedings of the 11th ACM Symposium on Cloud Computing (SoCC'20)* (pp. 328–343). Association for Computing Machinery. https://doi.org/10.1145/3458805.3476044.

CHAPTER 3

HYBRID SERVERLESS COMPUTING: OPPORTUNITIES AND CHALLENGES

Contents

INTRODUCTION

Hybrid serverless computing represents a paradigm shift in the way applications are developed, deployed, and managed. Combining the best of both serverless and traditional computing models, hybrid serverless computing offers a flexible, scalable, and cost-effective approach to application development. In traditional computing models, developers are responsible for managing the underlying infrastructure, including servers, storage, and networking. In contrast, serverless computing abstracts these concerns, allowing developers to focus solely on writing code and business logic. This abstraction is achieved through services like AWS Lambda, Azure Functions, and Google Cloud Functions, which automatically scale and manage the infrastructure based on the application's needs.

The hybrid serverless model integrates serverless functions with traditional server-based applications and services, enabling organizations to leverage the advantages of both approaches. This model allows for greater flexibility, as developers can choose the most appropriate computing paradigm for each component of their application. For instance, compute-intensive tasks can run on traditional servers, while event-driven functions are handled serverlessly. This hybrid approach can optimize performance, reduce costs, and enhance scalability. However, hybrid serverless computing also presents several challenges. One of the primary challenges is managing the complexity of integrating and orchestrating different computing models. Ensuring seamless communication and interoperability between serverless functions and traditional servers can be complex and require sophisticated architectural design. Additionally, monitoring and debugging applications in a hybrid environment can be more challenging due to the distributed nature of the system.

Security is another critical concern. With the increased surface area of a hybrid system, ensuring robust security measures are in place for both serverless and traditional components is paramount. Finally, organizations must also consider the cost implications of a hybrid approach, as it requires careful planning to balance the benefits of serverless computing with the potential costs associated with traditional server management.

3.1. CONCEPT OF HYBRID SERVERLESS COMPUTING

Cloud computing has developed from infrastructure services offered by cloud providers to a wide range of services required for application development. Hybrid cloud architectures, in which the components of an application are dispersed across several cloud providers, are becoming more and more popular as more businesses move their applications to the cloud. This could be because developers want to take advantage of unique features provided by various platforms, because they are attempting to avoid vendor lock-in, because they are consolidating applications that were independently developed across heterogeneous platforms, or because of regulatory constraints that require a hybrid on-premise and cloud architecture. The integration of edge platforms, IoT devices, and personal computers—an architecture known as hybrid computing—is a logical next step in this evolution, as shown in Figure 3.1.

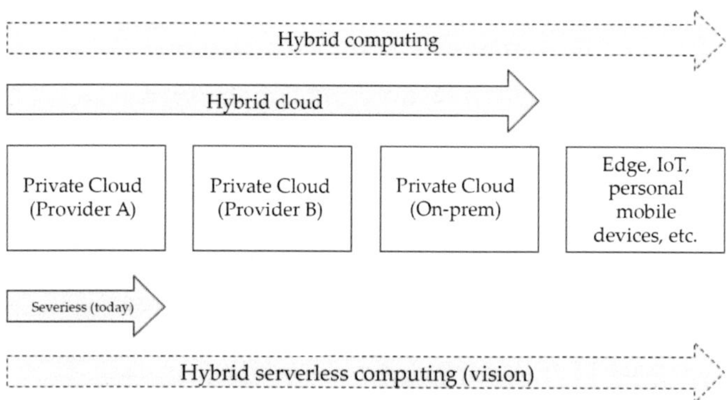

Figure 3.1. *Evolution of hybrid cloud and related areas.*

Source: https://arxiv.org/pdf/2208.04213.

From executing an application on a single public cloud provider to hybrid environments combining several public and private clouds, cloud computing has come a long way. We see this evolution continuing to include personal computers and edge devices, which we call hybrid computing. Currently, serverless computing is mostly restricted to apps that operate on a single provider's platform. We envision a hybrid serverless computing paradigm where applications spanning multiple clouds and devices are served by the serverless principles.

Less than ten years after public clouds first appeared, serverless platforms are a logical progression of cloud computing that emphasize pay-per-use, scalability, and simplicity with little to no knowledge of cloud servers. Serverless computing (Baldini I et al. 2017), primarily in the shape of serverless solutions like Knative Serving (Kaviani N, et al.) and Functions-as-a-Service (FaaS). 2019), users concentrate on creating and implementing their application logic while ignoring the majority of infrastructure issues. Because it enables developers to concentrate more on their application logic and less on non-differentiating platform configuration and operation, this has improved developer productivity. Applying serverless concepts to a hybrid environment, where heterogeneity and distribution amplify the difficulties associated with cloud native development, seems to have a lot of potential advantages. In general, the "serverless mindset" refers to building systems with an emphasis on business value and as little overhead as possible.

It is challenging to directly apply serverless concepts that were initially created for a single vendor platform to a hybrid environment. The same non-technical and technical forces driving the evolution of hybrid cloud and hybrid computing, however, will also compel developers of serverless applications to take a more comprehensive and diverse approach to the concept. According to Wade Tyler Millward (2022), the emerging hybrid cloud market has the potential to grow to a value of over a trillion dollars. However, we believe that serverless vendors face obstacles from both technical and business factors that limit the adoption of this expansive concept of hybrid serverless computing.

3.2. TRENDS IN CLOUD AND SERVERLESS COMPUTING

3.2.1. Cloud and Hybrid Cloud

Cloud evolved from early ideas of Utility (Parkhill DF 1966) and Grid Computing (Foster, et al. 2022). An early definition of cloud computing has similarities with the definition of serverless computing (Armbrust M et al.,2010):

- The appearance of infinite computing resources available on demand, quickly enough to follow load surges.
- The elimination of an up-front commitment by cloud users.
- The ability to pay for use of computing resources on a short-term basis as needed (e.g., processors by the hour and storage by the day) and release them as needed.

According to that definition, cloud computing (as well as others like Buyya R. et al. 2009)) developed into "a computer usage method where software and data are managed or stored on a network of servers.." Infrastructure-as-a-Service (IaaS) cloud computing got its start in 2006 when Amazon Elastic Compute Cloud became widely accessible through Amazon Web Services (AWS).

In the current era of hyperscalers, a small number of planet-scale public platform providers control the majority of the cloud market. The word "cloud" is frequently used to refer to for-profit public clouds like Microsoft Azure, AWS, and Google Cloud, which provide a range of hardware and software services that customers can use on a pay-per-use basis. Although this can all be done self-service and eliminates the need to manage physical data centers, users still need to be aware of, configure, and manage cloud resources. The majority of cloud native applications are constructed using a vertical, segmented stack of software services and infrastructure options found on each cloud provider platform. A wide range of services that are particular to each provider are provided by cloud providers. There are currently little to no industry standards, and services from different providers do not work together seamlessly. Although some managed open source software is offered by cloud providers, each one will have different features and tooling. It is difficult to transfer installed applications from one provider to another.

In actuality, this lack of compatibility might draw attention to the necessity of making apps more portable across cloud providers and expanding beyond a small number of hyperscale cloud providers. Many businesses today already use multiple cloud service providers. This may be intentional, as users will inevitably want to create hybrid or multi-cloud solutions to avoid vendor lock-in and take advantage of the best services available, or it may just be the outcome of certain industries' naturally uncoordinated adoption of cloud computing. Larger businesses have made large capital investments in their own private data centers, and using a hybrid system that combines public and on-premises clouds makes sense in many situations. Concerns about data privacy, industry-specific regulations, and changing legal landscapes are also becoming more and more urgent; initiatives such as GAIA-X aim to limit data use and computation to protect data sovereignty. Because of this, the hyperscale cloud providers and other outside suppliers are trying to make the process of developing hybrid or multi-cloud solutions less difficult.

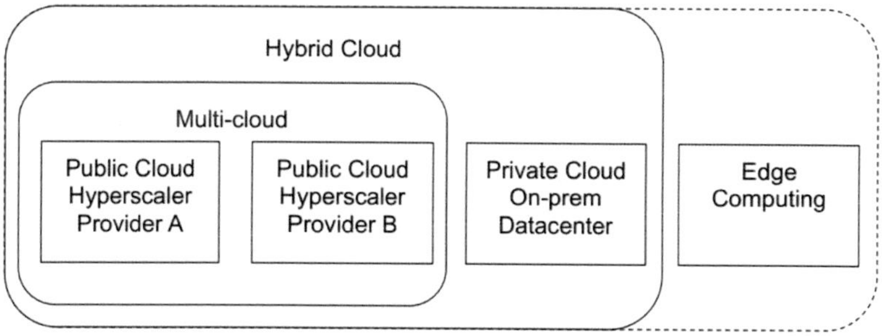

Figure 3.2. *Relations between public cloud, private cloud, multi-cloud, hybrid cloud, and edge computing.*

Source: https://arxiv.org/pdf/2208.04213.

Many terms are being defined to represent various viewpoints on this emerging, heterogeneous, distributed platform, including multi-cloud, hybrid cloud, polycloud, and supercloud (Kaur K, et al. 2017). In this context, public clouds, on-premise data centers, and edge services are all included under the umbrella term "hybrid cloud.." At IBM, hybrid cloud refers to the integration of on-premises, private, and public cloud infrastructure into a single, adaptable, and economically efficient IT system. The emphasis of Microsoft's definition is on app and data sharing between hybrid cloud environments. Certain individuals characterize hybrid cloud as encompassing "multi-cloud" setups, in which an enterprise employs multiple public clouds alongside their on-premise datacenter. The relationships between the various elements of hybrid computing are depicted in Figure 3.2.

Many in academia and business view hybrid clouds as dispersed platforms for developing applications that are not dependent on a single supplier and are made up of disparate services that can operate anywhere. For instance, Sky Computing's vision is based on the development of the Internet, and its objective is to use industry-wide protocols to connect cloud providers' and other heterogeneous cloud platforms' offerings (Stoica I, et al. 2021). Pemberton N., et al., "The RESTless Cloud." 2021) highlights the requirement for a POSIX-like industry standard for cloud APIs in order to facilitate interoperability. In a similar vein, Zhang Y. et al. 2021) searches for declarative approaches at a high level, enabling users to define their own clouds according to the needs of their applications. Hybrid cloud solutions are marketed by companies such as HPE GreenLake and Dell Technologies APEX. Crossplane is an open-source project that is presently in the Cloud Native Computing Foundation's (CNCF) incubation stage. It enables users to manage resources across multiple clouds via a high-level Kubernetes interface.

3.2.2. Computing Trends Toward Hybrid Computing

According to Mytton D 2020, there are between 10 and 100 million servers utilized across all public clouds, and there are even more in private clouds and on-site data centers. Globally, between one and three billion personal computers are in use. In addition to supporting increasingly sophisticated computing functions, modern computing devices also have constant Internet connectivity.

While there are many servers in hybrid clouds today that can be used to process large amounts of data, the number of personal computers (PCs), including laptops, smartphones, and Internet of Things (IoT) devices, is still growing.

As per Turner A's (2018) research, there are currently over 6.5 billion smartphone users worldwide, which translates to approximately 83% of the global population. There are currently many times more IoT devices than people, and this number is increasing quickly. In 2021, there were over 35 billion IoT devices, and by 2025, it is expected to have doubled.

Table 3.1. *Number of Computing Devices in 2022 Based on Estimates Available*

Computing paradigm	Number of devices (in billions)
Hybrid cloud	0.1–1B
Personal computing (PC)	1–3B
Smartphones	6–7B
IoT	> 35B

Source: https://arxiv.org/pdf/2208.04213.

Edge computing, which offers low latency and high bandwidth intermediate computing capabilities, is a crucial component in tying the cloud to consumer and Internet of Things devices. According to IDC, the global edge computing market is expected to reach $250 billion by 2024, growing at a compound annual growth rate (CAGR) of 12.5 percent during the 2019–2024 forecast period. Edge computing is also expanding quickly.

Computers are becoming more affordable, energy-efficient, and nearly always Internet-connected. Based on the previously mentioned numbers, we condense the variety of computing device types in Table 3.1.

Hybrid cloud computing is a subset of hybrid computing, which encompasses cloud and edge computing as well as any type of computing that has some sort of connection to the Internet, even if it's only temporary. Future developments could see the emergence or increased significance of other forms of computing, such as distributed computing based on Web3 and Blockchain, fog computing, the metaverse with AR/VR devices, and so forth. Within Figure 3.3 The relationship between hybrid computing, hybrid clouds, and various computing paradigms is demonstrated (Figure 3.4).

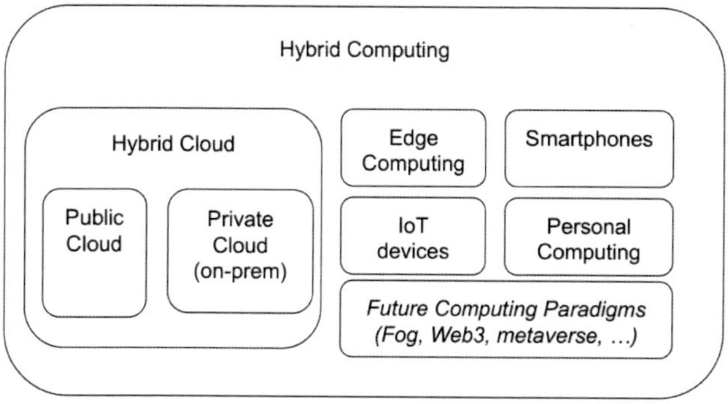

Figure 3.3. *Hybrid computing as a superset of hybrid cloud.*

Source: https://arxiv.org/pdf/2208.04213.

Figure 3.4. *Popularity of "serverless computing" and "hybrid cloud" in the last 15 years. (Google Trends).*

Source: https://www.researchgate.net/publication/362568575/figure/fig3/AS:11870 72404656128@1660031524348/Popularity-of-Serverless-computing-and-Hybrid-Cloud-in-the-last-15-years.ppm.

Any computing paradigm can be combined with hybrid computing to create applications that function seamlessly across various computing infrastructures connected by the Internet.

Serverless computing is becoming more and more popular alongside hybrid cloud, even though hybrid cloud definitions are changing and hybrid computing may change in the future. For instance, Google Trends indicates that the search terms "serverless computing" and "hybrid cloud" are becoming more and more popular. We hypothesize that serverless computing paradigms of the future will emphasize developers, be simple to scale, and be scalable.

3.3. THE CASE FOR HYBRID SERVERLESS COMPUTING

Previously, we defined serverless computing as a platform that executes code on-demand, automatically scales, and bills only for the time the code is executed, all while concealing server usage from developers. This perspective on serverless computing emphasizes the benefits of hiding complexity and shifting a large portion of the work related to infrastructure management, security, compliance, and application scaling to the cloud provider. It also focuses on simplifying compute. Current research (Schleier-Smith J, et al.

2021) projects that serverless computing will predominate and that abstractions that make cloud programming easier will be the way of the future for serverless. With a more expansive understanding of serverless and its economics, it is possible to contend that it is an advancement of the cloud platform itself and a vital component in luring the upcoming generation of developers to the cloud. Since its inception, serverless has promoted several values, one of which is simplifying cloud programming. The value of serverless computing, according to Tim Wagner, the former general manager of AWS Lambda and man credited with pioneering serverless compute, is increased productivity for application developers by "getting rid of undifferentiated heavy lifting" and enabling "capital efficient value creation.."

These days, "serverless" services go beyond Functions-as-a-Service (FaaS) and are provided by cloud providers. The executable component is expanded to containerized HTTP endpoints by managed serverless container runtimes like Google Cloud Run and IBM Code Engine, which facilitates the execution of more general-purpose code and lessens the emphasis on the low-latency startup requirements inherent in FaaS. With serverless storage becoming a more popular option and offering users the advantages of auto-scaling, fine-grained billing, and minimal configuration, accessing state from serverless functions in FaaS runtimes is also becoming simpler.

Serverless platforms are made available by open source communities and can operate on any cloud. Cloud providers occasionally offer these platforms as managed services. For instance, open source projects serve as the foundation for both IBM Code Engine and IBM Cloud Functions. Active industrial and research communities use open source serverless projects like Knative, OpenFaas, and Apache OpenWhisk. Open source software is now accessible from all cloud providers, which normalizes the situation and may lay the groundwork for application portability.

Additionally, providers offer planet-scale serverless systems that are independent of the cloud. Although traditional FaaS platforms have limitations on regional deployment, newer services like CloudFlare Workers will automatically migrate function code as needed using their current content distribution network. Users don't always need to know where Snowflake is running—it's a well-known planet-scale data warehouse with serverless features. Ecosystems of cloud-agnostic service providers might expand further in the future as participants can more quickly than today's hyperscalers specialize in solving particular issues for a particular industry. These products' success can be partly attributed to how simple it is to deploy application code globally with minimal low-level configuration. Serverless offers an ideal development platform that federates the heterogeneous, distributed hybrid cloud platform because of its focus on simplifying systems and enabling the transparent and elastic use of compute resources. Raising the abstraction level for developers to a programmatic interface to the cloud with minimal configuration needed to adhere to system-defined limits may be the biggest advantage of serverless computing for increased developer productivity. Concerns about developer productivity can be kept apart from platform optimizations by extending the application of serverless design principles beyond computation to Hybrid Computing.

3.3.1. Hybrid Serverless Architecture Design Principles

At least when it comes to FaaS platforms, the traditional serverless principles offer a simplified but naive view of compute where developers can abstract away worries about the distributed nature of the platform. In a hybrid cloud environment, it might not always be able to abstract away the distribution concerns due to longer latency times, more complex bug fixes that only become apparent at scale, or the requirement to give precise instructions on where to locate application components geographically. The overarching objectives of serverless remain relevant; however, in order to expose the essential abstractions that developers might need, the conventional principles of serverless design must be updated. We re-cast the traditional serverless design principles as follows:

1. ***Don't worry about infrastructure***: Beyond minimizing the need to configure compute, hybrid cloud serverless requires the need to abstract away the additional middleware, often deployed when provisioning primary services, across different cloud providers. For example, networking is often auto-provisioned when requesting a service component but today this only works within a single cloud provider. Identity management across cloud estates is also an open issue.
2. ***Don't worry about capacity***: Today, many serverless offerings beyond FaaS will auto-scale based on the workload requirements. For hybrid cloud serverless, developers will need to be aware of the differences in services across clouds, even those services (like ones based on open source) that are purportedly the same across providers. This means automated discovery and the ability to choose from the discovered options based on transparent optimizations becomes important.
3. ***Don't worry about idle***: Not paying for idle is beneficial for workloads that don't need resources to be provisioned all the time. This finer grained pricing model is beneficial to hybrid cloud serverless but

needs further refinement. First, it should apply to the entire hybrid cloud stack. Beyond charging GB-sec for compute or storage and egress costs for data, it may be necessary for the developer to be more aware of what type of hardware is available, e.g., GPU vs non-GPU, and pricing should reflect this. Also, scale-to-zero has impacts beyond direct costs; improving compute density may impact other factors like sustainable computing (Patros P, et al. 2021).

Keep in mind that these expanded serverless design principles are not intended to address every issue with running distributed applications; rather, they are meant to simplify things for developers. Rather, it offers an insight into how serverless can facilitate cloud evolution and streamline cloud native development. This can provide guidance on building a hybrid serverless architecture.

Let's use the hourglass metaphor from computer networking to represent the interface that cloud vendors provide to application developers as the waist of the hourglass. As Figure 3.5 illustrates, the waist was relatively low in the cloud application stack during a time when developers were creating apps using virtual machine abstractions. But in the serverless era, the vendor is responsible for much more through the serverless interface (like FaaS).

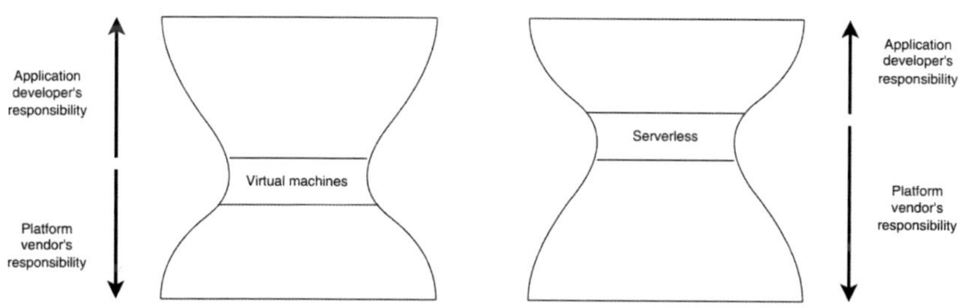

Figure 3.5. *Building cloud applications over a virtual machine abstraction requires the developer to be responsible for more of the application stack. Conversely, serverless abstractions give the platform vendor opportunities to optimize more of the stack.*

Source: https://arxiv.org/pdf/2208.04213.

Single-vendor serverless applications are inherently more likely because the vendor owns a far larger portion of the application stack. This is due to technical factors, such as the vendor's capacity to apply platform-level optimizations due to their visibility into the broader stack. Additionally, there are business incentives like pay-as-you-go serverless billing models, which only turn a profit if the vendor is able to oversee and manage the underlying resources.

The difficulty lies in overcoming the deeply ingrained prejudice against serverless applications from a single vendor. In this chapter, we contend that creating hybrid serverless applications that span vendor services can be done in two ways. While the standards-based approach is more reliable, vendor support is necessary for the compiler-based approach, which does not require any additional support from them.

3.3.2. Benefits to Application Developers and Platform Providers

A hybrid serverless architecture brings a number of benefits both to the serverless application developers and platform providers.

- Developers benefit from the flexibility to migrate their serverless applications to different platform vendors to take advantage of pricing differences. The choice of vendor is not a one-time decision, since an application may exhibit different load patterns as it evolves, and different vendors may offer pricing plans optimized for different classes of workloads.
- Similarly, an application may require different non-functional guarantees (such as throughput targets) or require different platform services (such as a global load balancer) as it matures from a proof-of-concept to a popular production application. Developers need flexibility to migrate vendors as their requirements evolve.
- A related point is that developers may want to deploy portions of their applications to the edge to improve user-perceived latency or leverage a combination of VMbased and serverless based resources for application execution (Raza A, et al. 2021). A hybrid architecture would facilitate more fine-grained deployment choices for portions of the application.
- Similarly, developers may have constraints on where parts of their application can be deployed. For example, there may be regulations that govern where health records can be stored, whether within a country or an on-prem datacenter managed by the company.
- Another developer benefit is the ability to mix and match services provided by different platform vendors rather than make the choice to deploy their entire application on a single platform. For example, they may choose the FaaS platform of one vendor, the logging service from another vendor, and the messaging service from a third one.

Regarding the last point, we still believe that developers should have a choice in how their applications are deployed, even though vendors may discourage such hybrid architectures with their pricing plans and there may be good performance reasons to deploy an entire application on a single platform. Additionally, we think that granting developers this option can help platform vendors in turn, particularly the expanding network of non-hyperscale vendors that are completing gaps in local and sector-specific offerings.

Specifically, today's serverless platforms must provide a wide range of services that developers might require. Vendors can provide specialized services without having to duplicate the whole stack of services required for an enterprise serverless application by making hybrid architectures more developer-friendly. For instance, by separating the specification of the quantum circuit from the underlying runtime system and offering transparent request autoscaling, FaaS can make it easier to integrate quantum computers as accelerators for already-existing enterprise applications (Grossi M et al. 2021). There are comparable benefits in other fields, such as serverless complex event processing. In this situation, platform vendors may become more competitive as a result of developer flexibility, which could lead to a positive feedback loop of reduced prices, more creative service offerings, and a rise in the use of hybrid serverless architectures.

3.3.3. Roadblocks to Hybrid Serverless Computing

In terms of hybrid cloud, the limitations of current serverless computing platforms are reflective of those of the cloud as a whole. Current multi-cloud surveys point to the trend toward hybrid cloud platforms and delineate particular difficulties. Table 3.2 provides a summary of the latter from two surveys.

Currently available serverless platforms are managed services that do not communicate across cloud provider boundaries.

These include AWS Lambda, Azure Functions, Google Cloud Functions, IBM Cloud Functions, and offerings based on open source software like OpenFaaS, Apache OpenWhisk, and Knative. This is reflected by the current use of serverless applications which typically use a single platform because:

1. Serverless relies heavily on a cloud provider's integrated ecosystem of databases, storage, etc. which are not entirely serverless.
2. Serverless applications are mostly built as extensions of already deployed cloud applications, to compose cloud services, or as features of cloud applications.

3. Its relatively easy to end up in anti-patterns of serverless applications design.

Interoperability across various serverless platforms is either not expected at all or is expected very little. The operational complexity of today's hybrid environments, which compels developers to use different tooling for each vendor, is a larger problem that includes this as well.

One cloud environment's experience cannot be transferred to another cloud. Present-day multi-cloud management solutions concentrate primarily on Kubernetes cluster management operations. For instance, the CNCF-incubating project Crossplane focuses on cross-provider resource management via Kubernetes operators, whereas SUSE Rancher assists in managing numerous Kubernetes clusters.

Table 3.2. *Summary of Practitioner Challenges for Hybrid Cloud from Recent Surveys*

Hybrid cloud challenge	Description
Security	Security across multiple clouds remains the highest priority concern as the attack surface is increased, and each cloud vendor has its own identity management and security controls that don't integrate across clouds
Integration complexity	Operating multiple clouds requires specialized skills that don't translate across clouds, and integration of edge components creates additional challenges that are not fully addressed by existing toolsets
Managing costs	Opaque pricing models and lack of comprehensive tools to understand and manage cloud costs makes it difficult to optimize cloud spending
Reduced visibility and control	Observability of deployed resources across clouds reduces the ability to understand what is deployed and how an application is operating
Application modernization	Integrating legacy applications with cloud is an existing problem that is exacerbated by multi-cloud. Even cloud native applications may have inertia and are not portable across different cloud providers

Source: https://arxiv.org/pdf/2208.04213.

A notable exception is Funqy, a Java-based library that uses the Quarkus runtime to let you write Java functions with a single API that is compatible with all FaaS implementations. Although code portability may be enhanced by this, the larger problems with hybrid cloud development remain unaddressed. A certain category of enterprise applications cannot be fully operated on a single public cloud because of financial reasons (e.g., current financial commitments to an on-site data center) and legal restrictions (Takabi H, et al. 2010). Nonetheless, disparate vendors' experiences with development (Raza A, et al. 2021), and the need to acquire non-transferable expertise across cloud estates leads to decreased developer productivity due to vendor and platform lock-in today's most popular serverless platforms.

3.4. TOWARDS A HYBRID SERVERLESS ARCHITECTURE

Using multiple servers and clouds at the same time (sometimes referred to as hybrid serverless multi-cloud) is feasible today, but it is not simple. The primary constraints stem, in part, from the challenges associated with advancing a common set of guidelines and shared abstractions in a setting as intricate as the hybrid cloud. Standards to enable cloud interoperability have long been developed, though most have had mixed results. However, we think that as cloud computing advances, knowledge about how to facilitate hybrid cloud deployments will increase. This understanding will likely involve agreement on interoperability standards, perhaps based on APIs offered by well-known open-source projects.

The trend toward solutions that operate across multiple cloud environments is validated by examples from the industry (Bernhardsson E 2022). Snap claims that their architecture is multi-cloud natively, enabling better pricing and regionalization. With its widespread cloud deployment, Snowflake, a data warehouse service, has surpassed AWS RedShift in market share.

Hybrid Serverless deployments for FaaS architectures have been the subject of recent research; Baarzi et al. The advantages of using a virtual serverless provider to combine serverless platforms from different clouds are discussed in (2021). Chard and associates. federate endpoints in the scientific computing domain in 2020 to carry out serverless operations. Perez along with others. (2019) goes one step further and permits the automatic scalability of distributed endpoints in addition to the deployment of functions on them.

More broadly, scholars are suggesting that the cloud should be understood as the combination of all cloud estates. As a "supercloud" or "sky computing," recent proposals place an emphasis on a consistent developer experience across several clouds: "the vision of a Sky full of computation, rather than isolated clouds."

We think that a convergence of serverless computing, hybrid cloud computing, and changing computing trends may result in hybrid serverless computing. This perspective holds that serverless principles are ingrained in the whole cloud stack, including data centers, edge computing, and Internet of Things devices. This helps to streamline cloud programming and create a clear division of responsibilities between the engineering work required to optimize cloud platforms and developer productivity/operator simplicity.

With the use of containers, Hybrid Serverless Computing unifies all computing paradigms. It offers a serverless computing approach by utilizing a compiler-based approach, which can help automate deployment provisioning across clouds, and a set of standards that enable improved interoperability between clouds.

Serverless encourages the "rental" view of cloud resources, which are used as needed and where an automated platform handles non-differentiating overhead management. It is our view that the rental model always makes sense, even for users that own their own platforms:

- Developer productivity is potentially improved because of a simplified model of the "rented" resources and how they are charged
- Serverless, in the form of FaaS, allows developers and platform operators a portable unit of compute that provides a common abstraction where requirements for improved developer productivity and platform operation meet. Whether it be function source code or containers (or any other unit of compute), this allows a higher degree of flexibility when an application is targeting a heterogeneous platform.
- Auto-scaling and in particular, scale-to-zero, provide value even if the platform is not shared among tenants. Higher utilization helps increase the value of a platform and can help lower costs. In addition, as sustainability becomes a higher priority, reducing the carbon footprint of the platform can also be accomplished by being more serverless.

The method for creating hybrid serverless computing is explained in this section, along with the features that are currently available and those that still require development.

- ***Observation:*** Nowadays, the majority of serverless applications mainly make use of one vendor's services. This is a result of utilizing a vendor's platform's cohesive ecosystem of services, which offers performance advantages and ease of use. Lock-in is also encouraged by pricing incentives such as volume discounts offered by the vendor.

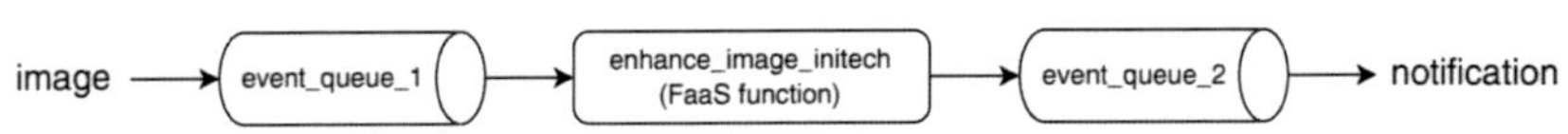

Figure 3.6. *A simple serverless application running on Initech's platform used as a running example.*

Source: https://arxiv.org/pdf/2208.04213.

- ***Hypothesis:*** It is not possible for a single vendor to offer every service with the functional and non-functional characteristics that application developers require. It is unrealistic to anticipate that a single vendor will provide the best-of-breed service in every way because there is too much continuous innovation in cloud services. It is asserted that compiler-based and standards-based methods will both be required.

3.4.1. Compilers and Standards: Two Ways to Achieve Hybrid Serverless Computing

3.4.1.1. Running Example

Imagine a basic serverless application that just says "Hello, World" and has an image processing function. The image may be converted to a different format or a thumbnail may be created by the function. In our example, we take into consideration a function that automatically improves an image by modifying the sharpening or exposure settings. Such a feature is offered by several cloud-based photo organization services.

Within the Figure 3.6, we observe that new images added to an event queue cause the serverless function "enhance_image" to be called. The improved output images are sent to a different event queue, where they could be stored or the user informed of the new image could be triggered by other functions.

The serverless platform of a single vendor is assumed to host all of the components, including the queues and functions, in this architecture. This vendor, let's call them Initech. Imagine that Acme, a different supplier, provides a better-looking image enhancement service. It's possible that Acme's service runs on specialized hardware to provide lower latency, is less expensive to operate, or employs a more sophisticated AI model for image processing. The Acme service can be integrated into this architecture in progressively more complex ways, which will be discussed in the following sections.

3.4.1.2. Implementation Step 1: Blocking API Call

Figure 3.7 illustrates one implementation in which we incorporate a blocking call to Acme's image enhancement service into the application running on Initech's platform.

This implementation has the advantage of being relatively simple, requiring no changes to other areas of the application or unique requirements of either Acme's service or Initech's platform. This is not a fully serverless application, which is a drawback. Specifically, the call to the blocking function is an anti-pattern that leads to double-billing and wasted compute (Baldini I et al. 2017).

3.4.1.3. Implementation Step 2: Event Bridge

The Acme service is now more serverless-friendly in this subsequent implementation. We assume that both vendors permit external calls to trigger FaaS functions but do not permit direct external access to their platform's queues. The final architecture is displayed in Figure 3.8 adds several more queues and features to the platforms of both vendors. Specifically, Acme's platform has an event queue that can start a serverless function to enhance the image. Additionally, the function output is sent to an event queue, which sets off a function that sends the improved image back to the Initech platform's application pipeline. Using event-driven design patterns, this implementation has the advantage of being a pure serverless architecture. The drawback that becomes clear when comparing Figs. The extra architectural elements that were added to bridge the event queues between Initech and Acme's platforms are Figures 3.7 and 3.8. The main application logic does not include these. The fact that the extra parts are exclusive to the hybrid platform is another drawback. These extra parts are unnecessary if we go back to using Initech's picture enhancement services. The deployment complexity is increased by adding and removing these components based on the service the developer decides to use (Figure 3.9).

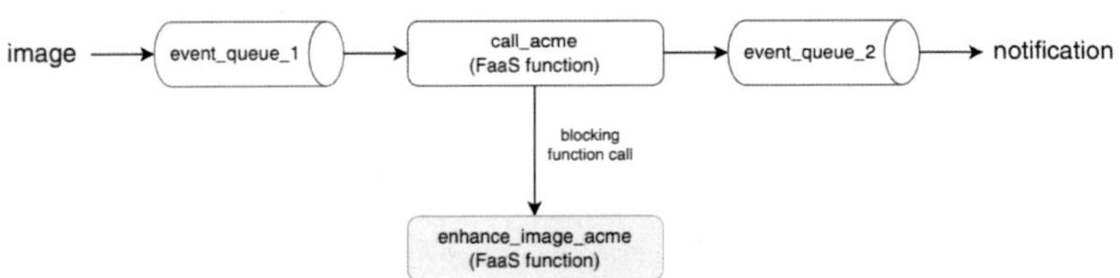

Figure 3.7. *A hybrid serverless application that spans two vendor platforms used as a running example. The clear diagram elements are those deployed on Initech's platform, while the gray elements are those running on Acme's platform.*

Source: https://arxiv.org/pdf/2208.04213.

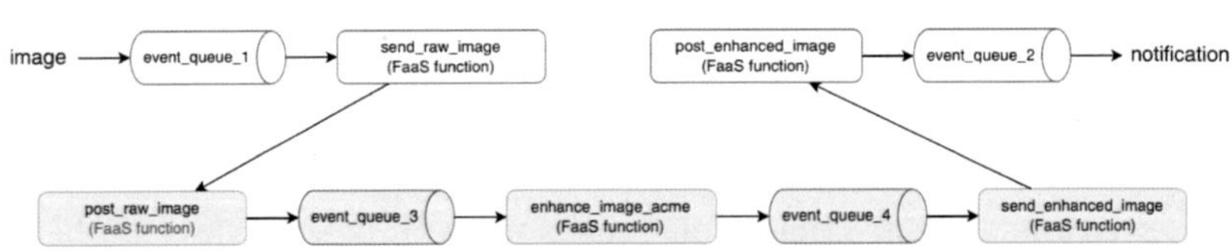

Figure 3.8. *A hybrid serverless application that adheres to serverless best-practices.*

Source: https://arxiv.org/pdf/2208.04213.

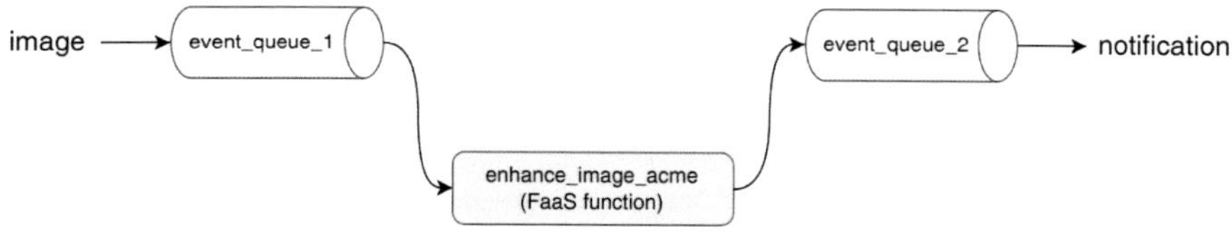

Figure 3.9. *Having vendors support a common eventing standard simplifies the hybrid serverless architecture.*

Source: https://arxiv.org/pdf/2208.04213.

3.4.1.4. Implementation Step 3: Event Standard

In this implementation, we assume that eventing is a widely used enough service that all serverless platform providers follow an eventing standard. This implies that, among other things, Acme's serverless function can publish events to Initech's event queue and subscribe to and be triggered by events in Initech's event queue. This implementation has the advantage of producing a much simpler architecture because it eliminates the need for additional components that would arise from choosing to deploy the application across multiple vendor platforms. This approach's clear drawback is that vendors must adopt and follow an eventing standard. The need to define an eventing standard presents an even more fundamental challenge. This could be an official standard released by a standards body, or it could be an already-existing event interface, like Knative Eventing, that becomes an ad hoc standard. It is still up for debate what the interface and semantics of a serverless eventing standard should be in order to support the variety of environments we want to support, such as resource-constrained IoT devices, secure on-premise data centers, and robust public clouds.

3.4.1.5. Implementation Step 4: Event Bridge with Compiler

The glue components in this implementation are created by a compiler and are used to connect the Initech and Acme platforms' application logic. Interestingly, as shown in Figure 3.10 The deployed architecture output from the compiler should resemble the Event Bridge implementation, while the application logic created by the developer should resemble that of the Event Standard implementation. This implementation has the advantage of shielding the developer from architectural complexities unrelated to the application logic. The drawback is that someone has to build the compiler in order to do this. Developers are also restricted to the vendors that the compiler supports since the compiler must have a native understanding of each vendor platform's capabilities.

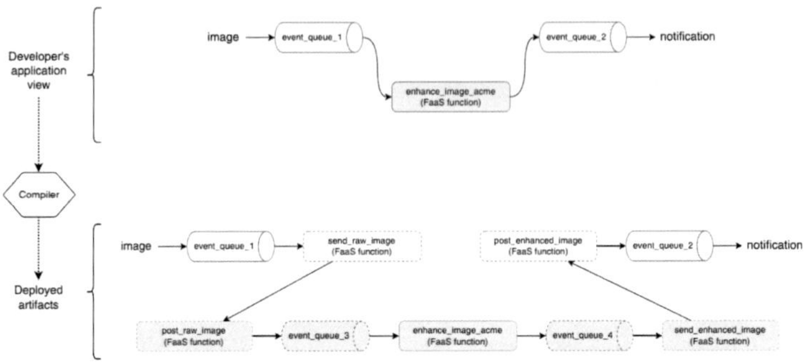

Figure 3.10. *In lieu of a common eventing standard, a compiler can help generate the artifacts needed to bridge vendor platforms. The generated artifacts, which are not part of the core application logic, are depicted with a dotted outline.*

Source: https://arxiv.org/pdf/2208.04213.

3.4.1.6. Implementation Step 5: Offline Service Selection

We now assume that image enhancement is a widely enough-used service in this implementation that vendors follow a well-defined serverless-friendly standard for this service. Stated differently, this service elevates to a first-class feature within a serverless platform. It should be noted that in actuality, other more fundamental backend services, like a key-value storage service, might establish themselves as industry standards before services like picture enhancement ones (Figure 3.11).

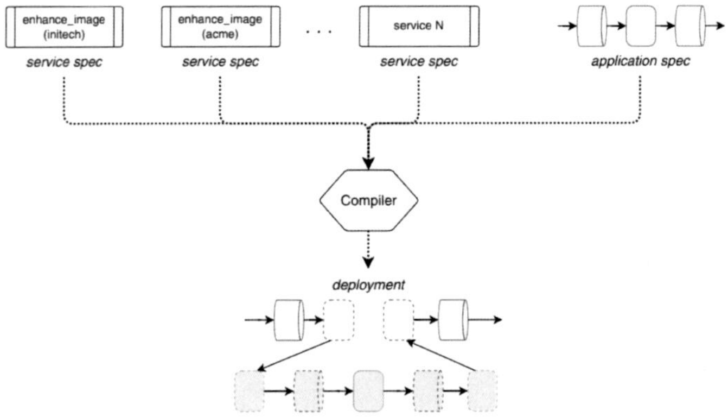

Figure 3.11. *The presence of serverless-friendly standards for service interface specifications and application requirements allows the compiler to select the optimal service across platforms.*

Source: https://arxiv.org/pdf/2208.04213.

This implementation adds a new feature: it can automatically choose the best service based on the non-functional requirements of the application by consulting a catalog of functionally equivalent options. Assume, for instance, that Acme's image enhancement service is more expensive while Initech's is slower. Developers can set a latency requirement in the order of hours and allow the compiler to select the less expensive Initech service if they are aware that offline batch processing is appropriate for the use case of the application. An application with less latency requirements, however, would pick to use Acme's service. The vendor-specific artifacts are generated and deployed automatically in both scenarios.

A standard describing the services is necessary in order to perform service selection. This standard should include both nonfunctional and functional specifications, such as the cost per invocation and response time estimates, as well as functional specifications like the input and output parameters. Even though some service interface standards, like WSDL and the recently proposed AsyncAPI, have been defined in the past, they are not currently widely used. We think there are still unanswered questions about the ideal format for the service interface specification, particularly in regards to serverless-specific issues like cold-start latencies.

Additionally, application developers must have a common method for defining the specifications for their applications. This is another open research challenge that must take into account factors like latency or cost limitations.

A compiler can decide on service selection and deployment once standards have been established for the applications and service interfaces.

There is also an open research challenge regarding the design of the compiler's service selection algorithm. How the methods in the literature (Sun L, et al.) are applied is unclear. 2014) must be expanded to take into account the needs of serverless architecture, including the overhead of extra queues and functions when bridging vendor boundaries and the range of hybrid environments, like the potential for sporadic connectivity when interacting with IoT devices.

3.4.1.7. Implementation Step 6: Runtime Optimizer

This implementation builds on the previous one by adding a component that keeps an eye on an application during runtime and modifies the deployment to keep it compliant with requirements. We now need a standard method to instrument each vendor's platform to monitor the behavior of the application at runtime, in addition to the service and application specifications needed in the previous step's implementation of the Offline Service Selection.

Furthermore, a standardized method for configuring and deploying services within a vendor's platform is necessary for this solution. As there is an alternative in which the compiler receives vendor-specific support, this can be left optional. This latter strategy restricts the range of vendors that the runtime optimizer can work with, but it does not alter the user experience for application developers (Figure 3.12).

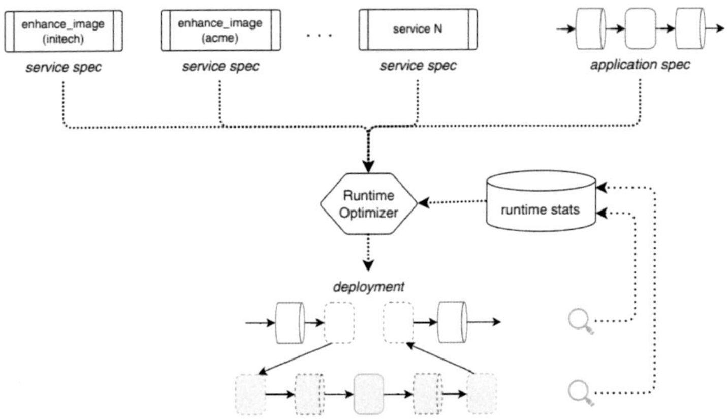

Figure 3.12. *An optimizer monitors application statistics at runtime and makes redeployment decisions based on changing service profiles and requirements.*

Source: https://arxiv.org/pdf/2208.04213.

The optimizer's design in at least two dimensions is an open research question. First, the optimization algorithms can draw from earlier work, just like in the previous implementation, but they must be expanded to account for serverless-specific behaviors and hybrid platform features. Second, since the optimizer is a runtime component, serverless best practices should be considered in its own architecture.

The above hybrid serverless application implementation sequence required a combination of vendor-adopted standards, compiler support, and custom implementations by the developer. These abilities are summed up in Table 3.3. The maturity of standards that are available and that vendors have adopted will determine the implementation strategy.

New capabilities, like the eventing bridging architecture in Implementation Step 2, are likely to follow a pipeline and start off as manual implementations. Compilers will embrace design patterns that emerge from common architectural designs, and as these patterns develop, the community will decide on unofficial or ad hoc standards to support these architectural patterns. This evolution of features is shown in Table 3.4. Since our goal is to show the pattern of development over time, the names of the features are not crucial. Take note that certain features, like "feature_4," might never be adopted as standards, while other features, like "feature_2," might never be promoted to compiler support. Although this progression is not specific to hybrid serverless applications, it offers a helpful framework to push towards the goal of hybrid serverless computing in spite of vendor resistance or community inertia.

Table 3.3. *A Summary of the Capabilities that were Implemented Manually or with the Help of Compilers and Standards*

Implementation	Custom code	Compiler support	Required standards
1: Blocking API call	API call		
2: Event bridge	Eventing		
3: Event standard			Eventing
4: Event bridge with compiler		Eventing	
5: Offline service selection		Service selection	+ Service, application
6: Runtime optimizer		Online replanning	+ Monitoring, deployment

Source: https://arxiv.org/pdf/2208.04213.

Compiler-based approaches can assist application developers in creating hybrid applications in the absence of standards by removing the need to worry about the specifics of bridging across vendor platforms. Implementation 4 exemplifies this methodology.

We can think of different strategies once standards are more developed. Implementation 3 results, for instance, when vendors only agree on an eventing standard, but Implementation 6 achieves the full hybrid serverless vision through a comprehensive set of standards on the services and platform.

It is our opinion that the current state of serverless platforms is changing too quickly for standards to encompass all of the functional and non-functional requirements for services and applications. Vendors might wish to provide platforms that are HIPPA-certified, use green energy, have specialized hardware for workloads involving machine learning training, or offer instances of quantum computing.

Developers will first implement all of these new innovations manually, and later, compilers with built-in knowledge of these vendor-specific features will support compiler-based approaches.

Developers can switch to the standards-based approach as these innovations become more commonplace and standards emerge. The shift from compiler-based to standards-based will continue.

Table 3.4. *An Illustration of how Capabilities Exercised by Hybrid Serverless Application Architectures will get Promoted From Manually Being Implemented by Application Developers, to Being Supported by Compilers, and Finally Getting Adopted as Ad-Hoc or Official Standards*

	Implemented manually	Supported by compilers	Adopted as standards
Time 1	feature_1		
Time 2	feature_2	feature_1	
Time 3	feature_3	feature_2	feature_1
Time 4	feature_4	feature_2, feature_3	feature_1
Time 5	feature_4, feature_5	feature_2	feature_1, feature_3
Time 6	feature_4	feature_2, feature_5	feature_1, feature_3

Source: https://arxiv.org/pdf/2208.04213.

3.4.2. Vision

The scope of Hybrid Serverless Computing will expand to encompass Edge Computing, IoT, and emerging new computing paradigms as various approaches mature. We anticipate that over an extended duration, various forms of computing (Serverless, Cloud, IoT, etc.) will eventually converge to form a Hybrid Computing paradigm that is just as user-friendly as Serverless Computing is now, giving rise to Hybrid Serverless Computing.

3.5. OPPORTUNITIES AND CHALLENGES OF HYBRID SERVERLESS COMPUTING

Many cross-disciplinary challenges, including those related to data placement, task scheduling, universal identity management, and code and data migration, are associated with a hybrid serverless architecture.

When bridging across serverless platforms from various providers, it is also necessary to address the impedance mismatch, taking into account non-functional characteristics like latency, scalability, availability, and cost. While optimizing for cold-start behavior has been studied, for instance, in the context of serverless functions deployed on a single platform, the emergent cold-start behavior when serverless functions operate across providers will be significantly impacted by scheduling and data placement at scale (Figure 3.13).

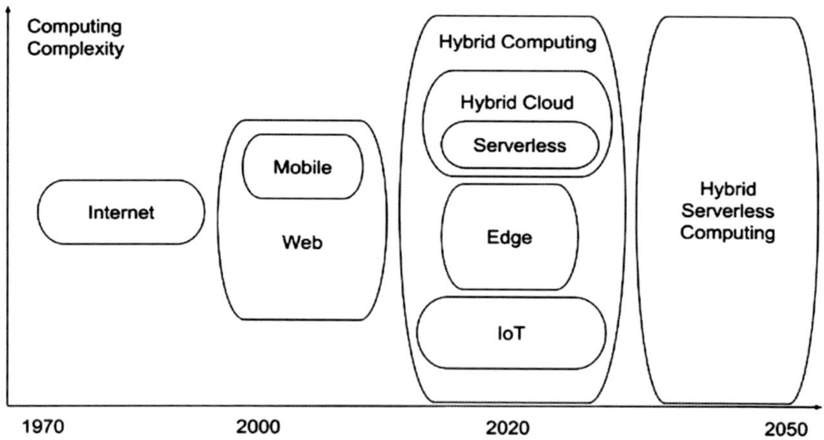

Figure 3.13. *Evolution of computing towards hybrid serverless computing.*

Source: https://arxiv.org/pdf/2208.04213.

Reconciling functional mismatches like security policies and messaging semantics is also necessary. There are a number of serverless computing opportunities and difficulties that have been noted. In this segment, we examine them in the framework of Hybrid Serverless Computing (HSC) and pinpoint fresh obstacles and unresolved research issues. We begin with a specific issue that we think is essential to the uptake of HSC.

3.5.1. Standards

For application developers, the current state of serverless standards and provider interoperability is disorganized. According to surveys, one of the biggest pain points for developers is complexity like vendor lock-in. They also use dozens of different tools and spend a lot of time maintaining their development environments. Many of the abstraction layers found in other, more established platforms are absent from serverless development.

Stickiness and vendor lock-in particular are becoming more and more of an issue. For instance, it can be costly to transfer large volumes of data out of one cloud provider, and certain features are provider-specific and not as well supported by other cloud providers. The process of developing a widely accepted standard will take time, but before standards are approved, they must develop naturally and adhere to a bottom-up methodology, much like the IETF Internet Standards, which standardize best practices and require several implementations. The practical evolution of Web Services standards can be observed in their creation by IBM, Microsoft, and other major corporations. Despite initial expectations that tooling would conceal the complexity of

SOAP, XML, and WS-* standards, RESTful Web services ultimately prevailed by improving upon simplicity and adding features that were lacking from the bottom up to already functional HTTP-related standards. The only way to successfully develop standards for Hybrid Serverless Computing is to base them on current implementations and advocate for similar simplicity.

The following are some of the key components that, in our opinion, ought to form the foundation of a new hybrid serverless computing standard.

- ***Basic code packaging standards:*** The CNCF Open Container Initiative (OCI) offers an open standard and is the only packaging format needed. Likewise, orchestration of containers is necessary. The most widely used open platform, Kubernetes, is quickly taking over as the accepted method for code packing. The primary benefit of using containers is that they can run smoothly in Kubernetes cluster environments in addition to giving developers the flexibility to package code and libraries in a container (Shepherd D 2022). To run their customers' containers, many cloud providers—if not all of them—offer Kubernetes services right out of the box.
- ***Service Specification Standards***: In addition to having a standard for code packaging and execution, it is essential because we anticipate that these containers will operate on various computing platforms. g. The Internet of Things, Cloud, Edge, and even consumer electronics like smartphones and pcs\. Should not have different, incompatible standards for each of these platforms. We anticipate that newer standards like AsyncAPI and OpenAPI will become more widely accepted and utilized in HSC.
- ***Open Source APIs as evolving standards***: The challenge of developing industry-wide standards stems from the rapid changes in the cloud native development landscape and the breadth of services offered. Sometimes the widespread use of a service leads to the creation of de facto standards; for instance, many platforms now support the S3 API for object storage. Scholars are suggesting that open source APIs be used as a starting point for developing workable standards that can change as a service becomes more or less popular. By using a community consensus approach, a domain is not restricted to a specification; instead, the specification develops (and ends) naturally as a result of real usage.

  Apart from the aforementioned building blocks, standardizing other elements of the hybrid serverless application, like eventing (e.g., Cloud Events), vendor deployments, application requirement definition, and runtime monitoring.

Together, academia and industry can develop best practices based on fruitful open source projects (for instance, by developing compiler-based approaches as we previously discussed) and transform unofficial standards into fruitful open international standards with the same degree of influence as previous Internet interoperable standards.

3.5.2. Foundational Challenges in Hybrid Serverless Computing

While many of these issues have been discussed and partially resolved in the context of one cloud server computing provider, we describe below how they vary in the context of Hybrid Serverless Computing (HSC).

Since 2017, a lot of progress has been made in the field of serverless computing research. Larger-scale experimentation is made possible by the abundance of open source platforms and the generous free tiers offered by cloud providers. For instance, Apache OpenWhisk is a well-known open source FaaS platform that is utilized in both academic and commercial contexts. It is included in offerings like Adobe I/O Runtime, IBM Cloud Functions, and Nimbella.

Scholars have delineated authentic workloads submitted to serverless platforms and the QoS-related conduct of authentic production platforms. The possible serverless attack surface is now better understood. Additionally, researchers have been working to optimize serverless job configuration. For instance, several disadvantages of serverless platforms were noted (Hellerstein JM et al. 2019) enumerated restrictions like I/O bottlenecks, communication through sluggish storage, lack of specialized hardware, and brief serverless function lifetimes. Future enhancements, including flexible code and data placement, support for heterogeneous hardware, long-running code support, SLAs, and security considerations, have also been noted.

The benefits of hybrid serverless are being studied in more recent work; for instance, scheduling stateless functions across heterogeneous (e.g., target platforms (Smith CP, et al.) and develop data-aware scheduling across various serverless target nodes. 2022). Mampage along with others. provides a thorough serverless model that is applied to the traditional resource management problem to incorporate fog and edge nodes (Mampage A, et al. 2022). According to them, workload modeling, resource scheduling, and resource scaling are the three main areas of challenge with serverless, which makes it perfect for resource management in a distributed cloud environment. This chapter examines the impact that a serverless viewpoint offers on the numerous opportunities and challenges that arise in any hybrid cloud environment.

- ***Cost:*** assumes a significantly new form in Hybrid Serverless settings, requiring optimization across several cloud providers rather than just one, and considering on-premise resources in the event that they are available. This is complicated by the fact that different serverless providers have different tuning knobs and pricing structures to reduce resource consumption while the system is idle as well as during execution.

Cold start, resource constraints, and scalability: an application running in an HSC environment faces distinct and more complicated challenges than one running in a standard serverless environment. Multiple environments may have very different cold starts, which increases complexity but also presents a chance for dynamic routing that accounts for resource constraints and cost. Developers must manage various scaling policies from various providers. The development of automated tools for observability and scalability can help close the gap between this approach and the serverless promise of relieving the developer of scalability concerns.

- ***Security***: It's a complicated problem for serverless computing, and it gets even more complicated in an HSC environment with varying function isolation levels among providers, the requirement for multiple provider accounts, and various access control methods. With more components, a typical FaaS platform has a potentially larger attack surface, which grows even larger in a hybrid environment. Using on-premise resources to manage mission-critical tasks that call for security and privacy is one way to find a solution.
- ***Heterogeneity:*** How to distinguish between edge, on-prem, and cloud deployment methods, security, privacy, access control, and quality of service.
- ***Legacy systems***: How current systems can work together and be integrated into HSC, including current serverless computing applications. Although serverless code operating in HSC platforms should make it simple to access legacy Cloud and non-cloud systems, how can one migrate current applications to fully utilize HSC?
- ***Service Level Agreements (SLAs)***: It's still challenging to provide QoS guarantees in a serverless environment. An even greater challenge for a developer is to provide QoS guarantees across various serverless platforms: First, some providers might have SLAs on a specific set of serverless services, rather than other sets of services. Secondly, a service level agreement (SLA) offered by one supplier might differ from another (e.g., 99.9% uptime as opposed to 99.99% uptime). Third, the QoS-considered dimensions might not

be accessible in some areas (e.g., GDPR). It may be necessary to use an SLA formalism and a set of SLA transformations that are simple for application developers to comprehend and alter in order to provide an SLA across the application's end-to-end flow across various HSC platforms.

- ***Serverless at the Edge***: The use of serverless platforms at the edge has advanced recently (Wang B, et al. 2021). We do, however, view this as a challenging problem because the computing resources and connectivity of HSC platforms might be more diverse. As a result, in order to facilitate device and cloud mobility, code operating at one edge device and in the cloud may be virtualized rather than merely embedded. That could result in particular demands that redefine the cost. For instance, energy consumption might matter more than speed.
- ***Orchestration***: When migrating to HSC environments, serverless applications will require more sophisticated tooling for the orchestration of resources and services due to their increasing complexity. Additionally, there is a chance to select resources based on their availability, optimize for cold starts and performance, reliability, and cost, and take advantage of scaling opportunities while maintaining cost and performance SLAs.
- ***Developer experience with tools and integrated development environments (IDEs)***: Although some progress has been made, there is still a long way to go before developers can fully create, test, monitor, and debug serverless applications (Lenarduzzi V, et al. 2021). In order to allow developers to debug across platforms and services locally, HSC must raise the abstraction level and create new techniques.
- ***Observability***: Because functions in an HSC environment run for shorter periods of time, there will be orders of magnitude more of them running, which makes it more difficult to spot issues and bottlenecks. Dependencies between functions and their executions have been identified with the aid of recent work on call and causal graphs. To comprehend the behavior of the application across environments and the interdependence among components in an HSC, event correlation across this intrinsically distributed environment is required.
- ***State***: Real applications frequently call for a state. The management of state in HSC stateless serverless functions is unclear, especially since it could be necessary to access a state created on one platform

from another. Although serverless computing has the potential to be portable, data gravity and/or legal requirements that specify where state must reside make state management more challenging. The capacity to migrate state may have a significant impact on an application's cost and performance, necessitating improvements in the efficiency with which existing stateless functions can exchange state. These days, serverless functions rely on a bottleneck called a proxy store. The difficulty of developing stateful serverless apps may be lessened by using stateful programming models like actors.

- ***Recovery Semantics***: To guarantee application execution success and enable recovery from failures, it is essential to identify recovery semantics in an HSC setting, such as exactly once, at most once, and at least once semantics.

3.5.3. High-Impact Challenges in Academia and Industry

High-impact opportunities and challenges for research in academia and industry that may be critical to evolving Serverless Computing and Hybrid Cloud into Hybrid Serverless Computing (HSC):

- ***Interface description***: What should the interface to custom services look like? Should it include functional specifications, such as the input and output parameters, and non-functional ones, such as the cost per invocation and response time estimates? What is common across multiple services and vendors? What could be standardized?
- ***Application and solution descriptions***: How could application developers define the requirements and composition of their applications as they solve business problems? What is common across vendors that could be standardized for vendor runtime monitoring and vendor deployment interfaces?
- ***Continuous Integration/Continuous Deployments (CI/CD) pipelines***: As diversity of HSC deployments increases it becomes very important to automate them with CI/CD pipelines. This is a key challenge identified for the future of cloud engineering (Bermbach D et al. 2021), and is gaining some attention in serverless settings (Dalla Palma S, et al. 2022). With HSC, the complexity increases as it includes deployments to multiple clouds, edges, and other upcoming Hybrid Computing environments.
- ***Container adaptation***: Can containers be adapted to run in all possible computing environments, from public cloud to edge to IoT devices? How to manage tradeoffs in resources (CPU, memory,

network) versus cost and energy usage. Can security be maintained across multiple environments in one simple consistent way? Can new upcoming packaging formats like WebAssembly (Wasm) with common system-level interface (such as WASI and related proposed APIs) be used?

- ***Container orchestration***: Can cold-start and other related challenges (such as container security when compared to virtual machines) be addressed to make container-based and container orchestration successful long-term?
- ***Compiler optimizations***: How can HSC compilers optimize the selection of services based on application requirements? What would be the designs and implementations of such compilers? What optimizations could be applied? To what degree can we optimize applications to take full advantage of diverse distributed resources? How transparent are such compiling and optimizations for developers and to what degree can they support observability and developer productivity? For example, could monitoring be done in a standard way and still support multiple platforms?
- ***Sustainable and energy-aware environment-friendly computing***: as HSC environments are growing in complexity and diversity there is great opportunity to not only optimize for cost but also for environmental impact. The challenges in this area are already identified for serverless computing providers must make it easier to discover energy usage of energy by computing resources and schedule to use green resources.
- ***Everything-as-a-Software***: As "Software is Eating World" (Andreessen M 2022) does that mean that HSC hardware is abstracted and treated as a software resource that can be managed with uniform HSC software tooling and treated as software code? Can existing approaches such as Infrastructure as Code (IaC) be extended to contain all of HSC and go beyond infrastructure to represent any relevant resources as software code?
- ***Ease-of-use***: Simplicity of serverless computing is the main reason why it is popular. To what degree can we retain serverless simplicity in HSC? We do not only have multiple cloud and hybrid clouds environments but also edge and other emerging computing paradigms. One particular vision worth outlining as a grand challenge for HSC programming model outlined in (Jonas E, et al. 2017) is identifying that what users want is the simplicity of being

able to work locally and use a simple button to deploy remotely: "… students simply wish they could easily "push a button" and have their code—existing, optimized, single-machine code—running on the cloud.." The diversity of environments comprising HSC make transparently providing tools and runtime support to improve developer productivity (García-López P, et al. 2020) even more challenging.

- ***Next Generation Tooling, Productivity and Developer Experience***: How does the decreasing cost of running containers impact developer experience? The cost for 1 GB of memory per hour is estimated to be less than $0.01 in the near future (about $0.06 in, 2022) (Slominski A, et al. 2019). However, one cost is unlikely to change, which is developer time per hour. It is crucial for HSC to support consistent experience for developers regardless of where containers are running: local, remote, cloud or edge. Ideally, developers can have a consistent local and remote development experience (aka transparency) where they use identical code and tooling across these different estates. Is it possible to create common ground based on compilers and standards that allow interoperability between providers in a serverless cloud, similar to what Internet Protocol did for the Internet?
- ***Artificial Intelligence (AI) and Machine Learning (ML)***: as complexity of HSC environments is growing it becomes a great target to apply AI/ML techniques to not only do compiler-based or dynamic optimizations but also to better understand how developers and customers are building applications and solutions. For example, recent trends that focus on building Intelligent assistants that can help developers (Finnie-Ansley J, et al. 2022) use the best practices for building and evaluating code (Chen M et al. 2021), help customers discover vulnerabilities (Pearce H, et al. 2021), repair bugs (Prenner JA, et al. 2021), understand choices in deploying solutions and optimizing configurations (Akhtar N, et al. 2020), and provide easy-tounderstand recommendations based on monitoring data available. These techniques can serve as building blocks to address the challenges in a HSC setting. Another opportunity is to use AI/ML to gain better understanding of HSC applications operations by extending existing serverless observability solutions in Application Performance Management (APM) (Thurner P 2022), artificial intelligence for IT operations (AIOps), and related areas.

Today, serverless gives us direction for creating the cloud platform of the future. We believe that Hybrid Serverless Compute offers a broad perspective on how we can streamline cloud programming by combining a platform designed to maximize resource utilization for Hybrid Cloud and other scenarios with a set of higher-level abstractions. We discussed prospects and difficulties for further study. Further research on FaaS platforms running on hybrid platforms spanning multiple clouds and Edge, more general approaches to serverless resource management, and serverless as a bridge for integrating traditional enterprise compute stacks with a variety of distributed compute platforms like HPC, quantum compute, and complex event processing are some examples of how these can be applied in more specialized domains for future directions.

By establishing computing standards that enable the construction of hybrid serverless computing solutions anywhere, there is a significant chance to create an open-standards and open-source hybrid serverless computing platform with an impact comparable to that of the Internet. When certain computing niches are dominated by current providers, some components of hybrid serverless computing might not be built on open standards. However, Hybrid Serverless Computing might offer a single set of standards and abstractions that offer long-term winning alternatives. One provider probably won't be able to create hybrid serverless computing solutions. To support Hybrid Serverless Computing, the best solutions probably need to be standardized and require a wide range of computing resources.

REFERENCES

1. Akhtar, N., Raza, A., Ishakian, V., & Matta, I. (2020). COSE: Configuring serverless functions using statistical learning. In *IEEE INFOCOM 2020—IEEE Conference on Computer Communications* (pp. 129–138). Toronto, ON, Canada. https://doi.org/10.1109/INFOCOM41043.2020.9155363.
2. Amazon Web Services. (2024). Aurora Serverless. https://aws.amazon.com/rds/aurora/serverless/ (accessed on 1 August 2024).
3. Andreessen, M. (2011). Why software is eating the world. Andreessen Horowitz. https://a16z.com/2011/08/20/why-software-is-eating-the-world/ (accessed on 1 August 2024).
4. Apache Software Foundation. (2016). OpenWhisk. https://openwhisk.apache.org/ (accessed on 1 August 2024).
5. Armbrust, M., Fox, A., Griffith, R., et al. (2010). A view of cloud computing. *Communications of the ACM, 53*(4), 50–58. https://doi.org/10.1145/1721654.1721672.
6. AsyncAPI. (2024). AsyncAPI Initiative for event-driven APIs. https://www.asyncapi.com/ (accessed on 1 August 2024).
7. AWS RedShift Serverless. (2024). https://aws.amazon.com/redshift/redshift-serverless/ (accessed on 1 August 2024).
8. Baarzi, A. F., Kesidis, G., Joe-Wong, C., & Shahrad, M. (2021). On merits and viability of multi-cloud serverless. In *Proceedings of the ACM Symposium on Cloud Computing* (pp. 600–608). Seattle, WA, USA. https://doi.org/10.1145/3472883.3487002.
9. Balakrishnan, H., Chen, K., Dogar, F. R., Freedman, M. J., Maggs, B. M., Mazières, D., & Vutukuru, M. (2021). Revitalizing the public internet by making it extensible. *SIGCOMM Computer Communication Review, 51*(2), 18–24. https://doi.org/10.1145/3464994.3464998.
10. Baldini, I., Castro, P., Chang, K., et al. (2017). Serverless computing: Current trends and open problems. In S. Chaudhary, G. Somani, & R. Buyya (Eds.), *Research Advances in Cloud Computing* (pp. 1–20). Springer. https://doi.org/10.1007/978-981-10-5026-8_1.
11. Baldini, I., et al. (2017). The serverless trilemma: Function composition for serverless computing. In *Proceedings of the 2017 ACM SIGPLAN International Symposium on New Ideas, New Paradigms, and Reflections on Programming and Software* (pp. 89–103). NY, USA. https://doi.org/10.1145/3133850.3133855.
12. Bermbach, D., et al. (2021). On the future of cloud engineering. In *2021 IEEE International Conference on Cloud Engineering (IC2E)* (pp. 264–275). https://doi.org/10.1109/IC2E52221.2021.00044.

13. Bernhardsson, E. (2022). Storm in the stratosphere: How the cloud will be reshuffled. *Erik Bernhardsson Blog*. https://erikbern.com/2021/11/30/storm-in-the-stratosphere-how-the-cloud-will-be-reshuffled.html (accessed on 1 August 2024).
14. Bloomberg. (2020). Worldwide spending on edge computing will reach $250 billion in 2024, according to a new IDC spending guide. https://www.bloomberg.com/press-releases/2020-09-23/worldwide-spending-on-edge-computing-will-reach-250-billion-in-2024-according-to-a-new-idc-spending-guide (accessed on 1 August 2024).
15. Buyya, R., Yeo, C. S., Venugopal, S., Broberg, J., & Brandic, I. (2009). Cloud computing and emerging IT platforms: Vision, hype, and reality for delivering computing as the 5th utility. *Future Generation Computer Systems, 25*(6), 599–616. https://doi.org/10.1016/j.future.2008.12.001.
16. Castro, P., Ishakian, V., Muthusamy, V., & Slominski, A. (2019). The rise of serverless computing. *Communications of the ACM, 62*(12), 44–54. https://doi.org/10.1145/3368454.
17. Chard, R., et al. (2020). funcX: A federated function serving fabric for science. In *Proceedings of the 29th International Symposium on High-Performance Parallel and Distributed Computing* (pp. 65–76). https://doi.org/10.1145/3369583.3392683.
18. Chen, M., et al. (2021). Evaluating large language models trained on code. https://doi.org/10.48550/ARXIV.2107.03374.
19. Cisco. (2022). *2022 Global Hybrid Cloud Trends Report*. https://www.cisco.com/c/en/us/solutions/hybrid-cloud/2022-trends.html (accessed on 1 July 2024).
20. Cisco. (2024). Multicloud is the new normal. https://www.cisco.com/c/dam/global/en_uk/solutions/cloud/overview/cloud_business_cloud_advisor_infobrief_eng_FY18Q3.pdf (accessed on 1 August 2024).
21. Cloud Security Alliance. (2021). How to Design a Secure Serverless Architecture. https://cloudsecurityalliance.org/artifacts/serverless-computing-security-in-2021/ (accessed on 1 August 2024).
22. CloudEvents. (2024). https://cloudevents.io/ (accessed on 1 August 2024).
23. CloudFlare Workers. (2021). https://workers.cloudflare.com/ (accessed on 1 August 2024).
24. Crossplane. (2023). https://crossplane.io/ (accessed on 1 August 2024).
25. Dalla Palma, S., Catolino, G., Di Nucci, D., Tamburri, D. A., & van den Heuvel, W. J. (2022). Go serverless with RADON! A practical DevOps experience report. *IEEE Software*. https://doi.org/10.1109/MS.2022.3170153.

26. Datadog. (2022). Machine Learning Based Monitoring. https://www.datadoghq.com/solutions/machine-learning/ (accessed on 1 August 2024).
27. Dell Technologies. (2024). APEX. https://www.dell.com/en-us/dt/apex/index.htm (accessed on 1 August 2024).
28. Djemame, K., Parker, M., & Datsev, D. (2020). Open-source serverless architectures: An evaluation of apache openwhisk. In *2020 IEEE/ACM 13th International Conference on Utility and Cloud Computing (UCC)* (pp. 329–335). https://doi.org/10.1109/UCC48980.2020.00052.
29. Findstack. (2022). 21+ Internet of Things statistics, facts & trends for 2022. https://findstack.com/internet-of-things-statistics/ (accessed on 1 August 2024).
30. Finnie-Ansley, J., Denny, P., Becker, B. A., Luxton-Reilly, A., & Prather, J. (2022). The robots are coming: Exploring the implications of OpenAI Codex on introductory programming. In *Australasian Computing Education Conference* (pp. 10–19). Virtual Event, Australia. https://doi.org/10.1145/3511861.3511863.
31. Fisher, T. (2021). Introducing the first integration of Instana's enterprise observability platform with IBM Watson AIOps. Instana. https://www.instana.com/blog/introducing-the-first-integration-of-instanas-enterprise-observability-platform-with-ibm-watson-aiops/ (accessed on 1 August 2024).
32. Flexera. (2022). Trends in cloud computing: 2022 state of the cloud report. https://www.flexera.com/blog/cloud/cloud-computing-trends-2022-state-of-the-cloud-report/ (accessed on 1 August 2024).
33. Foster, I., & Kesselman, C. (2004). *The Grid: Blueprint for a New Computing Infrastructure*. Morgan Kaufmann. https://www.amazon.com/Grid-Blueprint-Computing-Infrastructure-Elsevier/dp/1558604758 (accessed on 1 August 2024).
34. GAIA-X. (2024). https://www.bmwk.de/Redaktion/EN/Dossier/gaia-x.html
35. García-López, P., Slominski, A., Shillaker, S., Behrendt, M., & Metzler, B. (2020). Serverless end game: Disaggregation enabling transparency. *arXiv*. http://arxiv.org/abs/2006.01251 (accessed on 1 August 2024).
36. Google Cloud. (2024). Cloud Run. https://cloud.google.com/run (accessed on 1 August 2024).
37. Google Trends. (2024). Hybrid cloud and serverless. https://trends.google.com/trends/explore?date=all&q=%2Fg%2F11c0q_754d,Hybrid%20Cloud (accessed on 1 August 2024).

38. Grossi, M., Benedetti, L., Bezzi, M., Carpineti, R., Cervini, P., & Giardina, M. (2021). A serverless cloud integration for quantum computing. *ArXiv Preprint*. https://arxiv.org/abs/2107.02007.
39. Hassan, H. B., Barakat, S. A., & Sarhan, Q. I. (2021). Survey on serverless computing. *Journal of Cloud Computing, 10*(1), 39. https://doi.org/10.1186/s13677-021-00253-7.
40. Hellerstein, J. M., et al. (2019). Serverless computing: One step forward, two steps back. *CIDR 2019*.
41. Hewlett Packard Enterprise. (2024). HPE GreenLake—Edge-to-cloud platform. https://www.hpe.com/us/en/greenlake.html (accessed on 1 August 2024).
42. IBM Cloud Functions—Overview. (2021). https://www.ibm.com/cloud/functions (accessed on 1 August 2024).
43. IBM. (2022,). Artificial intelligence for IT operations (AIOps). https://www.ibm.com/cloud/learn/aiops (accessed on 1 August 2024).
44. IBM. (2022). What is hybrid cloud? https://www.ibm.com/cloud/learn/hybrid-cloud (accessed on 1 August 2024).
45. IBM. (2024). Code engine. https://www.ibm.com/cloud/code-engine (accessed on 1 August 2024).
46. IDC. (2024). Personal computing devices—Market share. https://www.idc.com/promo/pcdforecast (accessed on 1 August 2024).
47. Ishakian, V., Muthusamy, V., & Slominski, A. (2018). Serving deep learning models in a serverless platform. In *2018 IEEE International Conference on Cloud Engineering (IC2E)* (pp. 257–262). Orlando, FL. https://doi.org/10.1109/IC2E.2018.00052.
48. Jonas, E., Pu, Q., Venkataraman, S., Stoica, I., & Recht, B. (2017). Occupy the cloud: Distributed computing for the 99%. In *Proceedings of the 2017 Symposium on Cloud Computing* (pp. 445–451). New York, NY, USA. https://doi.org/10.1145/3127479.3128601.
49. Kaur, K., Sharma, S., & Kahlon, K. S. (2017). Interoperability and portability approaches in interconnected clouds: A review. *ACM Computing Surveys, 50*(4), 49:1–49:40. https://doi.org/10.1145/3092698.
50. Kaviani, N., Kalinin, D., & Maximilien, M. (2019). Towards serverless as commodity: A case of Knative. In *Proceedings of the 5th International Workshop on Serverless Computing (WOSC '19)* (pp. 13–18). https://doi.org/10.1145/3366623.3368135.
51. Kehoe, B. (2019). Serverless is a state of mind. Medium. https://ben11kehoe.medium.com/serverless-is-a-state-of-mind-717ef2088b42 (accessed on 1 August 2024).

52. Klingler, R., Trifunovic, N., & Spillner, J. (2021). Beyond @ CloudFunction: Powerful code annotations to capture serverless runtime patterns. In *Proceedings of the Seventh International Workshop on Serverless Computing (WoSC7) 2021* (pp. 23–28). Virtual Event, Canada. https://doi.org/10.1145/3493651.3493669.
53. Knative Eventing. (2024). https://knative.dev/docs/eventing/ (accessed on 1 August 2024).
54. Knative. (2024). https://github.com/knative (accessed on 1 August 2024).
55. Kuntsevich, A., Nasirifard, P., & Jacobsen, H. A. (2018). A distributed analysis and benchmarking framework for apache openwhisk serverless platform. In *Proceedings of the 19th International Middleware Conference (Posters)* (pp. 3–4). NY, USA. https://doi.org/10.1145/3284014.3284016.
56. Lenarduzzi, V., & Panichella, A. (2021). Serverless testing: Tool vendors' and experts' points of view. *IEEE Software, 38*(1), 54–60. https://doi.org/10.1109/MS.2020.3030803.
57. Lenarduzzi, V., Daly, J., Martini, A., Panichella, S., & Tamburri, D. A. (2021). Toward a technical debt conceptualization for serverless computing. *IEEE Software, 38*(1), 40–47. https://doi.org/10.1109/MS.2020.3030786.
58. Lin, W. T., et al. (2018). Tracking causal order in AWS lambda applications. In *2018 IEEE International Conference on Cloud Engineering (IC2E)* (pp. 50–60). Orlando, FL. https://doi.org/10.1109/IC2E.2018.00027.
59. Linthicum, D. (2019). Serverless computing's dark side: Less portability for your apps. InfoWorld. https://www.infoworld.com/article/3336498/serverless-computings-dark-side-less-portability-for-your-apps.html (accessed on 1 August 2024).
60. Luthra, M., Hennig, S., Razavi, K., Wang, L., & Koldehofe, B. (2020). Operator as a service: Stateful serverless complex event processing. In *2020 IEEE International Conference on Big Data (Big Data)* (pp. 1964–1973). https://doi.org/10.1109/BigData50022.2020.9378130.
61. Mampage, A., Karunasekera, S., & Buyya, R. (2022). A holistic view on resource management in serverless computing environments: Taxonomy and future directions. *ACM Computing Surveys (CSUR)*.
62. Microsoft Azure. (2024). Azure SQL database serverless. https://docs.microsoft.com/en-us/azure/azure-sql/database/serverless-tier-overview?view=azuresql (accessed on 1 August 2024).
63. Microsoft Azure. (2024). What is hybrid cloud computing—Definition. https://azure.microsoft.com/en-us/resources/cloud-computing-dictionary/what-is-hybrid-cloud-computing/ (accessed on 1 August 2024).

64. Millward, W. T. (2022). Red Hat CEO Matt Hicks: Partners key to $1 trillion open hybrid cloud market. CRN. https://www.crn.com/news/cloud/red-hat-ceo-matt-hicks-partners-key-to-1-trillion-open-hybrid-cloud-market (accessed on 1 August 2024).
65. Mytton, D. (2020). How much energy do data centers use? David Mytton. https://davidmytton.blog/how-much-energy-do-data-centers-use/ (accessed on 1 August 2024).
66. Nimbella. (2024). Serverless Cloud Platform for Developers. https://nimbella.com/opensource (accessed on 1 August 2024).
67. O'Reilly. (2019). O'Reilly serverless survey (2019): Concerns, what works, and what to expect. https://www.oreilly.com/radar/oreilly-serverless-survey-2019-concerns-what-works-and-what-to-expect/ (accessed on 1 August 2024).
68. Obetz, M., Patterson, S., & Milanova, A. (2019). Static call graph construction in AWS lambda serverless applications. In *11th USENIX Workshop on Hot Topics in Cloud Computing (HotCloud 19)*. Renton, WA. Available: https://www.usenix.org/conference/hotcloud19/presentation/obetz (accessed on 1 August 2024).
69. Opara-Martins, J., Sahandi, R., & Tian, F. (2014). Critical review of vendor lock-in and its impact on adoption of cloud computing. In *2014 International Conference on Information Society (i-Society 2014)* (pp. 92–97). https://doi.org/10.1109/i-Society.2014.7009018.
70. OpenFaaS. (2024). https://www.openfaas.com/ (accessed on 1 August 2024).
71. Parkhill, D. F. (1966). *The Challenge of the Computer Utility*. Addison-Wesley Publishing Company.
72. Patros, P., Spillner, J., Papadopoulos, A. V., Varghese, B., Rana, O., & Dustdar, S. (2021). Toward sustainable serverless computing. *IEEE Internet Computing, 25*(6), 42–50. https://doi.org/10.1109/MIC.2021.3093105.
73. Pearce, H., Tan, B., Ahmad, B., Karri, R., & Dolan-Gavitt, B. (2021). Examining zero-shot vulnerability repair with large language models. https://doi.org/10.48550/ARXIV.2112.02125.
74. Pemberton, N., Schleier-Smith, J., & Gonzalez, J. E. (2021). The Restless cloud. In *Proceedings of the Workshop on Hot Topics in Operating Systems* (pp. 49–57). https://doi.org/10.1145/3458336.3465280.
75. Pérez, A., Risco, S., Naranjo, D. M., Caballer, M., & Moltó, G. (2019). On-premises serverless computing for event-driven data processing applications. In *2019 IEEE 12th International Conference*

on Cloud Computing (CLOUD) (pp. 414–421). https://doi.org/10.1109/CLOUD.2019.00073.

76. Prenner, J. A., & Robbes, R. (2021). Automatic program repair with OpenAI's Codex: Evaluating quixBugs. https://doi.org/10.48550/ARXIV.2111.03922.
77. Protocol. (2022). How snap made its old stack disappear. https://www.protocol.com/enterprise/snap-microservices-aws-google-cloud (accessed on 1 August 2024).
78. Quevedo, S., Merchán, F., Rivadeneira, R., & Dominguez, F. X. (2019). Evaluating apache openWhisk—FaaS. In *2019 IEEE Fourth Ecuador Technical Chapters Meeting (ETCM)* (pp. 1–5). https://doi.org/10.1109/ETCM48019.2019.9014867.
79. Raza, A., Matta, I., Akhtar, N., Kalavri, V., & Isahagian, V. (2021). SoK: Function-as-a-service: From an application developer's perspective. *Journal of Systems Research, 1*(1). https://doi.org/10.5070/SR31154815.
80. Raza, A., Zhang, Z., Akhtar, N., Isahagian, V., & Matta, I. (2021). LIBRA: An economical hybrid approach for cloud applications with strict SLAs. In *2021 IEEE International Conference on Cloud Engineering (IC2E)* (pp. 136–146). https://doi.org/10.1109/IC2E52221.2021.00028.
81. Schleier-Smith, J., Zhang, Y., et al. (2021). What serverless computing is and should become: The next phase of cloud computing. *Communications of the ACM, 64*(5), 76–84. https://doi.org/10.1145/3406011.
82. Shahrad, M., et al. (2020). Serverless in the wild: Characterizing and optimizing the serverless workload at a large cloud provider. In *2020 USENIX Annual Technical Conference (USENIX ATC 20)* (pp. 205–218). Available: https://www.usenix.org/conference/atc20/presentation/shahrad (accessed on 1 August 2024).
83. Shepherd, D. (2022). Introducing Acorn | Acorn labs. https://acorn.io/introducing-acorn/ (accessed on 1 August 2024).
84. Singhvi, A., Balasubramanian, A., Houck, K., Shaikh, M. D., Venkataraman, S., & Akella, A. (2021). Atoll: A scalable low-latency serverless platform. In *Proceedings of the ACM Symposium on Cloud Computing* (pp. 138–152). NY, USA. https://doi.org/10.1145/3472883.3486981.
85. Slominski, A., Muthusamy, V., & Isahagian, V. (2019). The future of computing is boring (and that is exciting!). In *2019 IEEE International Conference on Cloud Engineering (IC2E)* (pp. 97–101). https://doi.org/10.1109/IC2E.2019.00023.
86. Smith, C. P., Jindal, A., Chadha, M., Gerndt, M., & Benedict, S. (2022). FaDO: FaaS functions and data orchestrator for multiple serverless edge-

cloud clusters. In *2022 IEEE 6th International Conference on Fog and Edge Computing (ICFEC)* (pp. 17–25).

87. Snowflake. (2024). https://www.snowflake.com/ (accessed on 1 August 2024).
88. Spillner, J. (2017). Practical tooling for serverless computing. In *Proceedings of the 10th International Conference on Utility and Cloud Computing* (pp. 185–186). Austin, Texas, USA. https://doi.org/10.1145/3147213.3149452.
89. Stoica, I., & Shenker, S. (2021). From cloud computing to sky computing. In *Proceedings of the Workshop on Hot Topics in Operating Systems* (pp. 26–32). https://doi.org/10.1145/3458336.3465301.
90. Sun, L., Dong, H., Hussain, F. K., Hussain, O. K., & Chang, E. (2014). Cloud service selection: State-of-the-art and future research directions. *Journal of Network and Computer Applications, 45*, 134–150. https://doi.org/10.1016/j.jnca.2014.07.019.
91. SUSE. (2024). SUSE Rancher Kubernetes cluster management platform. https://www.suse.com/products/suse-rancher/ (accessed on 1 August 2024).
92. Taibi, D., Kehoe, B., & Poccia, D. (2020). Serverless: From bad practices to good solutions. *ArXiv Preprint*. https://arxiv.org/abs/2009.08422 (accessed on 1 August 2024).
93. Takabi, H., Joshi, J. B. D., & Ahn, G. J. (2010). Security and privacy challenges in cloud computing environments. *IEEE Security & Privacy Magazine, 8*(6), 24–31. https://doi.org/10.1109/MSP.2010.186.
94. Tariq, A., Pahl, A., Nimmagadda, S., Rozner, E., & Lanka, S. (2020). Sequoia: Enabling quality-of-service in serverless computing. In *Proceedings of the 11th ACM Symposium on Cloud Computing* (pp. 311–327). NY, USA. https://doi.org/10.1145/3419111.3421306.
95. Thurner, P. (2022). Seamless AI-powered observability for multicloud serverless applications. Dynatrace News. https://www.dynatrace.com/news/blog/seamless-ai-powered-observability-for-serverless/ (accessed on 1 August 2024).
96. Turner, A. (2018). How many people have smartphones worldwide (July 2022). https://www.bankmycell.com/blog/how-many-phones-are-in-the-world (accessed on 1 August 2024).
97. Wang, B., Ali-Eldin, A., & Shenoy, P. (2021). LaSS: Running latency-sensitive serverless computations at the edge. In *Proceedings of the 30th International Symposium on High-Performance Parallel*

and Distributed Computing (pp. 239–251). NY, USA. https://doi.org/10.1145/3431379.3460646.

98. WebAssembly. (n.d.). WebAssembly (abbreviated Wasm). https://webassembly.org/ (accessed on 1 August 2024).
99. Wikibon Research. (2018). Building the hybrid serverless multiclouds of the future. https://wikibon.com/building-hybrid-serverless-multiclouds-future/ (accessed on 1 August 2024).
100. Yussupov, V., Breitenbücher, U., Leymann, F., & Müller, C. (2019). Facing the unplanned migration of serverless applications: A study on portability problems, solutions, and dead ends. In *Proceedings of the 12th IEEE/ACM International Conference on Utility and Cloud Computing* (pp. 273–283). https://doi.org/10.1145/3344341.3368813.
101. Zhang, Y., Sani, A. A., & Xu, G. H. (2021). User-defined cloud. In *Proceedings of the Workshop on Hot Topics in Operating Systems* (pp. 33–40). https://doi.org/10.1145/3458336.3465304.

CHAPTER 4

A TAXONOMY OF PERFORMANCE FORECASTING SYSTEMS IN THE SERVERLESS CLOUD COMPUTING ENVIRONMENTS

Contents

INTRODUCTION

The environment (or platform) of serverless cloud computing controls the resource management of its various clients, who typically submit their applications as collections of functions (tasks). A customer has the option to submit his application as a single function or as a collection of tasks. Every collection of functions (tasks) is compiled into a Directed Acyclic Graph (DAG), where each edge denotes a dependency between two functions and each node represents a function that represents a specific task. For these resource management systems, the choices made by resource forecasting engines or performance forecasting systems (PFS) are crucial. But predicting future resource availability is a challenging task. Numerous PFS projects utilize multiple computer resources in multiple dimensions. From a software engineering perspective, new code can be written to integrate PFS projects' forecasting services on Serverless (Edge) Cloud platforms since the majority of them have already been designed for performance forecasting of resources on Distributed Computing Environments like Peer-to-peer, Queue systems, Clusters, Grids, Virtual Machine Organizations, and Cloud systems. This chapter discusses the taxonomy used to describe the PFS architecture. In order to realize their adaptation in Serverless (Edge) Cloud Computing, the taxonomy is used to classify and identify the approaches that are used in the implementation of the current PFSs in Distributed Computing Environments.

4.1. BACKGROUND AND RELATED WORK OF SERVERLESS COMPUTING PLATFORMS

Serverless clouds, also known as Serverless Computing Platforms (SCP's), have become a well-liked way to launch apps on the cloud. With PFS's assistance, SCP's internal server can perform Resource Management more effectively. It can also independently scale computational resources finely, with high availability, fault tolerance, and only charging for actual computing time. SCPs use ephemeral infrastructure, like MicroVMs or application containers from Containers as a Service (CaaS), to make such capabilities a reality. Better server utilization is promised by the SCP architecture because cloud providers can efficiently distribute client workloads to occupy available capacity, saving both client costs and vendor energy. Due to the serverless architecture's ability to provision fine-grained resources on demand and charge only for actual computing time, it ensures equitable and generous hosting costs.

The necessary middleware platforms, like CaaS, are a type of virtualization based on containers, where users receive containers as a service from a serverless cloud provider. Utilizing SCP, it is possible to deploy, host, and scale resources for discrete operations referred to as "micro-services" on a demand basis. Granular infrastructure for each micro-service is provided by CaaS platforms through the creation and management of temporary infrastructure (containers) holding user code and dependent libraries (Oakes E. et al. 2017). Micro-service requests must be created, destroyed, and load balanced amongst server resources by the SCP. In order to provide a fair service to the clients, the total number of micro-service invocations, runtime, and memory utilization are metered (charged) to the nearest second.

The Resource Management System (RMS) internal operations of a Serverless provider can be broadly characterized as follows. An event triggers the sending of a request or requests to the API gateway in order to call the appropriate function or functions in accordance with the established rules. It is essential to complete Performance Forecasting for each available worker node before scheduling any function(s). The function(s) (or job task(s)) should then be submitted to the best set of performing worker nodes. Here, a provider can use the Performance Forecasting Algorithms that are currently available to forecast how well the function(s) or job task(s) will perform in the future. If he is eager to employ a machine learning forecasting algorithm, then all of the previous load data Independent Data Tuples (IDPs) of each worker node must be archived in a relational database. This is because a particular machine learning (ML) predictor must be trained immediately prior to use. Because the provider has a server (which we incorrectly refer to as serverless) to manage all the cloud nodes, this is quite feasible in a serverless cloud environment. Nevertheless, the Serverless provider does not need to archive a sizable historical collection of load data from the worker-nodes if he employs an analytical (mathematical) forecasting model.

The purpose of the SCPs is to facilitate highly scalable, event-driven applications. These applications are made up of brief, stateless processes that are started by events produced by users, middleware, sensors, or micro-services. Among its use cases are the following: chatbots, backend APIs, multimedia processing, data pipelines, Internet of Things data collection, continuous integration and deployment services (CI/CD), etc.

Workload characterization methods and forecasting models in SCPs have been developed extensively using analytical modeling and machine learning techniques. It is noted that performance forecasting on SCPs is challenging and that hardware heterogeneity-related performance variance must be addressed (Jonas E. et al. 2019). Numerous researchers have identified how pay-as-you-go pricing models, combined with the sophistication of serverless job deployments, lead to a major risk: unpredictable costs and spans. SCPs make budgeting more difficult than with virtual machines (VMs) because they require organizations to forecast service utilization in order to determine hosting costs. Runtime forecasting accuracy and serverless workload performance variance are inescapably linked scenarios.

The main causes of performance variance are heterogeneity in the hardware, resource contention, and provisioning variation. Ou and Farley discovered that IaaS cloud performance variance is caused by heterogeneous CPUs hosting identically labelled virtual machine types on Amazon EC2. The issue with "provisioning variation" in IaaS clouds was recognized by Rehman et al. Provisioning variation is the result of resource contention caused by the stochastic nature of virtual machine placements, which results in different multi-tenancy across physical servers. Schad et al. demonstrated how resource contention from VM multitenancy and variation in provisioning cause unpredictable performance of Amazon EC2 virtual machines. The CPU Steal metric has been shown by Ayodele et al. and Lloyd et al. to be a useful tool for identifying resource contention from multi-tenant virtual machines.

As part of preliminary research on Serverless Cloud computing, the effectiveness of FaaS platforms for hosting different types of workloads has been assessed. Numerous scientists have examined the performance consequences of hosting workflows for scientific computing. Others have looked into FaaS performance for neural network training, machine learning inference, and even natural language processing. To facilitate the cost comparison of SCP versus IaaS cloud, Boza et al. designed CloudCal. It is a tool to calculate hosting costs on IaaS (reserved), IaaS (on demand), and FaaS platforms for workloads that are service-oriented (Boza EF et al. 2017,). To compare hosting costs to FaaS deployments, the CloudCal can be used to determine the minimum number of virtual machines (VMs) required to maintain a specified average request latency.

Alternatively, the case studies have been used to compare the expenses of operating particular application workloads on IaaS, FaaS, and PaaS. Cordingly et al. characterized the variation in workload performance amongst FaaS platforms. To estimate the runtime and cost of the FaaS workload, he had employed their Linux time accounting method.

With the exception of serverless computing platforms, numerous forecasting engines have already been developed to predict performance on DCEs. These forecasting engines can be used appropriately by the providers to forecast the computing resources of SCPs with some necessary modifications. Because any such forecasting engine can be adapted in any DCE from a software perspective, we therefore optimistically count on and consider any forecasting engines that are currently used in the DCEs in this survey. The Resource Type Taxonomy, shown in Figure 4.3, explains how adaptable PPEs are at the top of the hierarchy.

The simple fact is that all of the cloud resources are being overextended by Forecasting Engines' (FEs') demand for Serverless clouds. As such, the Performance Prediction must take various FE types into account. Therefore, if forecasts of multiple resources are needed for the SCP internal server, they must be performed using a middleware platform like CaaS, which grants access to various FEs. It is necessary for the FE developers to consider new performance metrics that are suitable for serverless cloud environments.

In the current study, we not only examine a large number of FEs that have previously been used in the DCEs to forecast computer resources, but we also classify them using a number of developed taxonomies in an attempt to define and organize the FEs in relation to various resource and application levels and to inspire researchers to experiment with novel forecasting techniques.

4.2. BASIC DIFFICULTIES AND CHALLENGES IN SCPS

Because the Serverless (edge) cloud (or SCP) is heterogeneous and distributed, finding forecasting solutions is fundamentally difficult. This is due to fundamental variations in the various tasks and resources offered by Serverless (edge) cloud platforms (also known as SCP). Performance prediction systems would greatly benefit from easy access to the archived information profiles of a specific Serverless (edge) cloud (or any DCE).

However, historical data suggests that their efficacy is dependent on how well they are used. The truth is that no forecasting algorithm can be completely accurate. It's also common knowledge that certain algorithms work better and more quickly than others when it comes to achieving a given specialized goal. For example, using Modeling Workloads for the Grids to forecast the runtimes of parallel batch job tasks in a homogeneous cluster (Song B et al., 2004). For this reason, it is wise to consider combining several algorithms to get the best result.

In the past, it might have been possible to predict the runtime of a brief job task with just one reading of point-valued variables. But since DCEs like clusters, grids, and serverless (edge) cloud (or SCP) applications involve lengthy job tasks, these variables might only be able to represent a specific point in time, which could lead to inaccurate results. Accordingly, it makes sense to create pertinent Serverless cloud performance metrics that span a specific amount of time (Seneviratne S and Levy DC, 2011).

For the proper designing of the Forecasting Engines (FEs), it is imperative to address the following list of problems which require the solutions in terms of the nature of the Serverless (edge) cloud environments.

1. Forecasting of different variables such as latency (queue waiting time, resource set up time, runtime and communication time), throughput, event arrival rate, average throttle, energy consumption, resource efficiency (utilization), communication time of MPIs of DAGs, data transfer time (remote input devices), user cost.
2. Forecasting of errors of the predicted resources in the system. If we can collect information on possible forecasting errors, then it is possible to make statistical corrections for the forecasting errors of resources.
3. If possible, novel metrics should be designed to suit the different specialized SCP. In conventional parallel computing, function's runtime and system utilization are appropriate. However, in the SCP, we may require to update such traditional metrics, because the Serverless cloud is a dynamic environment.
4. The FEs of Serverless cloud environments must forecast the quality of service.
5. The FEs of Serverless cloud environments must forecast the overheads of the system.
6. The FEs of Serverless cloud environments must forecast the availability of the required data storage.

4.3. THE TAXONOMY OF PERFORMANCE FORECASTING SYSTEMS

The FEs have been analyzed under three different taxonomies, namely the Design methodology of forecasting engines, Forecasting algorithm, Resource hierarchy tree.

4.3.1. Classification of PFS by the Design Methodology of Forecasting Algorithms

Our goal is to predict the job task's (function's) performance for each of the potential hosts for DCE (Peer-peer, Queue system, Cluster, Grid, VM, Clouds, including Serverless Clouds). There are two main strategies to achieve the design goal: the Explicit Forecasting Method and the Implicit Forecasting Method.

4.3.1.1. Explicit Forecasting Method

The Explicit method directly forecasts a performance metric for each host in the Distributed Computing Environment for the job task (or function). They consist of things like runtime, cost, and end-to-end latency, for example. After that, a host is chosen based on how well they forecast.

4.3.1.2. Implicit Forecasting Method

The Implicit method makes the assumption that some task-independent host metric may be used to rank the job task's (or function's) performance on each of the potential hosts. For example, the background load that is currently being measured as a result of this can be considered a task-independent metric, as recommended by Wolsi's NWS for the submission of short job tasks. However, this method is not entirely reliable for lengthy job tasks because the background load of the computer node can fluctuate without warning. There are two branches to the Explicit Method. The resource-oriented method and the application-oriented method are these.

4.3.1.3. Application-Oriented Versus Resource-Oriented Method

The relationship between the dependencies involved in selecting the right host to execute a task is depicted in Figure 4.1. The decision lies in whether to forecast at the resource availability node-level or the runtime node-level. This also establishes if resource- or application-oriented forecasting should be used. The variable background load determines how long a job task takes to complete in a time-shared computer node. As a result, along with other relevant characteristics, it is necessary to gather and store in a database the average background load of the job task.

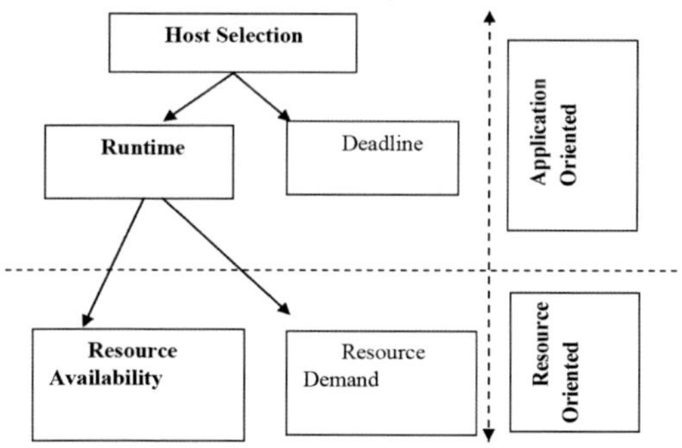

Figure 4.1. *Dependencies of forecasting.*

Source: Rajalakshmi Krishnamurthi, Adarsh Kumar, Sukhpal Singh Gill, and Rajkumar Buyya. Serverless Computing: Principles and Paradigms. Springer. https://doi.org/10.1007/978-3-031-26633-1.

The resource-oriented method forecasts the background load of the prospective job task. This has a direct bearing on estimating the amount of available CPU resources or capacity. Forecasting the resource level using the resource-oriented method is possible regardless of the quantity of job tasks that are ongoing at any given time. Following the resource level (e.g., host load) is anticipated, an estimate of the runtime can be made.

When using an application-oriented approach like Smith's, it is necessary to use advance search techniques to find previous job tasks that are comparable to the future job task in order to estimate the runtime of the prospective job task.

Our needs are restricted to the computer nodes of peer-peer, grid, cluster, or serverless (edge) cloud computing environments. These are the only environments in which the forecasting algorithms can be utilized successfully. Since the CPU and disk IO loads for each DCE user as well as the system administrator (or root user) are periodically collected, resource-level analysis has become more transparent and straightforward. We are therefore encouraged to take into consideration the available forecasting opportunities under a resource-oriented method as this indicates that the quality of resource collection has improved.

With resource-oriented forecasting, specific resources (e.g., host load) that exhibit strong epochal behavior; hence, statistical methods can be applied to the host load forecasting process. It is possible to use a simpler linear mathematical/statistical forecasting model on each sampling unit (time step) of CPU-bound job tasks in computer nodes, regardless of whether they belong to any DCE, because the load profiles of these tasks often exhibit consistent behavior. The results can then be aggregated with the necessary adjustments to reflect the behavior and existence of disk r/w segments.

One benefit of the application-oriented approach is that it directly affects the performance metric (runtimes, deadlines, etc.) that the scheduler is ultimately concerned with. Because the measurements and forecasts generated by this method are specific to the job task (function), they cannot be applied to other job tasks (functions). This historical data is gathered independently for every job task that is executing on a specific computer node. Since each node collects the system's periodic measurements, it is always possible to borrow measurement data. This indicates that other forecasting advisors have access to or are able to share the measurement data.

Metrics that are more closely aligned with the actual parameters are forecasted in application-oriented forecasting and can be utilized to inform scheduling decisions (e.g., end-to-end latency, runtime, CPU utilization). When forecasting resources, it is important to consider their availability (e.g., host load) needs to be estimated beforehand and then translated into the runtime of a specific job task. This conversion could result in a decline in forecasting accuracy. However, by enhancing the underlying CPU and disk load (resource) measurement system, a better model that more accurately forecasts the runtime/ latency can be achieved in the computer-nodes of DCEs. As a result, the OS kernel's Division of Load (DOL) feature makes it possible to collect more data, particularly regarding user loads, which facilitates the creation of a more accurate resource-oriented model.

4.3.2. Forecasting Approaches Trained from Historical Execution

Traditionally, prediction algorithms have been modeled using analytical and mathematical models. However, Wolski et al.'s early research has demonstrated that the CPU load is strongly correlated with time, suggesting that modeling historical data for forecasting is a promising avenue. Dinda's work also demonstrates the viability of load forecasting based on historical data and the use of linear time series, such as autocorrelation models, in forecasting. To realize the characteristics of historical archived data, statistical analysis can be applied. For example, statistical analysis of past data is used to model workloads for grid systems and forecast queue wait times in space-shared environments. In order to utilize the gathered historical data for analysis and simulation in a methodical and analytical manner, workload modeling is presented. Numerous streams exist for modeling. AI techniques, for example, can be applied. Kurowski et al. developed the Grid Performance Forecasting System (GPRES), which is based on the expert systems' architecture. Using the data mining rules, it is quite possible to locate datasets that are similar. Li et al. have employed the Distance Function to group related jobs and resources. Using historical data, the Genetic Search Algorithm looks for specific weights of the closest neighbors. The pertinent literature contains the algorithm's specifics. The ML forecasting models branches off to the following major types. They are the Spatial Temporal Correlation Models (STC) and the models that analyze data as independent data tuples (datasets) (IDT).

4.3.3. Resource Type Taxonomy (Resource Type Hierarchy Tree)

Users of distributed computing environments, such as those found in serverless clouds, make use of a variety of basic resources. (1) Processor time (CPU), (2) Memory, (3) Disk (access cost), and (4) Network bandwidth per CPU are the four categories. Since every fundamental resource type has unique traits and behaviors as well as distinct purposes, it is possible to forecast performance for each type of resource separately. The time-shared method and the space-shared method are the two ways to share the resources. The way the CPU in a desktop computer divides up its work tasks is an illustration of a time-shared resource (functions). In this instance, a few jobs with comparable priorities are executing round-robin style within the designated time slots or time slices. The space-shared CPU, on the other hand, is limited to one job task at a time. The next CPU that becomes available might be assigned to the next job task. A cluster computing system, which manages several CPUs in a space-shared fashion, is a good example of this. Space-shared resources include disk storage and network bandwidth. Homogeneous clusters and other well-connected homogenous resources may be found in the computing cloud. The resource can also be dedicated or shared. One type of dedicated resource would be a cluster of nodes that is always available for HPC tasks. For example, a cluster (Cloud Bigtable cluster) or a collection of uniform and scalable worker nodes may be found in the Google Serverless Cloud. There are various metrics that can be used to define the usage of a specific resource. As a result, it's critical to gauge these resources using pertinent and predictable metrics. The dynamic resource forecast levels on the Distributed Computer System, or DCE hierarchy, are displayed in Figure 4.3. The lowest level (L-0) of resources includes CPU, Memory, Disk space, and I/O bandwidth per computer node. Computer nodes, network bandwidth, and disk storage units are all included in Level-1 (L1). Level 2 (L-2) is where the data storage is located. The Clusters and the Grids are located on Level-3 (L-3). There are virtual organizations at Level-4 (L-4). Serverless clouds remain above them, at the very top level. It is simple to adapt some of the Cluster and Grid PFSs designed to predict Level-0 and Level-1 basic resources to predict the same basic resources of serverless clouds.

- **Level-0**: This level consists of the basic elements such as CPU, memory etc.
- **CPU**: CPU, which is available for a new job task (of a parallel application), can be predicted on a single node by using Dinda, Smith et al., ASKALON, OpenSeries and StreamMiner, DIMEMAS, eNANOS, MWGS, GPRES, Li et al., PACE, PPSKel, FREERIDE-G, Minh and Wolters, FAST, Forecasting of Variance, AWP, FVMRRP, WP_ARIMA, UPVM_Energy Efficient, DRDPred or TPM.

Several of the mathematical and analytical algorithms, as well as forecasting methodologies, are utilized. Unfortunately, the majority of the approaches call for the analysis of workload flow data from time series (STC). Time series (STC) workload data sets can also be used in Serverless clouds to forecast request (event) rate and end-to-end latency. Thus, the Box Jenkin's models are employed with specific machine learning and heuristic techniques in the two aforementioned scenarios. Barister, SPOCK, STOIC, Atomic forecasting suite for cloud resource provisioning, etc. are a few examples. However, in serverless clouds, a function's end-to-end latency is comprised of several time components, including cold start, computation, communication, and storage, making its correlation with CPU load a complicated phenomenon. The Serverless cloud resources are therefore displayed at the top of the tree.

- **Memory**: This basic metric can be forecast on a single node by using PACE, FAST or OpenSeries and StreamMiner.
- **Disk**: In FREERIDE-G predict the disk space access cost (time) or the data retrieval time.
- **I/O Bandwidth per Node**: Both Network I/Os and Disk I/Os inherit I/O Bandwidth per node.
- **Level-1**: At this level, there are 3 main resource components that can be predicted either using the parameters of the level-0 or directly.
- **Machine/Node**: The availability of a computer-node can be forecast directly using historical data as the service provider expresses the time intervals in the day that the machine is available for Grid/Cloud users. NWS or OpenSeries and StreamMiner predicts the availability of computer-nodes. The availability of computer-node can be forecast after performing L-0 level forecasting on CPU, memory, or disk (access cost) resources.
- **Network Bandwidth**: This metric can be forecast by using NWS, Faerman et al., PACE, EDG ROS, FREERIDE-G, FAST, Vazhkudai and Schopf or PDTT.
- **Data Storage Unit**: A large amount of replica data is stored in different Hierarchical Storage Management (HSM) systems. The access latency consists of two major components and they are network access cost and storage access cost. In EDG ROS, the forecasting of storage access cost is conducted by CrossGrid data access estimator. FREERIDE-G can forecast the data storage access time.
- **Level-2**: At this level, there is a single resource component that can be forecast either using the parameters of the level-0 and level-1 or directly.
- **Data Storage Facility**: The forecasting of the access cost of the Data storage facility is done through the forecasting of individual data storage units at level-1. If a data storage unit consists of several individual computer-nodes, after predicting the disk space access cost of each machine at level-0, the total data storage access time can be calculated.
- **Level-3**: The resources at this level can be forecast either using the forecast information of level-0, level-1 and level-2 or directly. The Grid systems belong to this level.

- **Cluster (Parallel Application's Total Runtime)**: DIMEMAS can forecast the communication and computational times of a MPI parallel application. Smith et al., eNANOS, Li et al., Minh and Wolters or PQR2 predict the parallel job's runtime. MWGS or GPRES forecast the parallel job's runtime.
- **Cluster (Parallel Application's Required Number of Nodes)**: The MWGS or RBSP forecasts a parallel application's required number of computer-nodes. The suitability of a DAG parallel application to a particular cluster of nodes (of a loud) can be forecast using the GAMMA Model therefore, it also belongs to level-3.
- **Cluster (Available Memory):** PQR2 or eNANOS forecast the available memory.
- **Cluster (Queue Wait Time)**: In the available PFSs, the queue waiting time is defined for a space-shared cluster of computer-nodes and therefore it belongs to level-3. Downey, Smith, ASKALON, Li et al., QBETS or eNANOS forecasts the queue waiting time. Also, MWGS or GPRES forecast the queue wait time.
- **Grids**: The resource prediction is conducted at level-0, level-1 and level-2.

On a Grid, Sanjay and Vadhiya, or HIPM, predicts the runtime of the MPI parallel job. On a Grid, GIPSY predicts the runtime of parameter sweep applications. LaPIe has the ability to predict how long an MPI parallel application will take to communicate in total on a Grid or Cloud.

- **Level-4**: The suitability of a particular VO requirement to be forecast using the forecast information of the levels below them (level-0, level-1 and level-2).
- **Level-5**: **Serverless (Edge) Cloud Level**: The most suitably the Cloud resources can be predicted using information at level-0. Besides the Cloud resources can be forecast using the forecast information of level-1, level-2, level-3 and level-4.

Archipelago predicts a DAG of serverless cloud functions' latency and deadline. Based on moving window Linear Regression (LR), the SPOCK prediction scheme can accurately predict the average request rate in the 500s window on serverless clouds. STOIC can predict deployment times or overall response times from the edge to the cloud with accuracy. Das and associates. have created models (POEC) to precisely predict costs and end-to-end latencies (communication, computing, and cloud storage time) for operations that move from edge to cloud. Our survey includes access to the SONIC as well as numerous other performance prediction systems.

4.4. SURVEY

PFS for Serverless (edge) clouds is our main area of interest. The resources of an upper level (branch) typically inherit the resources of the lower level, so from a fundamental software engineering point of view, it is essential to take into account the PFSs that are associated with the lower branches of the Resource type hierarchy tree of Figure 4.3. Consequently, the PFSs that are intended to forecast the resources of the lower levels can be used to forecast the resources of the helm of the tree by modifying specific code. As a result of its continued leadership (Figure 4.3), the serverless (edge) cloud inherits all resources at lower tiers. We have therefore included in our survey all PFSs that are intended to forecast resources at lower levels. Put differently, every PFS that has been created for every DCE is included in our survey.

Tables 4.1 and 4.2 include the survey summary that was completed using the Taxonomy.

Table 4.1. *The Classification of Performance Forecasting Approaches*

Performance Forecasting Model	Category of the Predict Model					Input Metrics/Training Data	Res. Type	Class of Job (Time/ Space Shared)
	Machine learning model				Analytical Mo			
	STC	IDT	Selection of data (Man./ Auto.)					
			Man	Auto				
Archipelago					Y	Given the execution time of a function and the SLA, they model how requests of the function arrive to determine the minimum number of sandboxes needed. They make an assumption that request inter-arrival times follow an exponential distribution and model the number of requests expected in a given time interval T as a Poisson distribution	Worker node availability	Functions of DAG (space)

CPU cap control in serverless computing					Y	(1) the "throttled time" of each worker node obtained from the underlying operating system, and (2) the number of "unprocessed functions" in the queue of each worker	Latency (CPU, memory)	Functions of DAG (space)
Performa optimization for serverless edge-cloud					Y	Input data size For training: upload time, cold start time, warm start time, compute time, storage time and the time to send the results from the edge device to the cloud IoT Core, including the network transfer time and the framework-induced overhead	Latency (CPU, memory)	Functions on the smart edge devices (space)
SPOCK					Y	Rate of requests	Deadline (CPU, memory)	ML based web services and applications with multiple request types
STOIC	Y			Y		Batch size, historical runtimes of functions	CPU, bw memory	Functions of DAG (space)
Barista	Y			Y		Work loads Number of requests	CPU, memory	Functions (space)
Mahmoudi and Khazaei	Y			Y		Task arrival rate, response time, maximum concurrency level, initialization time	CPU, bw memory	Functions (space)
Skedulix		Y		Y		Function compute time Framework overhead, file size	CPU, bw, memory	Functions of DAG (space)
Fifer		Y		Y		Past arrival rates	CPU, memory	Functions of DAG (space)
Sonic					Y	Each function's memory foot print, compute time, intermediate data size, fan-out type/degree etc.	Latency Memory	Functions of DAG (space)

Downey		Y		Y		Jobs' historical runtimes, queue times, cluster size and details of their processors are collected from the similar sites to plot the distribution of total allocation time of jobs in log space	Queue	Parallel jobs (space)
Dinda	Y			Y		(1) Historical host load data is automatically stored. (2) Free load runtime of the new job task needs to be recorded	CPU	short j. tasks (100 ms to 10 s) (time)
NWS	Y			Y		Historical values of CPU usage, memory usage, TCP end-to-end bandwidth and latency, and connection time are stored automatically	CPU avail- ability, BW	Parallel j tasks (time)
Faerman	Y			Y		Historical information of data transfer NWS measurements such as TCP end-to-end bandwidth and latency and the connection time are automatically stored	BW	Appli. with data transfer infor. (time)
Vazhkudai and Schopf	Y			Y		GridFTP logs, disk throughput observa- tions and network throughput data are automatically stored	BW	Appli. with data transfer infor. (time)
Smith		Y		Y		Sets of template attri- butes and their profiles of historical workload are automatically stored	CPU Queue	Parallel job (space)
DIMEMAS					Y	Sets of computation bursts and calls to MPI primitives. Descript. of application architecture	CPU and BW	MPI parallel jobs (space)
Predict. of variance	Y			Y		CPU load time series is automatically and online stored on each node	CPU	Parallel jobs (time)
LaPIe					Y	Communication latency, message gap according to message size and number of processors	BW	MPI parallel jobs (time)

ASKALON		Y		Y		Job tasks' historical information such as, job task names, runtimes, input parameter sizes, processor speeds are automatically stored from previous actual runs. If the historical information is not available then it is manually supplied from one of the identical machines	CPU (total) and queue	Parallel jobs (time)
Li et al.		Y		Y		The profiles of historical workloads are automatically stored	CPU Queue	Parallel job (space)
PDTT	Y			Y		Network bandwidth time series is automatically and online recorded at constant width time intervals	BW	Data intensive (time)
eNANOS		Y		Y		Statistical and data mining predictors need the same inputs: job name, user name, group name, no. of processors, job and script names automatically stored as load profiles	CPU Memory, queue	MPI parallel jobs (space)
OpenSeries and StreamMiner		Y		Y		Historical values of workload such as CPU idleness, percentage of free virtual memory, machine availability (switched on or off) and user presence indicator (logged on or off). The attribute selection process which has 3 phases can be semi-automated	CPU, memory and CPU availability	Parallel jobs (time)
GPRES		Y		Y		Historic jobs are categorized according to static or dynamic template attributes. Then the mean of values estimated parameters are calculated for each category. Categories with specific set of values fed to knowledge database as rules and this can be automated	CPU Q ueue	Parallel jobs (space)

MWGS	Y			Y		User-name, submission time, job ID, number of nodes requested, user-predicted job runtime, actual job runtime are the input to generate two Markov chains for the runtimes and num. of nodes. Data collection and generation process can be automated	Queue No. of nodes CPU (total)	Parallel jobs (space)
GAMMA					Y	Computational and network traffic information of the application and the cluster and costing parameters	Cluster	Parallel job (space)
PACE					Y	Software code of the applications and machine and environmental details	CPU, bw queue Mem	MPI parallel J. (time)
TPM					Y	FLPs of the job tasks and machine environmental details. Disk IO maps of the job tasks	CPU, Disk	Parallel job (space/time)
PPSkel					Y	The records of execution activities of the CPU usage, memory consumption and MPI message exchanges are taken from the same program	CPU BW Mem	MPI parallel jobs (time)
EDG ROS					Y	Characteristic details of CPU, network and storage	Disk BW	Remote data processing appli. (time)
Sanjay and Vadhiyar		Y		Y		Available CPUs and available BWs are automatically measured for all processors and links at periodic intervals. The calculated coefficients are used in the total runtime equation	CPU and BW	MPI parallel jobs (time)
PQR2		Y		Y		Application and system-specific attributes such as cluster name, CPU clock, amount of memory, location of data, CPU speed, memory speed, disk speed, number of threads. The data sets can be collected automatically	CPU Mem, disk	MPI parallel jobs (space)

QBETS	Y					Historical data profiles of similar jobs. The data is collected online: collection can be automated	Queue	Parallel jobs (space)
FREERIDE-G					Y	No. of storage nodes, dataset size, network BW, execution speed, disk speed, no. of computing nodes, and the corresponding values of the outputs	Disk BW CPU	Remote data processing appli. (space)
Minh and Wolters		Y		Y		Original inputs: user_name, group_name, queue_name, job_name, Intermediate parameters: historical database size (N), no of nearest neighbour jobs K, the factor α and β Training parameters: user_name, group_name, queue_name, job_name, point_of_separate, N, K, α, β The traces are collected automatically and training parameters are calculated automatically	CPU	Parallel jobs (space)
HIPM		Y		Y		Data/activities of the workflow application, such as type (e.g., metric multiplication), name, arguments, problem size, preparation time, user name, grid site, submission time, queue time, external load, processors, execution time can be automatically collected and the predictor can be trained fast using Bayesian network	CPU and BW	Workflow job (time)
RBSP		Y		Y		Job's input variables, number of machines under consideration are inputs to the regression equation. The collection of the training data can be automated	Cluster	MPI parallel jobs (time)

AWP	Y			Y		Historical workload points are collected online	CPU	Parallel jobs (time)
FAST					Y	Dynamically collected data such as CPU speed, workload, BW, available memory, batch system	CPU Memo-ry BW	Parallel jobs (space)
GIPSY		Y		Y		(a) Initial training sample selection can be automated (b) Selection of the model may be automated subjected to the condition. The selected models can be run until the predicted runtime error converges, and then the most suitable model will be selected.	CPU	Parameter sweep jobs (space)
Forecasting of the QoS					Y	The current measure-ment of the balance of resources of all the nodes (CPU, mem etc.)	CPU, mem-ory	Parallel jobs (space)

Source: Rajalakshmi Krishnamurthi, Adarsh Kumar, Sukhpal Singh Gill, and Raj-kumar Buyya. Serverless Computing: Principles and Paradigms. Springer. https://doi.org/10.1007/978-3-031-26633-1.

Table 4.2. *The Classification of the Resource Types*

Forecasting model	**Res. type**	**Res. level**	**Predicted metrics**	**Centralized/ decentral-ized**	**Homoge-neous/ het-erogeneous**	**Dedi-cated/ shared**
Archipelago	Worker node avail-ability	L-5	Worker node availability	Decentralize	Homogeneous	Dedicated
CPU cap control in serverless comput-ing	CPU, memory	L-5	Latency	Decentralize	Homogeneous	Dedicated
Performa optimiza-tion for edge-cloud serverless	CPU, memory	L-5	Latency	Decentralize	Homogeneous	Dedicated
SPOCK	CPU, memory	L-5	Deadline	Decentralize	Homogeneous	Dedicated

STOIC	CPU, memory, BW	L-5	Overall execution time	Centralized	Homogeneous	Dedicated
Barista	CPU, memory, BW	L-5	Execution time	Centralized	Homogeneous	Dedicated
Mahmoudi and Khazaei	CPU, memory, BW	L-5	Average response time, probability of cold start, and the average number of function instances in the steady-state	Centralized	Homogeneous	Dedicated
Skedulix	CPU, memory, BW	L-5	Function execution time, network latency	Centralized	Homogeneous	Dedicated
Fifer	CPU, memory	L-5	Required number of containers	Centralized	Homogeneous	Dedicated
Sonic	BW, CPU	L-5	Optimal performance/cost Low latency	Centralized	Both	Dedicated
Downey	Queue	L-3	Queue time	Centralized	Homo	Dedicated
Dinda	CPU	L-0 L-0	Host load Job task's runtime	Both	Both	Both
NWS	CPU availability BW	L-1, L-1, L-1	CPU availability, TCP end-to-end throughput, TCP end-to-end latency	Decentralize	Hetero	Shared
Faerman	BW	L-1	Data transfer rate	Decentralize	Hetero	Shared
Vazhkudai and Schopf	BW	L-1	Data transfer rate	Decentralize	Hetero	Shared
Smith	CPU and Queue	L-3, L-3	Job's runtime, Queue time	Centralized	Homo	Dedicated
DIMEMAS	CPU and BW	L-3	Job's runtime	Centralized	Homo	Dedicated

Forecasting of variance	CPU	L-0	CPU load mean and variance over a time	Decentralize	Hetero	Shared
LaPIe	BW	L-4	MPI job's communication makes span	Decentralize	Hetero	Shared
ASKALON	CPU CPU (total) Queue	L-0 L-3 L-3	Job task's runtime Job's runtime Queue time	Centralized	Hetero	Dedicated
Li	CPU, queue	L-3 L-3	Job's runtime Queue time	Centralized	Homo	Dedicated
PDTT	BW	L-1	Data transfer time between 2 nodes	Decentralized	Hetero	Shared
eNANOS	CPU, memory, queue	L-3, L-3, L-3	Job's runtime Memory Queue time	Centralized	Homo	Dedicated
OpenSeries and StreamMiner	CPU, memory, CPU avail-ability	L-0 L-0 L-1	Idle % of CPU Memory Availability of PCs	Decentralized	Hetero	Shared
GPRES	CPU, queue	L-3 L-3	Job's runtime Queue time	Centralized	Homo	Dedicated
MWGS	Queue, no. of nodes, CPU (total)	L-3 L-3 L-3	The arrival time of job No. of nodes Job's runtime	Centralized	Homo-	Dedicated
GAMMA Model	Cluster	L-3	1. For each clus-ter G (γ_a/γ_m) 2. Total usage cost	Centralized	Homo-	Dedicated
PACE	CPU, memory, BW, queue	L-0, L-0, L-1, L-3	Job task's runtime Memory Communication time Queue time	Decentralized	Hetero	Shared

TPM	CPU, disk	L-0 L-0	Load profiles of future Job tasks Disk access time	Decentralized	Hetero	Shared
PPSke	CPU, BW, memory,	L-0, L-0, L-0	MPI job task's runtime (CPU, communication and memory)	Decentralized	Hetero	Shared
EDG ROS	Disk, BW	L-1 L-1	Data retrieval time and communication time	Decentralized	Hetero	Shared
Sanjay and Vadhiya	CPU and BW	L-4	Job's runtime	Decentralized	Hetero	Shared
PQR2	CPU, memory, disk	L-3, L-3, L-3	Job's runtime, memory Disk space	Decentralized	Hetero	Shared
QBETS	Queue	L-3	Probability of past queue wait times reaching the confidence level (95%) of the predicted queue wait times and the RMS error of job tasks that delays less than the predicted value	Centralized	Homo	Dedicated
FREERIDE-G	Disk, BW, CPU	L-0, L-1, L-0	Data retrieval time, communication time, and data processing time	Decentralized	Hetero	Shared
Minh and Wolters	CPU	L-3	Job's runtime	Centralized	Homo	Dedicated
HIPM	CPU and BW	L-4	Job's runtime	Decentralized	Hetero	Shared
RBSP	Cluster	L-3	No of machines	Centralized	Homo	Dedicated
AWP	CPU	L-0	Load profile	Decentralized	Hetero	Shared

FAST	CPU, memory, BW	L-0, L-0, L-1	Processing run-time, memory, Communication time	Decentralized	Hetero	Shared
GIPSY	CPU	L-4	Job's runtime	Decentralized	Hetero	Shared
Forecasting. Of QoS	CPU, Mem etc.	L-0, L-0	Future available balance of resources (CPU, mem etc.)	Decentralized	Hetero	Shared

Source: Rajalakshmi Krishnamurthi, Adarsh Kumar, Sukhpal Singh Gill, and Rajkumar Buyya. Serverless Computing: Principles and Paradigms. Springer. https://doi.org/10.1007/978-3-031-26633-1.

4.4.1. The Surveyed Performance Forecasting Systems

We have examined the systems listed below in our survey. Three sections have been identified: Analytical/Mathematical Models, Machine Learning Models: Spatial Temporal Correlation (STC), and Machine Learning Models: Utilization of Independent Data Tuples (IDT).

4.4.1.1. Analytical/Mathematical Models

- **Archipelago** (Serverless clouds)
- **CPU Cap Control in Serverless Comp. Platform** (Serverless clouds)
- **Performance Optimization for Edge-Cloud Serverless Platforms (POEC)** (Edge-Cloud)
- **SPOCK** (Serverless clouds)
- **SONIC** (Serverless clouds)
- **PACE** (Clusters and Grids)
- **The Task Profiling Model (TPM)** (Clusters and Grids)
- **DIMEMAS** (Single Machines/Clusters)
- **LaPIe** (Clusters and Grids)
- **ASKALON** (Single Machines/Clusters)
- **GAMMA** (Clusters)
- **Performance Forecasting with Skeletons (PPSkel)** (Clusters and Grids)
- **Performance Forecasting Model for FREERIDE-G** (Grids)
- **Fast Agent's System Timer (FAST)** (Grids)

- **Forecasting of the QoS** (Grids)
- **EDG Replica Optimization Service (ROS)** (Grids).

4.4.1.2. Machine Learning Models: STC

- **STOIC** (Edge-cloud)
- **Barista** (Serverless clouds)
- **Mahmoudi and Khazaei** (Serverless clouds)
- **Atomic forecasting suite for cloud resource provisioning** (Clouds)
- **Wolski** (DCE)
- **Dinda** (Clusters and Grids)
- **Modelling Workloads for Grid Systems (MWGS)** (Parallel Computers with Batch Queue Systems)
- **Forecasting of Variance** (Grids)
- **Forecasting of Data Transfer Time (FDTT)** (Data Grids)
- **Adaptive Workload Forecasting in Confidence Window (AWP)** (Grids)
- **QBETS** (for Parallel Computers with Batch Queue Systems).

4.4.1.3. Machine Learning Models: (IDT)

- **Skedulix** (for Serverless clouds)
- **Downey** (Clusters)
- **Fifer** (Serverless clouds)
- **Smith** (Single Machine/Cluster)
- **Li's data mining method** (Clusters)
- **eNANOS** (Clusters)
- **OpenSeries and StreamMiner** (Desktop Grids)
- **GPRES** (Clusters)
- **Faerman** (Collection of Distributed Resources)
- **Vazhkudai and Schopf** (Data Grids)
- **PQR2** (Clusters)
- **Sanjay and Vadhiyar** (Grids)
- **Minh and Wolters** (Backfilling parallel systems)
- **Hybrid Intelligent Forecasting Model (HIPM)** (Grids)
- **Regression-Based Scalability Forecasting (RBSP)** (Clusters)
- **Grid Information Forecasting System (GIPSY)** (Grids).

4.5. ANALYSIS OF THE SURVEY

We take into consideration the PFS that are currently in use in the RMS of the Serverless Cloud Platforms since our goal is to analyze the survey results. We also take into account PFSs that are utilized on DCEs in our survey because it is feasible to upgrade them to be compatible with Serverless Cloud Environments. We discovered that it is difficult to accurately estimate the forecasting information in the serverless cloud environment after examining more than 50 different PFSs. Tables 4.1 and 4.2 contain the tabulated results of our analysis.

In our analysis, the majority of PFSs predicted the job task's runtime (or, in the case of serverless clouds, the end-to-end latency of a function). The queue waiting time for the Parallel job has been predicted by eight PFSs on the clusters. The runtime of the Parallel job has been predicted by 7 PFSs on the clusters. One PFS on each cluster has predicted the total computational and communication time for MPI parallel jobs. Two PFSs on the clusters have predicted the amount of memory that is available. Two PFSs on a Grid have predicted the total computational and communication time for MPI parallel jobs. 8 PFSs have forecasted the communication time between two points. One PFS on the Grid has predicted the entire communication time (LaPIe). Three PFSs have forecasted the memory of the computer node. Four PFSs have projected the number of PCs that will be available. A single PFS has predicted whether a parallel application to a cluster (GAMMA model) is appropriate. Also, there is an attempt to forecast the resources' quality of service.

4.5.1. Meeting the Challenges

4.5.1.1. Appropriate Performance Metrics for the Serverless Computing Environments

Introducing metrics that work in a serverless cloud environment is essential. Because we can modify their forecasting methods to perform forecasting on Serverless clouds, it is crucial to examine the forecasting mechanisms of other DCEs. In the Resource level taxonomy (Figure 4.3), forecasting algorithms that remain below that level of the DCS tree's resource type hierarchy may be modified to make predictions of resources at that level.

We discovered that several PFSs have unique metrics. For example, Yang and colleagues. have projected the variation in CPU load over a future time period as well as the average CPU load over a specific time period. Yang along with others. have created a forecasting method that uses anticipated means and variances in the shared networks to predict the effective bandwidth over the data transfer time interval. It is easy to modify this forecasting method to predict the time it will take for data to move from edge devices to the cloud. Wu et al. predicted the CPU load inside a specific confidence window over n time steps. Since their AHModel computes the Mean sq\. Error of forecasting over n and w steps, it is particularly applicable to clusters and serverless clouds, which are typical execution environments for lengthy job tasks.

The new metric that Seneviratne and Levy developed for the TPM, called the "individual Free Load Profile or FLP," of upcoming job tasks, has been a crucial component. It is simple to modify this forecasting method for use with serverless cloud platforms.

The GAMA model aids in predicting which cluster will work best for a given MPI parallel application. With the GAMMA Model, a group of computer nodes in a serverless cloud can be predicted.

A set of MPI tasks or a workflow's total communication time can be predicted using the LaPIe model, which is the new metric. The communication time of a DAG in a serverless cloud can also be predicted using this method.

By utilizing the probability of previous queue wait times reaching the confidence level (95 percent) of the predicted queue wait time, QBETS has developed a new metric to predict the delay times on the queue.

4.5.1.2. Forecasting of the Bandwidth (Communication Time)

Fewer PFSs have been used to forecast network bandwidth than the run time of job tasks (functions). It is crucial to have the best possible upstream network time (latency) from the smart (mobile) devices to the serverless cloud server when using edge cloud computing. To achieve this goal, the network bandwidth forecasts below—which were made at the lower rungs of Figure 4.3's Resource type hierarchy tree—can be modified. Data transfer times can be predicted using regression-based techniques. Yang et al.'s forecasting is based on the NWS forecasting engines and spans a specific time period, which makes it more applicable to serverless edge clouds than other forecasting methods. Level L-1 data transfer forecasting using linear regression has been carried out by Faerman et al. NWS has predicted the TCP end-to-end bandwidth, latency, and connection time at resource level L-1. Vazhkudai and Schopf employed the multivariate regression technique in their predictors.

Numerous attempts have been made to predict the communication time or bandwidth since Wolski developed NWS. The PACE toolkit at L-1 (Figure 4.3) can be used to predict how long a job task will take to communicate. LaPIe at L-4 can forecast the total communication time of a group of MPI tasks or a workflow. FAST forecasts communication times without taking background congestion into account.

4.5.1.3. Forecasting of Multiple Metrics

Multiple parameters are predicted simultaneously by the GPRES, eNANOS, and PACE. It might be necessary to predict multiple parameters when different classes of applications operate in the same DCE. For example, it might be necessary to forecast several metrics in Clusters, Grids, Clouds, and Serverless Clouds. These prediction systems have the drawback of not being resource-specific, which makes it difficult to fine-tune them and potentially reduces forecasting accuracy.

4.5.1.4. Forecasting of Data Access

The amount of time needed to access replicated data from any serverless cloud location is known as the data access time (or Grid, or Cloud). This might represent a specific bottleneck for high-performance computing. For the purpose of efficiently reading data, it is therefore necessary to forecast the access times for the Hierarchical Storage Management (HSM) systems. Two PFSs that are included in this study are the Forecasting Model for FREERID-G and the EDG Replica Optimization Service.

4.5.2. Taxonomy

4.5.2.1. Resource Type Hierarchy Tree (Resource Type Taxonomy)

In order to schedule resources in Serverless clouds effectively and efficiently, it is necessary to forecast a number of resource types. The resource type hierarchy tree shown in Figure 4.3 indicates that forecasting techniques appropriate to a given level can be applied to all levels below it as well as to resources at that level. Forecasting techniques that have been effectively applied to the computer resources of Grids, clusters, peer-peer engines, virtual machines, queue systems, etc. must therefore be taken into account because these systems are all below the top level, which is made up of Serverless clouds and Serverless edge clouds.

The forecasting done on a lower leaf in the Figure 4.3 tree can be transferred to a higher leaf without losing information because the metrics on a leaf at a higher level depend on the metrics on a leaf at a lower level. For example, it is possible to predict the CPU load, memory usage, and disk usage—all of which fall under Level-0—in order to determine the availability of a specific computer node (which is assigned to Level-1). However, the value forecast at Level-1 may not provide the forecasting data, such as CPU or memory capacity. Similarly, the predicted CPU capacity, memory capacity, or disk access cost of a specific node (of that cluster) cannot be derived from this information even if the most appropriate future cluster is selected using the Gamma model (at Level-3). Since the information is so closely entwined in the upper levels of the tree in Figure 4.3, it is either very difficult or impossible to accurately separate them.

As a fundamental or basic measurement (CPU load, disk load, memory capacity, etc.) of the system, a metric of the lowest level (Level-0) of the tree is easily and directly measurable. Its attributes are also fully comprehensible. As a result, their predicted value has a higher accuracy than the higher levels. Take Dinda, PACE, PPSKel, and TPM, for example. It is best to forecast at the lowest level of the tree and transfer the forecast results to the top level without sacrificing accuracy for Serverless clouds (Level-5). As a result, it is simple to modify PFSs (Level-0) that are designed to forecast fundamental metrics at the lowest level (Level-0) for the purpose of predicting application performance on Serverless clouds.

A higher-level resource's behavior becomes complex because it depends on a wide variety of metrics that are associated with the lowest level. Because of this, it is challenging to assess or predict its behavior at a higher level.

Similar to this, basic lower levels can conduct the highest level forecasting, to which Serverless clouds belong, and then transfer the results to the highest level in a meaningful way. As a result, it is simple to modify the forecasting techniques that have already been created to predict the usage of basic resource elements like CPU, memory, and disk usage for computer nodes to forecast the resources for serverless clouds.

Our research has shown that, due to the difficulty of accurately forecasting at higher levels of the tree, only a small number of PFSs are available for use in this capacity (Figure 4.3). For example, only one PFS is available at level-4 to forecast the computational and communication times of a parallel application on the Grid. On the Grid, there is only one PFS available for estimating a workflow's execution time.

The CPU resource or job task's runtime is predicted by 18 applications at Level-0, the lowest level of the tree. In order to predict the communication time between two points, at least nine PFSs are used at Level-1. There are two PFSs at Level-1 that forecast the access time to data storage. Two PFSs at Level-0 are able to forecast the memory that is available on a computer node.

Because independent resource predictions are simpler and more accurate at the lowest level than those at higher levels, it is therefore preferable to perform forecasting at the lowest level in Serverless cloud platforms (SCP). The prediction of resources at the lowest level is more important for a heterogeneous collection of resources (a grid of heterogeneous computer nodes) than it is for a homogeneous set of resources because the latter will behave in a more sophisticated manner with many different dependencies, making accurate forecasting at the higher level a challenging task.

4.5.2.2. Forecasting Approach Taxonomy

There are two main categories of forecasting methodologies. They are machine learning approaches and mathematical or analytical approaches. They are the forecasting engines that analyze individual data sets (tuples) and the STC family. The types are shown in detail in Figure 4.2. In Table 4.1, we have tallied them based on their own attributes.

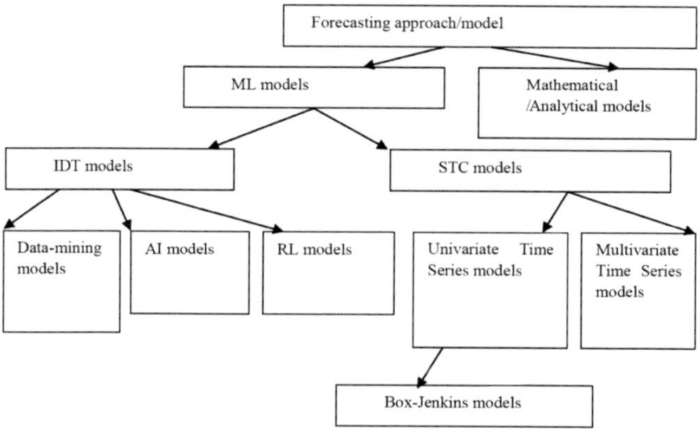

Figure 4.2. *Forecasting approach taxonomy.*

Source: Rajalakshmi Krishnamurthi, Adarsh Kumar, Sukhpal Singh Gill, and Rajkumar Buyya. Serverless Computing: Principles and Paradigms. Springer. https://doi.org/10.1007/978-3-031-26633-1.

The source code for the job tasks and the hardware configuration of the computer are used by Nudd et al.'s developed analytical model, the PACE toolkit, to simulate forecasting. Given that clients are not particularly interested in processing source code or configuring hardware to simulate prediction, Seneviratne et al. could be a worthwhile endeavor. The created Task Profiling Model reflects the behavior of both CPU and disk loads by using Free Load Profiles rather than source code. The GAMMA model, which selects the best cluster for a given parallel application, is another intriguing analytical model (Gruber and Tran, 2004). The LaPIe predicts an MPI parallel application's network BW metric.

Automating the process of gathering training data is essential for Machine Learning prediction systems to ensure the effectiveness of the forecasting systems. While it takes a few minutes to train an ML PFS, once trained and operational, ML models can be highly competitive in the market. The forecasting algorithm must be applied to the highest level of the tree when using it (Figure 4.3). For example, a cluster at level-3 can have its queue time and job total runtime forecast. Nevertheless, because a Grid at level 4 is a network of diverse resources, Smith's prediction algorithm cannot be used. Sanjay and Vadhiyar use a Grid to forecast job runtime at Level-4. The prediction algorithms at level-0 must, however, be applied in order to independently forecast the runtime of each job task (function) on each worker node in a serverless cloud.

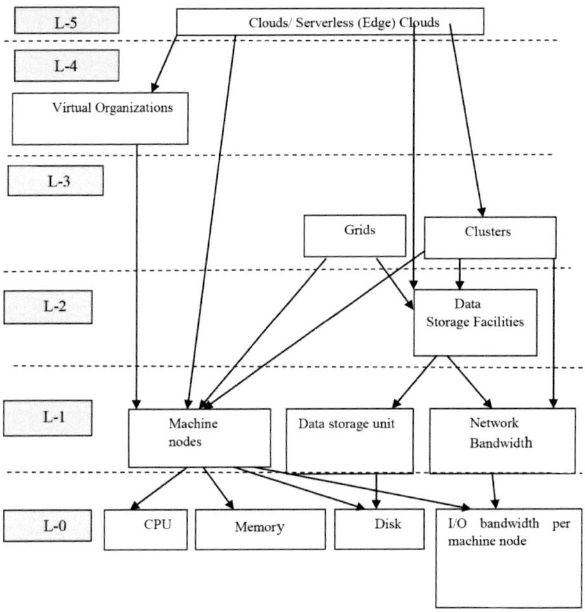

Figure 4.3. *Resource hierarchy tree (resource type taxonomy).*

Source: Rajalakshmi Krishnamurthi, Adarsh Kumar, Sukhpal Singh Gill, and Rajkumar Buyya. Serverless Computing: Principles and Paradigms. Springer. https://doi.org/10.1007/978-3-031-26633-1.

The other crucial point is that, in contrast to a Serverless (edge) cloud, which is made up of groups of homogeneous clusters, and the Grid, which is a dynamic and heterogeneous collection of resources, Level-3 prediction algorithms could very well be modified for the forecasting of SCP resources.

REFERENCES

1. Andrzejak, A., Domingues, P., & Silva, L. (2006). Predicting machine availabilities in desktop pools. In *IEEE/IFIP Network Operations & Management Symposium (NOMS 2006)*, Vancouver, Canada.
2. Andrzejak, A., Graupner, S., & Plantikow, S. (2006). Predicting resource demand in dynamic utility computing environments. In *International Conference on Autonomic and Autonomous Systems (ICAS'06)*, Santa Clara, USA.
3. Ayodele, A. O., Rao, J., & Boult, T. E. (2015). Performance measurement and interference profiling in multi-tenant clouds. In *2015 IEEE 8th International Conference on Cloud Computing* (pp. 941–949).
4. Badia, R. M., Labarta, J., Gimenez, J., & Escalé, A. F. (2003). DIMEMAS: Predicting MPI applications behavior in grid environments. In *Workshop on Grid Applications and Programming Tools (GGF8).*
5. Barnes, B. J., Rountree, B., Lowenthal, D. K., Reeves, J., Supinski, B., & Schulz, M. (2008). A regression-based approach to scalability prediction. In *22nd International Conference on Supercomputing (ICS '08)*. ACM, Kos, Greece.
6. Boza, E. F., Abad, C. L., Villavicencio, M., Quimba, S., & Plaza, J. A. (2017). Reserved, on demand or serverless: Model-based simulations for cloud budget planning. In *2017 IEEE Second Ecuador Technical Chapters Meeting (ETCM)* (pp. 1–6).
7. Calheiros, R. N., Masoumi, E., Ranjan, R., & Buyya, R. (2015). Workload prediction using ARIMA model and its impact on cloud applications' QoS. *IEEE Transactions on Cloud Computing*, *3*, 449–458.
8. Carvalho, M., Miceli, R., Maciel Jr, P. D., Brasileiro, F., & Lopes, R. (2010). Predicting the quality of service of a peer-to-peer desktop grid. In *10th IEEE/ACM International Conference on Cluster, Cloud and Grid Computing (CCGrid)*. IEEE Comput. Soc., Melbourne, Australia.
9. Das, A., Imai, S., Patterson, S., & Wittie, M. P. (2020). Performance optimization for edge-cloud serverless platforms via dynamic task placement. In *2020 20th IEEE/ACM International Symposium on Cluster, Cloud and Internet Computing (CCGRID)* (pp. 41–50).
10. Das, A., Leaf, A., Varela, C. A., & Patterson, S. (2020). Skedulix: Hybrid cloud scheduling for cost-efficient execution of serverless applications. In *2020 IEEE 13th International Conference on Cloud Computing (CLOUD)* (pp. 609–618).

11. Desprez, F., Quinson, M., & Suter, F. (2002). Dynamic performance forecasting for network-enabled servers in a heterogeneous environment. In *International Conference on Parallel & Distributed Processing Techniques & Applications (PDPTA)*, Las Vegas, USA.
12. Eyupoglu, C. (2019). Big data in cloud computing and Internet of Things. In *2019 3rd International Symposium on Multidisciplinary Studies and Innovative Technologies (ISMSIT)* (pp. 1–5).
13. Faerman, M., Su, A., Wolski, R., & Berman, F. (1999). Adaptive performance prediction for distributed data-intensive applications. In *ACM/IEEE International Conference on Supercomputing*, Portland, OR, USA.
14. Fahringer, T., Jugravu, A., Pllana, S., Prodan, R., Seragiotto, C. Jr, & Truong, H. L. (2005). ASKALON: A tool set for cluster and grid computing. *Concurrency and Computation: Practice and Experience*, *17*, 143–169.
15. Feng, L., Kudva, P., Silva, D. D., & Hu, J. (2018). Exploring serverless computing for neural network training. In *2018 IEEE 11th International Conference on Cloud Computing (CLOUD)* (pp. 334–341).
16. Gruber, R., & Tran, T. M. (2004). Parameterization to tailor commodity clusters to applications. *EPFL Supercomputing Review*, *14*, 12–17.
17. Gunasekaran, J. R., Thinakaran, P., Kandemir, M. T., Urgaonkar, B., Kesidis, G., & Das, C. (2019). Spock: Exploiting serverless functions for SLO and cost-aware resource procurement in public cloud. In *2019 IEEE 12th International Conference on Cloud Computing (CLOUD)* (pp. 199–208).
18. Gunasekaran, J. R., Thinakaran, P., Nachiappan, N. C., Kandemir, M. T., & Das, C. R. (2020). Fifer: Tackling resource underutilization in the serverless era. In *Proceedings of the 21st International Middleware Conference*. Association for Computing Machinery, Delft, Netherlands.
19. Hendrickson, S., Sturdevant, S., Harter, T., Venkataramani, V., Arpaci-Dusseau, A. C., & Arpaci-Dusseau, R. H. (2016). Serverless computation with openLambda. In *Proceedings of the 8th USENIX Conference on Hot Topics in Cloud Computing*. USENIX Association, Denver, CO.
20. Hsieh, S. Y., Liu, C. S., Buyya, R., & Zomaya, A. Y. (2020). Utilization-prediction-aware virtual machine consolidation approach for energy-efficient cloud data centers. *Journal of Parallel and Distributed Computing*, *139*, 99–109.
21. Jonas, E., Schleier-Smith, J., Sreekanti, V., Tsai, C. C., Khandelwal, A., Pu, Q., Shankar, V., Carreira, J., Krauth, K., Yadwadkar, N. J., Gonzalez,

J., Popa, R. A., Stoica, I., & Patterson, D. A. (2019). Cloud programming simplified: A Berkeley view on serverless computing. *arXiv:1902.03383*.

22. Kim, Y. K., Hoseinyfarahabady, M. R., Lee, Y. C., & Zomaya, A. Y. (2020). Automated fine-grained CPU cap control in serverless computing platform. *IEEE Transactions on Parallel and Distributed Systems*, *31*, 2289–2301.
23. Kumar, J., Singh, A. K., & Buyya, R. (2020). Ensemble learning based predictive framework for virtual machine resource request prediction. *Neurocomputing*, *397*, 20–30.
24. Kurowski, K., Oleksiak, A., Nabrzyski, J., Kwiecien, A., Wojtkiewicz, M., Dyczkowski, M., Guim, F., & Corbalan, J. (2005). Multi-criteria grid resource management using performance prediction techniques. In *CoreGrid Integration Workshop*, Pisa, Italy, Nov 2005.
25. Li, H., Groep, D., & Wolters, L. (2007). Mining performance data for metascheduling decision support in the grid. *Future Generation Computer Systems*, *23*, 92–99.
26. Li, H., Sun, J., & Sun, B. L. (2009). Financial distress prediction based on OR-CBR in the principle of K-nearest neighbors. *Expert Systems with Applications*, *36*, 643–659.
27. Mahgoub, A. Y., Shankar, K., Mitra, S., Klimovic, A., Chaterji, S., & Bagchi, S. (2021). SONIC: Application-aware data passing for chained serverless applications. In *USENIX Annual Technical Conference*, 2021.
28. Mahmoudi, N., & Khazaei, H. (2020). Performance modeling of serverless computing platforms. *IEEE Transactions on Cloud Computing*, *10*, 2834–2847.
29. Malawski, M., Gajek, A., Zima, A., Balis, B., & Figiela, K. (2020). Serverless execution of scientific workflows: Experiments with HyperFlow, AWS Lambda and Google Cloud Functions. *Future Generation Computer Systems*, *110*, 502–514.
30. Nudd, G. R., Kerbyson, D. J., Panaefstathiou, E., Perry, S. C., Harper, J. S., & Ewilcox, D. V. (2000). PACE—A toolset for the performance prediction of parallel and distributed systems. *High Performance Computing Applications*, *14*, 228–252.
31. Nurmi, D. C., Brevik, J., & Wolski, R. (2007). QBETS: Queue bounds estimation from time series. In *SIGMETRICS '07: International Conference on Measurement & Modeling of Computer Systems*. Springer, San Diego, CA, USA.
32. Oakes, E., Yang, L., Houck, K., Harter, T., Arpaci-Dusseau, A. C., & Arpaci-Dusseau, R. H. (2017). Pipsqueak: Lean lambdas with large libraries. In

IEEE 37th International Conference on Distributed Computing Systems Workshops (ICDCSW 2017).

33. Ou, Z., Zhuang, H., Lukyanenko, A., Nurminen, J. K., Hui, P., Mazalov, V., & Ylä-Jääski, A. (2013). Is the same instance type created equal? Exploiting heterogeneity of public clouds. *IEEE Transactions on Cloud Computing*, *1*, 201–214.
34. Palmer, N., Sherman, M., Wang, Y., & Just, S. (2015). Scaling to build the consolidated audit trail: A financial services application of Google Cloud Bigtable.
35. Prodan, R. (2007). Specification and runtime workflow support in the ASKALON grid environment. *Scientific Programming*, *15*, 193–211.
36. Rehman, M. S., & Sakr, M. F. (2010). Initial findings for provisioning variation in cloud computing. In *2010 IEEE Second International Conference on Cloud Computing Technology and Science*, 30 Nov–3 Dec 2010 (pp. 473–479).
37. Rodero, I., Guim, F., & Corbalán, J., & Labarta, J. (2005). eNANOS: Coordinated scheduling in grid environments. In *Parallel Computing: Current & Future Issues of High-End Computing, ParCo, 2005.*
38. Sanjay, H. A., & Vadhiyar, S. (2008). Performance modeling of parallel applications for grid scheduling. *Journal of Parallel and Distributed Computing*, *68*, 1135–1145.
39. Sanjay, H. A., & Vadhiyar, S. (2009). A strategy for scheduling tightly-coupled parallel applications on clusters. *Concurrency and Computation: Practice and Experience*, *21*, 2491–2517.
40. Schad, J., Dittrich, J., & Quiané-Ruiz, J. A. (2010). Runtime measurements in the cloud: Observing, analyzing, and reducing variance. *Proceedings of the VLDB Endowment*, *3*, 460–471.
41. Scheuner, J., & Leitner, P. (2020). Function-as-a-Service performance evaluation: A multivocal literature review. *Journal of Systems and Software, 170*, 110708. https://doi.org/10.1016/j.jss.2020.110708.
42. Seneviratne, S. (2009). *A Framework for Load Profile Prediction for Grid Computing* (PhD thesis). Sydney University.
43. Seneviratne, S., & Levy, D. C. (2011). Task profiling model for load profile prediction. *Future Generation Computer Systems, 27*, 245–255. https://doi.org/10.1016/j.future.2010.09.008.
44. Seneviratne, S., Levy, D. C., Hong, W., De Silva, L. C., & Hu, J. (2021). Introduction of the new OS kernel internals for the new metrics for the performance prediction on the distributed computing environments. In V.

M. Petrova (Ed.), *Advances in Engineering Research*. Nova Science and Technology.

45. Seneviratne, S., Levy, D., & Rajkumar, B. (2015). Taxonomy of performance prediction systems for parallel and distributed computing systems. In J. G. Barbosa (Ed.), *Grid Computing Techniques and Future Prospects*. Nova Science Publishers.
46. Song, B., Ernemann, C., & Yahyapour, R. (2004). Parallel computer workload modelling with Markov chains. In *International Conference on Job Scheduling Strategies for Parallel Processing* (pp. 47–67). Springer.
47. Steffenel, L. A. (2005). *LaPIe: Communications Collectives Adaptées aux Grilles de Calcul* (PhD thesis). INPG.
48. Ullah, Q. Z., Shahzad, H., & Khan, G. M. (2017). Adaptive resource utilization prediction system for infrastructure as a service cloud. *Computational Intelligence and Neuroscience, 2017*, 1–12. https://doi.org/10.1155/2017/4523795.
49. Vazhkudai, S., & Schopf, J. M. (2003). Using regression techniques to predict large data transfers. *High Performance Computing Applications, 17*, 249–268. https://doi.org/10.1177/1094342003017002006.
50. Wolski, R. (1998). Dynamically forecasting network performance using the network weather service. *Cluster Computing, 1*, 119–132. https://doi.org/10.1023/A:1019027103127.
51. Wolski, R., Spring, N., & Hayes, J. (1999). The network weather service: A distributed resource performance forecasting service for metacomputing. *Future Generation Computer Systems, 15*, 757–768. https://doi.org/10.1016/S0167-739X(99)00027-4.
52. Wolski, R., Spring, N., & Hayes, J. (2000). Predicting the CPU availability of time-shared Unix systems on the computational grid. *Cluster Computing, 3*, 293–301. https://doi.org/10.1023/A:1019077924697.
53. Wu, Y., Hwang, K., Yuan, Y., & Zheng, W. (2010). Adaptive workload prediction of grid performance in confidence windows. *IEEE Transactions on Parallel and Distributed Systems, 21*, 925–938. https://doi.org/10.1109/TPDS.2009.150.
54. Yang, L., Schopf, J. M., & Foster, I. (2005). Improving parallel data transfer times using predicted variances in shared networks. In *Fifth IEEE International Symposium on Cluster Computing and the Grid (CCGRID05)* (pp. 734–740). IEEE Computer Society. https://doi.org/10.1109/CCGRID.2005.1558640.

CHAPTER 5

OPEN-SOURCE SERVERLESS FOR EDGE COMPUTING

Contents

INTRODUCTION

A more distributed service model known as edge computing has replaced the centralized cloud computing model due to the exponential growth of real-time and data-intensive services. This shift is driven by Internet-of-Things (IoT) devices and new technologies like those used in self-driving cars. In fact, edge computing relies on resource-constrained nodes rather than a centralized cloud data center approach in an attempt to move data processing closer to the source in order to avoid potential bottlenecks and latency caused by the transport and computation of large data volumes. Furthermore, IoT data usually result in the deployment of multiple applications with different computational demands that are frequently met by the same computing platform. These applications are deployed in multiple networks situated in various locations. The flexibility required by the Internet of Things domain is granted by edge computing, which offers local data computation and storage with the option to transfer the collected data to a centralized cloud computing platform if necessary.

Edge computing can host multiple applications at once and offer a range of network locations and functions. In actuality, edge computing does not require a specific location for deployment.

Edge nodes, for instance, can be found in local data centers, WiFi hotspots, radio towers, and network routers. As long as it can handle a computational workload, any nearby device with processing power can function as an edge node. Whether they are public clouds or telecom operator (Telco) cloud facilities, edge computing layers are usually positioned between user devices (more than tens of millions of points of presence) and centralized computing datacenters.

Because of their heterogeneity and the kind of network environment they are connected to (usually Local Area Network (LAN) environments), device computing resources are challenging to use and manage. Edge computing based applications can be designed with real-time and interactive features, as well as temporal and spatial proximity to end users, to meet the demands of use cases like video analytics, healthcare, industrial control, and multimedia services.

This is made possible by the variety of deployment configurations that are available. The establishment of the Industry Specification Group (ISG) on Multi-Access Edge Computing (MEC) at the European Telecommunications Standards Institute (ETSI) in late 2014 marked the beginning of the standardization process for this computing paradigm. According to the ETSI ISG MEC definition, MEC is situated at the network's edge and provides application developers and content providers with computing power and an IT service environment, much like in a cloud computing scenario.

Typically, MEC is characterized by:

- ***On-Premises***: An edge application can be isolated from the rest of the network while still having access to local resources. When it comes to requirements for machine-to-machine communication, these isolation boundaries can be a useful feature. This might apply to safety or security systems where a high degree of privacy and resilience is required.
- ***Proximity***: Edge computing, which allows for physical proximity to data sources, is especially effective at processing data for big data analytics. It also offers direct device access when required by certain business logic.
- ***Lower latency***: An advantageous latency reduction is also offered by the previously mentioned proximity feature. In addition to decreasing the likelihood of traffic bottlenecks on the platform, this can logically enhance service responsiveness and user experience.
- ***Resource efficiency***: The optimization of resource usage is essential because edge devices typically have limited hardware.

A core component of edge computing is resource efficiency. However, the number of concurrent applications and users in an edge system is severely limited by the conventional method of service provisioning through virtual machines (VMs). In actuality, virtual machines lack efficiency due to their frequent overprovisioning by design, which can result in significant computational overhead and prolonged boot times. Deploying applications in containerized packages—processes that encapsulate applications with their runtimes and execute them directly on the host system—is becoming a more and more popular method of resolving these problems. As a result, containers maintain separate file systems while sharing the same host system kernel. Because of this feature, containers can start up to ten times faster than virtual machines while using less resources. Serverless computing is a new deployment paradigm that heavily leverages containers.

A serverless computing approach dynamically provisioned computing resources, configuration, and management services at runtime by the platform. Function as a service (FaaS), an event-driven allocation model, is what makes this possible. This new model bears some resemblance to the popular software as a service (SaaS) paradigm; however, it places greater emphasis on auto scalability and event-based architecture, resulting in a platform that is akin to a back-box that is separate from the underlying servers (i.e., serverless), at least as far as developers and end users are concerned. Developers of serverless applications, as opposed to earlier approaches where resource configuration and provisioning must be carefully planned during application design, can actually concentrate only on the services logic, which is typically divided into atomic modules and wrapped into containers. The platform itself handles infrastructure provisioning and maintenance activities in a transparent manner for developers and end users. Because cloud providers handle the maintenance of the hardware infrastructure, even complex applications that rely on the FaaS paradigm are designed and released as a set of functions hosted in containers. These functions can be dynamically loaded on demand, frequently with parallel execution, without incurring additional overhead due to control and management of the application deployment at the operating system level.

Therefore, serverless computing makes edge services more accessible to developers of applications, providing them and IT/operations teams with a fine-grained deployment model that spares the application developer from the overhead of provisioning, updating, and managing hardware infrastructure. With its emphasis on flexible provisioning and efficient resource usage, the FaaS approach makes serverless computing a promising deployment paradigm for edge scenarios.

FaaS can use containerization's extremely flexible configuration and speed to adjust resource allocation to the actual needs of the service. This feature is especially useful for short-term, event-triggered tasks, like those found in IoT scenarios. In actuality, serverless computing enables the dynamic processing of data streams from Internet of Things (IoT) devices, which may transmit messages periodically or randomly, be event-triggered, and inactive for the majority of the time.

After these messages are received, the required serverless modules may be activated, taking into account the warm and cold start operational modes. The user is given the impression of high availability when the warm start mode is chosen because the application-hosting containers are kept operational after initialization. In contrast, cold start configurations save resources by deleting those containers after a predetermined amount of time if no application requests are received. A cold start strategy, though, might make some laten.

This tutorial aims to give a thorough overview of the state-of-the-art in open-source serverless technologies for edge computing. Our goal is to investigate potential ways to implement serverless applications on edge nodes, with an emphasis on Internet of Things data—one of the main applications for edge computing. Additionally, we analyze the advantages and security constraints of serverless computing and offer some insights on new lightweight virtualization technologies. Lastly, we offer a summary of the state-of-the-art in multiclouds, a possible new setting for serverless technologies, for edge and cloud interworking.

Hence, the contribution of this work consists of the following points:

- The analysis of the currently available open-source serverless platforms, providing a comparison of their features, benefits and disadvantages.
- A detailed description of OpenFaaS, the most used open-source server platform, based on Kubernetes.
- An overview of new lightweight technologies as potential alternatives to containers for serverless application on the edge.
- The analysis of serverless computing on edge nodes' benefits and drawbacks from a security perspective. The description of a state-of-art serverless application for IoT data.
- A discussion on the current ways to interconnect edge and cloud platforms and the role of serverless computing in this scenario.

We present the available open-source options for implementing a serverless application in an edge computing scenario, emphasizing OpenFaaS in particular since it is the most adaptable and user-friendly framework out of all the open-source serverless computing platforms currently in use. Additionally, we demonstrate how to implement a serverless function in OpenFaaS and outline the various templates that are offered by this serverless platform. We examine the alternatives to containers for serverless application deployment, examining the features, advantages, and disadvantages of these novel lightweight virtualization technologies as well as their application in OpenFaaS (Figure 5.1).

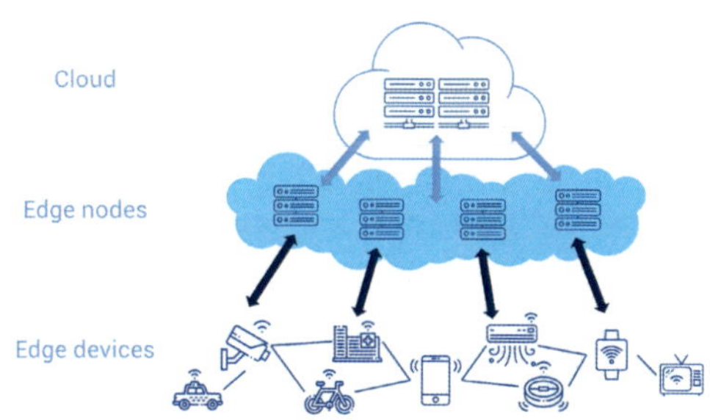

Figure 5.1. *Edge computing location.*

*Source: https://miro.medium.com/v2/resize:fit:1400/0*8pz8vkPhwdlPhsw_.png.*

5.1. OPEN-SOURCE SERVERLESS PLATFORMS: CHARACTERISTICS AND PERFORMANCE

In cloud computing, serverless computing has brought in a new era. Cloud computing uses efficient multiplexing and economies of scale to provide end users with large-scale, low-cost computing and storage services. By enabling providers to dedicate only the necessary resources to a specific application and use those resources for the brief period of time necessary to carry out an invoked function, serverless computing elevates multiplexing and scalability to a new level. In response to user requests, resources are dynamically scaled. When there is no demand, serverless computing achieves nearly zero resource cost and scales to as many instances as needed to meet the traffic demand, in contrast to traditional cloud deployment models that deploy many computing instances well in advance. Serverless computing may therefore be economical and scalable.

According to the Cloud Native Computing Foundation (CNCF), serverless computing offers developers the ability to create, launch, and operate applications on demand without having to worry about server management, in addition to scalability and multiplexing. A portion of the infrastructure is dynamically allocated for function execution upon the occurrence of an event. The fundamentals of resource management, such as. function execution, data transmission, and resource allocation are separated from the user. On their public clouds, several cloud service providers (CSPs) provide serverless computing platforms. One such platform is Amazon Web Services (AWS) Lambda, an event-driven serverless platform that allows applications to be implemented, deployed, and executed on-demand as Docker containers in any supported language. Many open-source serverless platforms are emerging that enable developers to freely deploy and manage functions on self-hosted clouds, as public serverless platforms run the risk of vendor lock-in. However, developing functionalities that work well takes a great deal of skill and a thorough understanding of platform frameworks and performance-affecting features. Differentiating between various scenarios and choosing the appropriate serverless platform can be difficult for a service developer.

To help developers choose suitable open-source platforms to deploy efficient services, we systematically identify and analyze the salient characteristics of several popular open source serverless platforms (i.e., Knative, Kubeless, Nuclio and OpenFaaS) and compare their performance. Our key contributions include:

- We provide an understanding of the platform frameworks and interaction between different components of four popular open-source serverless platforms.
- We analyze the salient features of each platform, such as the built-in workload-based auto-scaling mechanism and the event processing model inside the function pod.
- We evaluate the performance of different service exporting and

auto-scaling modes, and analyze the root cause of performance gap among different serverless platforms.

- We give several insights for future work, such as autoscaling and metric collection.

5.1.1. Open-Source Serverless Platforms

Serverless computing platforms, like Alibaba Cloud Function Compute, Google Cloud Functions, Azure Functions, and Amazon Web Services (AWS) Lambda, are available on many cloud service providers' (CSPs) public cloud servers. The serverless functions that developers create and implement must be based on the database, storage, and message queuing services that CSPs offer. The risk of vendor lock-in results from this.

There is a high degree of reliance on particular CSPs for the deployed serverless functions, making it challenging to move them to other public clouds or self-hosted clusters. More flexibility and unrestricted function deployment and management on self-hosted clouds are made possible by open-source serverless systems.

Open-source serverless platforms still face a few obstacles, though: (1) developing effective functions requires a thorough understanding of the platform's features; (2) managing and maintaining serverless platforms independently requires extensive knowledge of the platform's infrastructure and frameworks; and (3) choosing the right platforms for a given usage scenario can be challenging due to the variability of open-source serverless platform performance. To assist developers in selecting appropriate serverless platforms for the deployment of effective services, it is therefore necessary to examine the key features of well-known open-source serverless platforms and compare their performance.

5.1.2. Platform Characteristics

We specifically choose four open-source serverless frameworks, i.e., based on their rich feature set, community vibrancy, and recent popularity. Knative, Kubeless, Nuclio, and OpenFaaS, in order to examine their features.

5.1.2.1. Dependency on Kubernetes

An open-source system called Kubernetes is extensible and portable that makes declarative configuration easier while automating deployment and management of workloads that are containerized. Function pods, which are Kubernetes' atomic deployable units, are orchestrated and managed by the majority of open-source serverless platforms using Kubernetes. The essential

Kubernetes services that serverless platforms rely on are displayed in Figure 5.2 Configuration management, service discovery, auto-scaling, pod scheduling, traffic load balancing, network routing, and service roll-out and roll-back are among the uses for these Kubernetes services.

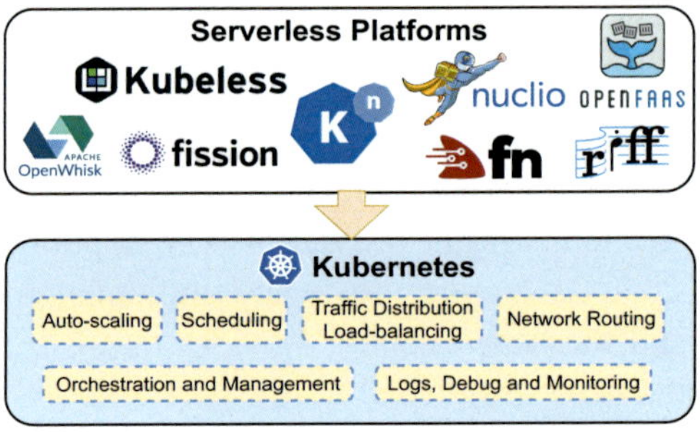

Figure 5.2. *Serverless platforms and underlying Kubernetes services.*

Source: https://arxiv.org/pdf/2106.03601.

Resource-based auto-scaling is supported by Kubernetes-based serverless platforms because of the horizontal pod auto-scaler (HPA) feature. Figure 5.3 displays the HPA framework. Every node's Kubelet gathers each pod's resource metrics.

The API server provides these metrics to HPA. A percentage of the pod's requested amount for that resource or a raw value could be used as the auto-scaling threshold. The HPA automatically notifies the Development controller to scale the number of pods when the CPU or memory usage of a specific function pod surpasses the threshold.

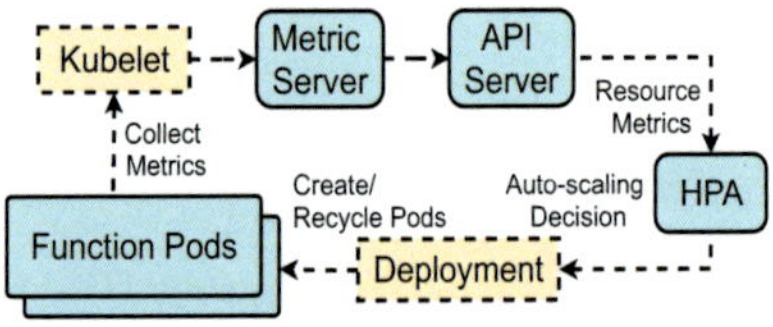

Figure 5.3. *Horizontal pod auto-scaling framework.*

Source: https://arxiv.org/pdf/2106.03601.

5.1.2.2. Salient Features of Serverless Platforms

Table 5.1 summarizes salient features of four widely-known open-source serverless platforms.

Table 5.1. *Comparison of Popular Open-Source Serverless Platforms*

Feature	Nuclio	OpenFaaS	Knative	Kubeless
Queue inside Function Pod	✔	✔	✔	✖
Support for Multiple Workers in Function Pod	✔	✖	✔	✖
Function Startup Policy	Warm Start	Cold/Warm Start	Cold/Warm Start	Cold Start
Service Export Method	Ingress Gateway/NodePort	API Gateway/Ingress Gateway	Ingress Gateway	Ingress Gateway
Runtime Metric Collection	Metric Server	Metric Server/API Gateway	Metric Server/Queue-proxy	Metric Server
Auto-scaling Mode	CPU/Memory	CPU/Memory/RPS	CPU/Memory/Concurrency/RPS	CPU/Memory
Scale-to-zero	✖	✖	✔	✖

Source: https://arxiv.org/pdf/2106.03601.

1. **Nuclio**

   Figure 5.4 displays Nuclio's primary components. There are several worker processes and one event listener in each function pod. New events are received by the event listener, which routes them to worker processes. On a multi-core worker node, several worker processes operating in parallel could greatly increase performance. The worker process number is defined in the configuration file and is set to be static. Although Kubernetes HPA supports resource-based auto-scaling, workload-based auto-scaling is not included in the open-source version. Nuclio provides two methods for triggering functions: (1) calling the function directly through the ingress controller, which can route traffic to various back-end pods based on the load balancing rule that has been pre-established (e.g., round-robin, random, and least connection first) and (2) using NodePort, a function's specific assigned cluster-wide port, to send requests straight to function pods. Netfilter load balances incoming requests at random when using the NodePort method.

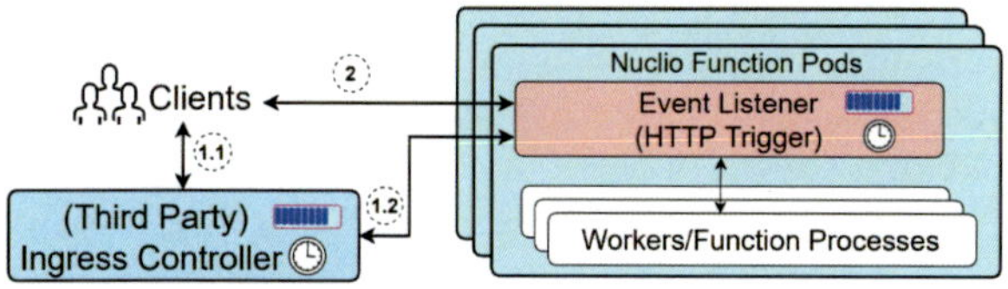

Figure 5.4. *Nuclio framework.*

Source: https://arxiv.org/pdf/2106.03601.

2. **OpenFaaS**

   Figure 5.5 displays the main elements of OpenFaaS. The functions are accessible through the API gateway, which also gathers traffic data. The controller for OpenFaaS function pod management is called Faas-netes. For auto-scaling, Prometheus and AlertManager are employed.

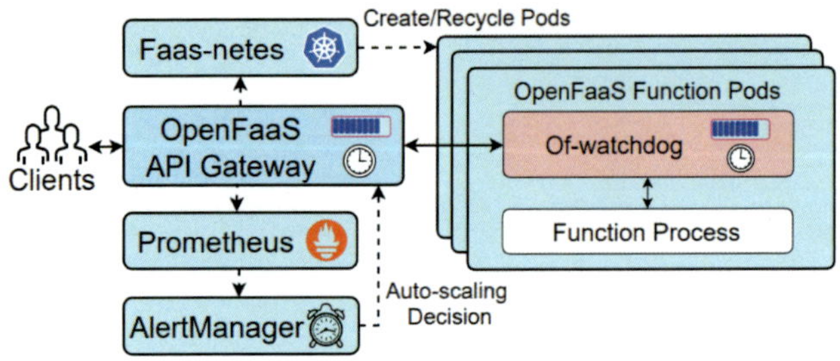

Figure 5.5. *OpenFaaS framework.*

Source: https://arxiv.org/pdf/2106.03601.

A single container running both the function process and the of-watchdog is present in each function pod. A small server called Of-watchdog serves as the point of entry for incoming requests and routes them to the function process. There are three modes of operation for Of-watchdog. HTTP, serialization, and streaming. The function process in HTTP mode is only ever forked once at the start and is kept warm throughout the function pod's life cycle. Every request results in the forking of a new function process in both the streaming and serializing modes, which has a negative impact on performance and causes a large amount of cold-start latency. The evaluation results indicate that the streaming or serializing mode has a throughput that is approximately 10× lower than the HTTP mode. A built-in auto-scaling feature based on requests-per-second (RPS) is available in OpenFaaS. Prometheus uses the API gateway to scrape traffic metrics. In accordance with the auto-scaling rule specified in the configuration file, AlertManager receives the RPS metric from Prometheus and sends an alert to the API gateway. After handling the alert, the API gateway calls the Faas-netes to adjust the function replicas' size. It should be noted that the scale-to-zero feature—which is exclusive to the commercial version—is not supported by the open-source version. OpenFaaS Pro.

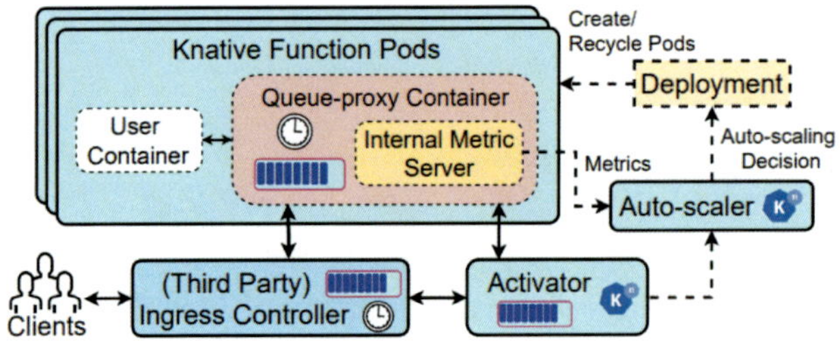

Figure 5.6. *Knative framework.*

Source: https://arxiv.org/pdf/2106.03601.

3. **Knative**

This is the Knative framework in Figure 5.6. The queue-proxy container and the function container are the two containers that make up each function pod. Incoming requests are queued by the queue-proxy, a sidecar container, and then forwarded to the function container. Despite experiencing queuing latency, the queue-proxy offers a buffer to manage traffic surges. Furthermore, the queue-proxy gathers metrics and makes them available through a basic HTTP server, i.e., internal measurement system. The user container houses several workers who handle requests concurrently. Lower performance is the result of a higher communication overhead between the queue-proxy container and function container compared to Nuclio and OpenFaaS process models. An inherent feature of Knative is auto-scaling. Both the concurrency mode and the RPS mode are supported by Knative Pod Autoscaler (KPA). Using the auto-scaling algorithm, the auto-scaler retrieves metrics from function pods and determines the replica number. After receiving the auto-scaling decision, the deployment controller modifies the pod count. Scale-to-zero functionality, which recycles all pods of inactive functions, is supported by Knative. The ingress controller forwards new requests for idle functions to the activator so that they can be buffered. Next, the autoscaler is triggered by the activator, potentially increasing the idle function's scale from zero. Upon restarting the function, the activator forwards the request that has been buffered to the pod. Scale-to-zero increases cold start latency even though it uses fewer resources.

4. **Kubeless**

Another open-source platform built on top of Kubernetes is called Kubeless. Figure 5.7 outlines the essential elements and Kubeless's operational model. Regarding ingress controllers, there are numerous choices. After testing both the Traefik and Nginx ingress controllers, we decide on Traefik because of its superior performance. Kubeless does not support scale-to-zero and instead uses Kubernetes HPA for auto-scaling.

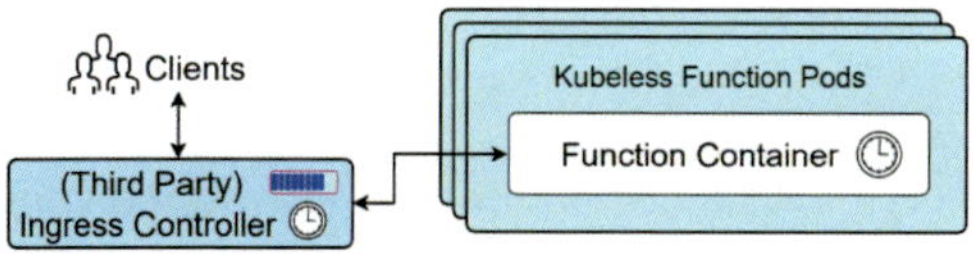

Figure 5.7. *Kubeless framework.*

Source: https://arxiv.org/pdf/2106.03601.

5.1.2.3. Service Exporting and Network Routing

1. *Service Exporting*

   Because they are dynamic entities, function pods can be created and destroyed at any time as a result of failures, auto-scaling, etc. In order to access the pods that perform the same function, Kubernetes offers services as an abstraction. Services can be exported in two ways: (1) by assigning a NodePort to the service, which directs incoming traffic to the entry node and allows the kernel stack to manage traffic load balancing amongst active pods; (2) by using the API gateway/ingress controller to act as the entry point and exporting services with designated URLs. An external public IP address can be used to access the serverless platform's API gateway/ingress controller from outside the cluster. Upon receiving an incoming request, the API gateway/ingress controller loads-balances and routes the packet to an active pod instance on the back end after determining the service associated with the request based on the URL.

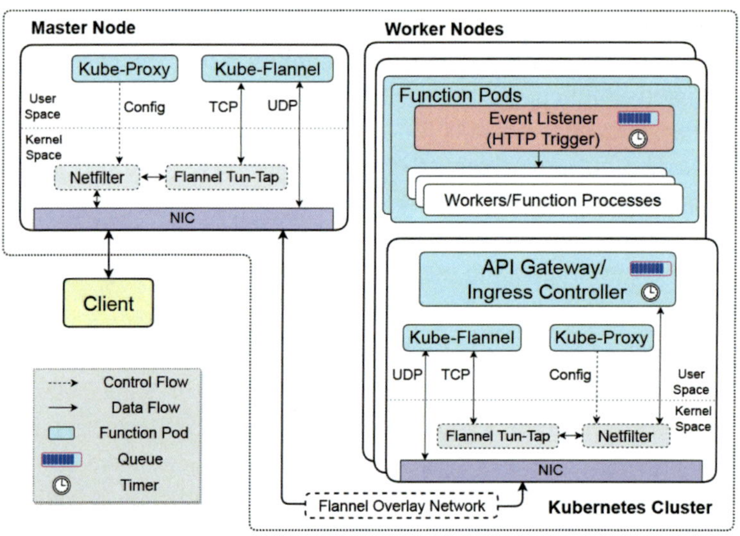

Figure 5.8. *Network routing (Flannel mode) to export the services.*

Source: https://arxiv.org/pdf/2106.03601.

2. *Network Routing*

   Flannel is a basic Kubernetes overlay networking framework that routes traffic to function pods; Figure 5.8 explains it. The routing and load-balancing rules must be configured by the Kube-Proxy pod, that is to say. the destination IP of incoming request packets is altered by the netfilter destination network address translation (DNAT) rules. The Kube-Flannel pod is in charge of intercepting packets and encapsulating and decapsulating UDP traffic as it enters or leaves the physical network interface.

5.1.3. Performance Evaluation

The overall performance of several open-source serverless platforms is first contrasted. The performance results of various service exporting modes and auto-scaling modes are used to analyze the core cause of the differences in performance between various serverless platforms.

5.1.3.1. Experimental Setup and Workload Description

We evaluate the serverless platforms on the CloudLab testbed consisting of one master and two worker nodes, each of them equipped with Intel CPU E5-2640v4@2.4GHz (10 physical cores), running Ubuntu 16.04.1 LTS (kernel 4.4.0-154-generic). We build all four serverless platforms on Kubernetes (v1.20.0), using the latest version available at the time of writing. Several serverless functions of Python 3.6 runtime are implemented. We use wrk to generate HTTP workloads for invoking serverless functions.

5.1.3.2. Performance

1. *HTTP Workload*

   We implement an HTTP workload function that could fetch a four-byte static webpage from a local HTTP server on the master node in order to assess the baseline performance of various serverless platforms. In order to ensure a fair comparison, we restrict the function pod to a single instance, turn off auto-scaling, and set the queue size and timeout parameters (50K requests, 10s timeout) at the ingress gateway and function pod components for every platform. We further limit it to one worker per pod for Nuclio and Knative. Each experiment lasts two minutes, during which we warm up for one minute and measure for another. There are twenty repetitions of the experiment. The throughput for a range of concurrent connections and the latency profile at a concurrency level of 100 are displayed in Figure 5.9. While OpenFaaS and Knative can queue requests at ingress/gateway components, Nuclio can only do so within the function pod, giving it the lowest 99 percent ile latency within 500 ms. Because there are lines at the gateway and watchdog components, OpenFaaS exhibits a heavy tail. Lower throughput is the result of more client retries caused by Kubeless dropping connections at the ingress. Because there isn't a queue inside the Kubeless function pod, the latency with Kubeless is lower.

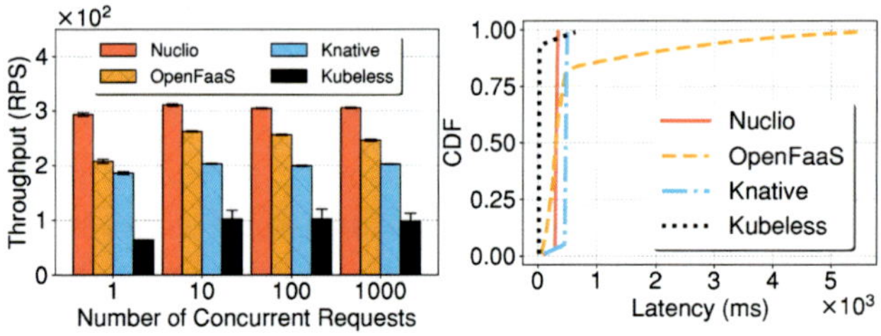

(a) Throughput. (b) Latency (concurrency = 100).

Figure 5.9. *Performance of HTTP workload function. Error bars indicate standard deviation over 20 runs.*

Source: https://arxiv.org/pdf/2106.03601.

2. *Latency Breakdown of Single Request*

We examine the overhead delays in serverless function processing across various platforms. We dissect the function pod's internal processing delays. In this experiment, we send a single request for the hello-world function using curl, and we capture the packets on the function pod's worker node using tcpdump. Four timestamps are recorded, i.e., , (1) when the request enters the function pod; (2) when the function runtime begins; (3) when the function runtime concludes; and (4) when the function pod sends the response. Figure 5.10 displays the average time intervals between these timestamps after the experiment is repeated 20 times. The function's actual run-time (0.001ms) is the same for all frameworks. On the other hand, there are differences in the function response delay (the amount of time it takes for the function's response to leave the pod) and function initiation time (the amount of time it takes for a request to be sent to the function instance). This is dependent upon how the function instance shares and packages the data. Kubeless has a very high packet forwarding delay to the function instance because of forking-per-request.

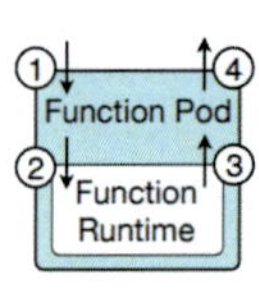

Process	1→2	2→3	3→4
Nuclio	0.63	0.001	0.54
OpenFaaS	1.32	0.001	0.93
Knative	1.30	0.001	0.62
Kubeless	4.96	0.001	2.63

Figure 5.10. *Latency breakdown of function execution (ms).*

Source: https://arxiv.org/pdf/2106.03601.

5.1.3.3. Auto-scaling

We compare the features of workload-based and resource-based auto-scaling under various workload characteristics in order to examine the auto-scaling capabilities offered by various serverless platforms. We use the same HTTP workload function as:

1. *Workload-based Auto-scaling*

   Workload-based auto-scaling is supported by both OpenFaaS and Knative. Whereas Knative uses concurrency as a workload-based auto-scaling metric, OpenFaaS uses RPS. the number of concurrent requests. We gave these platforms' auto-scaling configuration parameters equal settings to ensure a fair comparison. We conduct the experiment for 60 seconds using wrk to send a constant stream of requests (with 100 concurrent requests and 100 RPS requests). We watch the throughput, CPU and memory usage, and number of pod instances every two seconds. Figure 5.11 shows that OpenFaaS simply scales up one instance at a time, taking 26s to reach 10 instances, whereas Knative scales multiple instances at once, reaching 10 instances rapidly (in 12s). Because OpenFaaS's auto-scaling process chain is longer (i.e., , Prometheus → AlertManager → API gateway → Faas-netes), OpenFaaS has a greater scaling latency than Knative. Knative has more memory pressure even though the scaled instances appear to have the same CPU utilization. This results from variations in Python proxies and runtimes. , the of-watchdog in OpenFaaS and the queue-proxy in Knative).

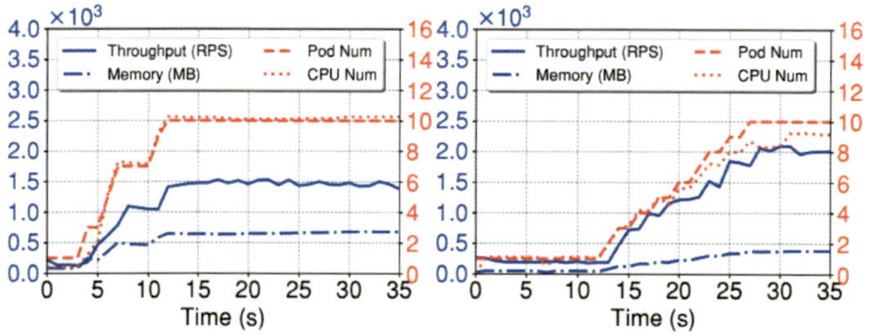

Figure 5.11. *Workload-based auto-scaling.*

Source: https://arxiv.org/pdf/2106.03601.

2. *Resource-based Auto-scaling*

   These platforms, all built on top of Kubernetes, allow resource-based auto-scaling. The CPU threshold in this experiment is set at fifty percent, and we use CPU usage as the HPA metric. As Figure 5.12 demonstrates, the auto-scaling behavior is consistent across all platforms, with the exception of Kubeless auto-scaling attempts to increase the number of instances by two at a time until it hits the maximum. However, the CPU utilization factor, which is dependent on the serverless platform-specific elements like event-listener, of-watchdog, and queue proxy, determines how long each step takes. Compared to Knative and OpenFaaS, Nuclio can scale more quickly (in 40s) despite being comparatively more CPU hungry. Due to the fork-per-request model and lack of function pod queuing, Kubeless experiences high latency and packet loss, which lowers throughput and CPU utilization. As a result, auto-scaling performance suffers.

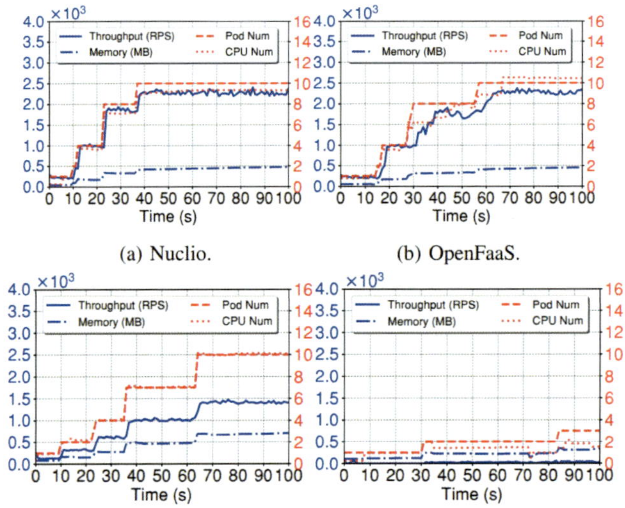

(a) Nuclio. (b) OpenFaaS.

(c) Knative. (d) Kubeless.

Figure 5.12. *Resource-based auto-scaling.*

Source: https://arxiv.org/pdf/2106.03601.

5.2. BEYOND CONTAINERS: LIGHTWEIGHT VIRTUALIZATION TECHNIQUES

Since containers are lighter and faster than virtual machines, they are the de facto standard for virtualization when deploying serverless functions. However, as several reports have demonstrated, using a shared kernel may present certain security and isolation risks in addition to higher latency when launching the containers from the beginning (cold start). New lightweight virtualization technologies have therefore been proposed as alternatives to virtualization in order to meet the requirements of system security as well as quick resource and provisioning efficiency. Micro virtual machines (microVMs), minimal hypervisors, and unikernels are some of these substitutes.

5.2.1. Unikernels

A more rapid and secure virtualization solution than containers has been proposed: unikernels, which are runtime environments with a minimal surface area. But unikernels become less flexible and useful when the design decision is made to remove support for dynamic forking, which forms the foundation of the standard multi-process abstraction found in traditional UNIX applications. Additionally, recent studies have shown that unikernels may also have security vulnerabilities due to operating directly in the kernel ring, since privilege separation is impractical and potentially harmful kernel functions could be called from virtualized applications. The IBM Nabla project was motivated by unikernels technology, which has enhanced isolation by substituting a specialized, unikernel-optimized hypervisor, Nabla Tender, for a general-purpose hypervisor (e.g., QEMU). In order to facilitate sandboxed applications, Google gVisor additionally uses Sentry, a specialized guest kernel, to run in user space. Actually, it retrieves and transfers all system calls from the sandboxed applications to the host kernel, allowing gVisor's customized kernel to handle them safely.

5.2.2. Kata Containers

Using microVMs to isolate container processes and namespaces, Kata Containers is a promising lightweight virtualization technology. With this approach, a single sandbox will combine the isolation provided by virtual machines with the speed of containerization. Actually, each instantiated Pod in Kata Containers' runtime (kata-runtime) launches a Kernel-based Virtual Machine (KVM), supporting a variety of hypervisors, including minimal ones made especially for serverless deployments. The most popular serverless hypervisor at the moment is Firecracker, a simple, open-source Virtual Machine Monitor built in Rust that uses KVM virtualization to deploy and manage microVMs. Like unikernels, Firecracker's design minimizes device emulation to offer each microVM quicker startup times and less memory usage.

5.2.3. Integration in Serverless Platforms

These new virtualization technologies can already be integrated into serverless platforms. For instance, by utilizing the Kubernetes Runtime Class feature, both Knative and OpenFaaS enable the configuration of multiple runtimes. To enable the runtimeClassName feature flag in Knative, all that needs to be done is edit the feature flags ConfigMap and apply that flag to the desired service.

- Code 1: OpenFaaS gVisor Profile

```
kind: Profile
apiVersion: openfaas.com/v1
metadata:
    name: gvisor
    namespace: openfaas
spec:
    runtimeClassName: gvisor
EOF
```

  To apply the desired runtime class in OpenFaaS, as demonstrated in Code 1, a Profile needs to be created and enabled. Next, as demonstrated in Code 2, OpenFaaS will deploy the serverless function using the chosen lightweight technology by referring to the defined Profile by its runtimeClassName in the serverless function YAML stack file. When utilizing lightweight virtualization technologies in a production setting, caution must be exercised. Actually, there are still certain impediments and immaturity. It is currently important to highlight that there are significant compatibility limitations with Kata Containers and the Firecracker hypervisor in Kubernetes, which have led to numerous issues.

- Code 2: OpenFaaS stack file

```
provider:
  name: openfaas
  gateway: \url{http://127.0.0.1:8080}

functions:
  gvisorfunction:
    image: functions/alpine:latest
    annotations:
      com.openfaas.profile: gvisor
```

5.3. SERVERLESS SECURITY FOR EDGE COMPUTING

The data produced by end devices is processed and stored closer to these devices in an edge computing environment, which results in quicker processing, quicker response times, and less network traffic. But distributing data across large networks, like those found in edge scenarios made up of numerous connected devices, is a difficult task that may give rise to security problems. Due to the intricacy of these networks, data protection and security control are extremely difficult because every device in the cluster is a potential attack vector. Furthermore, when deploying services on the edge, security and isolation become crucial requirements due to the typical multi-tenancy of the edge computing paradigm. Some of the security vulnerabilities of edge computing are:

- Denial of Service (DoS) attacks
- Data tampering
- Insecure communication between devices
- Updates' late reception and implementation
- Weak credentials for protection.

5.3.1. Serverless Security Advantages for Edge Computing

Security benefits may result from the use of serverless computing for edge layer service deployment. Adopting the serverless paradigm can greatly reduce the surface exposed to attackers because serverless functions are typically atomic, ephemeral, and stateless. To be sure, attacks are still possible in serverless environments, but this paradigm logically shortens the window of opportunity that the adversary has to retrieve target data from functions. The edge layer is more resilient to conventional DoS attacks thanks to the serverless methodology. Features like serverless autoscaling can strengthen an application's resistance to DoS attacks, which overload the servers in an attempt to disrupt the service. However, if owners of serverless applications are charged for resources used, a countermeasure must be implemented to safeguard the platform from Denial of Wallet attacks (DoW), which aim to rationally increase application owners' expenses.

5.3.2. The Tradeoff between Security and Performance

The serverless platform in use's performance and security are significantly impacted by the execution environment selection. Different virtualization technologies are available, each with varying degrees of isolation between users and applications. There is clearly a trade-off between performance and environmental security in this situation. Virtual machines (VMs), for instance, provide robust boundaries and a high degree of isolation at a relatively low startup overhead. Conversely, alternative solutions like unikernels and containers can be implemented more quickly and ensure optimal resource usage, albeit at the expense of less robust isolation barriers. Recent years have seen the introduction of new lightweight virtualization technologies like Google gVisor, IBM Nabla, Amazon Firecracker, and Kata Containers in an effort to overcome these limitations and jointly provide good levels of security and performance. These innovative approaches, which were previously covered in the previous section, use micro virtual machines (VMs) to host multiple containers in a single, highly isolated jailer that is controlled by an efficient minimal hypervisor (Kata Containers with Firecracker). In the absence of a guest kernel, Nabla and gVisor intercept and handle the majority of system calls made by sandbox application containers. Specifically, gVisor only uses 53 of the 237 system calls that are available, which reduces the amount of interface that interacts with the host OS kernel by over 75% and the attack surface that is exposed, all while offering a startup time that is comparable to that of using containers. However, these solutions are still in their infancy and will not be widely used in serverless deployments.

5.3.3. The Cold versus Warm Start Problem

Regarding serverless warm and cold start modes, one more security-related factor needs to be taken into account. Warm-weather containers, for example. Containers—which are maintained in a running state to continue fulfilling requests—are being used in serverless deployments more frequently due to their notable efficiency gains and reduction in startup times. Warm start modes actually preserve connections between invocations or make use of local caches. Warm container benefits come at the expense of the serverless platform's security, though. Warm containers maintain some disk space in the /tmp/ location to share state across different function invocations, even though they reset the default values in the filesystem upon function completion. Thus, these systemically shared data could be used to launch persistent attacks. Application owners can prevent such vulnerabilities by disabling the ability to recycle the execution environment and execute the same function more than once, especially when working on security-sensitive tasks. For instance, the authors provide a serverless monitoring framework that uses OpenFaaS to prevent the use of sensitive data in third-party security analytics platforms. In order to provide secure poly-instantiation in warm start settings, this work modifies the containers that the FaaS runtime uses to enforce lightweight processes and storage isolation within the container. In conclusion, it should be mentioned that switching from warm start to cold start instantiated containers may not always be possible, particularly for tasks requiring a quick turnaround time, as this can result in a sizable latency and instability penalty.

5.4. OPPORTUNITIES

5.4.1. Pure Pay-per-use

IoT applications with unpredictable workloads seem incompatible with static container provisioning, which charges even when the container is idle. Naturally, dynamic auto-scaling can help reduce costs, but inaccuracies in over-

and under-provisioning are probably the reason why additional fees persist or QoS is jeopardized. This becomes even more problematic when there are large spikes in workload that are expected from the application. Increasing capacity seems to be the only practical solution, but it comes at a high cost. However, with serverless, the fee is determined by real triggered events, i.e., the allotted resource, and the frequency of function execution. With serverless, achieving price predictability for IoT is more achievable since a fixed, minimal fee is always paid for each event or transaction, regardless of whether the workload is fluctuating or steady, assuming a traffic control camera that records the license plates of cars that violate the law and uploads the images to the cloud for processing. The resource provisioning process will be extremely difficult because such actions will occur frequently at midnight, spiky during rush hours, and consistently throughout the day. Such variability won't have an impact on the imposed cost if the processing is handled by the precise scalability of Serverless, which prevents over-provisioning and pays for idle times.

5.4.2. Always-on Mitigation

Because of the difficulties associated with deployments related to the environment, Internet of Things use cases like Smart Irrigation Systems are designed to function on devices with limited power and computational resources. Batteries or renewable energy sources like solar panels will probably power them. Single-board computers (SBCs) like Raspberry Pis will handle computations and orchestration. In addition, they have programs that run occasionally—not constantly—to gather data, like soil humidity. These restrictions won't work with traditional deployments, where the application must always be operational, even in the absence of an event. Additionally, a certain amount of unused resources will always be used in this manner. Edge nodes will be able to extend their lifespan and conserve their limited resources thanks to serverless architecture and the scale to zero feature. By only provisioning resources when a trigger, like sensing, is pulled and then de-provisioning unused resources, serverless computing can reduce energy consumption. This benefit of Serverless offers an additional perspective on its appropriateness for applications that are event-driven.

5.4.3. Event-driven Applications

Serverless can be a perfect fit for sensor and actuation-based Internet of Things applications because of their event-based nature. In typical cloud services, e.g., function invocation is heavily reliant on back-end systems for mobile applications, events like API calls, and data storage. The majority of IoT applications, however, are event-driven. One excellent example of a sensing-driven application is the decision-making process for farm management in Smart Agricultural Farming, where the management system is activated by variations in temperature and humidity, failing which it does nothing. According to Serverless terminology, this means that the sensor can decide in advance, based on local data acquisition, whether to initiate a series of function invocations; if not initiated, no resources are used on the Serverless platform. In a further scenario where the cloud and an edge system are involved, the remote sensor may always cause the edge system to execute a specific function (using humidity/temperature data). The edge system can then decide whether or not to escalate the situation to the management system by triggering a function in the cloud platform. In every instance, Serverless's architecture seamlessly aligns with the sense-decide-act paradigm, a common feature of numerous useful Internet of things applications.

5.4.4. Stateless Life-cycle

The invoked functions in an edge designed for event-driven Internet of Things applications are performing tasks like image processing that do not require knowledge of past occurrences. The monitor in a road vehicle monitoring system is looking to call an image processing function in order to examine the license plate number in an input image. This function loads repetitive code and libraries as if it were being created from scratch and doesn't require any prior task knowledge. As required by IoT events, stateless functions only have one task to complete. Therefore, statelessness can be significantly transformed to the edge through Serverless. The fundamental resource abstraction of serverless, which depends on containers and unikernels, has the potential to quicken this transition. These abstractions are designed to be stateless on purpose.

5.4.5. Parallelizing Computation

The added value of Serverless functions is their ability to parallelize computation with independent execution. Functions are typically fairly underpowered on their own, but when the problem is decomposed and processing is parallelized, Serverless becomes even more advantageous for parallelized Internet of Things use cases—especially when the problem space is conducive to this type of decomposition. Consider Defense IoT (DIoT) and its Equipment Tracking Systems, which are made possible by edge computing. It's critical to act swiftly to initiate an event as soon as a hazard is detected in order to track tracked equipment, including vehicles, ambulances, tactical devices, etc. prior to taking any action. In addition to performing mission-related tasks, such equipment will need to operate autonomously and respond rapidly. Mission-critical Internet of Things applications are likely to react slowly in the absence of parallelizm.

Equipment with serverless capabilities will take advantage of these tasks' parallelism and decomposition. In this case, serverless architecture is even more useful since it can handle the scalability of the invoked function in the event that peers receive several alarms with similar details.

5.4.6. Storage Isolation

Applications for the Internet of Things, like Smart Traffic Monitoring, are always gathering data. A vast quantity of data is shipped with the application to be scaled up in traditional deployments in the event of bursty workloads. Regardless of storage waste, it may be difficult to promptly launch a new instance using this method. The situation becomes even more problematic when the machine is provisioned from distant devices task offloading), requiring the data to be shipped, and enforcing additional traffic jams. With serverless, computation and storage are decoupled and can be swiftly scaled and provisioned independently.

5.4.7. Fine-grained Auto-scaling

Resource constraints are one of the main issues with edge devices. Conventional virtual machines were obviously not the ideal solution because of their large memory footprint and challenging scalability (i.e , making additional copies of the same service on a device) at the cost of duplicating a substantial amount of data, such as the application environment and operating system. Because the overhead of launching and stopping replicas is significantly lower than that of fully functional virtual machines, Serverless will support small footprint and fine-grained auto-scaling by relying on lightweight abstractions like containers and, more recently, unikernels like microVM. This holds even more promise when Serverless adopts the function as computation principles that the microservices architecture has advanced.

5.4.8. CPU-bound Applications

In serverless environments, the amount of CPU needed for each instance is pre-defined before a function is deployed. Thus, the CPU requirements of an application are always known to a Serverless enabled platform. This CPU specification, which is supported by automatic scalability, has made the Serverless well-suited for CPU-bound cloud applications. IoT use cases with CPU-intensive functionalities can also take advantage of this enabler to prevent wasting resources (e.g., provisioning (memory or data) in scaling techniques. Pedestrian monitoring systems used by self-driving cars can be an excellent example. The purpose of the system is to initiate events that contain surrounding area images, which must be processed by the edge device that is integrated into the vehicle (e.g., Motor Control Unit (ECU). Processing is done to identify potential cross-street pedestrians, other vehicles' trajectories that could end up colliding with us, etc. Such CPU-bound applications can be embedded in edge nodes and effectively made Serverless so that they can scale up/down the CPU-bound functions proportionately.

5.4.9. Bursty Workloads

Regarding the type of workload, eighty-one percent of Serverless use cases are bursty hectic schedules, a fiery or flash crowd. The primary reason for this is the seamless and precise scalability that comes with Serverless, which eliminates lengthy wait times and offers accurate resource allocation, respectively. This is why Serverless deployments are a great fit for IoT use cases that may experience spikes in workload. Use cases exposed to intermittent events, like traffic or crowd control systems, require continuous monitoring. An important event may go unnoticed, for example, if a timely reaction is lacking. Conventional IaaS/PaaS solutions might only be able to manage spikes by overstuffing the system, for example regarding service replicas that are constantly active, as their auto-scale features might produce a latency that isn't suitable for the demands of the application.

This is made worse in edge domains where overprovisioning is even less desirable due to edge nodes' lower resource availability compared to cloud counterparts. Due to its ability to take advantage of statistical multiplexing of bursty workloads through scale-to-zero during idle times and fast up-scale during peaks, serverless computing offers significant advantages to use cases susceptible to flash crowd effects. Therefore, to handle such burstiness, edge computing orchestrators will use Serverless functions rather than clumsy heavyweight virtualization and ineffective resource reservation solutions.

5.4.10. Custom-made Solutions

The requirements for edge frameworks differ based on the Internet of Things use case, environmental constraints, locality requirements, etc. In light of this, edge nodes from public cloud services that are located in a restricted geographic area won't be able to meet the demand for edge frameworks designed with specificity anytime soon. For example, while data transmission between agricultural facilities can be difficult, connecting to a cloud-hosted Serverless system can be even more difficult. Thankfully, specialized serverless solutions like OpenFaaS can ease the load on serverless at the edge, eliminating the need for communication with inaccessible clouds. Tailored solutions are also adjusting to work with edge nodes that have limited resources. Faas is a lightweight platform that functions even without an orchestrator for Kubernetes. Estimates also support their good performance, with them being used in 53% of Serverless use cases and becoming more popular than cloud services.

5.4.11. Cloud to Edge Integration

While some IoT use cases—like smart farming—tend to remain isolated at the network's edge, other use cases necessitate smooth integration and communication with the cloud. For mobile edge computing, which requires both cloud and edge computations, such as task offloading, this is especially necessary to enable data persistence or access infinite computation, to mention a few. Although they were initially created for the cloud, existing serverless platforms are now adapting to this need and enabling a serverless-enabled edge platform that is integrated with the cloud. AWS IoT Greengrass, which uses Lambda Functions internally, is a successful example. This will assist clients in carrying out their work on edge nodes until resources become available, at which point it will begin to offload to the cloud. The client is intended to be able to see the seamless transition between edge and cloud. Additionally, the system can withstand sporadic cloud connectivity. The integration no longer prevents Serverless from being implemented in edge computing.

5.5. OPEN ISSUES

5.5.1. Cold Starts

Some latency-sensitive Internet of Things applications are not suitable for the scale to zero technique and subsequent cold start of Serverless functions, despite the fact that it is widely regarded as a successful accomplishment in the cloud landscape. That being said, scaling to zero seems like a two-edged sword. One advantage is that it uses less energy. Conversely, the initial call to the function will result in a cold startup, delaying current technologies by tens or even hundreds of milliseconds. Batch applications designed to resize an image stored in the storage, for example, do not experience this delay. However, for latency-sensitive Internet of Things applications controlled by an embedded edge device, such delays may result in performance degradation. An edge device in an autonomous vehicle, for example, undoubtedly wants to make decisions quickly (e.g., pressing the brake pedal) to prevent collisions rather than conserve energy, which is plentiful in an electric vehicle and, therefore, is considered a secondary need. Therefore, if avoiding high latency (or jitter) is essential, the cold start needs to be fixed before implementing serverless edge computing. It appears that customers are more concerned with cost than latency these days, which explains why Serverless is so popular despite the cold startup bottleneck. Only 2% of Serverless use cases, according to estimates, are meant for real-time applications. However, the research community has not remained silent and has put forth a number of intriguing solutions, including function pinging, warm starts, pre-loading essential packages for the container, using more agile unikernels (or Web Assembly-based resources) in place of containers, and reducing overhead during the development phase, to mention a few.

5.5.2. Impracticable Cost-efficiency

According to estimates from the cloud domain, Serverless's cost-effectiveness (41%) accounts for a significant portion of its appeal, compared to performance (23%), which is appealing given its pure pay-as-you-use business model. But (1) high performance is needed for mission-critical IoT use cases, like healthcare, in order to anticipate major incidents before they really happen.

Since edge computing frameworks are meant to be customized and open-source, they are likely to embrace these solutions without regard to financial considerations.

Additionally, this might lessen the importance of cloud offerings in the market going forward, removing the financial component of public cloud offerings. For example, a private farm with local resources and Serverless enabled won't pay itself. Rather, their deployment concerns will likely move from cloud cost-efficiency to edge high performance.

5.5.3. Continuous Workloads

While applications with event-driven execution are recognized as appropriate IoT use cases for serverless computing, some IoT use cases—like traffic control systems—have ongoing executions. It's unclear if Serverless is more affordable in these kinds of situations. Assume that there are no expected idle periods and that the edge node must constantly respond to incoming workload. Functions will be called repeatedly by such executions. The truth is that constant function calls will not improve serverless cost efficiency; rather, they will deteriorate it.

According to investigations, always-on resources will be more effective for continuous executions until serverless platforms find more effective resource scheduling schemes.

Given that the billing is based on both the execution time and the allocated resource, the inefficiency in terms of costs is accentuated in long-running functions. Stateless executions will cause the obtained latency to increase regardless of the cost. A resource provisioner must search for new resources for each instance creation due to statelessness.

5.5.4. Edge Artificial Intelligence (AI)

Whether it is federated or central machine learning at the edge AI is a rapidly growing field for predictive IoT solutions. Utilizing cloud services such as Serverless for lengthy AI tasks won't be cost-effective because, according to investigations, training and testing machine learning at the edge with computationally constrained resources will require a lot of input/output, which will take time. While serverless processing is meant to function well for CPU-bound, short-running tasks, edge AI processing will entail significant I/O-intensive, long-running tasks. But the lack of awareness seems profound. Although I/O-intensive applications are not considered worthy of being delivered to Serverless, research indicates that they make up a greater proportion of Serverless use cases than CPU-bound applications.

5.5.5. Location-Agnostic

The devices will be dispersed throughout the environment and will be able to communicate with one another in the edge landscape. It has always been debatable to minimize the communication overhead, and for example, efforts must be made to inform the edge nodes of their offloading choices. On the other hand, serverless platforms don't care about network communications and are more concerned with resource customization. While there is a logically centralized controller in the cloud that makes decisions about resource provisioning on an infinite basis, task offloading and load distribution are actually possible at the edge. Furthermore, because of the statelessness, executions ignore server affinity and deny new instances of peers from previous locations. Let's say that the edge node chooses to assign peers to handle resource provisioning for a function because it wants to save energy or because there aren't enough resources available. In this instance, the edge node performing the function has a significant impact on the function's execution time, communication overhead, and energy consumption. The composition of functions (i.e, function-to-function interactions) can also add complexity to resource optimization. Whereas location-aware resource provisioning is crucial in many edge applications, serverless architecture doesn't seem to account for these kinds of concerns.

5.5.6. Energy-Agnostic

Resource efficiency through fine-grained embedded scalability in the cloud is one of the primary benefits of serverless computing. Cloud services take into account the memory and CPU allotments on the underlying Serverless platform. But at the periphery, energy and latency are issues—even the most significant ones in specific IoT use cases like Smart Farming, which rely on battery-operated sensors and suffer from their short lifespan. Energy-aware function provisioning is necessary for the adoption of Serverless at the edge; otherwise, the Serverless-enabled edge device may sacrifice energy in an attempt to locate edge nodes with less processing and memory allocated. It appears that when Serverless moves to edge computing, cloud-driven performance metrics like boot time, concurrent requests, and scalability need to be reviewed.

5.5.7. Distributed Networking

The search for peer-to-peer communications to share state, offload tasks, and send data is crucial because many Internet of Things applications are distributed. For example, a vehicular ad-hoc network (VANET) necessitates remote function calls on peers in order for the vehicles to interact and determine the optimal routing. But Serverless cloud-based designs are ignoring this requirement, leading to ineffective function communications. Functions in the current Serverless architecture must communicate with one another through storage systems or intermediary functions. Luckily, this problem seems to be transient, as initiatives like Serverless Supercomputing will investigate it.

5.5.8. Data-Shipping Architecture

In serverless edge computing, data and storage must be handled regardless of networking constraints. Serverless computing would prioritize CPU and memory requirements over storage provisioning strategies, which are crucial in the distributed edge. The issue would arise from stateless performance combined with a lack of server affinity.

Applications in the cloud similarly preserve their (remote) states by storing data in storage systems like DynamoDB, but in the event of an emergency, this state needs to be preserved closer. Due to this flaw, edge devices with Serverless capabilities may send enormous volumes of data to the remote device for each function call. This barrier is also present when functions interact with one another through function composability. For example, if an application consists of a series of function calls from the user's initial input to the final output, the transfer cost is paid once for a monolithic application running in a virtual machine or container, but may need to be paid several times when using serverless, i.e, if each function call is carried out on a separate (edge) node, in between any two successive function calls.

Strong data centers and fast communications enable the cloud to easily handle these constraints, but in the distributed edge, data shipping presents challenges, especially for mist computing. A fully distributed edge network without a central controller is referred to as a mist network. It is suggested that all CPU, RAM, and data requirements be taken into account when determining the data transmission. Processing may shift to the data location if an enormous amount of memory needs to be read or if the CPU on an edge device is oversubscribed.

5.5.9. Resources Specifications

It was discovered by AWS Lambda, the pioneer, that each invoked function can carry out a task for a maximum of fifteen minutes. Although considered quite sufficient for IoT with event-driven and short-running tasks, McGrath et al. also raised the question, "Is function termination time of 15 minutes efficient?" However, specific use cases, like data analytics, may not be adopted with this limitation. On the other hand, it might not always be required to follow cloud providers' protocol of, say, keeping a function warm for fifteen minutes. Furthermore, function size and level of concurrency may become problematic at the edge. Fortunately, there won't be much of a challenge because open-source solutions will make things easier by enabling complete customization to tailor the platform to the particular use case. This field has a thriving open source community that is making great strides toward the objective of creating serverless platforms that can be tailored to any need. For example, the previously mentioned OpenFaaS now provides a lighter version called faas that can function flawlessly even on very resource-constrained edge devices like Raspberry Pis.

5.5.10. Reliability and Fault Tolerance

Errors happen in both cloud and edge environments; the distinction lies in the level of dependability. Such incidents are prevented in cloud data centers by several tiers of underlying virtualization and constant, meticulous server and application monitoring. However, fault rolerance techniques are very limited in the edge, and in order to achieve the desired level of resiliency, we envision more robust solutions that need to be defined. Palade et al. express concern that fault tolerance—which is crucial in, say, mission-critical Internet of Things applications—won't be given enough consideration by current Serverless platforms. Given the real-time nature of Internet of Things applications, failing to handle failures of this kind could be disastrous. If a function's container failed, or more seriously, if a function's edge node failed, how is the lack of that covered by Serverless platforms?

5.5.11. Resource Inefficiency

Efficient and flexible resources that can be quickly provisioned, started, and operated are crucial for use cases that require real-time processing and low latency, like Fleet Monitoring in the DIoT. The difficulty is doubled by edge nodes' computation-limited nature. This is due to the fact that although cloud computing offers limitless and potent resources, resource saturation is more likely to occur in the edge. Using container provisioning was a significant step toward increasing efficiency in situations where heavy hypervisor-based machines cannot be launched by edge devices like SBCs. The drawback of containers, however, is that while a specially designed container cannot be heavy in and of itself, prerequisites like Docker engines can be, especially when the Serverless platform is introduced on top of them. In order to reduce the startup time, unikernels are putting forward practical solutions that do away with the middle layer, like Docker engine. The microVM that AWS Firecracker unveiled can achieve a respectable boot-up time (e.g., 125ms) and an effective memory footprint; however, there is disagreement over the latter and its difficult orchestration. Nevertheless, greater agility is unavoidably required from Serverless platforms as well as virtualization.

5.5.12. Security

Serverless computing is supported in the cloud by Trusted Execution Environment (TEE) platforms and firewalls, but devices are exposed in weak edge networks. Microservices are more vulnerable due to their distributed architecture and anticipated multi-tenancy, especially when functions are implemented on containers, which have less isolation than virtual machines (VMs). There are efforts to create microVMs or unikernels in an attempt to logically isolate microservices. The latter uses a combination of technologies, including cgroups, namespaces, seccomp-bpf, iptables, and chroot, to specifically guarantee an isolated environment. Furthermore, because the functions are thought to be dispersed throughout the edge network, their ephemerality will at least prevent continuous data leakage, but the transmission pattern between them may make them even more vulnerable. That being said, security assurances must still be provided before enabling Serverless at the edge.

5.5.13. No GPU Support

The majority of for-profit Serverless platforms don't provide APIs that let computation be transferred to specialized hardware—like GPUs and FPGAs—that might be more effective for the job at hand. Due to this restriction, Serverless edge cannot be used for GPU-based real-time streaming applications. Examples of these applications are Smart Supply Chain Systems, which track and monitor the whole supply chain, from suppliers to distributors and retailers, and are outfitted with real-time information. It seems that serverless architecture needs to be reconsidered for these sectors, particularly at the edge, by expanding programming paradigms to be more universally applicable to a variety of hardware targets while maintaining the current degree of abstraction. Differentiated pricing plans and more adaptable billing and accounting schemes than those that are currently available may also be necessary for commercial systems.

5.5.14. Function Triggering

With HTTP being the most popular type with a 46 percent share, cloud-driven serverless manages function triggering through HTTP APIs, cloud events, scheduled events, etc. In actuality, HTTP APIs belong to the request/reply family of communication patterns, whereas MQTT and other subscribe/reply patterns are more commonly used in the Internet of Things. Open-source platforms and cloud services like AWS GreenGrass and KubeEdge, respectively, have realized this need and are bridging the gap.

5.6. HANDLING CLOUD-EDGE INTERWORKING

The benefits that edge computing offers for a wide range of features inherited from the architecture, such as low-latency response, bandwidth savings, and improved user quality of experience (QoE) and quality of service (QoS), are driving its continued adoption. Edge environments typically have constrained hardware resources, which makes serverless functions an ideal application. There has been some work done to standardize concepts related to edges. The definition provided by the European Telecommunications Standards Institute (ETSI), i.e, the Radio Access Network's Multi-access Edge Computing (MEC) system (RAN). The OpenInfra Foundation Edge Computing Group has also published a whitepaper on the specification, design, and testing of edge computing. Furthermore, through the EdgeX Foundry, the Linux Foundation for the Edge (LF-Edge) seeks to standardize edge computing architecture for the Industrial Internet of Things (IIoT). There are additional possible hazards and issues that need to be addressed because the edge is operating with fewer resources. For example, systems may malfunction or go offline, resources may run out, or new tasks may demand more resources than are currently available. Edge nodes frequently connect to a central cloud, also known as the edge's backend, in order to solve these issues. It's true that combining cloud and edge can offer higher service levels. While the cloud can handle jobs that don't require a quick response or resource-hungry tasks, the edge side can provide local computation and quick response times. Since that data storage can be too heavy for the edge side, it can also be moved to the cloud. The cloud generally manages the orchestration of the entire ecosystem, since one or more edge devices may be connected to multiple environments.

5.6.1. Connecting Cloud and Edge

There are numerous open-source solutions available for configuring the cloud and edge connection. Many factors need to be considered, as there is no one best solution. The final decision can be made based on various factors, such as the use case, the hardware and software that is available, the application requirements, or the knowledge of a particular technology. Possible open-source solutions for setting up the connection are:

1. *Software Defined Network (SDN) or Software Defined Wide Area Network (SDWAN) infrastructure.*

   They make it possible to separate the control plane from the data plane, giving the network flow more precise control. SDN controllers can be integrated into cloud and edge environments such as Kubernetes clusters or OpenStack clouds, or they can be deployed as standalone instances using open-source tools like Open Network Operating System (ONOS) or OpenDayLight (ODL). Network Function Virtualization (NFV) and SDN approaches are frequently combined, particularly for 5G and mobile network solutions.

2. *Virtual Private Network (VPN) or Virtual Extensible Local Area Network (VXLAN)*

   You can also use these methods to establish the connection. By encrypting or encapsulating the packets traveling through the public internet, they both enable communication to devices situated in various private networks as though they were directly connected. Open vSwitch (OVS) and Open VPN (OVPN) are the most popular open-source tools.

3. *Service Mesh*

   An additional option is to make use of an open-source service mesh such as Consul or Istio. They provide functions similar to VPNs, allowing private networks to be connected while data is encrypted. They also provide extra features like load balancing, traffic management, observability, and service discovery. They can be seamlessly integrated with public and private clouds as well as Kubernetes clusters, as they were designed for cloud-native applications.

4. *Middleware*

   Middleware is one type of software that can be used to achieve specific use cases and coordinate communications between clouds and edges. Installing a middleware framework across all involved entities or using it as a stand-alone intermediate layer are the most popular configuration options. The latter typically denotes communications that are encrypted end to end. Open-source middleware that is frequently used includes EdgeX Foundry, Open IoT, and ONEedge.

5. *Physical or virtual routers*

   Routers can be used to control communications by combining firewall rules and protocols such as Border Gateway Protocol (BGP). Although the idea behind managing network flow is the same as that of SDN, all operations are carried out directly at the router level in this scenario, negating the need for a centralized controller. OpenWRT and IPFire are two open-source examples.

5.6.2. Cloud and Edge Interactions

Most serverless function deployments use containers, and Kubernetes plays a major orchestration role in these deployments. A single worker node might require fewer resources than an entire cluster with the necessary control plane, but there are several frameworks available, and their deployment might vary if carried out on the edge. Thanks to the connection established with one of the workable solutions, an edge worker node can join a cloud cluster. Similarly, an entire edge cluster can connect to other cloud-hosted resources or exchange data with other edge clusters to form what is known as a cluster federation. Data exchange is implied by interactions between the cloud and edge, all while attempting to save bandwidth. In this case, some data transmission—such as control plane messages or application health checks—may be required for the system to operate correctly. Depending on the use case, cloud and edge interactions can differ significantly. Although edge sensors and devices can gather and process data locally, the cloud is always the best option for long-term storage, statistics, or the execution of computationally demanding tasks. Other examples of data transmission between edge and cloud include backups and data replication, as well as forwarding tasks, like in situations where edge resources are insufficient. Another important factor is the manner and timing of the edge's decision to communicate with the cloud. The edge may wait for an idle period, based on event triggers that have been pre-specified, or once more when the amount of resources being used exceeds a predetermined threshold. Usually, middleware or algorithms are used to manage the interactions. They typically collaborate with Prometheus-like monitoring systems. In other situations, such as when using Content Delivery Network (CDN) or edge caching, data must be moved from the cloud to the edge, usually with the goal of enhancing QoS and QoE. The objective is to offload servers in the cloud while maintaining content closer to end users to enable rapid availability. Updates must be made frequently to the content stored at the edge using pre-established methods such as First-In-First-Out (FIFO). The more recent resources are eliminated in FIFO to create room for the newest information. Maintaining the most often accessed logic, in which the most requested elements are accessible for a longer period of time than the less requested ones, is an additional strategy. It's worth mentioning the scenario where communication is required between several edges. Collaborative Edge Computing (CEC) is a recently introduced paradigm that involves multiple edges working together in a distributed working model to share resources for tasks that are too big for a single edge to handle.

REFERENCES

1. Aditya, P., Akkus, I. E., Beck, A., Chen, R., Hilt, V., Rimac, I., Satzke, K., & Stein, M. (2019). Will serverless computing revolutionize NFV? *Proceedings of the IEEE, 107*(4), 667–678. https://doi.org/10.1109/JPROC.2019.2895936.
2. Agache, A., et al. (2020). Firecracker: Lightweight virtualization for serverless applications. In *17th USENIX Symposium on Networked Systems Design and Implementation (NSDI '20)* (pp. 419–434). USENIX Association.
3. Aggarwal, V., & Thangaraju, B. (2020). Performance analysis of virtualization technologies in NFV and edge deployments. In *2020 IEEE CONECCT* (pp. 1–5). https://doi.org/10.1109/CONECCT49016.2020.9249930.
4. Al-Ali, Z., Goodarzy, S., Hunter, E., Ha, S., Han, R., Keller, E., & Rozner, E. (2018). Making serverless computing more serverless. In *International Conference on Cloud Computing (CLOUD)* (pp. 456–459). IEEE. https://doi.org/10.1109/CLOUD.2018.00065.
5. Allen, S., et al. (2018). CNCF Serverless Whitepaper. Retrieved from: https://github.com/cncf/wg-serverless/blob/master/whitepapers/serverless-overview/cncf_serverless_whitepaper_v1.0.pdf (accessed on 1 August 2024).
6. Artuñedo, D., et al. (2021). *Edge Computing for 5G Networks, v1.0.* Technical Report, 5GPPP Technology Board Working Group.
7. Aslanpour, M. S., Gill, S. S., & Toosi, A. N. (2020). Performance evaluation metrics for cloud, fog and edge computing: A review, taxonomy, benchmarks and standards for future research. *Internet of Things, 12*, 100273. https://doi.org/10.1016/j.iot.2020.100273.
8. Bahman, J., Jingtao, S., & Rajiv, R. (2020). Serverless architecture for edge computing. In *Edge Computing: Models, Technologies and Applications* (pp. 249–264). Institution of Engineering and Technology. https://doi.org/10.1049/pbpc033e_ch12.
9. Baldini, I., Castro, P., Chang, K., Cheng, P., Fink, S., Ishakian, V., Mitchell, N., Muthusamy, V., Rabbah, R., & Slominski, A. (2017). Serverless computing: Current trends and open problems. In *Research Advances in Cloud Computing* (pp. 1–20). Springer. https://doi.org/10.1007/978-3-319-55755-0_1.
10. Baresi, L., & Filgueira Mendonça, D. (2019). Towards a serverless platform for edge computing. In *2019 IEEE International Conference on Fog Computing (ICFC)* (pp. 1–10). https://doi.org/10.1109/ICFC.2019.00016.

11. Baresi, L., Mendonça, D. F., & Garriga, M. (2017). Empowering low-latency applications through a serverless edge computing architecture. In *European Conference on Service-Oriented and Cloud Computing* (pp. 196–210). Springer. https://doi.org/10.1007/978-3-319-71003-0_13.
12. Benedetti, P., Femminella, M., Reali, G., & Steenhaut, K. (2021). Experimental analysis of the application of serverless computing to IoT platforms.
13. Benedetti, P., Femminella, M., Reali, G., & Steenhaut, K. (2022). Reinforcement learning applicability for resource-based auto-scaling in serverless edge applications. In *2022 IEEE International Conference on Pervasive Computing and Communications Workshops and Other Affiliated Events (PerCom Workshops)* (pp. 674–679). https://doi.org/10.1109/PerComWorkshops54810.2022.00094.
14. Buyya, R., Srirama, S. N., Casale, G., Calheiros, R. N., Simmhan, Y., Varghese, B., Gelenbe, E., Javadi, B., Vaquero, L. M., & Netto, M. A. S. (2018). A manifesto for future generation cloud computing: Research directions for the next decade. *ACM Computing Surveys (CSUR), 51*(5), 1–38. https://doi.org/10.1145/3242736.
15. Castro, P., Ishakian, V., Muthusamy, V., & Slominski, A. (2019). The rise of serverless computing. *Communications of the ACM, 62*(12), 44–54. https://doi.org/10.1145/3358802.
16. Castro, P., Ishakian, V., Muthusamy, V., & Slominski, A. (2019). The rise of serverless computing. *Communications of the ACM, 62*(12), 44–54. https://doi.org/10.1145/3359780.
17. Chard, R., Skluzacek, T. J., Li, Z., Babuji, Y., Woodard, A., Blaiszik, B., Tuecke, S., Foster, I., & Chard, K. (2019). Serverless supercomputing: High performance function as a service for science. *arXiv preprint arXiv:1908.04907*. https://arxiv.org/abs/1908.04907.
18. Cicconetti, C., Conti, M., Passarella, A., & Sabella, D. (2020). Toward distributed computing environments with serverless solutions in edge systems. *IEEE Communications Magazine, 58*(3), 40–46. https://doi.org/10.1109/MCOM.001.1900568.
19. Deng, S., Zhao, H., Fang, W., Yin, J., Dustdar, S., & Zomaya, A. Y. (2020). Edge intelligence: The confluence of edge computing and artificial intelligence. *IEEE Internet of Things Journal*. https://doi.org/10.1109/JIOT.2020.2999303.
20. Dizdarević, J., Carpio, F., Jukan, A., & Masip-Bruin, X. (2019). A survey of communication protocols for internet of things and related challenges of

fog and cloud computing integration. *ACM Computing Surveys (CSUR), 51*(6), 1–29. https://doi.org/10.1145/3362274.

21. Djemame, K., Parker, M., & Datsev, D. (2020). Open-source serverless architectures: An evaluation of Apache OpenWhisk. In *2020 IEEE/ACM 13th International Conference on Utility and Cloud Computing (UCC)* (pp. 329–335). https://doi.org/10.1109/UCC50840.2020.00055.
22. Duplyakin, D., Ricci, R., Maricq, A., Wong, G., Duerig, J., Eide, E., Stoller, L., Hibler, M., Johnson, D., Webb, K., et al. (2019). The design and operation of CloudLab. In *USENIX Annual Technical Conference (ATC)* (pp. 1–14). USENIX Association. https://doi.org/10.5555/3333217.3333218.
23. Eismann, S., Scheuner, J., van Eyk, E., Schwinger, M., Grohmann, J., Herbst, N., Abad, C., & Iosup, A. (2020). Serverless applications: Why, when, and how? *IEEE Software*. https://doi.org/10.1109/MS.2020.3003612.
24. Eismann, S., Scheuner, J., van Eyk, E., Schwinger, M., Grohmann, J., Herbst, N., Abad, C. L., & Iosup, A. (2020). A review of serverless use cases and their characteristics. *arXiv preprint arXiv:2008.11110*. https://arxiv.org/abs/2008.11110.
25. El Ioini, N., Hästbacka, D., Pahl, C., & Taibi, D. (2020). Platforms for serverless at edge: A review. In *1st International Workshop on Edge Migration and Architecture (EdgeWays 2020)*.
26. Fraga-Lamas, P., Fernández-Caramés, T. M., Suárez-Albela, M., Castedo, L., & González-López, M. (2016). A review on internet of things for defense and public safety. *Sensors, 16*(10), 1644. https://doi.org/10.3390/s16101644.
27. Ghobaei-Arani, M., Souri, A., & Rahmanian, A. A. (2020). Resource management approaches in fog computing: A comprehensive review. *Journal of Grid Computing, 18*(1), 1–42. https://doi.org/10.1007/s10723-019-09491-1.
28. Glikson, A., Nastic, S., & Dustdar, S. (2017). Deviceless edge computing: Extending serverless computing to the edge of the network. In *International Systems and Storage Conference*.
29. Glikson, A., Nastic, S., & Dustdar, S. (2017). Deviceless edge computing: Extending serverless computing to the edge of the network. In *Proceedings of the 10th ACM International Systems and Storage Conference (SYSTOR '17)*. Association for Computing Machinery. https://doi.org/10.1145/3087556.3087567.
30. Guerzoni, R., Trivisonno, R., & Soldani, D. (2014). SDN-based architecture and procedures for 5G networks. In *1st International Conference on 5G for Ubiquitous Connectivity* (pp. 209–214).

31. Hall, A., & Ramachandran, U. (2019). An execution model for serverless functions at the edge. In *International Conference on Internet of Things Design and Implementation* (pp. 225–236).

32. Hassan, B., & Askar, S. (2021). Survey on edge computing security. *arXiv preprint arXiv:2107.10368.* https://arxiv.org/abs/2107.10368 (accessed on 1 August 2024).

33. Hellerstein, J. M., Faleiro, J., Gonzalez, J. E., Schleier-Smith, J., Sreekanti, V., Tumanov, A., & Wu, C. (2018). Serverless computing: One step forward, two steps back. *arXiv preprint arXiv:1812.03651.* https://arxiv.org/abs/1812.03651 (accessed on 1 August 2024).

34. Hendrickson, S., Sturdevant, S., Harter, T., Venkataramani, V., Arpaci-Dusseau, A. C., & Arpaci-Dusseau, R. H. (2016). Serverless computation with OpenLambda. In *8th USENIX Workshop on Hot Topics in Cloud Computing (HotCloud '16)*. USENIX Association.

35. Hong, C. H., & Varghese, B. (2019). Resource management in fog/edge computing: A survey on architectures, infrastructure, and algorithms. *ACM Computing Surveys, 52*(5). https://doi.org/10.1145/3301282.

36. Huang, Y., Geng, J., Lin, D., Wang, B., Li, J., Ling, R., & Li, D. (2017). LOS: A high performance and compatible user-level network operating system. In *Proceedings of the First Asia-Pacific Workshop on Networking (APNet)* (pp. 50–56). https://doi.org/10.1109/APNet.2017.16.

37. Jung, R., et al. (2017). RustBelt: Securing the foundations of the Rust programming language. *Proceedings of the ACM on Programming Languages, 2*(POPL), 1–34. https://doi.org/10.1145/3009838.

38. Li, J., Kulkarni, S. G., Ramakrishnan, K. K., & Li, D. (2019). Understanding open source serverless platforms: Design considerations and performance. In *Proceedings of the 5th International Workshop on Serverless Computing (WOSC '19)* (pp. 37–42). Association for Computing Machinery. https://doi.org/10.1145/3341691.3341712.

39. Li, J., Kulkarni, S. G., Ramakrishnan, K. K., & Li, D. (2019). Understanding open source serverless platforms: Design considerations and performance. In *Proceedings of the 5th International Workshop on Serverless Computing (WoSC)* (pp. 37–42). Association for Computing Machinery. https://doi.org/10.1145/3341691.3341712.

40. Li, J., Li, D., Wu, W., Ramakrishnan, K. K., Geng, J., Gui, F., Wang, F., & Zheng, K. (2019). Sphinx: A transport protocol for high-speed and lossy mobile networks. In *IEEE 38th International Performance Computing and Communications Conference (IPCCC)* (pp. 1–8). IEEE. https://doi.org/10.1109/IPCCC.2019.8917414.

41. Li, J., Li, D., Yu, Y., Huang, Y., Zhu, J., & Geng, J. (2018). Towards full virtualization of SDN infrastructure. *Computer Networks, 143*, 1–14. https://doi.org/10.1016/j.comnet.2018.06.015.
42. Li, X., Ma, Z., Zheng, J., Liu, Y., Zhu, L., & Zhou, N. (2020). An effective edge-assisted data collection approach for critical events in the SDWSN-based agricultural Internet of Things. *Electronics, 9*(6). https://doi.org/10.3390/electronics9060925.
43. Lloyd, W., et al. (2018). Serverless computing: An investigation of factors influencing microservice performance. In *IEEE International Conference on Cloud Engineering (IC2E)* (pp. 159–169). IEEE. https://doi.org/10.1109/IC2E.2018.00035.
44. Manner, J., Endreß, M., Heckel, T., & Wirtz, G. (2018). Cold start influencing factors in function as a service. In *2018 IEEE/ACM International Conference on Utility and Cloud Computing Companion (UCC Companion)* (pp. 181–188). https://doi.org/10.1109/UCC-Companion.2018.00035.
45. Marin, E., Perino, D., & Pietro, R. (2021). Serverless computing: A security perspective.
46. McGrath, G., & Brenner, P. R. (2017). Serverless computing: Design, implementation, and performance. In *IEEE 37th International Conference on Distributed Computing Systems Workshops (ICDCSW)* (pp. 405–410). IEEE. https://doi.org/10.1109/ICDCSW.2017.82.
47. Mohanty, S. K., Premsankar, G., & di Francesco, M. (2018). An evaluation of open source serverless computing frameworks. In *2018 CloudCom* (pp. 115–120). https://doi.org/10.1109/CloudCom.2018.00029.
48. Mohanty, S. K., Premsankar, G., & di Francesco, M. (2018). An evaluation of open source serverless computing frameworks. In *IEEE International Conference on Cloud Computing Technology and Science (CloudCom)* (pp. 115–120). IEEE. https://doi.org/10.1109/CloudCom.2018.00030.
49. Nastic, S., Rausch, T., Scekic, O., Dustdar, S., Gusev, M., Koteska, B., Kostoska, M., Jakimovski, B., Ristov, S., & Prodan, R. (2017). A serverless real-time data analytics platform for edge computing. *IEEE Internet Computing, 21*(4), 64–71. https://doi.org/10.1109/MIC.2017.64.
50. Ning, Z., Kong, X., Xia, F., Hou, W., & Wang, X. (2019). Green and sustainable cloud of things: Enabling collaborative edge computing. *IEEE Communications Magazine, 57*(1), 72–78. https://doi.org/10.1109/MCOM.2019.1800284.
51. Palade, A., Kazmi, A., & Clarke, S. (2019). An evaluation of open source serverless computing frameworks support at the edge. In *IEEE World*

Congress on Services (SERVICES) (Vol. 2642, pp. 206–211). IEEE. https://doi.org/10.1109/SERVICES.2019.00037.

52. Perez, R., Benedetti, P., Pergolesi, M., Garcia-Reinoso, J., Zabala, A., Serrano, P., Femminella, M., Reali, G., & Banchs, A. (2021). A performance comparison of virtualization techniques to deploy a 5G monitoring platform. In *2021 Joint European Conference on Networks and Communications & 6G Summit (EuCNC/6G Summit)* (pp. 472–477). https://doi.org/10.1109/EuCNC/6G-Summit53000.2021.9463778.
53. Polinsky, I., Datta, P., Bates, A., & Enck, W. (2021). SCIFFS: Enabling secure third-party security analytics using serverless computing. In *Proceedings of the 26th ACM Symposium on Access Control Models and Technologies (SACMAT '21)* (pp. 175–186). Association for Computing Machinery. https://doi.org/10.1145/3406026.3406037.
54. Rimal, B. P., Maier, M., & Satyanarayanan, M. (2018). Experimental testbed for edge computing in fiber-wireless broadband access networks. *IEEE Communications Magazine, 56*(8), 160–167. https://doi.org/10.1109/MCOM.2018.1800227.
55. Sabella, D., Alleman, A., Liao, E., Filippou, M., Ding, Z., Gomes Baltar, L., Srikanteswara, S., Bhuyan, K., Oyman, O., Schatzberg, G., Oliver, N., Smith, N., Mishra, S. D., Thakkar, P., & Shailendra, S. (2021). *Edge Computing: From Standard to Actual Infrastructure Deployment and Software Development—Whitepaper 2021.*
56. Shi, W., Cao, J., Zhang, Q., Li, Y., & Xu, L. (2016). Edge computing: Vision and challenges. *IEEE Internet of Things Journal, 3*(5), 637–646. https://doi.org/10.1109/JIOT.2016.2579198.
57. Singh, J., Bello, Y., Hussein, A. R., Erbad, A., & Mohamed, A. (2021). Hierarchical security paradigm for IoT multi-access edge computing. *IEEE Internet of Things Journal, 8*(7), 5794–5805. https://doi.org/10.1109/JIOT.2021.3059204.
58. Tang, J., Yu, R., Liu, S., & Gaudiot, J. L. (2020). A container-based edge offloading framework for autonomous driving. *IEEE Access, 8*, 33713–33726. https://doi.org/10.1109/ACCESS.2020.2971315.
59. Wen, J., Liu, Y., Chen, Z., Ma, Y., Wang, H., & Liu, X. (2020). Understanding characteristics of commodity serverless computing platforms. *arXiv preprint arXiv:2012.00992*. https://arxiv.org/abs/2012.00992.
60. Zhang, Y., et al. (2018). KylinX: A dynamic library operating system for simplified and efficient cloud virtualization. In *USENIX Annual Technical Conference (ATC '18)* (pp. 173–186). USENIX Association.

CHAPTER 6

ACCELERATING AND SCALING DATA PRODUCTS WITH SERVERLESS

Contents

INTRODUCTION

Hardly a company exists that does not use analytics and data in one way or another to either directly enhance its user experience and products or to help it make better, more informed decisions. Data teams will differ substantially in terms of their roles, structure, workflows, tech stack, and output depending on how mature the data operations are. The stage of the data journey will therefore largely depend on the data requirements of the company.

The ability to answer questions about products or business and compute metrics either ad hoc or systematically is the most basic requirement for data. The crucial position involved in these duties is that of the data analyst. The perfect analyst moves quickly through uncharted territory and through data to produce insights that can be presented as a dashboard or a single analysis.

Further, the data needs will inevitably evolve in terms of:

1. **Scale**—supporting more teams with faster time to insights.
2. **Complexity**—increasing volume and complexity of data, domains and analysis.
3. **Requirements**—data quality, metrics standardization, continuous tracking.

The data team will grow by adding new roles and technologies in response to these changing needs. The majority of the time, the new positions in the data team will be focused on data science, data engineering, analytics engineering, and BI development.

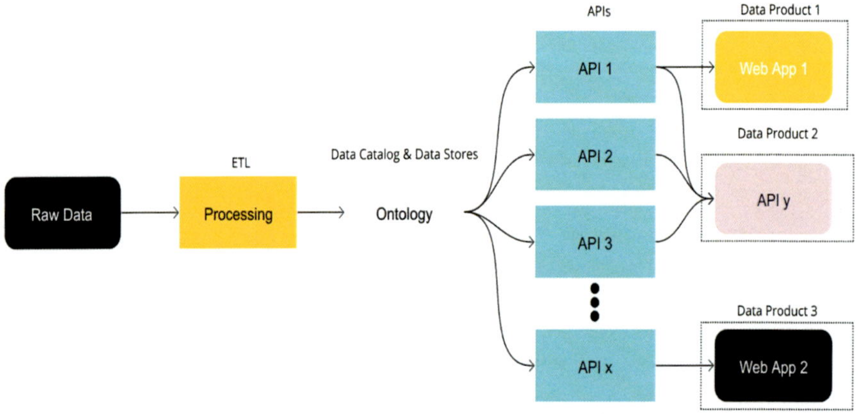

Figure 6.1. *Data flow used for developing data products.*

Source: Rajalakshmi Krishnamurthi, Adarsh Kumar, Sukhpal Singh Gill, and Rajkumar Buyya, Serverless Computing: Principles and Paradigms, ISBN 978-3-031-26632-4.

The application of software engineering concepts to the development, management, and provision of data and related capabilities will be greatly aided by data engineers.

Version control of the code and the establishment of standard guidelines and procedures will ideally result in reliable workflows with completely visible and monitored data pipelines. In order to create interactive dashboards and applications that represent data models across all domains served to the organization, analysts, analytics engineers, and BI (business intelligence) developers will collaborate closely.

By utilizing advanced modeling techniques and machine learning, data scientists can increase the depth and breadth of the insights that are produced. These will usually be provided to the business as extra data points for current deliveries or as interactive web applications.

Data and team deliveries will eventually be considered data products as the data team and capabilities grow. As a result, solid data, product, and engineering principles will be established, pushing the team's technological requirements even higher.

At this level of data maturity, a data science team's primary duties include creating data products that are needed to influence important business metrics within an organization, personalize user experiences, and inform decisions. A portfolio of data products that are intended for use by more than just data specialists (analysts, researchers, etc.) fulfill this responsibility.) but also by teams and decision-makers who depend on these data products as downstream dependencies in order to carry out their daily tasks. (Johnson J et al.,2021).

Therefore, in order to increase business performance while maintaining maintainability, the data science team must produce new features at a high rate of change that can be tested and implemented.

Figure 6.1. depicts the fundamental data flow that is utilized for these data products' quick prototyping and interoperability. We have demonstrated that using this modular strategy in conjunction with serverless technology can reliably produce data products at scale with a small team.

A shared data model and a data foundation are two actions that will greatly enhance the development process and are crucial to the flow in Figure 6.1. Our first step is to create a conceptualization of the data model, or what we call our ontology, which will be shared by the data team and the organization's data products as a whole.

The data ontology, which is initially derived from business knowledge and discussions with important stakeholders, is essential for creating a foundation that can be utilized for numerous projects. The process of developing and managing a shared data model is depicted in Figure 6.2, and it is essential for remaining relevant and giving other teams access to the correct data. Building a data foundation that subsequently translates into standardized and widely understood entities, attributes, and relationships requires iterating to improve on the shared data models.

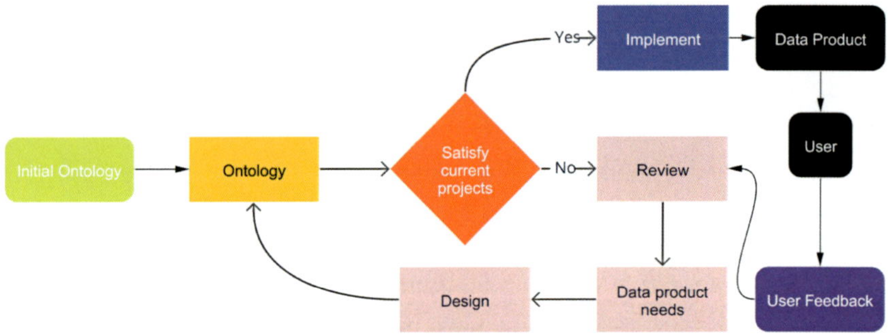

Figure 6.2. *Methodology for a shared data model and its continuous improvement.*

Source: R. Krishnamurthi et al. (eds.), Serverless Computing: Principles and Paradigms, Lecture Notes on Data Engineering and Communications Technologies 162, https://doi.org/10.1007/978-3-031-26633-1_6.

This work fills a recognized vacuum in the literature by providing an all-inclusive set of serverless solutions that can efficiently deliver data products at the enterprise level. For each cloud provider, there are comprehensive books covering various topics related to the delivery of data products.

These topics may include data science, data engineering, or general aspects of Google cloud development.

On the other hand, our group can offer comprehensive solutions that not only incorporate various Google cloud services, but also expand the fundamental components for straightforward migrations and applications to alternative cloud providers, as well as reducing vendor lock-in. Furthermore, the recommended architecture and solutions offer a production-ready solution because they have been tested on a real-world application.

6.1. DATA PRODUCTS AND THEIR ARCHITECTURE

By taking a broad approach and considering all of our data teams' outputs as designed products, or data products, we can break down tasks into manageable components and increase the maintainability of each deliverable.

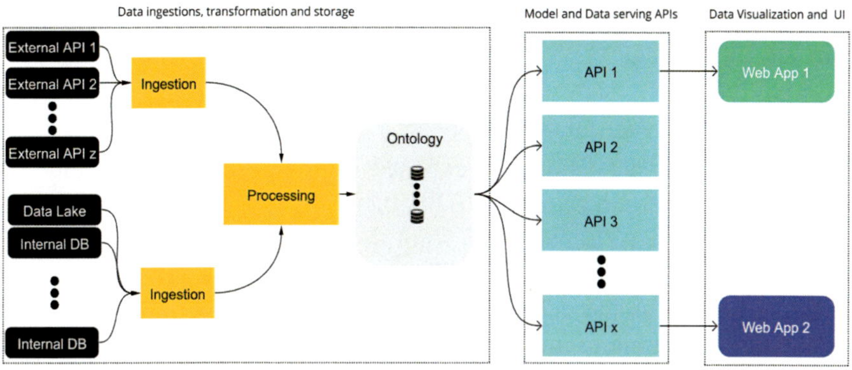

Figure 6.3. *Generic architecture used for our data product and fundamental building blocks.*

Source: R. Krishnamurthi et al. (eds.), Serverless Computing: Principles and Paradigms, Lecture Notes on Data Engineering and Communications Technologies 162, https://doi.org/10.1007/978-3-031-26633-1_6.

In order to fulfill this goal, the team had to select a cloud architecture that would allow for the production and maintenance of general data products by the company while minimizing the amount of additional work needed to maintain the infrastructure.

In order to manage this requirement, the following paradigms were considered:

1. Infrastructure must be established as code in version-controlled repositories, that includes CI/CD capabilities. GitHub and GitHub Actions are used for this purpose.
2. Solutions based on container orchestration (e.g., Kubernetes) are preferred when implementing custom applications.
3. Serverless solutions for data processing, app serving and model training are to be preferred.

The mentioned considerations allowed the team to create a generic structure in which all our current data products can be developed, and this approach has some clear advantages regarding the team output in comparison to its size.

Furthermore, serverless technology with auto-scaling features enables the use of only the resources needed at any given time, thereby lowering compute costs as well as the implied carbon footprint of the services that are created. This is because idle servers consume a large amount of energy when virtual machines (VMs) or traditional data center solutions are used. Figure 6.3 depicts the generic architecture used for a data product. The underlying idea of the suggested architecture is that, provided the data ontology is maintained as current, many of the APIs created for one data product can be recycled or repurposed for other data products in the future. The concepts of scalability and reusability are shared by all data products.

Since a unified data model is exposed in the APIs to our various data products—and in certain cases, the APIs themselves are the product—we are able to decouple the API consumers from the complexities of the data thanks to the architecture shown in Figure 6.3. Another use case that can be handled by the same model is the delivery of dashboards and reporting, which come straight from the ontology into managed solutions like Looker or Data Studio (i.e., serverless).

The group determined that there are three primary types of components that can be considered as essential elements of the architecture shown in Figure 6.3, specifically:

- ***Data ingestion, transformation, and storage***

  Since most of our applications involve multiple data sources—both internal and external—that must be integrated in order to produce actionable insights, this is likely the biggest challenge when developing data products. It involves making calls to APIs to input data, process it, and then store it so that our data products can use it. Reusable components include the Docker images for the services, the code created for ingesting the data (including storage and API calls), and the coordination of the various tasks that involve ingestion and transformation. A use case where all analytics questions that have been solved are version controlled is also provided, giving the team access to a repository of answers and a historical register of changes.

- ***Models and data serving APIs***

  Our solution must be reusable and extensible in order to share our data, features, embeddings, and models with other applications. As a result, an API was developed for every solution.

- ***Data visualization and UI***

  Our monitoring, data, and model outputs must be regularly made available to data professionals, stakeholders, workers, and users, in addition to other applications (like personalization). Small web applications with specialized functions are developed for these kinds of situations. These applications, such as Looker, DataStudio, and others, are containerized programs designed to deliver information in a way that requires less effort and solves a problem beyond the scope of traditional dashboard applications.

6.2. SERVERLESS BUILDING BLOCKS FOR DATA PRODUCTS

To make the description of the actual study cases easier to understand, we go over the specifics of each of the major components that make up our architecture here. The Google Cloud Platform's (GCP) solutions serve as the foundation for the architectures.

It is anticipated that the general building blocks covered in this section can be applied to different cloud services. This work offers a table with alternative 1 offerings to GCP services, either through other cloud providers or self-hosted options, to aid in the development of such applications and the search for equivalent services (see Table 6.1).

Table 6.1. *Equivalent Service Offerings Among Google Cloud Platform, Azure, Amazon Web Services, and Self-Hosted Options*

GCP	Azure	AWS	Self-hosted
Dataproc	Synapse	EMR[a]	Apache Spark
Composer	Data Factory	MWAA[b]/Glue	Apache Airflow
Kubernetes Engine	AKS[c]	EKS[d]	Kubernetes
Dataflow	Stream Analytics	Kinesis Data Analytics/Glue	Apache Beam
Cloud SQL	Database for PostgreSQL	RDS[e]/Aurora	PostgreSQL
App Engine	App Service	Elastic/Beanstalk	
Cloud Run	Container Instances	Fargate/Lambda/SAM[f]	

Source: Rajalakshmi Krishnamurthi, Adarsh Kumar, Sukhpal Singh Gill, and Rajkumar Buyya, Serverless Computing: Principles and Paradigms, ISBN 978-3-031-26632-4.

[a]Elastic MapReduce

[b]Amazon Managed Workflows for Apache Airflow

[c]Azure Kubernetes Service

[d]Elastic Kubernetes Service

[e]Relational Database Service

[f]Serverless Application Model

Since some of the services (e.g., Dataproc) offer self-managed versions, we would like to clarify that all solutions described are serverless, which means that the cloud provider offers managed solutions with no need for server management or resource allocation (e.g., Dataproc Serverless). The word serverless is omitted on many occasions for a clear and simple exposition.

6.2.1. Data Ingestion, Storage, and Transformation

This building block's primary goal is to coordinate a series of actions that transform unprocessed data into a useable ontology that can accommodate a broad range of diverse downstream use cases. Our data lake is receiving data streams from different products across the company. Our sources of raw data are kept in a data lake that is managed by a central data team.

A set of transformations and processing steps is applied to the raw storage in order to transform the data to a state that feed into our downstream data products. A non-exhaustive list of transformations include:

- Imputing missing data and entity resolution.
- Formatting data and other transformations.
- Computing metrics, statistics, and features.
- Joining data across product domains, financial systems, and other sources to create our ontology.
- Monitoring data quality

The transformed data is stored using three main services:

- **BigQuery**: Google Cloud's petabyte scale, serverless data warehouse that powers a great deal of our processing needs by providing a highly parallel and scalable execution model, that executes processing requests across thousands of machines, through a single SQL programming interface. This simple interface allows users, across many data roles, to analyze large quantities of data, which can scale to any organization size. The data ontology can then be transformed and exposed through a simple interface, which greatly improves iteration cycles and data discovery.
- **Cloud Storage:** distributed and highly scalable object storage, that is often used to stage data before loading to BigQuery or other services.
- **Cloud SQL:** managed relational database service, which is utilized as backend, to power our in-house API's and web applications.

Every transformation must be planned at a specific frequency, such as weekly or daily, along with the storage of the derived data asset. The team required a way to coordinate our workflows in order to do this. (Osman MA, Mohd Noah SA, Saad S 2022). This work suggests using Airflow for workflow orchestration. Among data professionals, Airflow is a widely used workflow scheduling framework. Workflows in Airflow are represented as directed acyclic graphs, or DAGs for short. DAGs are directed graphs that specify the sequence in which a number of tasks are executed within the graph, with each task being defined by a particular operator. Tasks, operators, and DAGs are all configured in Python. In particular, a Google Kubernetes Engine cluster (GKE) hosting Cloud Composer, a managed Airflow instance from Google Cloud, is utilized.

- The managed solution offers a high degree of workflow execution flexibility at a low maintenance cost. It enables the team to concentrate on developing workflows and adding value to the company for the majority of its time. Additionally, the team uses open-source execution operators contributed by the community as part of the solution.
- Tasks on GKE can be carried out using specially created container images, maintaining Airflow's orchestration capabilities. All members of the organization are welcome to contribute these images, which can then be shared in a centrally located and easily accessible Container Registry. g. GCR stands for Google Container Registry. Then, different teams can use these pictures again. This makes it easier to execute custom processing, integrate data, and perform machine learning tasks like training and model evaluation. The Airflow-provided KubernetesPodOperator is utilized for execution. With the help of this operator, distinct GKE Node Pools can be allocated according to the workload, supporting a wide range of workflows with possibly disparate hardware needs. Costs can be kept to a minimum by auto-scaling the node pools to zero when they are idle. We can also run a lot of compute-intensive workflows concurrently thanks to the auto-scaling nodes.
- Airflow offers pre-configured operators that can be used with Big Data tools like Apache Spark and Apache Beam, as well as with their serverless equivalents in CGP, which are Dataproc Serverless and Dataflow.

Our complete solution for data processing and ingestion is implemented as follows:

- Contributions for DAG workflow files are made to a single GitHub repository. A wide range of tasks could be included in each DAG, such as processing data in BigQuery, transferring or processing data using Spark or Beam Jobs, or executing unique data integration workflows using containerized images and custom Python code. The workflow files that are required to carry out these various workflows are additionally added to the central repository. As long as Airflow can be used to integrate and carry out the task at hand, each team member is free to select the optimal set of tools.

- GitHub Actions, which enables the definition of a set of unique actions to be carried out when a pull request is merged on the repository's main branch, is used to achieve continuous integration.
- The main actions are:
  - copying DAGs and other workflow files to the Cloud Composer environment.
  - building and pushing custom workflow container images to the container registry, in order to make them available for Airflow workers, when executing some specific task.

The combined solution offers a way for data professionals to quickly update and maintain data workflows. There are other aspects that are not covered in this chapter but for the sake of completeness are stated here:

- ***Logging***: All DAG logs are provided by Airflow, and these are particularly helpful for troubleshooting. Furthermore, Google Cloud Operations Suite offers a monitoring, metrics, and logging solution when integrated with one of the other managed services (like Dataflow).
- ***Security***: A central security team monitors the current Kubernetes versions and recommends upgrades based on emerging security issues, in addition to putting best practices into action. Furthermore, updated versions of the managed services are released on a regular basis; however, in most cases, this necessitates testing the code to ensure compatibility with updated versions and requiring intervention to change the version being used.
- ***Scalability***: The resources allotted for each service are overseen by the cloud provider; users typically do not manage these resources. It is possible to regulate the parameters within which the cloud provider distributes resources, though; this choice is tied to budget distribution according to project significance and necessary pipeline updating frequency.

6.2.2. Models and Data Serving Using APIs

The second fundamental building block serves to enable the team to share our ontology with other data teams and applications that depend on machine learning models or personalization to function. The steps below are the strategy applied to this building block:

- Create a repository that contains the API code, where Python is used alongside API frameworks such as FastAPI, Flask, etc. The repository contains enough information to create a Docker image for the application.
- Use GitHub Actions for continuous integration: it triggers on pull request to merge on main branch, builds of the Docker images, stores them in the registry, and deploys to Google Cloud Run
- GitHub offers "secrets," a way for us to store the credentials of the service account that performs the image builds using Google Cloud Build and deployment to Google Cloud run.

With the help of this solution, we can provide data to applications at run-time (e.g., web applications). Use cases like recommendation engines and machine learning model evaluation can be served straight from our team project with little maintenance required.

6.2.3. Data Visualization and User Interfaces

The work of a data science team includes a lot of storytelling and data visualization. It could be used to show the outcomes of an A/B test, assess the efficacy of a model, or provide an interactive example of a concept. Our task is to determine the most effective medium for clearly communicating our message.

There are several approaches to solving this problem, and although there are third-party solutions that guarantee this, our best option is to give analysts and data scientists the greatest amount of expressive freedom.

To achieve maximum expressive freedom, let the data professionals use the tools (web apps, dashboards, etc.) that they are most comfortable using to create the experiences. This approach requires support for multiple frameworks and languages, shifting the complexity from the data professionals to the deployment process.

Each data scientist or analyst will own the code that creates the custom images and CI/CD code for its deployment to App Engine in order to handle the increased complexity on the deployment side. Our data engineers' templates and their prior experience with other web apps the team has developed served as the foundation for this code.

In order to accommodate a dynamic mix of web frameworks, libraries, and programming languages, the following approach was developed:

6.2.3.1. Dashboard solutions:

The only additional step needed by the data professional to create this kind of visualization, aside from setting up the necessary tables in BigQuery, is the seamless integration of Looker and Google Data Studio with BigQuery.

6.2.3.2. Web Applications:

- Create a repository that contains the required files for creating a docker image (e.g., Docker file, packages requirement file, etc.).
- Use Github Actions to deploy the solution to Google Cloud App Engine.
- Using Google Cloud Identity and access management, user membership in privileged groups, integration with Okta, a single sign-on solution, and Identity-Aware Proxy solutions, access control to individual applications is achieved. The latter can be set up to provide access to an entire organization through the auto-scale features of Google Cloud App Engine and Google Workspace.

6.3. REAL-WORLD EXAMPLES, DATA PRODUCTS CATALOGUE

An overview of a few chosen applications from our data products catalog can be found in this section. An implementation card and a general business context are included with every application for convenient reference. The cards have the following use case-neutral format:

- **Context:** A brief description of the business need that is addressed.
- **Architecture:** A diagram and a description of the product building blocks.
- **Remarks:** Results that were obtained with the selected architecture.

Every example relates to a data product in our portfolio; only the most pertinent study cases are shown, and while a straightforward structure is provided for replication, the same architecture can support more intricate solutions.

The following examples are to be studied:

- **Data Processing Foundation for Analytics:** data product that is deployed in order to maintain our ontology.
- **Ontology Visualization:** a visual map of our ontology for the company to explore.
- **Data Lineage Visualization:** it provides a visual reference for the dependencies of each table (Lineage).

- **Community Analytics:** analysis of the pulse of the company's sentiment on different social networks.
- **Recommendation System:** powering personalization of our market place

The results achieved with the presented architecture and suggested services are the following: approx. 80 pipelines (DAGs) that spawn 90 datasets totaling 2700 tables that serve the business analytics needs of an entire organization. The internal web applications see up to approximately about 300 active users overall and 300 per app. There are 100 dashboards available. The volume of the external serving APIs (like Recommender) ranges from 100 to 3000 QPS (queries per second). With a staff of just 7 data professionals, all services are offered with a monthly uptime percentage 3 of at least 99.99 percent.

6.3.1. Data Processing Foundation for Analytics

Our team, like many data specialists in the software industry and beyond, is tasked with drawing conclusions from a vast and ever-expanding amount of diverse data. Our company's core software product generates complex, event-based, non-relational usage and performance data, but it also depends on multiple transactional systems to run our business. These systems handle things like sales, licenses, accounts, and metadata for e-commerce content. Furthermore, a wealth of product feedback is offered in numerous pertinent online channels (such as our own forums and third-party social media) because of the sizable and engaged user community for our products. Furthermore, new products and their instrumentation are regularly released into the market; timely information regarding these developments is highly beneficial to decision makers. The features and needs of the pertinent data processing workflows, which handle tasks like inference-based data cleaning, data collection via storage and APIs, and feature engineering using combinations and aggregations of multiple data sources, frequently differ greatly from one another. Tasks can process datasets as large as terabytes or as small as kilobytes, and computations can take minutes or hours (even with parallelism).

The team has enabled machine learning, data science, reporting, and interactive data exploration app use cases by utilizing these diverse and expanding data sources, even at the beginning of our data science and engineering team and our data foundation. The team had to deal with these demands in spite of limited engineering resources—particularly at first—and assistance from other data teams that was mostly restricted to data governance, storage, and ingestion and integration tasks (for certain data sources). As a result, we had to put in place a productive strategy to deal with the scalability of our data sources in terms of development and maintenance resources as well as time to insights.

This solution was created to facilitate the continuous growth of our team and foster cooperation between members, stakeholders, and other data professionals in order to maximize our impact and make efficient use of our expanding resources. Moreover, it was intended to offer a single location where our data processing pipelines and their infrastructure could be created, maintained, and developed—even by a small team—that is easily extensible with their preferred set of tools and accessible to all interested colleagues who are data specialists. Along with ensuring the pipelines operated reliably through orchestration, monitoring, logging, and alerts, version control and continuous integration solutions also had to guarantee the reproducibility and compatibility of data pipeline development contributions to our data foundation. This data foundation offers an extensible set of reusable data processing solutions and processed data outputs for end-to-end efficiency. These serve as building blocks for the various data use cases that have been previously discussed. These needs have been successfully met by the solution, and given its design, our team anticipates that it will scale even further to support future development and new use cases.

6.3.1.1. Implementation card

1. *Context*

   We develop advanced use cases, such as interactive apps, machine learning models, and reporting, based on a rapidly expanding volume and variety of data from multiple diverse data sources. Meanwhile, the team needed to empower our partners' and stakeholders' work as well as our own, while also taking into account our limited but expanding engineering resources. The efficient, scalable, and reusable solutions to our data processing needs were thus given top priority by our team, guaranteeing fast developer velocity, low maintenance costs, and maximum data quality.

2. Architecture

   Figure 6.4 shows the entire architecture of our data processing foundation. Our solutions for data ingestion and collection, transformation, storage, workflow orchestration, version control, and continuous integration serve as the fundamental building blocks.

- GitHub and GitHub Actions are used for version control and continuous integration.
- For orchestration, Google Cloud Composer (managed Apache Airflow) is utilized, along with custom operators and alerts to boost developer velocity even more. Occasionally, data quality issues are resolved through the creation and parsing of DAGs.

- The majority of internal data sources are either stored in Google BigQuery or have integrations with it. BigQuery is widely utilized for data processing and storage in our pipelines, with custom Airflow operators to expedite DAG development, because of its effectiveness and user-friendliness. In order to efficiently address data quality issues, documentation is kept in a standardized format in query files, parsed, and injected into pertinent data discovery interfaces. Python-based query conversion is then utilized to automate the application of pertinent processing.
- Our data pipelines use Kubernetes for containerized applications with different hardware requirements and dependencies. Custom, reusable utilities and the appropriate Airflow operator are used. Our use cases include feature engineering and other data processing (e.g., specialized NLP tasks), machine learning batch inference, and data collection via APIs.
- Our data processing pipelines' outputs are typically kept in BigQuery for later use. They are repurposed as components of other pertinent pipelines, for ad hoc analysis, custom interactive apps, machine learning inference features, Looker and Google Data Studio dashboard reporting, and other use cases in data science.

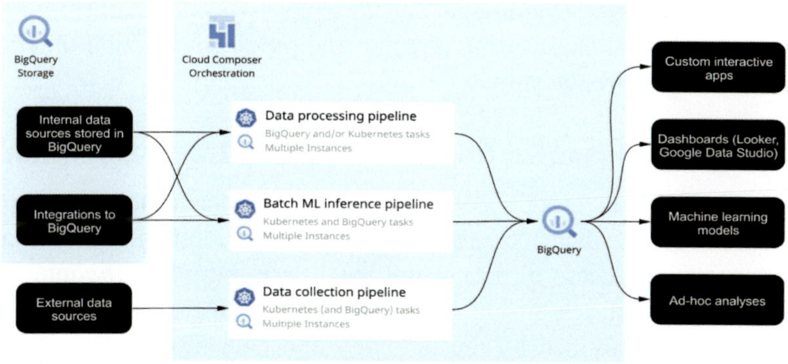

Figure 6.4. *General architecture for the data processing foundation and its analytics use cases, with data flow shown using black arrows.*

Source: R. Krishnamurthi et al. (eds.), Serverless Computing: Principles and Paradigms, Lecture Notes on Data Engineering and Communications Technologies 162, https://doi.org/10.1007/978-3-031-26633-1_6.

3. *Remarks*

Serverless solutions have proven to be an ideal match for our data processing requirements, as they efficiently handle the various forms of scaling that are necessary. With the chosen architecture, a small team has been able to generate actionable insights quickly, while maintaining high data quality, reliability, reusability, and scalability. This has enabled use cases such as dashboards, machine learning, and customized interactive apps, and it has also empowered other stakeholders and collaborators.

- The open source Apache Airflow project, which serves as the foundation for Google Cloud Composer, is highly customizable, easy to learn, and extensible, according to our team and other collaborators from a variety of backgrounds.
- We have found that BigQuery offers competitive performance for our typical use cases while requiring a significant reduction in development resources compared to Apache Spark workflows.
- In addition to other forms of data processing, our team has discovered that our Kubernetes orchestration with Google Cloud Composer is applicable for deploying machine learning batch inference as well. If the additional complexity of specialized ML inference deployment solutions is not required, our models can be deployed simply and effectively by reusing this method along with our custom utilities. Using this method, our team deployed our user segmentation models and discovered additional benefits, such as a smooth integration with the feature engineering pipeline and pipelines utilizing the model's batch inference outputs.

6.3.2. Ontology Visualization and Business Logic Compliance

Understanding the data model is one of the biggest obstacles to the enterprise's efforts to democratize data access and literacy, in addition to granting everyone in the organization access to data. High level descriptions of the interactions between various entities inside the enterprise or software that the team is developing are provided by the ontology and data model. A network can record these entities and their interactions. The network can then be shown for qualitative relationship analysis, compliance assessment, or any other decision-making process that needs to know the complete context of a user—that is, all the entities connected to them during their use of the product—for that user. Our main objective is to provide an interactive map of our ontology so that all of our colleagues can use it to discover how we view our customers, tell a story using networks, and intuitively untangle complex relations. It is accomplished by offering sophisticated data visualizations and adhering to the architecture shown in Figure 6.5.

6.3.2.1. Implementation card

1. *Context*

   A visual depiction of the intricate connections a user has with various components of our products or services would be beneficial to some of our data product users who lack understanding of our ontology. The solution to this problem is to offer sophisticated network graph visualizations through a web application. It uses various colors and icons to visualize the relationships between the nodes in our ontology, representing it as a network. The outcomes enable us to quickly determine a customer's context (such as usage, transactions, and interactions).

2. Architecture

   In this architecture, the three main building blocks are in use in the following way:

- Data processing block: An additional workflow is used to create a database of entities (nodes in the network), relationships (edges in the network), and metadata for each entity. A DAG in Airflow orchestrates the pipelines that compute our data ontology.
- Three APIs that grant access to the network representation of our ontology (data model) utilize the three databases.
- A web application that provides an interactive Visualization of the network using D3.js, the app calls the provided APIs and displays the network and metadata. The user can report anomalies or tell stories with the data by using the formatting and coloring options provided for various use cases.

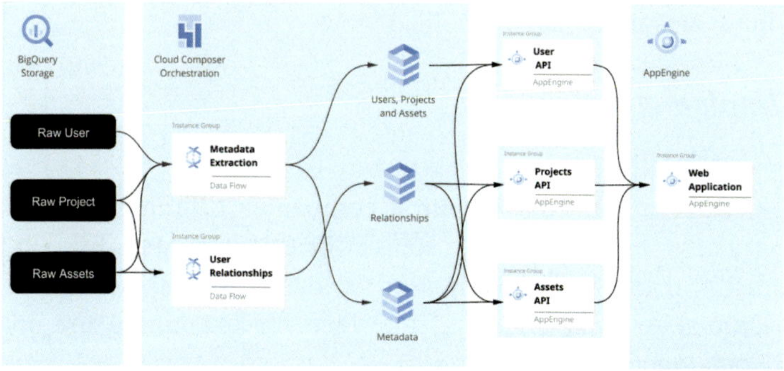

Figure 6.5. *Generic ontology visualization and business logic compliance.*

Source: Rajalakshmi Krishnamurthi, Adarsh Kumar, Sukhpal Singh Gill, and Rajkumar Buyya, Serverless Computing: Principles and Paradigms, ISBN 978-3-031-26632-4.

3. *Remarks*

- Providing an interactive visualization has had multiple impacts on the way our data products evolve:
- The subnetworks and underlying network can be utilized as a knowledge graph for machine learning tasks that come later (like recommender systems).
- The team can swiftly explain the data at hand and the relationships between various entities thanks to the data visualization.
- Since they give non-data professionals an easy way to investigate what information is available about our customers, network visualizations are frequently used in the fields of compliance, fraud, and money laundering applications (e.g., who have not paid for a service required to contribute to a project in a given company).

6.3.3. Community Analytics

These days, it is typical for end users of any kind of product or service—software included—to have a noticeable online presence across a variety of community and social media platforms. These may include public platforms like Twitter, YouTube, Instagram, Reddit, Discord, Stack Overflow, and others, or specific discussion forums run by the service provider. Users express their opinions about products in natural language text, which makes it difficult to analyze manually. However, automated analyses using natural language processing (NLP) open up the possibility of gaining insights on the aforementioned points at scale using techniques like sentiment and opinion mining, topic tracking, or user network analysis. These insights can then be used, among other things, to inform a product roadmap that addresses important issues, prioritizes user pain points, or innovates in the most practical ways.

6.3.3.1. Implementation card

1. *Context*

   Customer satisfaction with a company's offerings is crucial to its success. Having a single source for this insight is difficult because users share their thoughts on various platforms and services. It is crucial to offer a unified interface for examining the company's social media activity.

2. *Architecture*

   Providing analytics of user's post in social media that relate to a company is achieved using the following steps, as illustrated in Figure 6.6.

- Data ingestion: custom services that ingest the data from common social platforms are orchestrated by Cloud Composer and run periodically (e.g., daily).
- A number of natural language processing (NLP) models are applied on the collected texts at post and thread level: sentiment analysis, topic modelling, semantic similarity, etc. Search indices are built from the dataset and incrementally updated.
- Results of model inference, original posts, and other structural information (threads, subforums, etc.) are transferred to a supporting database in Cloud SQL.
- The user is presented with the data via a web application and a Slack bot, which provide personalized topic search and filtering, sentiment analysis, trend identification, trend detection, custom alerts for specific product features, and other features.
- The apps positioned at the front serve the purpose of partially automating the creation of periodicals, which are then utilized to share the community's pulse with internal stakeholders.

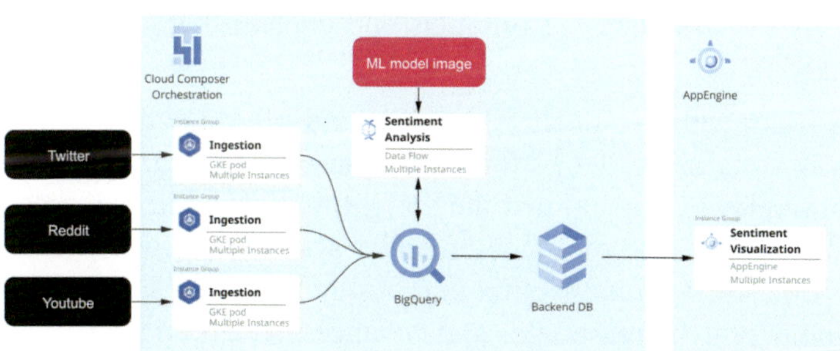

Figure 6.6. *Architecture for a community analytics application.*

Source: R. Krishnamurthi et al. (eds.), Serverless Computing: Principles and Paradigms, Lecture Notes on Data Engineering and Communications Technologies 162, https://doi.org/10.1007/978-3-031-26633-1_6.

3. *Remarks*

   The main impacts we see from this application are:

- Community managers' job of keeping an eye on social media trends is made much easier by tools that streamline search and post analysis, give a single, searchable source, and prioritize content based on sentiment and volume.
- Product managers can truly understand product feedback at scale and in fine detail by having access to a broad view of various product

aspects as well as the ability to break down the overall view down to the level of a single post.

- Marketing managers plan, carry out, and evaluate the results of focused user engagements by using our community analytics to monitor overall sentiment trends toward the company brand.
- In order to inform strategic planning and execution, senior executives receive a comprehensive, periodic, and data-driven view of the most important topics in the user community for a specific time period, along with insight from competitor communities.
- The application provides access to APIs that are used by a number of other internal stakeholder teams. These teams need sentiment analysis-based measures of the health of the product to complement the current orthogonal metrics, such as quality assurance and customer success.

6.3.4. Recommendation System

It can be challenging for users to find pertinent content without becoming overwhelmed by the vast array of products and content that are available on marketplaces.

Providing users with personalized content and offerings that are tailored to their needs is a major challenge for marketplaces, as it makes it easier for end users to find relevant content that they might find valuable and interesting. This help can take the shape of a recommender system, which is widely used by companies like Amazon and Netflix and has evolved into a standard in the e-commerce industry to increase sales and enhance user experience.

End users use explicit means, like star ratings, to communicate their level of satisfaction. They also use implicit means, like browsing history and search patterns, to communicate their level of satisfaction on the marketplace. With the use of matrix factorization (ALS) and implicit ratings, collaborative filtering via a latent factor model is made possible, ultimately leading to the characterization of both items and users. Because every user is unique and has different needs, a recommender system enables the marketplace to tailor its marketing to each individual user, improving user satisfaction and loyalty as well as engagement and retention. (Bell R, Koren Y, Volinsky C, 2009).

1. *Context*

   Tools are typically included with a marketplace experience to improve the user's ability to locate what they're looking for. In addition to search capabilities, a recommendation engine can help users find relevant content based on how they interact with the marketplace app or website. Among various methods for developing a recommendation system, a collaborative filtering strategy that relies on the implicit feedback of the user was chosen as the foundation.

2. *Architecture*

The implicit rating is calculated by adding together the user's wishlist, views, purchases, and usage of the item that they have purchased. This is accomplished by running a DAG on Cloud Composer (Airflow) that creates the necessary aggregations and runs the Spark code that generates recommendations for every user, filters the items (such as those they have already purchased), and provides embeddings for additional recommendations based on similarity. Figure 6.7 depicts the system's general architecture. The recommendations and embeddings, which are intermediate results, are kept in different Cloud SQL instances to support the APIs that the marketplace front-end will call and expose. We can use the Data Processing Block and the APIs Serving Block, two of our building blocks, to implement this solution thanks to the chosen architecture.

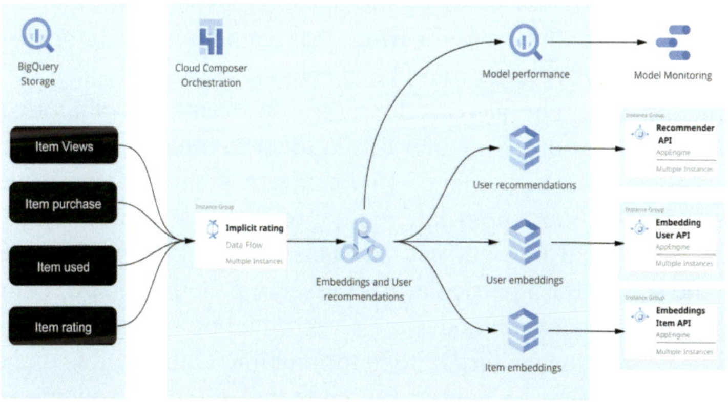

Figure 6.7. *Generic architecture for serving a recommendation system.*

Source: Rajalakshmi Krishnamurthi, Adarsh Kumar, Sukhpal Singh Gill, and Rajkumar Buyya, Serverless Computing: Principles and Paradigms, ISBN 978-3-031-26632-4.

3. *Remarks*

The model, the recommender architecture, and the marketplace interface can all be separated thanks to the chosen architecture. This lets us make tweaks and enhancements without changing the marketplace interface (gives a user ID and context, and gets the recommended items list). Additionally, the API is decoupled from the model and the similarity search—which allows changing the functionality to any of the existing options:

- Database of pre-computed values
- Call for a similarity search engine (e.g., Vertex AI Matching Engine)
- Custom code providing the search capability (e.g., custom API running Faiss library to provide similarity search.

A custom API was provided, which allows us to control the costs by running it in Google Cloud Run.

6.3.5. Data Lineage Visualization

It is complex to operate in a distributed and dynamic data landscape where data outages and asset changes frequently occur beyond the control of a single team. Consequently, downstream data assets may malfunction or inadvertently go stale. This may have a detrimental effect on data products that derive from a widely used data ontology and erode stakeholder data trust. It gets harder to comprehend the source data that feeds into the ontology and how the data is used downstream as the use cases of the ontology expand and the web of dependencies gets more cluttered. Fearing that something will go wrong downstream, more and more time must be spent carefully evaluating the risk of changing the ontology. The increased overhead prevents contributors from contributing to the current ontology and forces them to build everything from scratch. This problem can be lessened by having a complete data lineage, which provides users with an up-to-date picture of the data flows to and from particular data assets. Data lineage may be visualized as a directed graph, in which every node stands for a particular data asset, e.g., a dashboard, column, table, etc. Dependencies between nodes are represented by edges, whereby the source node is necessary for the target node to function. One possible example of this dependency would be an aggregated table that reads the rows from an upstream table. One can obtain a comprehensive understanding of all upstream and downstream dependencies by combining all of these dependencies. This complete dependency graph can be useful in addressing issues like how many dependencies there are upstream for a given data asset, how a single table update impacts downstream dependencies, how a particular metric was calculated, and which downstream dependencies were impacted by a particular incident.

1. *Context*

   As a step to ensure data quality, traceability and reproducibility of our pipelines, a data lineage retrieval and visualization tool has been built. Architecture Building data lineage and structuring it for visualization is achieved using the steps shown in Figure 6.8:

- **Metadata retrieval block:** Workflow metadata that is pertinent is retrieved and staged for further processing. Workflow metadata, such as those from our Airflow DAGs and the BigQuery processing history, make up this metadata.
- **Dependency retrieval block:** Data assets are mapped to upstream dependencies by parsing the workflow metadata. In this case, table and column level dependencies are retrieved using a SQL parser that was deployed via Cloud Run. In this step, column transformations are also retrieved. The Google Cloud Storage Bucket is used to stage dependencies. The KubernetesPodOperator is used to retrieve workflow dependencies, and it scales out the dependency building process by running multiple Pods on an autoscaling GKE nodepool.
- **Dependency graph building block:** Complete dependency graphs are then produced by combining the dependency mappings. This procedure is carried out in a manner akin to that of dependency retrieval. Onto a CloudSQL instance are pushed the dependency graphs.
- **Metadata retrieval block:** For every type of dependency, metadata is retrieved. The CloudSQL instance receives the results.
- **Data visualization block:** Google App Engine is used to deploy a web application. Users can search through table and column level dependencies, view metadata, and view the dependency graph through this application. Through an API that is set up on Cloud Run, the graph is made available to the web application.

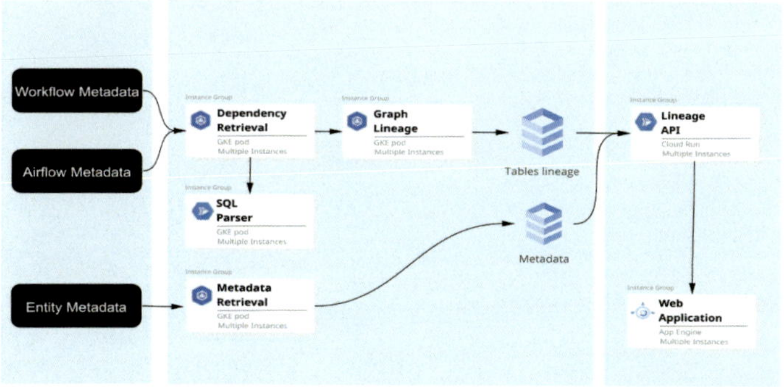

Figure 6.8. *Architecture for determining lineage and its visualization.*

Source: Rajalakshmi Krishnamurthi, Adarsh Kumar, Sukhpal Singh Gill, and Rajkumar Buyya, Serverless Computing: Principles and Paradigms, ISBN 978-3-031-26632-4.

2. *Remarks*

Our data lineage tool provides the following advantages:

- Discovery tool for data professionals (columns and feature dependencies) and fast onboarding of new colleagues
- Overview of the data dependencies and clear view of when a table was updated, which improves the prompt debugging of upstream data quality issues.

REFERENCES

1. Austrian, M., & Ryan, W. (2009). Cloud computing meets e-discovery. *Cyberspace Lawyer, 14*(6), 7–12.
2. Bell, R., Koren, Y., & Volinsky, C. (2009). Matrix factorization techniques for recommender systems. *Computer, 42*(8), 30–37. https://doi.org/10.1109/MC.2009.263.
3. Buyya, R., Yeo, C. S., & Venugopal, S. (2008). Market-oriented cloud computing: Vision, hype, and reality for delivering IT services as computing utilities. In *Proceedings of the 10th IEEE International Conference on High Performance Computing and Communications (HPCC 2008)* (pp. 5–13). IEEE CS Press, Los Alamitos, CA, USA, Dalian, China.
4. Johnson, J., et al. (2021). Billion-scale similarity search with GPUs. *IEEE Transactions on Big Data, 7*(3), 535–547. https://doi.org/10.1109/TBDATA.2019.2921572.
5. Melnik, S., et al. (2010). Dremel: Interactive analysis of web-scale datasets. In *36th International Conference on Very Large Data Bases* (pp. 330–339). Singapore.
6. Osman, M. A., Mohd Noah, S. A., & Saad, S. (2022). Ontology-based knowledge management tools for knowledge sharing in organizations—A review. *IEEE Access, 10*, 43267–43283. https://doi.org/10.1109/ACCESS.2022.3163758.
7. Plummer, D. C., Smith, D., Bittman, T. J., Cearley, D. W., Cappuccio, D. J., Scott, D., Kumar, R., & Robertson, B. (2009). Gartner highlights five attributes of cloud computing. *Gartner Report*, Vol G00167182, pp. 1–5.
8. Sreekanti, V., Wu, C., Lin, X. C., Schleier-Smith, J., Gonzalez, J. E., Hellerstein, J. M., & Tumanov, A. (2020). Cloudburst: Stateful functions-as-a-service. *Proceedings of the VLDB Endowment, 13*(12), 2438–2452. https://doi.org/10.14778/3407790.3407795.

CHAPTER 7

SERVERLESS COMPUTING USING MACHINE LEARNING

Contents

INTRODUCTION

Artificial intelligence and machine learning have long been the newest developments in computer science. Machine learning makes it possible for computers to identify patterns and trends in the data that is supplied during the training stage. Computers are programmed to use historical data to inform their decisions about fresh input. These choices are based solely on the information the computer learned during training and are made without the need for explicit coding. Both time and resources are needed for the training process. The primary components required for resource-intensive training are GPU, RAM, and CPU resources. It costs money to own each of these resources separately. Using cloud computing has emerged as a practical way to address this issue. By leasing resources for the necessary amount of time, cloud computing enables users to use resources for a fraction of the cost. An increasing number of models are being trained on the cloud as cloud computing becomes more and more popular. Because of this, more and more cloud instances—which need ongoing maintenance and monitoring—are being used by researchers and developers. It's also critical to remember that the cloud service provider only bears liability for the services' underlying hardware. The user is responsible for managing the operating system, updates, patches, and other software. Managing the libraries and their versions falls under this as well. One kind of service that lets users concentrate on creating solutions is serverless computing. Cloud service providers give the user a few options that are reasonably easy to customize to their specific needs, while abstracting the specifics of the underlying hardware and software infrastructure. This helps the developer because they can devote more of their time to solving the issue at hand rather than resolving unnecessary server-related issues. Furthermore, serverless computing can be carried out in private settings. This can be used to test several hypotheses concurrently, which benefits the developer.

7.1. UNDERSTANDING SERVERLESS MACHINE LEARNING

A new class of loosely coupled serverless services called serverless machine learning (ML) provides the computational and storage needs for AI-enabled goods and services. Batch inference pipelines, training pipelines, and feature pipelines are all coordinated and executed by serverless compute services. Reusable features, training data, models, and prediction logs are the results of these machine learning pipelines. In serverless machine learning, state is managed by a serverless feature/model store. Finally, online models that are reachable through network endpoints are supported by serverless model serving.

The primary cause of many data scientists' impasse in the model development and training phases is the absence of infrastructure support for quickly deploying models and prediction services using inference pipelines, as well as for quickly connecting models to data using feature pipelines. Data scientists can use only Python to implement machine learning-powered prediction services thanks to serverless machine learning (Figure 7.1).

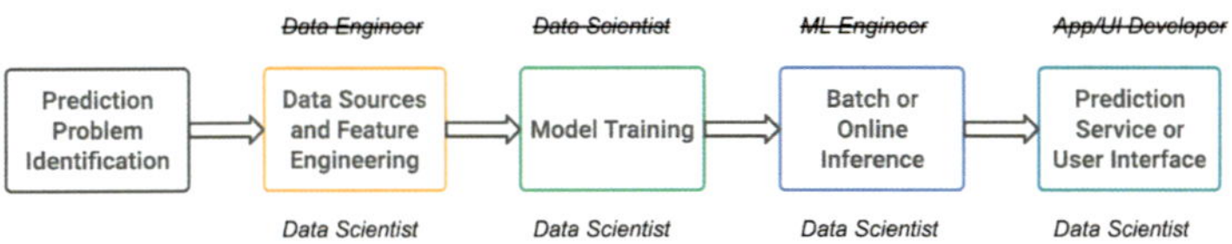

Figure 7.1. *Serverless machine learning enables data scientists, fluent in python, to build complete ml systems, from feature engineering to model training to inference and user interfaces.*

Source: https://www.serverless-ml.org/blog/what-is-serverless-machine-learning#:~:text=Serverless%20machine%20learning%20enables%20 Data,to%20inference%20and%20user%20interfaces.

A data flow of processing and storing steps is implemented by machine learning systems, commencing with input data, features, and trained models. The process concludes with a prediction service that utilizes the model and inference data, as well as a monitoring service that provides prediction logs for observability and debugging [Naik, Vidish, 2021].

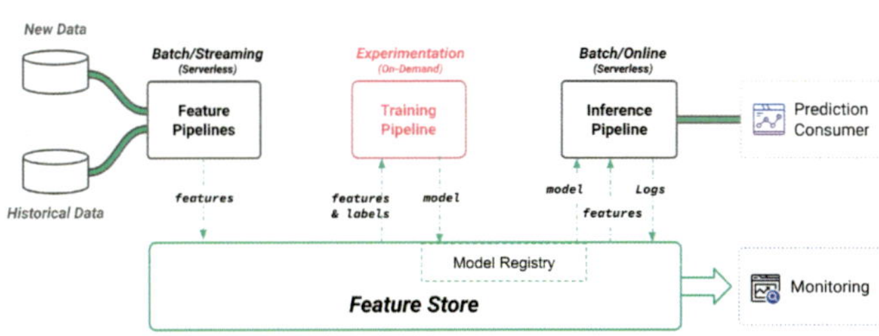

Figure 7.2. *Essentially all monolithic ML pipelines can be refactored into independent feature pipelines, training pipelines, and inference pipelines. These pipelines are decoupled sharing state through a feature store and model registry. The 3 pipelines can be scaled independently, run on a schedule or on-demand – training is often just run on-demand, while feature/inference pipelines are operational services that are either run on a schedule or run 24x7.*

Source: https://www.serverless-ml.org/blog/what-is-serverless-machine-learning#:~:text=Serverless%20machine%20learning%20enables%20 Data,to%20inference%20and%20user%20interfaces.

The machine learning pipeline stages are refactored into separate feature engineering, training, and inference pipelines in a serverless ML system. These pipelines exchange information by reading inputs from and storing outputs in a feature store or model registry. The feature store has the ability to store prediction logs, which consist of features and predicted labels, allowing for the tracking of models' accuracy, efficiency, and observability (Figure 7.2).

Not everyone is yet a good fit for serverless ML. A managed cloud offering, which allows the service to be deployed and managed inside the customer's cloud account, is absent from many serverless services. Because of this, some businesses will avoid utilizing SaaS services that handle sensitive client data.

7.1.1. MLOps without the Infra

To deploy ML in production, you do not need to learn Cloud Infrastructure or Kubernetes. To run a machine learning system in production, you must, nevertheless, understand the fundamentals of machine learning operations (MLOps) as well as how to put them into practice.

Versioning and testing of machine learning assets are two of MLOps' core tenets. Models and data (features) are the two most crucial resources. It is commonly known that you should version your machine learning models in order to run A/B tests on them and determine whether or not the newly trained model should take the place of the older one. Models in running machine learning systems usually need historical data (e.g., about a user) or contextual information (current trends). Thus, versioned data (features) are also required for your versioned models.

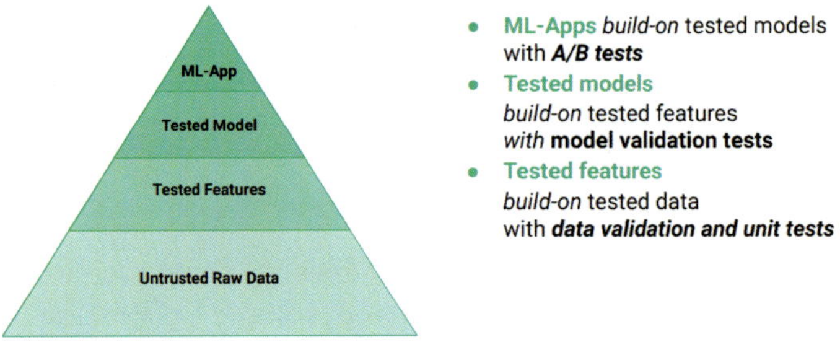

Figure 7.3. *Building ML systems means scaling this pyramid of testing. You should test your features before they are used by models. Models should be tested before used by ML-powered applications.*

Source: https://www.serverless-ml.org/blog/what-is-serverless-machine-learning#:~:text=Serverless%20machine%20learning%20enables%20Data,to%20inference%20and%20user%20interfaces.

Indeed, a hierarchy of dependencies exists amongst the models, data, and ML-Applications that employ the models. Features are the types of data that are used to train models and generate predictions from them. It is difficult to trust the models that are based on your features if you don't test them. Therefore, you should use unit tests for feature logic and data validation when testing your features. In a similar vein, models used in ML-enabled applications ought to be checked for bias and subpar performance. Therefore, before a model is used in an A/B test and deployed in production, it should pass validation tests (Figure 7.3).

7.1.2. Example Serverless ML System

We provide a Serverless ML online course at no cost. We developed both interactive and analytical machine learning systems during the course. Typically, analytical machine learning systems consist of a dashboard with updated predictions every hour or day. Examples of dashboards created from the course include ones that forecast the height of waves at an Irish beach, the sentiment of Bitcoin based on recent tweets, Poland's air quality, and the demand and price of electricity for the next 24 hours.

Once a day, these systems execute a feature pipeline to create a new Iris flower artificially and add it to the feature store. After that, a batch inference pipeline, which also runs once a day but follows the feature pipeline, downloads the trained iris model that predicts the type of iris flower based on four input features: sepal length, sepal width, petal length, and petal width. It does this by reading the single flower that was added that day. In order to determine whether the model predicted correctly, the actual flower (outcome) is read from the feature store and published to the same online dashboard as the model's prediction.

The interactive machine learning systems usually use a model that can be downloaded or hosted from Hopsworks and have a Gradio or Streamlit user interface (on Hugging Face Spaces or Streamlit Cloud). Usually, they gather input from the user, combine it with past features from Hopsworks Feature Store, and generate predictions for the user interface. Examples of systems developed during the course include those that forecast the cost of a home at a specific address in Stockholm, suggest songs for a specific Spotify playlist, extract vocals from a song or sound file, and forecast the likelihood that a Reddit post will be liked or not.

A monitoring dashboard is also included in all of the aforementioned systems to assess model performance, provide information on errors or bugs, and determine when to retrain models (Figure 7.4).

Figure 7.4. *The serverless ML services used in the earlier examples included: (1) Modal for the scheduled feature pipelines, (2) Collaboratory or Modal for training pipelines (run on-demand), (3) Hugging face (gradio/streamlit) or modal or for inference pipelines, and (4) Hopsworks as the serverless feature store, model registry, and model serving layer.*

Source: https://www.serverless-ml.org/blog/what-is-serverless-machine-learning#:~:text=Serverless%20machine%20learning%20enables%20Data,to%20inference%20and%20user%20interfaces.

7.1.3. Serverless ML Ecosystem

Numerous SaaS machine learning platforms exist that serve as the foundation for Serverless ML systems.

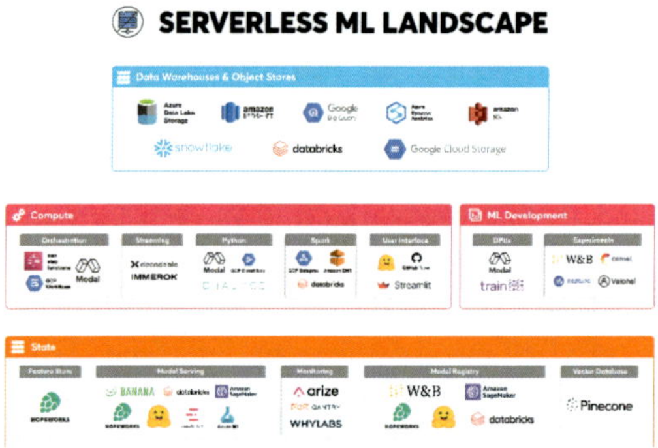

Figure 7.5. *Many companies are providing serverless services that can be plugged in together at the language API level. Here is a selection of some of the serverless ML products available today.*

Source: https://www.serverless-ml.org/blog/what-is-serverless-machine-learning#:~:text=Serverless%20machine%20learning%20enables%20Data,to%20inference%20and%20user%20interfaces.

We loosely group them into four categories in the figure below: ML Development services for model training and experiment management; compute layer for orchestrated pipelines (feature and inference pipelines); raw data layer (data warehouses and object stores); and state layer for features and models as well as model serving and model monitoring (Figure 7.5).

Data scientists can now create fully functional prediction services that leverage ML models instead of limiting themselves to training models in Jupyter notebooks with Serverless Machine Learning. Python proficiency is all that is required to create interactive, self-monitoring ML systems using Severless ML.

7.2. WORKING ON THE SERVERLESS MACHINE LEARNING

Building and implementing machine learning models without having to worry about maintaining servers or infrastructure is known as serverless machine learning, or serverless ML. This system refactors the machine learning pipeline stages into distinct feature engineering, training, and inference pipelines. By reading inputs from a feature store or model registry and saving their outputs, these pipelines exchange data. It makes use of serverless computing concepts, in which resource management, scalability, and server provisioning are automatically handled by the cloud provider. When it comes to running machine learning workloads with as little operational overhead as possible, serverless ML is especially well-liked (Figure 7.6).

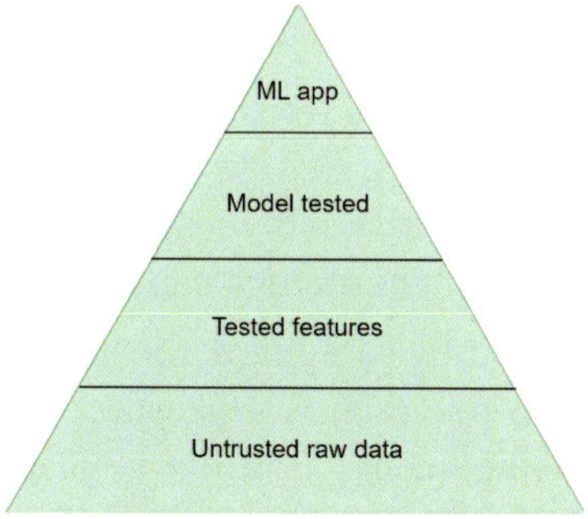

Figure 7.6. *Building ML systems.*

Source: https://www.educative.io/answers/how-does-serverless-machine-learning-work.

Here's how serverless machine learning typically works: (Figure 7.7).

- **Cloud provider:** Azure, Google Cloud, or AWS Lambda are frequently used for implementation. We can run code in response to events on these platforms without having to worry about managing servers.

- **Build a machine learning model:** To begin, we need to build and train a model utilizing various frameworks. Since serverless machine learning typically concentrates on predictions or classifications rather than model training, this model should be optimized for inference.
- **Model deployment:** Rather than deploying a model to a dedicated server, we package a model with inference code into a serverless function. This function is a little piece of code that can start scheduled jobs, HTTP requests, message queues, and other kinds of events.
- **Triggers:** The triggers that will cause the serverless function to be called should be specified. For instance, we design an HTTP endpoint that, upon receiving an HTTP request, forwards data to the ML model for predictions.
- **Scalability:** One of the main advantages of serverless computing is automated scaling. When the trigger happens, the cloud provider automatically supplies the resources required to process the request, guaranteeing that our model can manage fluctuating workloads without the need for manual intervention.
- **Cost optimization:** Since we only pay for the compute resources used during inference, it may be financially advantageous. We do not incur any expenses when there is no incoming traffic. Furthermore, free tiers are frequently offered by serverless platforms for a predetermined usage threshold.
- **Monitoring and logging:** We should set up monitoring and logging to make sure the serverless ML system operates as we had anticipated. Monitoring the quantity of invocations, execution duration, error rates, and other pertinent metrics can be part of this.
- **Security:** In order to safeguard the model, data, and serverless functions, the proper security measures must be put in place. It also entails putting access controls in place, encrypting data, and safeguarding API endpoints.
- **Versioning and deployment:** It's critical to maintain versions of serverless ML models and functions. This gives us the ability to revert to earlier versions in case problems occur.
- **Continuous improvement:** It gains from ongoing development, just like any other machine learning application. When necessary, we can release updated versions of the function and retrain a model using fresh data.

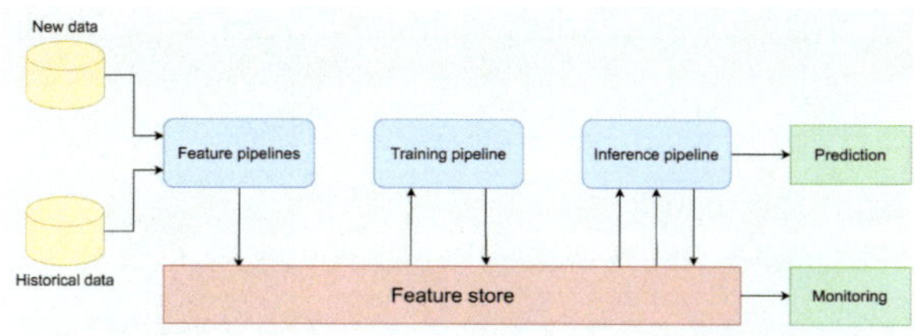

Figure 7.7. *Working of the serverless machine learning.*

Source: https://www.educative.io/answers/how-does-serverless-machine-learning-work.

7.2.1. Implementation

To utilize the scikit-learn model, simply define and load the model using the code below. The following is an illustration of how serverless machine learning functions (Figure 7.8).

```
1  # Import Libraries
2  import json
3  import pandas as pd
4  from sklearn import datasets
5  from sklearn.ensemble import RandomForestClassifier
6
7  # Use built-in dataset
8  iris = datasets.load_iris()
9  X, y = iris.data, iris.target
10 # Create and train a scikit-learn model by using the random forest classifier
11 model = RandomForestClassifier(n_estimators=100)
12 model.fit(X, y)
13 # Predict the function
14 def predict(InputData):
15     # Try the catch method
16     try:
17         # Convert the input data to a DataFrame
18         inputdf = pd.DataFrame([InputData])
19
20         # Make predictions using the loaded model
21         predictions = model.predict(inputdf)
22
23         return {'Prediction value': predictions.tolist()}
24     except Exception as e:
25         return {'Error': str(e)}
26
27 # Example input data
28 InputData = {"sepal_length": 5.1, "sepal_width": 3.5, "petal_length": 1.4, "petal_width": 0.2}
29
30 # Call the predict function with the input data
31 result = predict(InputData)
32 print(result)
33
```

Figure 7.8. *Implementation of serverless machine learning model.*

Source: https://www.educative.io/answers/how-does-serverless-machine-learning-work.

Explanation:

- **Lines 2–5:** We import the libraries.
- **Lines 8–9:** We use a built-in iris dataset.
- **Lines 11–12:** We create and train a scikit-learn model that RandomForestClassifier directly within the code.
- **Lines 14–25:** We define the predict function, which takes InputData, converts it into a DataFrame, and makes predictions using the

model. Instead of loading a model from a pickle file, we use the model object defined and trained in the code.

- **Lines 28–32:** Input data to test the model, so we call the function and print the result.

7.3. FAAS WITH MACHINE LEARNING

The way we model software and solutions has changed as a result of cloud computing. More economical, intelligent, and efficient solutions are always in demand. The next generation of built-in intelligent software is being driven by machine learning (ML), and "serverless" computing is revolutionizing the way we use cloud computing platforms to create applications that are more productive, simple, and efficient. A serverless cloud provider receives code uploaded at the function level, and the cloud provider handles the executing of the code by dynamically allocating resources. This is known as serverless computing. It's an event-driven model, meaning that in almost real time, your application will react to triggers and events. Functions as a Service is another name for this concept (FaaS).

Whether a project is using other cloud computing services or creates its own cloud application, there are many benefits to implementing a serverless architecture.

- **Savings:** Since most serverless solutions are usage-based, you only pay for the quantity and duration of function executions; idle servers are not billed.
- **Minimal administrative overhead:** development teams are distracted by server management. By removing server management from the deployment workflow, serverless computing allows you to concentrate solely on the logic.
- **Decentralized deployment:** Using a RESTFul interface, serverless architecture, which adheres to the Microservice Principle, enables you to deploy your model as a service. It conceals the implementation details and separates the service from other modules in addition to offering simple and quick deployment.
- **Auto scaling:** You don't have to worry about scaling when you use serverless architecture. It will transparently handle load spikes and keep your service operating smoothly even if the volume of requests increases dramatically.
- **Reusability:** You can use your models for a range of tasks because the service is only called via events and triggers.

In other words, going serverless transfers the most difficult aspect of maintaining server infrastructure to your cloud provider, who takes care of scaling, networking, resource allocation, and other issues.

Because of this, serverless computing frees you up to concentrate on developing features and applications rather than maintaining servers and other infrastructure. You should consider certain possible limitations of the serverless architecture when planning and budgeting for your project.

Make sure your cloud provider is compatible with the skills on your team and supports the languages and frameworks that are essential to your application.

To what extent is it simple to create, troubleshoot, and implement applications in the vendor's environment from your own? Can you easily integrate your serverless components with other parts of your application, like storage buckets, databases, and logging infrastructure? Do the management and administration tools offered by the cloud provider meet your needs?

Aside from these possible issues, the benefits outweigh the cost for many applications.

7.3.1. Serverless Architecture with Azure Functions

To give developers options for serverless computing, all of the major cloud vendors have already entered the market. These are just a handful of the things that are offered right now:

- Microsoft Azure Functions
- Alibaba Cloud Function Compute
- Amazon AWS Lambda
- Google Cloud Functions
- IBM Cloud Functions (using Apache OpenWhisk)

We'll look at Azure Functions in this section to see how simple it is to create and launch a cloud application. Microsoft's fully managed event-driven serverless compute solution, Azure Functions, makes it simple to run brief bursts of code in the cloud.

To link the invoked function with input data sources or output services, it makes use of built-in triggers (HTTP, timer, or any other event available from the sister Azure Event Hubs service) and bindings (Blob, Cosmos Db, Queue, and so forth) (Figure 7.9).

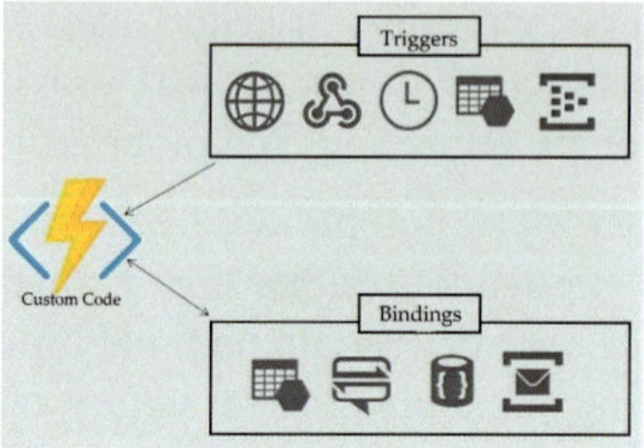

Figure 7.9. *Azure functions uses built-in triggers (HTTP, timer or any other event available from the sister azure event hubs service) and bindings (Blob, Cosmos Db, Queue and so on) to connect the invoked function with input data sources or output services.*

Source: https://contentlab.com/serverless-computing-an-introduction-to-faas-with-machine-learning/.

You can write functions in C, JavaScript, F, Java, and Python (preview version only) using Azure Functions. Using the user-friendly web interface or your preferred integrated development environment, you can test and debug locally. When your code is ready, there are many different deployment models available to you, such as ZIP upload, running straight from a package, continuous deployment via App Service continuous integration and many of the popular source code repositories, and more.

7.3.2. Building a Sample ML Function

We'll now show how to create a basic Python ML example solution using Azure Functions and a serverless architecture. We'll use the well-known machine learning example of categorizing and forecasting pictures of iris flowers.

An HTTP trigger will be utilized to deduce the species of iris flowers from a trained model. Based on the flower's features, the Azure Function is meant to determine the class and return the classification as an output (Figure 7.10).

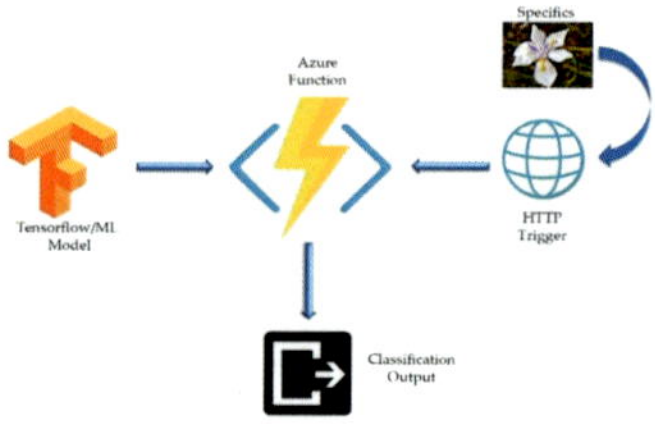

Figure 7.10. *ML example of classifying and predicting images of Iris flowers.*

Source: https://contentlab.com/serverless-computing-an-introduction-to-faas-with-machine-learning/.

To get started you'll need an active Azure subscription. To follow the example you'll also need the following tools installed in your development environment:

- Python 3.6
- Azure Functions Core Tools
- Azure CLI

Once you have the prerequisites installed, create and activate a virtual environment named .env:

```
python3.6 -m venv .env

source .env/bin/activate
```

Create a local function project by executing the following command:

```
func init predict-iris-function
```

Choose python for the runtime.

```
File Edit View Search Terminal Help
mehreen@mehreen-Inspiron-3542:~$ python3.6 -m venv .env
mehreen@mehreen-Inspiron-3542:~$ source .env/bin/activate
(.env) mehreen@mehreen-Inspiron-3542:~$ func init predict-iris-function
Select a worker runtime:
1. dotnet
2. node
3. python (preview)
Choose option: 3
python
Writing .funcignore
Writing .gitignore
Writing host.json
Writing local.settings.json
Writing /home/mehreen/predict-iris-function/.vscode/extensions.json
(.env) mehreen@mehreen-Inspiron-3542:~$
```

Now we need to create our desired function. Change the directory to the newly created folder and create a new function as follows:

```
func new
```

When prompted for a template, choose the "HTTP trigger" template. Name it predict_type.

```
File Edit View Search Terminal Help
(.env) mehreen@mehreen-Inspiron-3542:~$ cd predict-iris-function/
(.env) mehreen@mehreen-Inspiron-3542:~/predict-iris-function$ func new
Select a template:
1. Azure Blob Storage trigger
2. Azure Cosmos DB trigger
3. Azure Event Grid trigger
4. Azure Event Hub trigger
5. HTTP trigger
6. Azure Queue Storage trigger
7. Azure Service Bus Queue trigger
8. Azure Service Bus Topic trigger
9. Timer trigger
Choose option: 5
HTTP trigger
Function name: [HttpTrigger] predict_type
Writing /home/mehreen/predict-iris-function/predict_type/sample.dat
Writing /home/mehreen/predict-iris-function/predict_type/__init__.py
Writing /home/mehreen/predict-iris-function/predict_type/function.json
The function "predict_type" was created successfully from the "HTTP trigger" tem
plate.
(.env) mehreen@mehreen-Inspiron-3542:~/predict-iris-function$
```

Though it has been created, the function is empty. You can test and run it, but at this point it isn't doing what we need it to. This is where ML comes in. To support the model, a few libraries are needed. Append the requirements.txt file as follows:

```
azure-functions==1.0.0a5
azure-functions-worker==1.0.0a6
grpcio==1.14.2
grpcio-tools==1.14.2
protobuf==3.6.1
six==1.11.0
numpy
sklearn
scipy
```

You can just copy the model to the function directory.

Let's move ahead and code our main function:

```
import azure.functions
import pickle
import sys
import os

import numpy as np

def main(req: azure.functions.HttpRequest):

  # loading the model
  f = open('predict_type/model.pkl', 'rb')
  model = pickle.load(f)

  # request new features for sample
  sepal_length = float(req.params['slen'])
  sepal_width = float(req.params['swid'])
  petal_length = float(req.params['plen'])
  petal_width = float(req.params['pwid'])

  # setting new sample
  new_flower = [[sepal_length,
                 sepal_width,
                 petal_length,
                 petal_width]]

  # adding random features to match the training data
  n=40
  random_features = np.random.RandomState(0)
  new_flower_with_random_features = np.c_[new_flower,
    random_features.randn(1, n)]

  # getting prediction on the new sample
  prediction = model.predict(new_flower_with_random_features)

  return np.array_str(prediction)
```

The code is pretty self-explanatory. I just loaded a pre-trained model and added some random features that would match the training data. I invoke the function by specifying the values for new sample flower: sepal_length, sepal_width, petal_length and petal_width.

Before testing the function, change the scriptFile name in function.json file.

```
"scriptFile": "main.py"
```

Now that everything's in-place, install the required libraries and start the host function.

```
pip install -r
requirements.txt
func host start
```

```
File Edit View Search Terminal Help
(.env) mehreen@mehreen-Inspiron-3542:~/predict-iris-function$ func host start
```

It will only take a few seconds to apply the configuration and would provide you the URL at which it is listening.

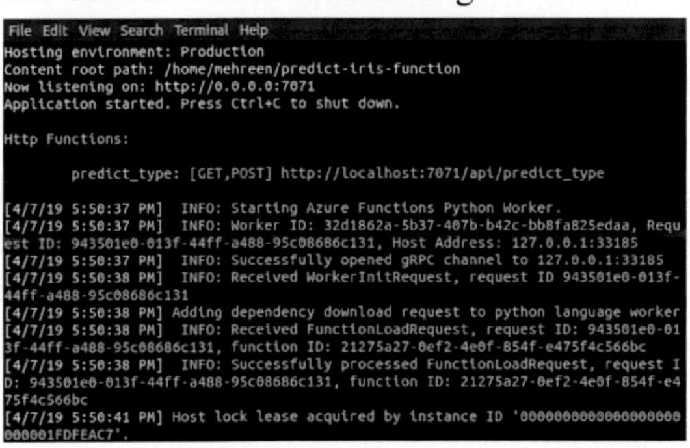

```
File Edit View Search Terminal Help
Hosting environment: Production
Content root path: /home/mehreen/predict-iris-function
Now listening on: http://0.0.0.0:7071
Application started. Press Ctrl+C to shut down.

Http Functions:

        predict_type: [GET,POST] http://localhost:7071/api/predict_type

[4/7/19 5:50:37 PM]  INFO: Starting Azure Functions Python Worker.
[4/7/19 5:50:37 PM]  INFO: Worker ID: 32d1862a-5b37-407b-b42c-bb8fa825edaa, Requ
est ID: 943501e0-013f-44ff-a488-95c08686c131, Host Address: 127.0.0.1:33185
[4/7/19 5:50:37 PM]  INFO: Successfully opened gRPC channel to 127.0.0.1:33185
[4/7/19 5:50:38 PM]  INFO: Received WorkerInitRequest, request ID 943501e0-013f-
44ff-a488-95c08686c131
[4/7/19 5:50:38 PM] Adding dependency download request to python language worker
[4/7/19 5:50:38 PM]  INFO: Received FunctionLoadRequest, request ID: 943501e0-01
3f-44ff-a488-95c08686c131, function ID: 21275a27-0ef2-4e0f-854f-e475f4c566bc
[4/7/19 5:50:38 PM]  INFO: Successfully processed FunctionLoadRequest, request I
D: 943501e0-013f-44ff-a488-95c08686c131, function ID: 21275a27-0ef2-4e0f-854f-e4
75f4c566bc
[4/7/19 5:50:41 PM] Host lock lease acquired by instance ID '0000000000000000000
000001FDFEAC7'.
```

Test the deployed model by executing the following:

curl -w 'n' 'http://localhost:7071/api/predict_type?plen=2.0&pwid=2.0&slen=2.0&swid=2.0'

You can also try and test the model by specifying different values for features.

```
File Edit View Search Terminal Help
mehreen@mehreen-Inspiron-3542:~$ curl -w '\n' 'http://localhost:7071/api/predict
_type?plen=2.0&pwid=2.0&slen=2.0&swid=2.0'
[
  "Iris-versicolor"
]
mehreen@mehreen-Inspiron-3542:~$ curl -w '\n' 'http://localhost:7071/api/predict
_type?plen=4.0&pwid=4.0&slen=4.0&swid=4.0'
[
  "Iris-virginica"
]
mehreen@mehreen-Inspiron-3542:~$
```

Observe the output on the other screen each time you pass the URL for inference. The HTTP trigger function is invoked and processes the request.

7.3.3. Publishing to Azure Functions

The function was written locally, and it was tested there as well. Publishing the local project to Azure Functions is the next step. You must have a local machine connection to Azure. You can choose which subscription to use for your service deployment when you sign into the Azure portal using Visual Studio Code. Once the portal is open, use the command pallet to look for Azure Functions: Deploy to Function App. Follow the instructions and give the function app, resource group, and storage account a unique name (you don't need a storage account for HTTP triggers, but you can for other events). You can view every Azure resource that has been created by looking at the output panel.

You can navigate to the Function App endpoint and pass your query parameters once it has successfully deployed. In order to publish your service on Azure, you can also use Azure Functions Core Tools and Docker to automatically build and configure the necessary binaries. Use the name of your Linux Function App to execute the following command.

```
func azure functionapp publish <APP_NAME> --build-native-deps
```

We discussed the idea of serverless computing in this section, along with some advantages of FaaS and some architectural considerations for serverless computing projects. We also saw how simple it is to create and test a function using Azure Functions, then publish it there to make your model available as an API. Our example illustrated how you might be able to take advantage of the potential power of microservices AI/ML applications by incorporating some machine learning components. You can also begin to see how serverless architecture in general, and Azure Functions specifically, can reduce DevOps headaches and expedite the development cycle: you can tailor language and deployment requirements to your team's best practices and strengths, and you don't have to worry about servers, containerization, or scaling.

7.4. DISTRIBUTED DOUBLE MACHINE LEARNING WITH A SERVERLESS ARCHITECTURE

V. Chernozhukov et al. (2018) discusses the DML application for model classes such as the interactive regression model, interactive instrumental variable model, partially linear regression model, and interactive regression model. Many model classes, including reinforcement learning, transformation models, generalized additive models, continuous treatment effects, dynamic treatment effects, Gaussian graphical models, difference-in-differences models, and many more, have recently been added to the DML framework and related techniques. Statistical inference for a causal parameter θ_0 is typically of interest in these

DML applications. The DML framework allows for the estimation of nuisance functions, denoted as η_0, while taking advantage of the excellent prediction quality of machine learning techniques to produce valid statistical inference for η_0.

As an example, we consider the partially linear regression (PLR) model as studied by P. M. Robinson. (1988):

$$Y = D\theta_0 + g_0(X) + U, \qquad \mathbb{E}(U|X, D) = 0, \qquad (7.1)$$

$$D = m_0(X) + V, \qquad \mathbb{E}(V|X) = 0, \qquad (7.2)$$

with outcome variable Y, treatment/policy variable D and the potentially high-dimensional vector of controls $X := (X_1, \ldots, X_p)$. The causal parameter of interest is θ_0. It measures the average treatment effect of D on Y, if D is conditionally exogenous. The confounding variables X affect D via the function $m0$ (X) and Y via the function g_0 (X). Figure 7.11 visualizes the interpretation in a causal diagram. The DML framework allows to obtain valid statistical inference for θ_0 while exploiting the excellent prediction quality of machine learning methods when estimating the nuisance functions $\eta_0 = (g_0, m_0)$. In the DML framework the nuisance functions $\eta_0 = (g_0, m_0)$ can be estimated with different ML-methods, e.g., V. Chernozhukov, et al. (2018) use random forests, regression trees, boosting, lasso, neural networks and ensembles of these methods. Depending on the structural assumptions on η_0, different ML-methods are appropriate.

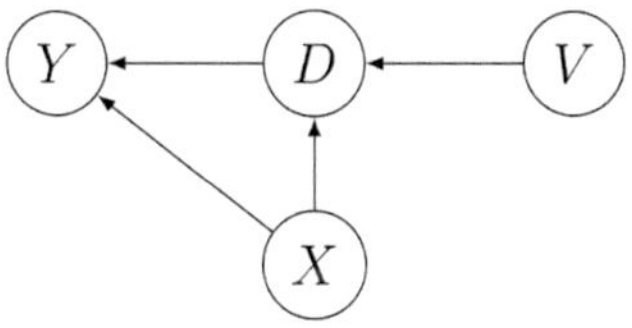

Figure 7.11. *Causal diagram for the PLR model.*

Source: Malte S. Kurz. 2021. Distributed Double Machine Learning with a Serverless Architecture. In Companion of the 2021 ACM/SPEC International Conference on Performance Engineering (ICPE '21 Companion), April 19–23, 2021, Virtual Event, France. ACM, New York, NY, USA, 7 pages. https://doi.org/10.1145/3447545.3451181.

A key component of the DML framework are so-called Neyman orthogonal score functions ψ $(W; \theta, \eta)$. The score functions identify the causal parameter of interest θ_0 as the unique solution to $E(\psi(W; \theta_0, \eta_0)) = 0$. Neyman orthogonality of ψ $(W; \theta, \eta)$ with respect to the nuisance functions η guarantees that there are no first-order effects of estimation errors in the nuisance functions on the estimation of the causal parameter θ_0.

Sample splitting is a crucial element of the DML framework, which serves to prevent biases resulting from overfitting. Further advice for applying repeated cross-fitting is provided in V. Chernozhukov et al. 2018. Because of this, it works especially well in distributed architectures where the computationally demanding inference tasks are carried out concurrently. In order to approximate nuisance functions in various sample splits, the estimation of typical DML models frequently necessitates the estimation and prediction of several hundred ML models. A challenging objective for a serverless DML implementation would be to make it so that, when using repeated cross-fitting, estimating the entire DML model doesn't take significantly longer than estimating the nuisance functions on a single fold. Such an objective can be accomplished in an on-demand setup without the need to start and maintain a sizable computing cluster, which is becoming expensive if left idle, thanks to the great elasticity of serverless cloud computing.

The DML algorithm with repeated cross-fitting can be summarized as follows (w.l.o.g. we assume that the number of observations N is divisible by the number of folds K):

1. For each $m \in [M] := \{1, \ldots, M\}$ draw a K-fold random partition $(I_{m,k})_{k \in K}$ of observation indices $[N] := \{1, \ldots, N\}$ of size $n = N/K$. Define $I^c_{m,k} := [N] \setminus I_{m,k}$ and for each k construct a ML estimator $\hat{\eta}_{0,k} = \hat{\eta}_0((W_i)_{i \in I^c_{m,k}})$.

2. For each sample split, compute an estimate $\tilde{\theta}_{0,m}$ of the causal parameter as the solution to the equation $\frac{1}{N}\sum_{k=1}^{K}\sum_{i \in I_{m,k}} \psi(W_i; \tilde{\theta}_{0,m}, \hat{\eta}_{0,k}) = 0.$

The final estimate for the causal parameter is obtain via aggregation $\tilde{\theta}_0 = \text{Median}((\tilde{\theta}_{0,m})_{m \in [M]})$.

Note that the number of nuisance functions, which need to be estimated with ML methods, depends on the considered model, e.g., for the PLR model we have $L = 2$ nuisance functions $\eta_0 = (g_0, m_0)$. The total number of ML fits is $M \times K \times L$, i.e., one ML estimation in each fold, of each repeated sample splitting and for each nuisance function. For example, V. Chernozhukov, et al. (2018) choose $K = 5$ (or $K = 2$) and $M = 100$, which for the PLR model with $L = 2$ nuisance functions amounts to 1000 (or 400) ML fits or for the partially linear instrumental variable model with $L = 3$ nuisance functions it amounts to 1500 (or 600) ML fits. Keep in mind that, with regard to the interactive regression models examined in Chernozhukov et al. (2018), additional annoyance functions must be calculated. As previously mentioned, our serverless DML prototype enables the parallelization of all 1000 machine learning tasks, potentially leading to a significant speedup in the estimation of DML models. In essence, the time required to estimate a single nuisance function for one fold in a single sample split could be nearly eliminated by repeatedly cross-fitting with five folds and 100 repetitions. Note that we do not require to transfer the estimated ML models for the nuisance functions $\hat{\eta}_{0,k}$, instead it suffices to return the predictions on the test datasets (i.e., for the observations indexed with $i \in I_{m,k}$) to evaluate the score function and solve for the causal parameter $\tilde{\theta}_{0,m}$in a second step.

Neyman orthogonal score functions for many model classes, like for example the PLR model, can be written as linear functions in the parameter θ, i.e.,

$$\psi(W;\theta;\eta) = \theta\psi_a(W;\eta) + \psi_b(W;\eta).$$

This common property forms the basis for a very general object-oriented implementation of DML models in the Python package DoubleML , which serves as a basis four our prototype DoubleMLServerless.

7.4.1. Serverless Double Machine Learning

Corresponding to PyWren [Eric Jonas, et al. In [2017], we present DoubleMLServerless, a prototype implementation designed for interactive use: the user runs a Python session on a local machine or server, but can also access high parallelism for the computationally demanding tasks during DML model estimation through an on-demand and pay-per-request interface. Compared to PyWren, which can execute nearly any kind of parallel task—for instance, map reduce—our implementation is more tailored to the particular use case of DML models. Serverless FaaS is offered by numerous cloud providers. Our Python-based DoubleMLServerless prototype, which extends the DoubleML package, makes use of AWS Lambda.

7.4.1.1. The Architecture of DoubleML-Serverless

Figure 7.12 provides a summary of DoubleML-Serverless architecture. We use AWS S3 object storage for data storage. We implement a DoubleMLDataS3 class in the DoubleML-Serverless package, which functions as a data backend. It mainly extends the DoubleML class DoubleMLData, from which it is derived, by providing methods for transferring datasets to and from AWS S3. The model classes, such as DoubleMLPLRServerless for the PLR model, add methods to the corresponding DoubleML package classes to enable AWS Lambda to be used for the ML estimation and prediction step. AWS region and the name of the deployed lambda function must be provided by the user upon initialization, in addition to the usual inputs for DoubleML model classes. The fit_aws_lambda() method can then be called to estimate the DML model. Each request is comprised of the sample splitting, names of target variables and confounders that are specific to the nuisance function, and a reference to the dataset on S3. The predictions for the corresponding test indices are returned by the lambda function.

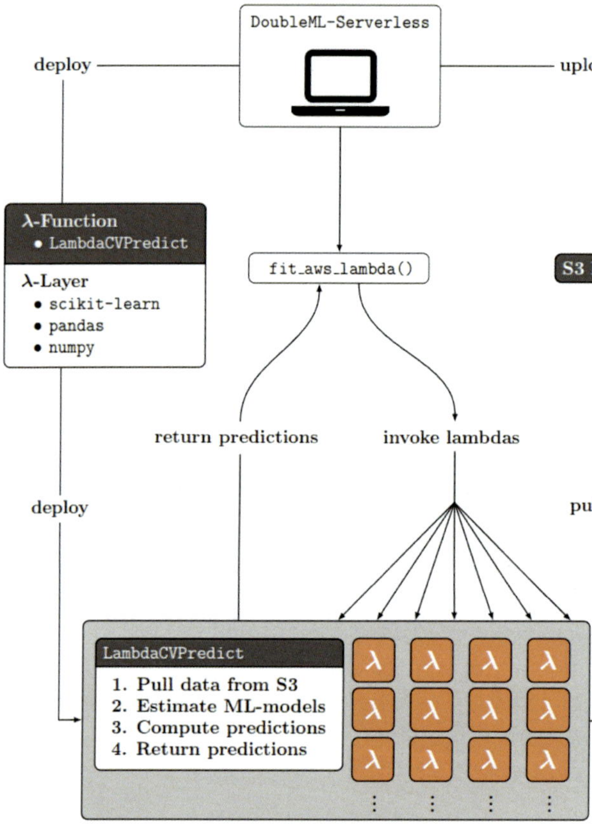

Figure 7.12. *DoubleML-serverless: architecture.*

Source: Malte S. Kurz. 2021. Distributed Double Machine Learning with a Serverless Architecture. In Companion of the 2021 ACM/SPEC International Conference on Performance Engineering (ICPE '21 Companion), April 19–23, 2021, Virtual Event, France. ACM, New York, NY, USA, 7 pages. https://doi.org/10.1145/3447545.3451181.

7.4.1.2. The Level of Scaling

Two distinct levels of scaling are available with our DoubleML-Serverless prototype implementation. The PLR class DoubleMLPLRServerless's level of scaling options are visualized in Figure 7.13. By selecting scaling = 'n_rep,' per-samplesplit scaling can be accomplished. For every nuisance function, it causes a lambda function to be called and a repeated sample split, i.e., for each of Figure 7.13's blue rectangles. Each time this kind of invocation occurs, *K* machine learning models are estimated and the corresponding test index predictions are returned. An alternative is to use scaling = 'n_folds * n_rep,' which will call a different lambda for every sample split, nuisance function, and single fold, i.e., for each orange rectangle in Figure 7.13.

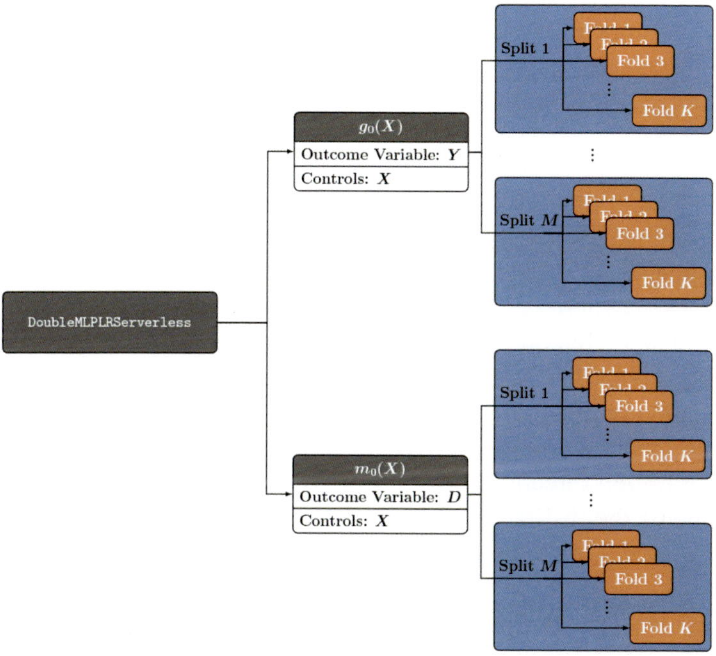

Figure 7.13. *DoubleML-serverless: level of scaling.*

Source: Malte S. Kurz. 2021. Distributed Double Machine Learning with a Serverless Architecture. In Companion of the 2021 ACM/SPEC International Conference on Performance Engineering (ICPE '21 Companion), April 19–23, 2021, Virtual Event, France. ACM, New York, NY, USA, 7 pages. https://doi.org/10.1145/3447545.3451181.

Reexamining the PLR model with $K = 5$ folds, $M = 100$ splits, and $L = 2$ nuisance functions, we can see that we either sent 200 requests or 1000 requests with $M \times K \times L$. The specific use case determines which scaling level is best. First off, based on the machine learning approach and dataset size, it is possible that the estimation of *K* machine learning models will take longer than the maximum runtime, in which case the per-sample-split scaling cannot be used. This is implied by the runtime limit of AWS Lambda. Additionally, there's always a cost versus. The user can adjust the estimation-time tradeoff by adjusting the memory allotted and the scaling parameter.

7.4.1.3. Deployment with AWS SAM

The AWS Serverless Application Model (AWS SAM) allows us to deploy our FaaS to AWS Lambda in a user-friendly manner. Serverless applications can be easily deployed to AWS Lambda with the help of AWS SAM, which is configured through template files. In order to visualize the architecture, we added an AWS SAM template to our prototype that deploys the following components (see Figure 7.12):

- A lambda function called LambdaCVPredict.
- A layer providing the Python libraries scikit-learn, pandas and numpy together with their dependencies.
- An S3 bucket for the data transfer (can be optionally generated, or an existing bucket is used).
- A role for the execution of the lambda function LambdaCVPredict which consists of the AWS-managed AWSLambdaBasicExecutionRole policy plus read access to the S3 bucket for data transfer.

The primary function called when estimating DML models on AWS Lambda is LambdaCVPredict. The primary benefit of using AWS SAM is that it only requires two calls for deployment: sam build and sam deploy guided. Furthermore, the AWS Serverless Application Repository offers an even easier deployment option directly based on the same SAM template. For estimating DML models, the listing in the AWS Serverless Application Repository functions as a kind of "bring me to the cloud" button.

7.4.2. Estimating Double Machine Learning Models with DoubleML-Serverless

To demonstrate our prototype implementation DoubleML-Serverless we revisit the Pennsylvania Reemployment Bonus experiment and estimate the effect of provisioning a cash bonus on the unemployment duration as studied in V. Chernozhukov, et al. (2018).

7.4.2.1. Experiment Setup

The experiment setup is based on the PLR model that was previously discussed. 500 regression trees are used in a random forest to estimate the nuisance functions g_0 and m_0. K = 5 folds and M = 100 splits are our choices. The following data is sent to LambdaCVPredict upon invocation:

- The name of the outcome variable, e.g., for g_0 the Y column.
- The names of the controls, e.g., for g_0 the X columns.

- The ML model to be estimated, e.g., random forest.
- The set of indices $I_{m,k}$.

In Listing 1 we provide sample code which demonstrates the syntax to estimate the described DML model with DoubleML-Serverless for the bonus dataset.

1. Listing 1: Estimation of a Partially Linear Regression (PLR) Model with DoubleML-Serverless.

```
from doubleml.datasets import fetch_bonus
from doubleml_serverless import DoubleMLDataS3, DoubleMLPLRServerless
from sklearn.base import clone
from sklearn.ensemble import RandomForestRegressor

df_bonus = fetch_bonus('DataFrame')
dml_data_bonus = DoubleMLDataS3(
    'doubleml-serverless-data', 'bonus_data.csv', df_bonus,
    y_col='inuidur1', d_cols='tg',
    x_cols=['female', 'black', 'othrace', 'dep1', 'dep2',
        'q2', 'q3', 'q4', 'q5', 'q6', 'agelt35',
        'agegt54', 'durable', 'lusd', 'husd'])
dml_data_bonus.store_and_upload_to_s3()

ml = RandomForestRegressor(n_estimators = 500, n_jobs=-1)
ml_g = clone(ml)
ml_m = clone(ml)
dml_lambda_plr_bonus = DoubleMLPLRServerless(
    'LambdaCVPredict', 'eu-central-1',
    dml_data_bonus, ml_g, ml_m,
    n_folds=5, n_rep=100)

dml_lambda_plr_bonus.fit_aws_lambda()
```

After the FaaS function LambdaCVPredict returns all requested predictions, the score function components for the PLR model at hand are obtained as follows: first, predictions are computed for all $i \in I_{m,k}$. These predictions are obtained by estimating the nuisance function based on the training indices $I^c_{m,k}$.

$$\psi_a(W_i;\hat{\eta}_0) = -(D_i - \hat{m}_0(X_i))(D_i - \hat{m}_0(X_i)),$$
$$\psi_b(W_i;\hat{\eta}_0) = (Y_i - \hat{g}_0(X_i))(D_i - \hat{m}_0(X_i)).$$

Using the evaluated score function components, we can solve for the parameter estimate

$$\tilde{\theta}_0 = \frac{-\sum_{i=1}^{N}\psi_b(W_i;\hat{\eta}_0)}{\sum_{i=1}^{N}\psi_a(W_i;\hat{\eta}_0)}.$$

Using the DoubleML package's functionalities, inference tasks based on the evaluated score function, such as computing standard errors and confidence intervals based on a multiplier bootstrap approach, could be completed quickly and locally.

7.4.2.2. Timings and Costs

Using the aforementioned bonus data example, we conducted a few tests on AWS Lambda to show the usefulness of our prototype DoubleML-Serverless. We pay particular attention to the two distinct scaling parameter settings, i.e., for per-sample-split scaling, use scaling = 'n_rep'; for per-fold scaling, use scaling = 'n_folds * n_rep.' Invocation counts for the aforementioned settings (K = 5 folds and M = 100 splits) are 200 and 1000, respectively. Because AWS Lambda scales other resources proportionately to the allocated memory, we also change the memory that the function has access to during runtime, which also affects CPU power. In Figures 7.14 and 7.15, boxplots are used to illustrate the estimation times and costs after each experiment is run 100 times.

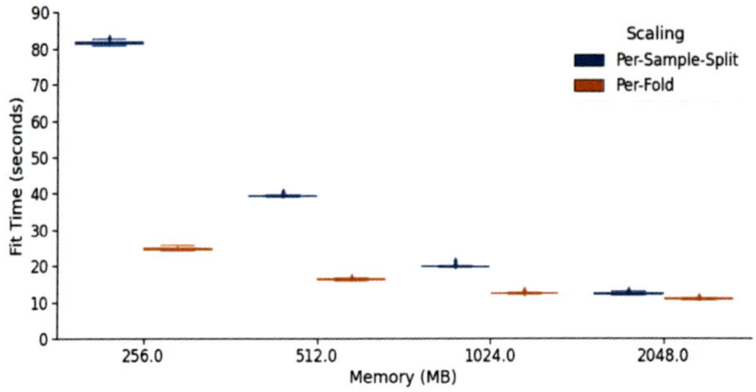

Figure 7.14. *Serverless fit times with different scaling and allocated memory.*

Source: Malte S. Kurz. 2021. Distributed Double Machine Learning with a Serverless Architecture. In Companion of the 2021 ACM/SPEC International Conference on Performance Engineering (ICPE '21 Companion), April 19–23, 2021, Virtual Event, France. ACM, New York, NY, USA, 7 pages. https://doi.org/10.1145/3447545.3451181.

It is evident from Figure 7.14 that increasing memory allocation reduces the overall estimation times for the DML models. However, the marginal improvement in the estimation times is decreasing which is a typical behavior as for example documented in [N. Akhtar, et al. (2020); V. Ishakian, et al. (2018)].

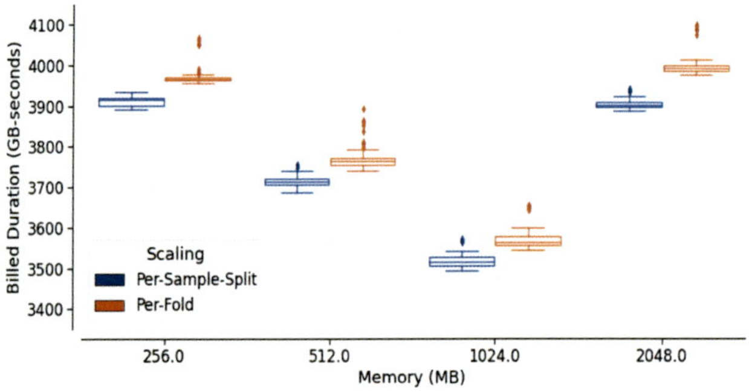

Figure 7.15. *Serverless costs with different scaling and allocated memory.*

Source: Malte S. Kurz. 2021. Distributed Double Machine Learning with a Serverless Architecture. In Companion of the 2021 ACM/SPEC International Conference on Performance Engineering (ICPE '21 Companion), April 19–23, 2021, Virtual Event, France. ACM, New York, NY, USA, 7 pages. https://doi.org/10.1145/3447545.3451181.

It's also critical to remember that speedier estimation does not always translate into higher expenses. Figure 7.15 illustrates how increasing memory allocation—512 MB or 1024 MB in place of 256 MB—could reduce estimation time while simultaneously lowering total estimation costs on AWS Lambda. For serverless computing with AWS Lambda, it is also common to observe that too low or high memory allocations result in higher costs. Based on this observation, cost optimization frameworks have been proposed. Figure 7.14 illustrates how the estimation times can be further reduced by selecting per-fold scaling when comparing the two different levels of scaling. It is noteworthy that the transition from per-sample-split to perfold scaling results in a negligible increase in costs (refer to Figure 7.15). One advantage of serverless computing is that it allows for significant concurrency increases without compromising billing, which is based on actual computing time and typically increases only slightly owing to additional overhead. More specific results for the least expensive scenario in our experiment—the one with 1024 MB of memory allotted and per-sample-split scaling—are given in Table 7.1. We can observe that, over the course of our experiment's 100 repetitions, the estimation time averaged 19 points82 seconds. The average response time was 19:09 seconds from the first lambda's invocation to the predictions we received from each of the 200 invocations. The average computation time for a single invocation was 17:16 seconds. Because of this, we are getting very close to the ambitious goal that, in this setting, estimating the DML model with repeated cross-fitting using serverless computing will only take slightly longer than estimating using a single sample split on a machine with a CPU power comparable to one lambda. The average estimation costs, as shown in Table 7.1, come to 3515.36 GB-seconds, or approximately 0.05858 USD at the current price of 0.0000166667 USD per GB-second that AWS charges in eu-central-1.

Table 7.1. *Serverless Fit Times and Costs with 1024 MB Memory and Per-Sample-Split Scaling (Mean, Min & Max in 100 Runs)*

	Mean	**Min**	**Max**
Fit Time (s)	19.82	19.53	21.49
Billed Duration (GB-s)	3515.36	3492.01	3571.42
Avg. Duration per Invocation (s)	17.16	17.05	17.44
Total Response Time (s)	19.09	18.81	20.76

Source: Malte S. Kurz. 2021. Distributed Double Machine Learning with a Serverless Architecture. In Companion of the 2021 ACM/SPEC International Conference on Performance Engineering (ICPE '21 Companion), April 19–23, 2021, Virtual Event, France. ACM, New York, NY, USA, 7 pages. https://doi.org/10.1145/3447545.3451181.

In this section, we delve into the characteristics, benefits, and drawbacks of the existing DoubleML-Serverless prototype implementation, and we also provide insight into possible future enhancements.

- **Reproducibility and seeds:** To achieve repeatable outcomes, the prototype includes a basic implementation of seeds. For a discussion of parallel random number generation, see the numpy documentation.
- **Launch cold and above the vs. warm invocations:** It is commonly known that utilizing serverless computing has a launch overhead, leading to timing discrepancies between "cold" and "warm" starts. We report timings for warm starts and refer to Eric Jonas, et al. (2019) for a discussion of the phenomenon.
- **Transfer of ML models:** Only a portion of the scikit-learn ML models are supported; the ML models are transferred at invocation using their string representation. An alternate strategy like pickling the students, akin to PyWren, could be used to transfer more advanced students.
- **Data transfer via payloads:** The test indices are transferred and the predictions are returned by the prototype using the payloads. This suggests certain limitations, which might be addressed by putting in place a data transfer via S3.
- **Distributed storage:** The datasets, which are loaded in every learning task, are stored in the Amazon S3 object storage. An alternative would be the AWS Elastic File System (EFS) which can be mounted directly for AWS Lambda calls [James Beswick. 2020].
- **Cost optimization:** The memory allotted to AWS Lambda is its primary configuration parameter. It's crucial to understand that AWS Lambda allots CPU power in direct proportion to memory capacity. As a result, both the overall execution time and the expenses are impacted by memory allocation. Discussions and proposal for cost optimization of serverless applications are provided in [H. Wang, D. Niu, and B. Li. 2019] and implementations of frameworks for cost optimization in A. Casalboni (2020). Our DoubleML-Serverless prototype could likewise be cost-optimized with similar methods.
- **Limits on runtime and memory:** There is currently a 15-minute maximum execution time on AWS Lambda. If the single fold estimation cannot be performed within this bound, then clearly our prototype is not usable. Assuming that the estimation of each task entails a similar amount of effort, the previously discussed scenario with $K = 5$ folds, 100 splits, and two nuisance functions translates to a total estimation time limit of approximately 10.5 days ($5 \times 100 \times 2 \times 15$ minutes). Be aware that AWS Lambda used to raise these limits on a regular basis.

- **Limits on memory:** The memory limit for AWS Lambda has been significantly increased from 3 GB to 10 GB [AWS. 2020]. This suggests that big data applications and models requiring a lot of memory are finding serverless computing to be more and more appealing. These memory limits don't pose a problem for DML applications that are used regularly. Nevertheless, DML is also utilized for very large datasets because it is especially well suited for causal inference in high-dimensional settings. It will be difficult to realize such estimates with our prototype in large, high-dimensional data sets.
- Parameter tuning for DML models: For DML models, hyperparameter tuning is also performed, as is customary in machine learning. It is possible to expand the prototype to accommodate serverless implementation that is efficient and allows for hyperparameter tuning.
- **DML models with multiple treatment variables:** Although the prototype implementation only allows for one treatment variable, it would be simple to extend to support multiple treatment variables, as DoubleML does.

Existing serverfull frameworks for distributed machine learning have a high entry barrier and are frequently expensive if used infrequently or inefficiently, which makes them unsuitable for many users, including econometricians, statisticians, and data scientists. This section delves into the use of serverless cloud computing in double machine learning model estimation. With our AWS Lambda prototype DoubleML-Serverless, statisticians, econometricians, and data scientists can leverage massive parallelism. It can be deployed effortlessly through AWS SAM, making it akin to a "cloud button," and it offers a pay-per-request pricing model.

REFERENCES

1. Akhtar, N., Raza, A., Ishakian, V., & Matta, I. (2020). COSE: Configuring Serverless Functions using Statistical Learning. In *IEEE INFOCOM 2020 - IEEE Conference on Computer Communications* (pp. 129–138). https://doi.org/10.1109/INFOCOM41043.2020.9155363.
2. AWS. (2020). AWS Lambda now supports up to 10 GB of memory and 6 vCPU cores for Lambda Functions. https://aws.amazon.com/about-aws/whats-new/2020/12/aws-lambda-supports-10gb-memory-6-vcpu-cores-lambda-functions/ (accessed on 1 August 2024).
3. Bach, P., Chernozhukov, V., Kurz, M. S., & Spindler, M. (2020). DoubleML–Double Machine Learning in Python. https://github.com/DoubleML/doubleml-for-py (accessed on 1 August 2024).
4. Beswick, J. (2020). Using Amazon EFS for AWS Lambda in your serverless applications. *AWS Compute Blog*. https://aws.amazon.com/blogs/compute/using-amazon-efs-for-aws-lambda-in-your-serverless-applications/ (accessed on 1 August 2024).
5. Casalboni, A. (2020). AWS Lambda Power Tuning. https://github.com/alexcasalboni/aws-lambda-power-tuning (accessed on 1 August 2024).
6. Chernozhukov, V., Chetverikov, D., Demirer, M., Duflo, E., Hansen, C., Newey, W., & Robins, J. (2018). Double/debiased machine learning for treatment and structural parameters. *The Econometrics Journal, 21*(1), C1–C68. https://doi.org/10.1111/ectj.12097.
7. Ishakian, V., Muthusamy, V., & Slominski, A. (2018). Serving Deep Learning Models in a Serverless Platform. In *2018 IEEE International Conference on Cloud Engineering (IC2E)* (pp. 257–262). https://doi.org/10.1109/IC2E.2018.00052.
8. Jonas, E., Pu, Q., Venkataraman, S., Stoica, I., & Recht, B. (2017). Occupy the Cloud: Distributed Computing for the 99%. In *Proceedings of the 2017 Symposium on Cloud Computing* (SoCC '17) (pp. 445–451). Association for Computing Machinery, New York, NY, USA. https://doi.org/10.1145/3127479.3128601.
9. Jonas, E., Schleier-Smith, J., Sreekanti, V., Tsai, C. C., Khandelwal, A., Pu, Q., Shankar, V., Carreira, J., Krauth, K., Yadwadkar, N., Gonzalez, J. E., Popa, R. A., Stoica, I., & Patterson, D. A. (2019). Cloud Programming Simplified: A Berkeley View on Serverless Computing. arXiv:1902.03383 [cs.OS]
10. Naik, V. (2021). Machine Learning Using Serverless Computing. *Master's Projects*, 993. https://doi.org/10.31979/etd.mywt-8ckw.

11. NumPy. (2021). Parallel Random Number Generation. https://numpy.org/doc/stable/reference/random/parallel.html (accessed on 1 August 2024).
12. Robinson, P. M. (1988). Root-N-Consistent Semiparametric Regression. *Econometrica, 56*(4), 931–954. https://doi.org/10.2307/1911232.
13. Wang, H., Niu, D., & Li, B. (2019). Distributed Machine Learning with a Serverless Architecture. In *IEEE INFOCOM 2019–IEEE Conference on Computer Communications* (pp. 1288–1296). https://doi.org/10.1109/INFOCOM.2019.8737391.

CHAPTER 8

WIRELESS SENSOR NETWORK AND SERVERLESS COMPUTING

Contents

INTRODUCTION

For many years, wireless sensor networks (WSNs) have been developed and have shown good performance, low power consumption, and congestion management. Nevertheless, a number of issues remain unresolved, including low hardware and software resource utilization throughout the WSN life cycle, highly-coupled engineering development, and inaccurate cost estimation of the device's lifetime. As a result, we first offer the conceptual framework for a serverless computing-based maintainability implementation for WSN. The ability to meet the WSN product's resource requirements during configuration, trial production, debugging, batch production, deployment, operation, and maintenance phases is referred to as maintainability implementation. Next, we go over how Serverless Computing can be implemented at the software functional level of WSN in order to eliminate hardware interference, significantly increase resource reuse, and decouple device operation and functional development. The idea of Serverless Computing can be applied to the development of WSN platforms from the standpoints of maintainability and cost control. These platforms can facilitate the functions of data management and collection into functional development that might profit from initial investment, thus cutting costs associated with design, manufacturing, and operation.

8.1. WIRELESS SENSOR NETWORK IN SERVERLESS COMPUTING

A wireless sensor network (WSN) in serverless computing represents an advanced and innovative approach to managing and analyzing data collected by spatially distributed sensors. These networks consist of numerous sensor nodes that monitor environmental conditions such as temperature, humidity, light, sound, vibration, pressure, and other physical parameters. Traditionally, data from these sensors is transmitted to a central server for processing and storage. However, integrating serverless computing into WSNs transforms this paradigm by leveraging cloud-based services that automatically manage the underlying infrastructure, allowing developers to focus solely on the application logic.

In serverless computing, also known as Function as a Service (FaaS), cloud providers like AWS Lambda, Azure Functions, and Google Cloud Functions handle the execution of code in response to specific events. This model is highly advantageous for WSNs, which typically generate sporadic and event-driven data. When a sensor detects an event (e.g., a sudden temperature spike), it can trigger a serverless function that processes the data, performs necessary computations, and stores the results or sends alerts as needed. This approach significantly reduces the need for constant server maintenance and can lead to cost savings since users only pay for the compute time they consume. One of the primary benefits of using serverless computing in WSNs is scalability. Serverless architectures automatically scale up to handle high loads and scale down during periods of inactivity, ensuring efficient resource utilization. This elasticity is particularly important for WSNs deployed in environments with variable data generation rates, such as agriculture, smart cities, or industrial monitoring. Furthermore, serverless computing enhances the reliability and availability of WSNs, as cloud providers typically offer robust fault tolerance and redundancy features.

Another critical advantage is the simplification of development and deployment processes. Developers can write modular functions that focus on specific tasks, such as data aggregation, filtering, or anomaly detection, without worrying about server management. These functions can be independently developed, tested, and deployed, fostering a microservices architecture that improves maintainability and flexibility.

However, integrating serverless computing with WSNs also presents challenges. Latency can be a concern, especially for real-time applications requiring immediate responses. While serverless functions execute quickly, the round-trip time to the cloud and back can introduce delays. Additionally, there are security considerations, as data transmitted between sensor nodes and cloud services must be encrypted to prevent unauthorized access and ensure data integrity.

8.1.1. Architecture and Design of Serverless WSNs

Integrating wireless sensor networks (WSNs) with serverless computing platforms represents a significant evolution in the way sensor data is managed, processed, and utilized. WSNs consist of numerous sensor nodes distributed across various environments to monitor and collect data on physical conditions like temperature, humidity, pressure, light, and more. Traditionally, these sensors transmit data to a centralized server or a cloud-based system for storage and analysis. The integration with serverless computing, also known as Function as a Service (FaaS), brings a transformative shift by leveraging the cloud's capability to automatically manage the underlying infrastructure, allowing developers to concentrate on writing application-specific code.

Serverless computing platforms such as AWS Lambda, Azure Functions, and Google Cloud Functions enable the execution of code in response to events, eliminating the need for developers to manage servers or worry about scalability issues. In the context of WSNs, this event-driven model is particularly advantageous as it aligns with the sporadic and sometimes unpredictable nature of sensor data generation. For instance, when a sensor node detects an event like a temperature anomaly or a change in pressure, it can trigger a serverless function to process the data immediately. This function can perform various tasks such as data filtering, aggregation, real-time analytics, or even triggering alerts and notifications.

One of the primary benefits of this integration is scalability. Serverless architectures inherently provide automatic scaling, which means that the system can efficiently handle varying loads of sensor data without manual intervention. During periods of high data influx, such as during a natural disaster or a sudden environmental change, the serverless platform can scale up to accommodate the increased load, ensuring timely processing and analysis. Conversely, during periods of low activity, the platform scales down, reducing costs since users only pay for the actual compute resources used.

Another significant advantage is the reduction in operational complexity and costs. In a traditional setup, maintaining the infrastructure for a WSN can be labor-intensive and expensive, requiring constant monitoring and management. Serverless computing abstracts away these responsibilities, allowing developers to deploy functions quickly without worrying about the underlying hardware. This not only reduces operational overhead but also accelerates the development cycle, enabling faster deployment of new features and improvements.

Security and reliability are also enhanced in a serverless WSN integration. Cloud providers offer robust security features, including data encryption in transit and at rest, identity and access management, and compliance with various industry standards. Additionally, serverless platforms are designed with high availability and fault tolerance, ensuring that sensor data processing remains reliable even in the face of infrastructure failures.

However, challenges such as latency, especially for real-time applications, need to be addressed. While serverless functions execute rapidly, the round-trip time to the cloud and back can introduce delays. Edge computing solutions can be combined with serverless architectures to mitigate this by performing initial data processing closer to the sensor nodes before sending refined data to the cloud.

8.1.2. Scalability and Flexibility:

Scaling serverless applications in response to varying data loads from wireless sensor networks (WSNs) involves several techniques that ensure efficient, reliable, and cost-effective data processing. The inherent nature of serverless computing platforms such as AWS Lambda, Azure Functions, and Google

Cloud Functions offers automatic scaling capabilities. These platforms dynamically allocate resources based on the volume of incoming events or data, which is particularly beneficial for WSNs that often experience fluctuating data loads. When a sensor detects an event, it triggers a serverless function that processes the data. As the data load increases, the platform automatically spins up additional instances of the function to handle the extra volume, ensuring seamless scalability without manual intervention.

One critical technique for scaling serverless applications is to optimize function performance. This involves minimizing cold start times, which are the delays that occur when a serverless function is invoked for the first time or after being idle. Developers can reduce cold starts by keeping functions warm through scheduled invocations, using provisioned concurrency (available in some platforms like AWS Lambda), or optimizing the function's initialization code. Another technique is to design functions to be stateless, enabling them to scale horizontally. Stateless functions do not rely on any previous state or context, allowing multiple instances to run concurrently without interference, thus improving scalability.

Partitioning data and workload distribution is another key technique. This involves dividing the data into smaller chunks that can be processed in parallel by multiple instances of serverless functions. Techniques such as sharding, where the dataset is split based on certain criteria (e.g., geographic location, sensor type), can help distribute the load evenly. Additionally, using message queues (e.g., Amazon SQS, Azure Queue Storage) and stream processing services (e.g., AWS Kinesis, Azure Event Hubs) allows for effective workload distribution. These services can buffer incoming data and ensure that serverless functions process data sequentially or in parallel, based on the data load, thereby maintaining performance during peak times.

Implementing event-driven architectures is also essential for scaling. WSNs generate data based on events, making event-driven models a natural fit. Using event sources such as API gateways, IoT hubs, or storage triggers, serverless functions can be automatically invoked in response to specific events. This model ensures that functions are only executed when necessary, optimizing resource usage and costs. Furthermore, configuring appropriate concurrency limits and throttling policies prevents overwhelming the serverless infrastructure, ensuring that the system scales gracefully under heavy load while maintaining reliability and performance.

Monitoring and logging play crucial roles in scaling serverless applications effectively. By continuously monitoring function performance, resource usage, and error rates using tools like AWS CloudWatch, Azure Monitor, or Google Cloud Monitoring, developers can gain insights into how the application scales under different conditions. Logs can help identify bottlenecks, inefficiencies, or potential failure points. Based on these insights, developers can fine-tune functions, adjust resource allocations, or implement additional scaling strategies to enhance performance.

Lastly, integrating serverless functions with other cloud services that support auto-scaling can further enhance scalability. For instance, combining serverless functions with managed databases, scalable storage solutions, and AI/ML services ensures that every component of the application can scale independently based on demand. This holistic approach to scalability leverages the strengths of the serverless model, providing a robust, responsive, and cost-effective solution for handling the dynamic data loads typical of WSNs.

8.1.3. Cost Efficiency

The analysis of cost savings achieved through serverless computing in wireless sensor network (WSN) deployments reveals several significant advantages that contribute to reducing both operational and capital expenditures. Serverless computing, provided by platforms like AWS Lambda, Azure Functions, and Google Cloud Functions, operates on a pay-as-you-go model where users are only charged for the compute time they consume. This model contrasts sharply with traditional server-based architectures, where costs are incurred for maintaining and operating servers regardless of their utilization.

One of the primary areas of cost savings in serverless WSN deployments is the elimination of server provisioning and maintenance costs. In traditional setups, maintaining a fleet of servers to handle the peak loads of data from sensor networks can be highly inefficient, as servers often remain underutilized during off-peak times. With serverless computing, there is no need to provision or manage physical or virtual servers. The cloud provider handles all infrastructure concerns, including server maintenance, patching, and scaling, thereby significantly reducing the costs associated with these tasks.

Another critical factor contributing to cost savings is the efficient resource utilization provided by serverless architectures. Serverless platforms automatically scale functions up or down in response to incoming data loads, ensuring that resources are allocated dynamically based on real-time demand. This elasticity means that during periods of low activity, costs are minimized as the infrastructure scales down. Conversely, during peak periods, the system scales up to meet the demand, but users are only billed for the actual compute resources consumed during these times. This model contrasts with the traditional approach of provisioning servers for peak capacity, which often leads to substantial waste in terms of idle resources.

Furthermore, serverless computing simplifies the development and deployment processes, which can lead to indirect cost savings. Developers can focus on writing code for specific functions without worrying about the underlying infrastructure. This focus reduces development time and complexity, enabling quicker iterations and faster time-to-market for new features and improvements. The reduced complexity also lowers the likelihood of errors and downtime, which can be costly in terms of both operational impact and potential revenue loss.

Operational costs related to energy consumption and cooling are also significantly reduced with serverless computing. Traditional server-based architectures require considerable energy to run and cool physical servers. In contrast, serverless computing offloads this responsibility to the cloud provider, who can achieve economies of scale and implement energy-efficient practices that are not feasible for individual organizations. These efficiencies translate into lower operational costs for businesses using serverless architectures.

Moreover, serverless computing facilitates better cost management through granular billing. With traditional server-based models, costs are often lumped together, making it challenging to attribute expenses to specific functions or projects. Serverless platforms, however, provide detailed billing information that allows organizations to track costs at a per-function level. This granularity enables better budget management and cost allocation, ensuring that resources are utilized efficiently and transparently.

Lastly, the serverless model's inherent high availability and fault tolerance reduce the costs associated with system outages and downtime. Cloud providers offer robust service level agreements (SLAs) that guarantee a high level of uptime. In a traditional setup, achieving similar levels of reliability would require significant investment in redundant infrastructure and failover mechanisms, further driving up costs.

8.1.4. Data Processing and Analytics

Implementing data analytics and machine learning (ML) models on serverless platforms for wireless sensor network (WSN) data presents a powerful approach to extracting actionable insights from sensor-generated data. Serverless computing, offered by platforms like AWS Lambda, Azure Functions, and Google Cloud Functions, enables on-demand processing and analysis without the need for managing infrastructure. This model is particularly advantageous for WSNs, which produce large volumes of data intermittently, making the scalable, event-driven nature of serverless architectures an ideal fit. To begin with, the data collected by WSNs needs to be ingested and preprocessed. This involves cleaning, filtering, and transforming the raw data into a format suitable for analysis. Serverless functions can be triggered by data ingestion events, such as new data being uploaded to cloud storage or streaming data from message queues like Amazon Kinesis or Azure Event Hubs. These functions can handle tasks such as removing noise from sensor readings, filling missing values, and aggregating data over specified intervals. The serverless model ensures that these preprocessing tasks scale seamlessly with the volume of incoming data, maintaining efficiency and cost-effectiveness.

Once the data is preprocessed, it can be stored in scalable storage solutions like Amazon S3, Azure Blob Storage, or Google Cloud Storage, where it remains accessible for further analysis. Serverless platforms can then be used to implement data analytics pipelines. For instance, AWS Glue, Azure Data Factory, and Google Cloud Dataflow provide serverless data integration services that can orchestrate complex ETL (extract, transform, load) workflows, combining and analyzing data from multiple sources.

Implementing machine learning models on serverless platforms involves several steps, starting with model training. Training ML models typically requires substantial computational resources and is often performed on dedicated services like Amazon SageMaker, Azure Machine Learning, or Google AI Platform.

These services provide managed environments for training models on large datasets, which can be stored in the aforementioned scalable storage solutions. Once trained, the models can be deployed to serverless functions for inference, enabling real-time or batch predictions.

For real-time predictions, serverless functions can be invoked by new data events. For example, when a new sensor reading is uploaded to cloud storage, it can trigger a serverless function that loads the trained ML model, performs inference, and outputs the prediction. This architecture allows for scalable, low-latency predictions without the need to maintain dedicated servers. Batch predictions can be handled similarly, where a serverless function processes a batch of sensor data, applies the ML model, and stores the results.

Serverless platforms also facilitate the continuous deployment and updating of ML models. When a new model version is trained, it can be seamlessly integrated into the serverless functions, ensuring that the latest and most accurate models are used for predictions. This continuous integration and deployment (CI/CD) approach helps maintain the efficacy of the analytics pipeline.

Security and monitoring are critical aspects of implementing analytics and ML on serverless platforms. Cloud providers offer robust security features, including encryption, access controls, and compliance certifications, ensuring that WSN data is protected. Monitoring tools like AWS CloudWatch, Azure

Monitor, and Google Cloud Monitoring provide insights into the performance and health of serverless functions, helping to identify and resolve issues promptly.

8.1.5. Latency and Performance Optimization

Minimizing latency in serverless wireless sensor network (WSN) applications is crucial to ensure timely processing and response to sensor data, particularly for real-time applications. The inherent architecture of serverless computing can introduce latency due to factors like cold starts, network delays, and function execution times. However, several strategies can be employed to mitigate these latencies and optimize the performance of serverless WSN applications.

1. **Optimize Function Code**: Efficient coding practices can significantly reduce the execution time of serverless functions. This includes minimizing the initialization code, using efficient data structures and algorithms, and reducing dependencies. Smaller and simpler functions tend to have shorter execution times and lower cold start latency.
2. **Provisioned Concurrency**: Cloud providers like AWS Lambda offer provisioned concurrency, which keeps a specified number of function instances warm and ready to handle requests. This approach reduces the cold start latency by ensuring that pre-initialized instances are available to process incoming events immediately.
3. **Edge Computing**: Deploying edge computing can reduce the latency by processing data closer to where it is generated. By offloading initial data processing to edge devices or gateways, the amount of data sent to the cloud is reduced, and the round-trip time is minimized. AWS Greengrass and Azure IoT Edge are examples of edge computing services that integrate with serverless architectures.
4. **Event-driven Architecture**: Utilizing event-driven models can streamline data processing. For instance, using message queues (e.g., Amazon SQS, Azure Queue Storage) or data streams (e.g., Amazon Kinesis, Azure Event Hubs) to buffer and batch incoming sensor data can help manage load spikes and ensure that serverless functions are triggered in a controlled manner.
5. **Reduce Function Overhead**: Minimizing the amount of work done within each serverless function invocation can reduce latency. This includes limiting the size of data processed in each invocation and using asynchronous processing where appropriate. For example, breaking down complex tasks into smaller, independent functions can reduce the execution time of individual functions.

6. **Efficient Data Storage and Access**: Choosing the right data storage solutions and optimizing data access patterns can also reduce latency. Using low-latency storage services like Amazon DynamoDB or Azure Cosmos DB for frequently accessed data ensures faster read and write operations. Additionally, employing caching mechanisms (e.g., AWS ElastiCache, Azure Cache for Redis) can further improve data retrieval times.
7. **Warmup Strategies**: Implementing warmup strategies, such as periodically invoking functions to keep them warm, can mitigate cold start issues. Scheduled invocations can be set up to keep function instances alive and reduce initialization latency during periods of low activity.
8. **Network Optimization**: Ensuring a robust and optimized network infrastructure can minimize latency caused by data transmission. This includes using geographically distributed data centers (edge locations) to process data closer to its source and optimizing network configurations for lower latency.
9. **Optimize External Dependencies**: Minimizing the reliance on external services or APIs that introduce latency can improve overall performance. Where external calls are necessary, optimizing these interactions and using asynchronous processing can help reduce their impact on function latency.
10. **Monitoring and Performance Tuning**: Continuous monitoring and performance analysis are essential to identify latency bottlenecks. Tools like AWS CloudWatch, Azure Monitor, and Google Cloud Monitoring provide insights into function performance and help pinpoint areas for optimization. Regularly reviewing and tuning serverless functions based on monitoring data ensures sustained low-latency performance.

8.1.6. Security and Privacy

Security is a critical aspect of deploying wireless sensor networks (WSNs) in serverless architectures. While serverless computing offers numerous benefits like scalability and reduced operational complexity, it also introduces unique security challenges. Addressing these challenges requires a combination of best practices and advanced security solutions. Here are the primary security challenges and their respective solutions in serverless WSN architectures:

1. **Data Transmission Security**:

- **Challenge**: Sensor data often travels over public or private networks, making it vulnerable to interception and tampering.

- **Solution**: Implement end-to-end encryption (E2EE) for data in transit using protocols such as TLS (Transport Layer Security). Encrypt data at the sensor level before transmission and decrypt it only at the destination.

2. **Data Integrity and Authenticity**:
- **Challenge**: Ensuring that the data collected by sensors has not been ltered or spoofed.
- **Solution**: Use cryptographic techniques like digital signatures and hash functions to verify the integrity and authenticity of the data. Each data packet can include a cryptographic hash, verified at the destination to ensure the data has not been tampered with.

3. **Function-Level Security**:
- **Challenge**: Serverless functions are executed in a multi-tenant environment, increasing the risk of cross-tenant attacks and unauthorized access.
- **Solution**: Implement the principle of least privilege by using fine-grained access controls and role-based access controls (RBAC). Ensure each function has the minimum permissions required to perform its task. Use AWS IAM roles, Azure Managed Identities, or similar tools to enforce these permissions.

4. **Event Injection**:
- **Challenge**: Malicious actors can attempt to inject fake events into the system to trigger unintended function executions.
- **Solution**: Validate and sanitize all inputs and events that trigger serverless functions. Implement strict validation checks to ensure that only legitimate events from authorized sources can invoke functions.

5. **Configuration and Secret Management**:
- **Challenge**: Mismanagement of configuration and secrets (like API keys and credentials) can lead to unauthorized access.
- **Solution**: Use managed secret storage solutions such as AWS Secrets Manager, Azure Key Vault, or Google Cloud Secret Manager to securely store and manage sensitive information. Ensure that secrets are not hard-coded in the functions but retrieved securely at runtime.

6. **Denial of Service (DoS) Attacks**:
- **Challenge**: Serverless architectures are susceptible to DoS attacks, which can overwhelm functions with excessive requests, leading to increased costs and degraded performance.

- **Solution**: Implement rate limiting and throttling policies using API gateways like AWS API Gateway or Azure API Management. These tools can limit the number of requests and help mitigate the impact of DoS attacks. Additionally, use CloudFront, Azure CDN, or Google Cloud CDN to distribute and balance the load.

7. **Logging and Monitoring**:

- **Challenge**: Limited visibility into function executions can make it difficult to detect and respond to security incidents.
- **Solution**: Use integrated logging and monitoring services like AWS CloudWatch, Azure Monitor, and Google Cloud Logging to gain insights into function performance and security. Set up alerts for suspicious activities and anomalies, and regularly review logs for signs of potential breaches.

8. **Third-Party Dependencies**:

- **Challenge**: Serverless functions often rely on third-party libraries and services, which can introduce vulnerabilities.
- **Solution**: Regularly update and patch all third-party dependencies. Use tools like AWS Lambda Layers or Azure Functions Bindings to manage dependencies securely and ensure they are up-to-date. Employ vulnerability scanning tools to detect and mitigate risks in third-party components.

9. **Data Privacy Compliance**:

- **Challenge**: Ensuring compliance with data privacy regulations (e.g., GDPR, CCPA) when processing sensor data in the cloud.
- **Solution**: Implement data anonymization and pseudonymization techniques where necessary. Ensure data processing activities are transparent and comply with relevant regulations. Use compliance management tools provided by cloud platforms to help monitor and enforce compliance.

10. **Function Isolation**:

- **Challenge**: Serverless functions often run in a shared environment, which can lead to isolation concerns.
- **Solution**: Ensure strong isolation between functions using containerization techniques and runtime security measures. Cloud providers typically manage this, but it's important to stay informed about the underlying security mechanisms and choose configurations that enhance isolation.

Securing serverless WSN architectures requires a multi-faceted approach that addresses the unique challenges of both WSNs and serverless computing. By implementing robust encryption, access control, event validation, and monitoring strategies, organizations can protect their data and infrastructure from potential threats. Regular updates, compliance with data privacy laws, and effective management of third-party dependencies further enhance the security posture of serverless WSN deployments. As serverless technologies and security practices continue to evolve, staying informed and proactive in implementing security measures is essential for maintaining a secure and resilient system.

8.2. SOFTWARE DEFINED NETWORKING FOR IMPROVED WIRELESS SENSOR NETWORK MANAGEMENT

Wireless sensor networks (WSNs) are made up of discrete nodes that sense and regulate physical parameters like temperature, pressure, and volume in order to interact with their surroundings. In order to accomplish the sensing task, the nodes must also communicate wirelessly with one another. They are also autonomous, though some user-driven data collection is possible. These nodes are equipped with wireless communication, sensing, actuation, and computation capabilities. WSNs are therefore becoming more and more crucial, particularly with the introduction of the Internet of Things (IoT), which is necessary for the monitoring of numerous objects in applications like intelligent transportation systems, smart farming, smart water networks, smart cities, smart health care, and smart power grids. Additionally, since wireless sensor nodes only need a small amount of energy, which is typically provided by integrated batteries, they are typically not connected to a power source. Although WSNs offer great application flexibility, their resource-constrained and application-specific architecture presents a research challenge. The resource-constrained nature of WSNs limits the extent to which they can be applied, despite the growing demand for their use. Although wireless sensor networks are widely used because deployment is made easier by the increased availability of embedded devices, their primary drawback is related to the resource limitations of the sensor hardware, specifically processing, memory, energy, and communication capabilities. But as more nodes are deployed, more problems related to managing large-scale WSNs emerge, like ensuring that nodes have the required Quality of Service (QoS) to function satisfactorily even as their numbers increase to extremely high levels. This is a crucial factor to take into account, particularly in industrial and medical applications where dependability and quality are essential.

Furthermore, these nodes will need to be adaptable to changes in their tasks in addition to processing data. As a result, during operations, when other tasks require priority, the nodes must be reprogrammable. When a new parameter needs to be sensed, it is challenging to re-task the vendor-specific sensor nodes currently used in WSNs. Given that WSNs use application-specific sensor nodes, task reprogramming would obviously necessitate removing each sensor from the water and reprogramming the embedded software in the sensor hardware. This approach would not be feasible given the requirement for large-scale WSNs. While some vendors have included Over The Air Programming (OTAP) techniques, the packet forwarding and data sensing protocols remain vendor-specific. In addition to being counterproductive—using unique programs and protocols would prevent the reuse of common functionalities, which, if possible, would speed up the prototyping and development of WSNs—the programmer would need to study and become familiar with the specific API functions. Mechanisms for maintainability and system self-healing must be used as part of the management of a large-scale WSN. The system should have the ability to adjust its parameters in response to changing circumstances, such as when energy resources become scarce and service quality is reduced. The way WSNs are currently configured presents a problem because data and control packets must all travel through a limited network band. It is a difficult task to develop a network management system for such a distributed WSN, especially on a large scale, and it is typically regarded as the second stage of project planning.

Due to the fact that every node in a WSN is designed to have every function, from the physical layer to the application layer, acting as a standalone system capable of network control and data forwarding, the aforementioned issues are inherent to WSNs. Even though these well-developed algorithms work well for small-scale, short-range WSNs, they lack flexibility and simplicity, which makes them difficult to manage when trying to implement low-power, long-range WSNs on a large scale. Many approaches have been studied and developed to address this issue with WSN management; some of these approaches center on the idea of Software Defined Networking (SDN). SDN is a cutting-edge networking architecture. Its foundation is the idea that the network should be divided into two distinct planes: the data plane, which forwards traffic packets, and the control plane, which chooses traffic routes. Because SDN was first created for conventional wired and wireless networks, it would be difficult to apply it to WSNs because of the limitations imposed by the architecture of the WSN, including scarce node resources.

In an attempt to provide management versatility and flexibility for wireless sensor networks, software-defined networking, or SDN, has been applied in certain cases (SDWSNs). Building a Network Management System (NMS) would be possible through integration of SDN, making it equivalent to adding another application to the control plane. Additionally, network administrators would prefer a centralized network view, which would be made possible. The benefits that SDN offers over conventional WSNs prompt ongoing research and development of applications for SDN-based WSNs. There has been little focus on how SDN might improve WSN management or the necessity of integrating SDN-based management architectures in WSNs, despite the fact that several management schemes for WSNs and the general SDN concept have been proposed and discussed in the last ten years. It is imperative that management solutions are thought through and developed for any network that is expected to scale up to thousands of nodes or more for use in various applications. There have been survey papers on general SDWSN aspects, but not enough attention has been paid to problems with WSN management based on SDN, which are essential to meeting the requirements of an effective WSN. Thus, in order to enhance the management of wireless sensor networks, this paper provides a survey of management techniques that have been applied with SDN and a brief review of contributions made to WSN management.

8.2.1. WSN Management

The configuration, maintenance, operation, and administration of the WSN's components and services should be integrated in an organized manner through the definition of a set of functions that are made possible by WSN management. A number of management techniques have been put forth to control the functionality found in WSN architectures. These techniques take into consideration WSN metrics like energy usage, system lifetime, data latency, fault tolerance, accuracy of data acquisition, QoS, and security. WSN management ought to be straightforward, compliant with the dynamic behavior of the network, and efficient with resources within the framework of MANNA (A management architecture for wireless sensor networks). The MANNA architecture looks at WSN management from three angles, defining functionality abstractions, and takes management policies for WSN services, functions, and models into consideration.

- WSN functionalities which include maintenance, configuration, sensor node operation (Sensing, processing, communication)
- Management levels which include application services and management of network elements (node clusters, data aggregation, network connectivity).
- Management of functional areas such as security, fault monitoring, performance and configuration.

8.2.1.1. Network Configuration Management

Network configuration, sensor node performance management, and maintenance management are all integrated into wireless sensor network configuration management. The network must be configured with field-like events and issues in mind in order to guarantee proper network operation. Environmental variation data, operational environment specification, topology discovery, synchronization, node programming, node self test, and node deployment are a few prerequisites for configuration management at the network level. It is simple to obtain information on the location of the nodes, their administration status, their usage status, and their energy level when the network is properly configured and maintained.

8.2.1.2. Topology Management

In addition to MANNA, the resource-demanding UPnP (Universal Plug and Play) protocol and a bridge are created by the Bridge of the SenSors (BOSS), a network management framework. This allows the resource-constrained sensor network to zero-configurely deploy its services to UPnP-based devices. Three components make up the UPnP-based architecture: the non-UPnP nodes in the WSN, the UPnP control point, and BOSS, which serves as the base node. Additionally, BOSS offers UPnP-based sensor network management services to the user. It is important to remember that the central management strategy is the foundation of both MANNA and BOSS. A distributed management scheme, also known as Management by Delegation (MdB), enables management tasks to be shared amongst WSN nodes. The central manager's workload is lightened by this configuration, but intelligent nodes or mobile agents are needed for the delegation process. To distribute management tasks for local execution on nodes and return the resultant data to the central management node, mobile agents are merely the code sections needed.

8.2.1.3. QoS Management

Performance management is combined with configuration management. The Quality of Service (QoS) and the caliber of the information gathered are the two primary goals of a WSN's performance management. Nonetheless, there is typically a trade-off between network lifetime, energy consumption, and quality of service. Depending on the environment, available resources, and service demand, management protocols may allow for a lower quality of service (QoS) during periods of energy scarcity, thereby prolonging the lifespan of the network. The hybrid data dissemination framework protocol RRP, the Sensor Network Management System (SNMS), the Simple Network Management Protocol

(SNMP), and the Wireless Sensor Network Management System (WinMS) are among the network management protocols that have been suggested for the QoS management of the WSN architecture. Many vendors support SNMP, a popular management protocol that offers effective management for TCP/IP-based networks. It can be used to manage both wired and wireless networks. It makes fault identification and network performance management possible. An effective system for managing network configuration, faults, and performance has been suggested: WSNManagement, which is based on SNMP protocols. While extending the lifespan of the entire sensor node system, the WSNManagement performance demonstrated efficiency in WSN management with a 5 percent reduction in packet loss and a 0.2 s reduction in delay time. For WSNs, delay-related quality of service is essential, particularly for real-time applications.

8.2.1.4. Energy Management

Software-based energy management has been proposed, which reduces the energy consumption of each sensor node by introducing a duty cycle that turns on and off the radio portion of the node on a regular basis. The network lifetime is increased by putting energy management plans and energy-saving protocols into practice. Power management protocols, such as SenOS, Appsleep, and energy level management, have been presented multiple times. These protocols give the WSN control over energy consumption, leading to energy efficiency. It has also been suggested to use a dynamic approach based on prediction for intelligent energy management. This method obtains information about a target state needed for optimized node sleep and sensing scheduling by estimating non-Gaussian and non-linear processes using a particle filter. This leads to increased energy efficiency over a longer network lifetime, and distributed node computing can be used to carry out additional optimization. Others have made comparable contributions to software duty cycling-based energy management; protocols like Sparse Topology and Energy Management (STEM) and SPAN allow sensor nodes to power down when they are not transmitting data. A functional network management system must be in place for a WSN to support these energy management strategies. The necessity for node synchronization has been made easier by advancements in network synchronization. Other energy management strategies, like energy harvesting and battery-based energy provisioning, have been introduced in recent years. The Energy Aware Adaptive Sampling Algorithm is one of the algorithms being developed to improve the energy harvesting technique and lead to network self-sustainability (EASA). This energy management strategy can be applied on any WSN, but it works best on power-hungry nodes that have the ability to harvest energy. It also requires the necessary power to process the algorithm.

8.2.1.5. Security Management

Because WSNs are primarily composed of ad hoc wireless networks with sporadic connectivity and resource constraints, security management is challenging to provide. This makes one vulnerable to risks that could be malicious, accidental, external, or even internal. This makes it possible for resources and data to be lost or altered, as well as for a denial of service attack to occur. Key management schemes, for instance, have been used to approach security management. To meet these requirements, a network with high security features should be created; however, the difficulty here is the bandwidth and energy limitations inherent in WSNs. As a result, security management must be based on effective key distribution, taking into account characteristics like bandwidth, sensor memory, transmission range, and the required know-how. Much more recently, key management was based on the Mobile Sink's optimal routing choice and dynamic clustering. The scheme satisfies storage efficiency and connectivity requirements while extending static key management to dynamic key management with enhanced flexibility. An additional contribution has been made by putting forth a hybrid key management scheme that increases the difficulty of breaking the key system by utilizing both the Polynomial Pool and Basic Random (PPBR) key pre-distribution techniques. The tree base path key establishment method is used in key management to address link connectivity issues.

8.2.1.6. Maintenance Management

Higher QoS and a longer network lifetime would be possible with maintenance management integrated into network management. Unexpected and expected network events, energy shortages, connectivity disruptions, and environmental changes are all major causes of faults in wireless sensor networks (WSNs). Therefore, it is important to configure, manage, and maintain the network in a way that promotes self-healing and fault tolerance. This will give the network a robust quality that will allow the WSN to continue providing useful information even in the event that some nodes disconnect from the network. Network monitoring is crucial to fault mitigation and maintenance management since it gathers data on the network's condition (e.g., link states, bandwidth, and node energy levels). In order to provide a visual depiction of the network state, various interfaces and tools have been created, including Mote-view, SNAMP, spy-glass, tinyviz, and nanomon. Systems that feature a central management scheme and send all analysis data collectively to a central server, like the mote-view and others, have the drawback of being passive and having limited configuration flexibility in the event of a fault. This can be viewed as a way for SDN to address this lack of flexibility, which is something that becomes apparent when this paper explores SDN-based management of WSNs. The need for energy efficiency in WSNs has led to the proposal of an Energy-efficient Passive MOnitoring SysTem (EPMOSt). EPMOSt, like WSNManagement, uses an SNMP agent to deliver monitoring data while using less energy. This energy efficiency guarantees a longer lifetime for network monitoring.

8.2.1.7. Comparison of WSN Management Systems

The above-discussed notable WSN management systems are compiled in Table 8.1 and assessed using the WSN design criteria. The table indicates that at least three of the requirements for an efficient management system are met by BOSS, Mobile Agent Based Power Management, WinMS, AppSleep, and EpMOSt, with WinMs being the most efficient of the management schemes.

Table 8.1. *Available WSN Management Systems Evaluation Against the Design Criteria*

Management Scheme	**Functionality**	**Energy Efficiency**	**Robustness**	**Scalability**	**Adaptability**
MANNA	Policy based framework, fault detection	NA	NA	NA	NA
BOSS	Network state retrieval, power management	Yes	Yes	No	Yes
Agilla	Event detection	Yes	No	No	Yes
Sectoral Sweeper	Switching node on/off	Yes	No	No	No
Intelligent Agent- Based Power Management	low power management	Yes	No	No	Yes
Mobile Agent Based Power Management	Policy based management	Yes	Yes	No	Yes

RRP	Data aggregation	Yes	No	No	No
SNMS	Health and event data collection	Yes	Yes	No	No
SNMP	Network function definition and monitoring	No	Yes	No	Yes
WSNManagement	Performance and fault management	No	Yes	No	Yes
WinMS	Synchronisation, local repair and state retrieval	Yes	Yes	Yes	Yes
SenOS	Triggering node on/off	Yes	No	No	No
AppSleep	Power Management	Yes	Yes	Yes	No
Energy level management	Power management	Yes	Yes	No	No
EASA	Self-sustaining energy management	Yes	Yes	No	No
MOTE-VIEW	Network state and visualisation	Yes	No	Yes	No
EPMOSt	Passive network monitoring	Yes	Yes	No	Yes

Source: https://www.ncbi.nlm.nih.gov/pmc/articles/PMC5469636/.

8.2.2. Network Management Based on SDN

The separation of the control plane from the data plane in WSN architecture forms the fundamental idea of Software Defined Networking (SDN). With the help of this new paradigm, the network's overall behavior can be controlled and managed by a logically centralized controller, which is a central program that serves as the Network Operating System (NOS). The data plane is home to network components like switches and sensor nodes, which do nothing more than forward data according to the controller's flow instructions. Unlike distributed management schemes, which may require individual network device configuration to change network behavior, this approach to network management enables network configuration to be performed globally. In Figure 8.1, the general basic architecture is displayed.

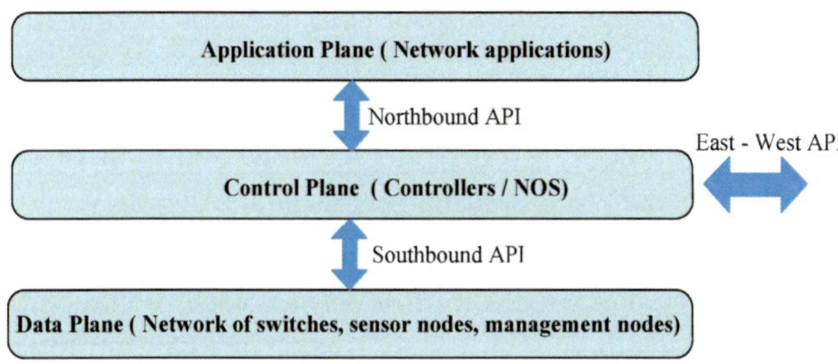

Figure 8.1. *SDN overall architecture.*

Source: https://www.mdpi.com/sensors/sensors-17-01031/article_deploy/html/images/sensors-17-01031-g001.png.

Application Programming Interfaces (APIs), which offer a functional interface between the application, control, and data planes, are integrated into the SDN architecture. The northbound APIs are located between the application and control planes, while the southbound APIs are located between the controller and the data plane. The controller and the data plane devices can exchange control traffic more easily thanks to the Southbound APIs. As a southbound interface, OpenFlow is widely used, and more OpenFlow-capable network infrastructure is being produced by most vendors. Controllers in the same domain or adjacent domains can communicate with one another thanks to East-West APIs. It is crucial to note that Software Defined Networking (SDN) aims to simplify network management and enable innovation through network programmability, rather than enhancing network performance. It's as simple to update network control and management as it is to install new computer applications. SDN increases flexibility by transforming network administration issues into programming problems. Other possible advantages of SDN in WSNs include:

- **Energy management:** Because WSN nodes have limited energy, sensor networks must use energy-efficient protocols. SDN can offer a way to manage WSN networks in an energy-efficient manner. This is made possible by the fact that a logically centralized control plane can lower the power used by nodes to maintain a localized view of the entire WSN. All routing protocols are managed by control plane functions, sparing nodes from adhering to application-specific protocols that, depending on traffic, may consume a lot of energy. At the control plane, alternative energy management strategies can also be used.

- **Configuration management:** The enhanced flexibility of SDN makes network management less complicated. It also makes it easier to implement new routing protocols without having to reconfigure the nodes, and it eliminates the need to compile separate versions of the same network applications for various sensor nodes. Because of this, implementing new management and control techniques is simple and leads to increased operational efficiency.

It can be difficult to manage a network when the network hardware is vendor specific. In order to apply intricate high-level network management policies, network operators must adapt to low-level hardware configurations that are vendor-specific. Changing the policies that are ingrained in the underlying network infrastructure presents challenges for network management schemes like the ones covered in the previous section. Application-specific networks with limited opportunities for innovation and improvement are the direct result. SDN has the potential to open up new options for network configuration and management. SDN helps to alleviate some of the challenges associated with network management by facilitating frequent and easy modifications to the state and functionality of the network, enabling high-level language network configuration, and offering visibility and control over the entire network, which facilitates network troubleshooting.

Network administrators must install and configure traditional wired and wireless networks using a set of low-level device commands found in the command line interface. This is a concern in particular when network conditions are continuously changing. In order to accommodate these changes, operators must manually modify configurations frequently, which opens the door to misconfiguration and errors when putting changes into practice. With SDN, utilizing a centralized controller makes it much simpler to incorporate new concepts and protocols into the network. Instead of requiring configuration for each network device in order to implement changes or integrate new services, SDN offers a global approach to network configuration management. Numerous studies and proposals have been made regarding the possible advantages of integrating SDN in wired and wireless networks. Many earlier studies on the use of SDN in computer network management have left space for future research on how SDN can improve and facilitate IoT management. a Machine to Machine

(M2M) infrastructure-focused SDN-based IoT management architecture. A centralized controller, M2M nodes, and a gateway connecting general nodes with non-M2M protocols to the controller make up the suggested framework. Without requiring the deployment of new infrastructure, the framework for routing reconfiguration was successfully tested.

8.2.3. WSN Applications and the Need for SDN-Based Management

Multiple sensing capabilities can be integrated by wireless sensor networks, supporting a wide range of practical applications. Given the resource-constrained nature of WSNs, this flexibility is accompanied by a number of research challenges in providing effective management for the application. SDN can be used in a variety of applications, including home networks, healthcare, the military, and environmental applications, thanks to the numerous advantages it brings to these management issues. We'll go over these application scenarios quickly and highlight the advantages of SDN-based management in these domains.

8.2.3.1. Environmental Applications

The measurement of physical parameters like temperature, vibration, sound, chemicals, and gases is a common use of WSNs in the environment. Applications for this have included the water and agriculture industries (for irrigation and animal monitoring, respectively), disaster relief applications (for monitoring and combating forest fires, earthquake detection and rescue operations), and the water industry (for developing smart water grids to enable efficient distribution and control of potable water). Additional uses include monitoring marine environments and controlling pollutants in the environment, both of which call for long-term unmanned WSN operations. These applications, however, might call for the deployment of sensors over very large areas, hostile environments, or even difficult-to-reach regions. This could lead to a dependence on the energy supply of the sensors, which would reduce network lifetime and the capacity to switch between tasks in the event of a node failure or a change in the requirements for sensing. Effective topology, energy, and maintenance management are therefore required, and SDN integration adds these capabilities to the application scenarios. In large-scale applications where energy is a critical factor, SDN-based management would enable a centralized network view of key parameters. SDN techniques offer efficient resource allocation through software duty-cycling and by making traffic engineering, congestion control, load balancing, and mobility management easier to use. In addition, SDN offers a functional interface that eliminates the need for extra hardware like FPGAs in order to achieve the sensor reprogrammability required for function switching.

8.2.3.2. Medicine and Health Care

The use of WSN in healthcare has been thought to have the potential to improve patient quality, particularly for elderly and chronically ill patients. In hospitals, WSNs can also be used for patient and physician tracking, which has the potential to save lives. Using implantable sensor systems to track patient activity and create Wireless Body Area Networks (WBANs) is one contentious use of WSNs in healthcare. The implementation of WBANs faces several challenges, including sensor maintenance after it is worn on the body, energy management for sensor batteries because charging them can be difficult for older people, who must remember to charge multiple sensors, insufficient bandwidth to transmit large amounts of medical diagnostic data, meeting QoS requirements for health monitoring hampered by WSN resource constraints, security and privacy of medical data, scalability issues, and challenges related to sensor mobility as patients go about their daily lives.

Based on the capability of providing energy and maintenance management from a central location—a task that could fall under the purview of hospital administration, for example—SDN-based management would offer a solution to several of these highlighted challenges. Moreover, SDN techniques are being developed to guarantee data accuracy and fault monitoring more effectively, as well as to minimize traffic overhead data and mitigate bandwidth issues. SDN offers a solution based on separation of destructive interfering nodes in light of the potential for implanting multiple body sensors in close proximity, which may result in interference affecting the QoS and application performance.

8.2.3.3. Military Applications

WSNs can be used in military applications to assess terrain, detect the presence of friendly or enemy forces, and detect the chemical makeup of weapons. WSN applications for defense IoT were highlighted, and these included fleet monitoring, energy management, fire control, inventory tracking, and troop health and safety management.

However, WSNs must satisfy operational requirements like robustness, ease of deployment, interoperability/adaptability, and most importantly security in order to be used in defense and security. By maintaining global control over the network infrastructure on the ground, SDN can be used to better manage system security and the issuance of new task protocols while the system is in operation. Because SDN-based management allows mobility algorithms to be configured and managed in a more resource-efficient global controller, it also makes it easier to deploy these algorithms to handle the constant movement of troops.

8.2.3.4. Wireless Home Networks

With the rise of smart homes and buildings in general, there has been a growing demand for WSNs for home use. Modern homes are made up of a network of motion, light, and temperature sensor nodes that can be integrated into appliances to add smart features. Users can operate these household appliances remotely by connecting this network to the Internet. But there is also a network of other communication technologies, like WiFi, ethernet, cellular, and power-line communications, in addition to a network of smart devices. The problem with a network this heterogeneous is that there isn't an automated system to enable network optimization by choosing the best communication technology to employ; instead, the user must typically make this decision by hand. Soetens and associates. have put forth an SDN-based management strategy that makes use of OpenFlow-enabled link switches to enhance management of such heterogeneous home networks. Additionally, it has been suggested that SDN techniques improve the design and administration of smart homes. The use of smart devices in homes is growing, which makes management more challenging, particularly with the introduction of video streaming services like Netflix and Youtube. The need for SDN-based smart home network management arises from user demand and control, which becomes a significant management factor. Furthermore, the competition for bandwidth among these user applications—voice, video, gaming, and others—leads to subpar service quality. Other SDN-based bandwidth allocation strategies, such as home slice, Network Assisted Video Streaming (NAVS), and SDN@home, have been proposed to manage home applications like voice and video and enhance quality of service.

8.3. MANAGEMENT OF WSNS BASED ON SDN

WSNs are made up of a network of sensors that are used to monitor various conditions, including air quality, pressure, and temperature. There could be hundreds or thousands of resource-constrained nodes in the sensor network. The management of the network topology, which requires us to take into account Quality of Service and network coverage in an environment with variable conditions and a limited energy supply, is another challenge introduced as the nodes are deployed in the field. This challenge is related to the inherent challenges of WSNs in terms of energy requirement, which is directly linked to network lifetime, the application specific nature with vertical integration, where manufacturers and vendors control the end products of the devices as well as the software and hardware of their infrastructure. To lessen these difficulties, it has been suggested that SDN integration be used with WSN. In order to ensure effective performance and resource allocation, integration of SDN would necessitate careful consideration of network management practices. The management functionality abstractions can be applied to the WSN architecture based on SDN to create managerial entities. This architecture is modified in Figure 8.2, which also emphasizes the management entities that will be taken into account when we review and assess SDN-based management for WSNs. The architecture demonstrates a centralized controller in an SDN-based WSN, giving management efficiency and a worldwide perspective of the whole network. While enabling technology management can be applied at every architectural level, network topology, energy, configuration, QoS, and security management are all centrally managed in the control plane. Enabling hardware can be installed in the data plane, such as SDN-enabled sensor nodes with multiple sensing capabilities, while programming and central management of the nodes for different applications can be done in the control plane.

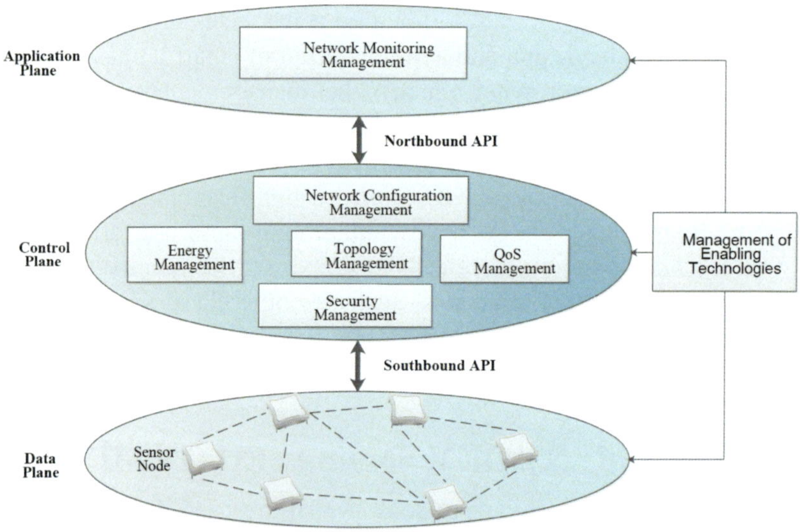

Figure 8.2. *An SDN-based wireless sensor network management architecture.*

Source: https://www.ncbi.nlm.nih.gov/pmc/articles/PMC5469636/bin/sensors-17-01031-g002.jpg.

8.3.1. Network Configuration Management

One functional area that will enable the sensor network to meet its necessary specifications is network configuration management. The first obstacle to meeting requirements in an SDN-based WSN architecture is SDN support for the WSN architecture. Since SDN was created for conventional networks, which are distinct from WSNs, the network must be configured in order to effectively support SDN. This is especially crucial for utilizing current network management architectures and protocols, which can give the SDN-based WSN an appropriate network management model. Configuring and expanding SDN functionality for wireless sensor applications has been the subject of several proposals. One such proposal is Sensor OpenFlow (SOF), a fundamental part of SDN-based WSNs that acts as a standard communication protocol between the data plane and control plane. The concept is based on two components: the control plane, which consists of a controller managing all network intelligence centrally, and the data plane, which is made up of sensors executing flow-based packet forwarding (Centralized Control). This makes it possible to fully program the data plane by allowing each sensor's flow table to be customized. The problem with this concept is that it is based on the core OpenFlow premise that the underlying network consists of IP routers and Ethernet switches, which are wired protocols better suited for data centers and cellular and enterprise backbones than WSNs. Furthermore, employing the centralized controller would prompt concerns about how security would be handled in the case of controller-focused attacks. Thus, there needs to be sufficient network security management in place.

Another solution to expand SDN functionality in wireless and mobile communications that has been prototyped is the Software Defined Wireless Network (SDWN), which supports SDN in Low Rate Wireless Personal Area Networks (LR-WPANs). To cut down on energy consumption, SDWN employs energy management strategies like duty cycling, in-network data aggregation, and cross-layer optimization. However, since the SDWN requires messages to be passed between the control and data layers, which may strain the already resource-constrained WSN, further research is necessary to adapt the SDWN architecture to integrate and configure SDN for WSNs to enable efficient energy use. The SDN-WISE (SDN-WIreless SEnsor network) technique allows sensor nodes to run applications that are not supported by stateless solutions by programming them as finite state machines. It offers an API that enables programmers to write code for the SDN controller in any language they choose, making network programming management easier and more flexible. This is particularly helpful for overseeing a vast and far-reaching wireless sensor network. The address-centric SDN protocols should be able to address the intrinsically data-centric WSN through the configuration of SDN-based WSNs. Using IP stacks like uIP, uIPv6 based on Contiki OS, and Berkley Low power IP (BLIP) based on Tiny OS for low power networks would be one way to solve this. IPv6-based low-power wireless personal area networks, or 6LowPANs, have been realized as a result of this integration. The 6LowPAN protocol has led to the proposal of various management architectures. These include the LowPAN Network Management Protocol (LNMP), 6LowPAN-SNMP, which is an expansion of the current SNMP protocol, and an additional SNMP-based network management architecture for 6LowPANs. Despite being used for different types of wireless networks, these management architectures serve as a model for creating an appropriate network management architecture for SDN-based WSNs.

Control flow management is another facet of network configuration. In wired SDN applications, a dedicated control channel is used for communication between the controller and the data plane; in wireless sensor networks (WSNs), control and data traffic use the same network path (in band). If not managed, this could present a problem for WSN control data because of changes in connectivity brought on by mobility, routing, link and node failures, and other similar network parameter variations. As a result, suggestions have been made to lower control traffic as a management technique.

8.3.2. Topology Management

WSNs are not the same as the traditional networks for which SDN was originally intended. With limited resources, WSNs process data (in-network processing) and communicate from node to node over the same channel. SDN makes it possible to separate the control plane from the data plane, but in WSNs, the control and data packets will still use the dynamic, resource-constrained WSN topology. The method used to manage the network topology should be able to accommodate node mobility, which causes changes in topology and includes handling erratic wireless links. These tasks ought to be coordinated with QoS management, which guarantees the network's resilience. SDN-based WSN topology management consists of managing the following:

8.3.2.1. Scalability and Localization Management

The architectures that have been reviewed thus far are predicated on an easily deployable and manageable flat topology with a centralized controller. Gante and associates. For example, implement intelligent SDWSN management to increase productivity and get around the challenges that come with standard WSNs. The proposed base station architecture for WSNs with an integrated controller serves as the foundation for the management scheme. Based on location data processed in the application layer of the architecture using localization techniques, the controller generates forwarding rules that are inserted into flow tables. Nevertheless, as networks grow to very large numbers of nodes, hierarchical topologies or those that offer a virtual overlay of the physical network must be integrated to enable effective scalability and localization. Flat topologies like this are only suitable for short-range and small-scale applications. There are a few network management architectures that use distributed multiple controllers instead of a single centralized controller in an effort to increase the efficiency of SDN-based WSN management. This eliminates the need for central communication of control data, allowing for effective scalability and a decrease in overhead. Because the WSN is not entirely dependent on a single controller, distributed controllers also enable effective security and QoS management, increasing the system's resilience to attacks and link failures to the central controller. Software Defined Clustered Sensor Networks (SDCSN), a hierarchical architecture, have been proposed to use multiple base stations acting as controllers and cluster heads. A large-scale collection of nodes is organized into clusters, each headed by a cluster head. Every cluster's sensor nodes are managed and coordinated by the cluster head, to whom all data processed within each cluster is directed. To effectively enable multiple controllers in the network, it is necessary to enable the sensor nodes to function as controllers in order to manage such an architecture. The drawback of this management strategy is that it may leave the cluster head open to attack, which could compromise network security. Nevertheless, self-stabilization strategies have been put forth to choose a new cluster head in the event of such an occurrence. In order to enhance network management flexibility and facilitate the integration of diverse functions, an architecture founded on network virtualization has been suggested. In essence, as illustrated in Figure 8.3, a virtual overlay topology based on a real physical WSN based on SDN can be constructed to specific requirements.

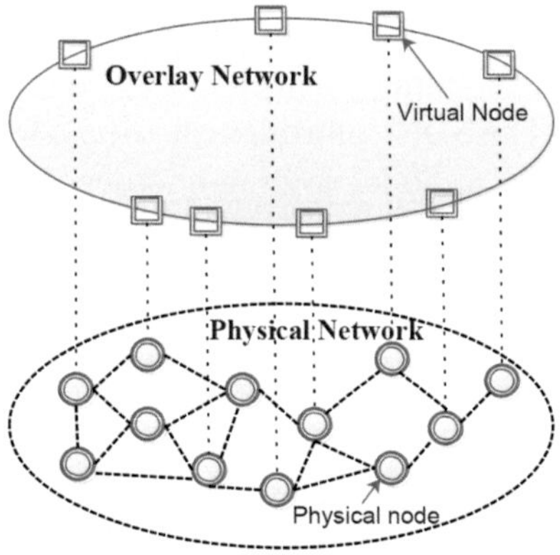

Figure 8.3. *Topology based on virtual overlay.*

Source: https://www.ncbi.nlm.nih.gov/pmc/articles/PMC5469636/bin/sensors-17-01031-g003.jpg.

Context-based logical clustering is another hierarchical architecture that has been suggested to control scalability. Unlike other clustering methods that allow clustering of adjacent nodes, this is based on logically clustering sensors according to context (gathered data type) regardless of their physical distribution based on HyperFlow. Context-based sensor clustering would enable resource and data sharing independent of network growth. Every cluster has a local controller, known as a logical sink in the virtual network overlay, that may be geographically dispersed but is logically synchronized. The performance analysis demonstrates how well this method increases network stability. In large-scale applications involving hundreds to thousands of nodes, sensor data lacking location information is particularly useless. SDN in WSNs offers the ability to apply suggested localization algorithms to obtain location data with a high degree of accuracy. Depending on the mapping data and accuracy level the algorithm provides, the localization algorithm to be used and managed can be distributed or centralized. In recent times, there has been research and proposal for a localization node selection algorithm that utilizes the SDN and the Cramer-Rao Lower Bound (CRLB) metric. The algorithm satisfies the requirement for energy conservation while utilizing the SDN controller's global network view, and the simulation results showed a notable improvement in the localization performance.

8.3.2.2. Mobility Management

It is vital to monitor and control node movement in an SDN-based WSN because sensor nodes are prone to movement, which can lead to variations in task execution and packet transmission. When integrating a mobility management scheme, managing the impact of nodes joining and departing the network on QoS, function execution, and other network attributes are among the challenges to be taken into account. The SDN controller can offer a few fixes and processing steps to stop issues related to nodes joining and departing the WSN. Mobility management in IP based WSNs based on TinyOS implemented and tested on a 6LoWPAN has been researched, taking into account IP support for nodes in SDN-based WSNs. A system grounded in IEEE 802.15. 4 standard has been researched and put into practice to control mobility in a distributed network architecture, showing promise for practical system implementation. Numerous studies on mobility management in SDN-based Wireless Cellular Networks (WCNs) have been published; it would be beneficial to investigate whether these management techniques can be used and integrated in SDN-based WSNs.

8.3.2.3. Communication Management

By incorporating SDN into the WSN topology, network management and operation with sensors from various manufacturers and architects can be accomplished with little to no difficulty in terms of compatibility problems. Due to the possibility of these nodes being densely populated and neighboring sensor nodes appearing extremely close to one another, an effective communication scheme must be implemented. While energy consumption and signal quality should be considered in the communication scheme, energy conservation should be the main priority in order to extend the lifetime of the network. For dense WSNs, multi-hop techniques based on short-range radio communication allow for lower energy consumption than direct communication. For node to cluster head communication in SDN applications using clustered hierarchical topologies, long range radio can be utilized. Because there is direct communication between each node and the cluster head (SDN local controller), this would enable network operation to continue even in the event that a few nodes in a cluster fail. In these kinds of situations, the suggested radio technology—such as LoRa, which is meant for Low Power Wide Area Networks—should also use less power (LPWAN). As demonstrated in Figure 8.4, a large low power WSN based on SDN can be managed using a hybrid of multi-hop techniques and long range radio, where multi-hop communication is implemented between nodes in a cluster and long range radio is used between cluster heads and the global controller.

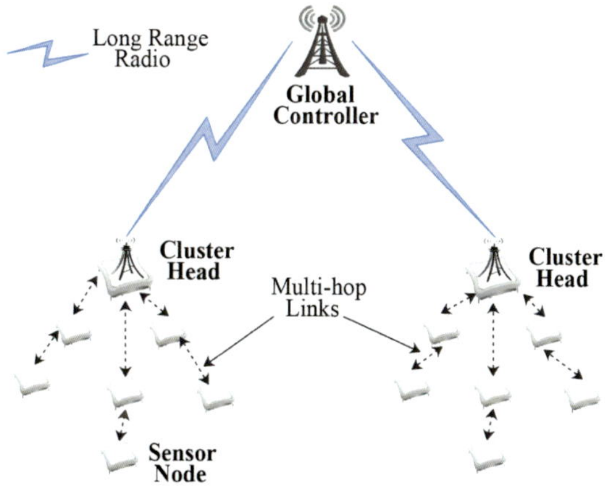

Figure 8.4. *Hybrid radio management.*

Source: https://www.ncbi.nlm.nih.gov/pmc/articles/PMC5469636/bin/sensors-17-01031-g004.jpg.

8.3.2.4. Network Monitoring

Network monitoring is critical to enhancing the manageability and simplicity of deploying a WSN based on SDN since it allows the management station to display all relevant sensor data, including specifics about the hardware, software, and battery level of each sensor node. Network monitoring apps for SDN have been created based on Openflow's ability to offer a mechanism for gathering statistics and flow level data. These applications can periodically query nodes through the controller. The frequency of these inquiries determines how accurate the information being tracked is. It has been suggested that methods like Payless can increase the effectiveness of this query process by reducing network overhead and accuracy monitoring. OpenSketch, OpenTM, FlowSense, and OpenNetMon are additional suggested network monitoring tools for conventional software-defined IP networks that are based on this idea. Research into these methods, or novel methods for monitoring SDN-based WSNs, has been scant and is still in its early stages. However, recent work has been presented on an SDN-based network measurement architecture for monitoring WSN data, including the delay resulting from each hop in a multi-hop configuration, the loss ratio for each link, and the routing path per-packet. Measurement tasks can be completed quickly and effectively thanks to TinySDM, a software defined measurement architecture based on the TinyOS platform that makes it simple to customize and execute a variety of measurement metrics.

8.3.2.5. SDN-Based Network and Topology Management Classification for WSNs

When integrating a management system into a network, classification criteria should be taken into account. The management function, controller configuration that best suits the architecture, and control traffic channel would all influence the management system selection. The architectures available for network and topology management of WSNs based on SDN are compiled and compared against classification criteria in Table 8.2.

Table 8.2. *SDN-Based Network and Topology Management Architectures*

Management Architecture	Management Feature	Controller Configuration	Control Traffic Channel	Configuration and Monitoring	Scalability and Localization	Communication Management
Sensor OpenFlow	SDN support protocol	Distributed and Centralized	in-band and out-band	√		√
SDWN	Duty cycling, aggregation and routing	Distributed	in-band	√		

SDN-WISE	programming simplicity, aggregation	Distributed	in-band	√		
Smart	Efficiency in resource allocation	Centralized	in-band		√	
SDCSN	Network reliability and QoS	Distributed	in-band		√	
TinySDN	in-band traffic control	Distributed	in-band		√	
Virtual Overlay	network flexibility	Distributed	in-band		√	
Context-based	network scalability and performance	Distributed	in-band		√	
CRLB	node localization	Centralized	in-band		√	
multi-hop	traffic and energy control	Distributed and Centralized	in-band			√
TinySDM	network task measurement	-	in-band	√		

Source: https://www.mdpi.com/1424-8220/17/5/1031.

8.3.3. Energy Management

Energy management is concerned with the various ways that SDN can be used to minimize energy consumption in a WSN that already has limited energy resources. There have been several suggestions for implementing energy management in the SDN controller for the worldwide energy balance used by the WSN. By allowing energy-consuming tasks like data traffic routing decisions to be handled by the controller and only assigning the energy-constrained sensor the task of forwarding data traffic, SDN integration in WSNs naturally lowers energy consumption. SDN-based WSN topology management includes the use of SDN for resource allocation control. In an effort to improve resource allocation, other topologies and architectures have also been proposed. For example, the SDWN and Smart both perform controller functions on the sink node, relieving the remaining sensor nodes of tasks like mobility management, localization, and quality of service, leading to energy-efficient operation. In a similar vein, a general framework based on OpenFlow has been proposed, with the controller located at the base station and center nodes integrating switching and communication functions with the controller in each cluster.

Another way to manage energy is to use software to establish control in a process known as duty cycling. This method focuses on controlling the sleep and wake states of the sensor nodes in order to minimize the amount of energy they consume. This method of managing WSNs has been suggested multiple times; however, SDN-based architectures depend on cross-layer communication between the decoupled control and data planes, which may necessitate a strong link in order to optimize the flow of control traffic. Additionally, energy savings through data aggregation may be required; employing techniques that turn nodes on and off may lead to unreliability in the communication links. A SDN-based architecture called multitasking for WSNs has been proposed to reduce energy consumption. The ability of a sensor node to perform multiple tasks simultaneously, resulting in distinct sensing outputs, makes multitasking possible. To attain a desired Quality of Sensing (QoSen), a task is performed collaboratively by multiple nodes. Three goals are considered when creating a Mixed Integer Linear Program (MILP): sensing scheduling, task mapping, and sensor activation. In addition, more work is being done on creating an online algorithm to manage the dynamics involving nodes joining or leaving the network (mobility or node failure). Simulation results indicate that this approach has an energy efficiency comparable to that of a globally optimized network, with the benefit of less overhead control data and rescheduling time.

To maintain the global view of the logically centralized controller, SDN-based management involves high control traffic overhead. This process consumes more energy during operation, which has an impact on the network's energy efficiency. By filtering redundancy and implementing a load-balancing routing mechanism in accordance with data flow distribution with the necessary QoS, the technique lowers overhead control traffic. The suggested SDN-based WSN prototype performed better in terms of energy efficiency during experiments. It is possible to expand and apply energy management strategies within each cluster, such as data aggregation and information fusion combined with multi-hop communication utilized in WSNs. The densely populated sensor nodes provide an opportunity for multi-hop links to transmit data at low power consumption. More recently, a wireless power transfer-based effective energy harvesting management method for SDN-based WSNs has been suggested. The mechanism extends the lifetime of the network by sending energy to sensor nodes through specialized wireless power transmitters. In order to enable maximum optimization while satisfying the minimum energy required by each sensor node, a utility function is defined to manage the energy distribution and the maximum energy required to charge the nodes. During each charge cycle, an energy-efficient scheduling system is integrated with the energy transmitters. The energy management plans available for SDN-based WSNs are contrasted in Table 8.3.

Table 8.3. *SDN-based Energy management schemes for WSNs*

Scheme	Features	Controller Architecture	Enabling Technology
SDWN	Duty cycling, data aggregation	Distributed	Software, Hardware
Smart	Resource allocation	Centralized	Software and Hardware
Multi-task	Resource allocation, QoSen, scheduling	Centralized	Software
SDWSN-RL	Load balancing, traffic control	Distributed	Software
Wireless power transfer	Energy harvest, Optimization, efficiency	Centralized	Software, hardware

Source: https://www.mdpi.com/1424-8220/17/5/1031.

8.3.4. QoS Management

All facets of guaranteeing a network's acceptable service delivery are covered by quality of service management. This covers event detection, robustness, maintenance, packet latency, tolerance and reliability management, and robustness. Because the SDN architecture is logically centralized, it enables the QoS management tasks to occur in the controller. In order to ensure network reliability, a mechanism for topology changes, node failures, bandwidth availability, and energy fluctuations must be integrated into the SDN-based WSN environment. The dependability of the SDN-based WSN architecture by utilizing continuous stochastic logic techniques and models based on continuous time Markov chain. The findings demonstrate that the quantity and failure rates of sensors and controllers have an impact on network reliability. A suggestion is made based on the findings to combine multiple dependable controllers as a strategy for reliability management.

The two categories of reliability management are task reliability and communication system reliability. Reliable communication can be managed by using techniques like redundant links and backup nodes. Function alternation is a self-healing mechanism that has been proposed to manage sensor task reliability by allowing neighboring sensor nodes to automatically take over tasks from damaged sensor nodes. In order to increase task reliability, the SDN controller can also offer information and a backup for sensing tasks. In SDN-based WSNs, neighboring sensor nodes can be retasked with replacing damaged or unreliable nodes by using the backup information. Performance reliability concerns in WSNs have been addressed and exploited through the use of the SDN OpenFlow concept. The concept is predicated on OpenFlow's built-in ability to regulate and track sensor traffic, enabling a dependable load balancing and routing system. The reliability of multi-hop and end-to-end communications in conventional WSNs is still an open problem that is challenging to manage. For this reason, flow-sensors, which generate fewer packets than typical sensors in order to reduce traffic overhead in constrained networks, have been proposed to produce better reliability than typical sensors. Robustness is a quality of service (QoS) parameter that describes a system's capacity to function as expected even in unpredictable environmental circumstances. It is vital to take into account variables influencing and interfering with the system and to keep an eye on the interference patterns in a suggested statistical machine learning technique in order to manage system robustness. Using this method, potential interference could be avoided based on prior interference-causing behavior patterns. While TinySDN has been proposed as a latency management solution, more research is needed in the areas of event detection and latency management.

8.3.5. Security Management

A logically centralized controller presents a security risk in WSNs based on SDN architecture because system QoS can be impacted by compromises in the controller, cluster-head in clustered topologies, or even the link to the controller. System unreliability may arise from a malicious attacker introducing false data and parameters into the network or causing a Denial of Service attack. A few contributions have been made to the management of security for SDN-based WSNs; for instance, they outline the necessity of security management for Internet of Things (IoT)-based SDN networks, both wired and wireless, and they suggest a security model for IoT SDN architecture. The suggested IoT architecture is expanded to include sensors that integrate the network security guaranteeing feature based on the concept of the grid of security embedded in every controller. A communication model is used to help structure the service distribution of security among nodes. The grid of security concept was previously introduced as a way to secure networks by guaranteeing that communication occurs between reliable devices independent of system policy control. The general idea is to decentralize network security management in order to maintain security in the event of a failure. Secure Multiparty Computation (SMC) has been integrated into SDN-based WSNs to protect private sensory data, which is another contribution to security management. The use of SMC to securely process sensory data between the web server and the SDN-based WSN is the main focus. For the purpose of conducting selection in SDN-based WSNs, a lottery SMC protocol is built, utilizing layered homophobic function encryption.

8.3.6. Management of Enabling Technologies

8.3.6.1. Enabling Software

Software plays a central role in SDN-based WSNs by facilitating the management and control of sensor nodes and providing the foundation for sensor operations. With the help of the SDN-based architecture, enabling software can be managed and controlled at the application, control, and data planes in a way that gives application programmers the ability to modify sensor functionalities by calling various programs that cause the sensor node to function like a tiny computer. Because sensor nodes have limited processing power and memory, this also requires the sensor nodes in the data plane to have an operating system, albeit a simpler one than that of personal computers.

The architecture of an SDN-based WSN can incorporate sensors thanks to a number of sensor operating systems. The protection of sensor nodes and memory management are impacted by the operating system selection; memory management can be either dynamic or static. Because static memory management cannot allocate memory at run-time, it is not flexible. However, static memory management is fixed and straightforward, making it useful for memory nodes that are limited. On the other hand, dynamic memory management offers flexibility by allowing memory to be allocated and released at runtime.

Because SDN-based WSNs allow for multiple function execution, memory protection is necessary to avoid mixing up process address spaces. TinyOS, which is written in nesC, is designed for embedded systems with constrained resources and low-power wireless sensors. Memory protection and static memory management are features offered by TinyOS. TinyOS has been used in SDN-based WSNs.

Using Contiki, it is shown that dynamic program loading and offloading is feasible in a network with limited resources. Although Contiki lacks a management mechanism for memory protection in between function executions, it does support memory block functions and dynamic memory management. Other operating systems that are available are LiteOS, Nano-RK, and MultimodAl system for NeTworks of In situ wireless Sensors (MANTIS). However, these operating systems are primarily used for regular WSNs and are not often implemented in SDN-based management of WSNs. The operating systems for sensor nodes that can be integrated into SDN-based WSN management are contrasted in Table 8.4.

Table 8.4. *Enabling node operating systems for SDN-based management of WSNs: A comparison*

OS	Language	Memory Management	Implementation for
TinyOS	NesC	Static	TinySDN, TinySDM, mobility
Contiki	C	Dynamic	SDN-WISE
MANTIS	C	Dynamic	-
Nano-RK	C	Static	-
LiteOS	Lite C++	Dynamic	-

Source: https://www.mdpi.com/1424-8220/17/5/1031.

Providing a global view of sensor nodes for effective program delivery when forwarding control data or updating node software for a new task is a crucial feature of SDN in WSNs. Because of this, the architecture makes it possible to deliver the program using Over The Air Programming (OTAP) techniques, which help to manage enabling software more effectively. OTAP is used in a reconfigurable SDWSN to download roles to nodes over a multi-hop wireless link. SDN-WISE, an SDN solution for WSNs, has been used to further demonstrate the efficiency of OTAP. SDN-WISE has been used in a practical demonstration to reprogramme WSNs so that different logical sensor networks can coexist while utilizing the same node hardware.

8.3.6.2. Enabling Hardware

The infrastructure of SDN-based WSNs includes hardware that is enabled, and the SDN-enabled sensor node is a crucial part of managing and enabling the SDN integration into WSNs. The SDN requirements must be met in both the node management and design, with a key component being the ability to reconfigure the node through wireless communications even after it has been deployed. Reconfigurable nodes for wireless sensor networks (WSNs) have been demonstrated. One such node is a modular sensor node that uses a Field Programmable Gate Array (FPGA) as its node control unit because FPGA hardware is re-configurable, unlike micro-controllers. This makes it possible for sensor hardware to be remotely reconfigured over wireless networks, which is necessary for SDN-based WSN management. Modern designs that run in ultra low power modes have been developed to lower the energy consumption of FPGAs. A node design with a soft core processor and the ability to be remotely reconfigured using OTAP techniques after deployment, based on the FPGA as the control unit, is another implementation of sensor re-configurability.

In recent years, more attempts have been made to suggest reconfigurable nodes (also known as SDN-enabled nodes) for use in SDN-based WSNs. TinySDN makes use of an SDN-enabled node divided into three sections: ActiveMessageC, a part of TinyOS that manages and provides a programming interface with radio hardware on the sensor; TinySdnP, which updates the flow table in response to a flow setup response; and TinyOS application, which generates data packets and sends them over the network. The node uses a modular FPGA and microcontroller combination to create an energy-efficient node that can be reprogrammed via OTAP to fulfill a variety of functions. The FPGA performs more complex data processing tasks, while the micro-controller modifies the behavior of the network. It has been suggested that SDN-based management for WSNs be implemented with additional enabling hardware, such as computer servers for role or task generation and communication modules for the multi-hop wireless link.

REFERENCES

1. Abu-Mahfouz, A. M., Olwal, T., Kurien, A., Munda, J., & Djouani, K. (2015). Toward developing a distributed autonomous energy management system (DAEMS). In *Proceedings of the 2015 IEEE AFRICON* (pp. 1–6). Addis Ababa, Ethiopia.
2. Akyildiz, I. F., Su, W., Sankarasubramaniam, Y., & Cayirci, E. (2002). Wireless sensor networks: A survey. *Computer Networks, 38*(4), 393–422. https://doi.org/10.1016/S1389-1286(01)00302-4.
3. Cardei, M., & Wu, J. (2006). Energy-efficient coverage problems in wireless ad-hoc sensor networks. *Computer Communications, 29*(4), 413–420. https://doi.org/10.1016/j.comcom.2004.12.025.
4. Chen, B., Jamieson, K., Balakrishnan, H., & Morris, R. (2002). Span: An energy-efficient coordination algorithm for topology maintenance in ad hoc wireless networks. *Wireless Networks, 8*(5), 481–494. https://doi.org/10.1023/A:1016542229220.
5. Cheng, B., Cui, L., Jia, W., Zhao, W., & Hancke, G. P. (2016). Multiple regions of interest coverage in camera sensor networks for tele-intensive care units. *IEEE Transactions on Industrial Informatics, 12*(3), 2331–2341. https://doi.org/10.1109/TII.2016.2574305.
6. Culler, D. E., & Mulder, H. (2004). Smart sensors to network the world. *Scientific American, 290*(6), 84–91. https://doi.org/10.1038/scientificamerican0604-84.
7. Dayal, P., & Kumar, P. (2015). Fault mitigation by topology management in WSN: A survey. In *Proceedings of the 2015 International Conference on Communications and Signal Processing (ICCSP)* (pp. 0836–0840). Melmaruvathur, India.
8. Donmez, M. Y., Isik, S., & Ersoy, C. (2013). Combined analysis of contention window size and duty cycle for throughput and energy optimization in wireless sensor networks. *Computer Networks, 57*(5), 1101–1112. https://doi.org/10.1016/j.comnet.2012.11.016.
9. Gante, A. D., Aslan, M., & Matrawy, A. (2014). Smart wireless sensor network management based on software-defined networking. In *Proceedings of the 2014 27th Biennial Symposium on Communications (QBSC)* (pp. 71–75). Kingston, ON, Canada.
10. Gao, S., Zeng, Y., Luo, H., & Zhang, H. (2016). Scalable control plane for intra-domain communication in software defined information centric networking. *Future Generation Computer Systems, 56*, 110–120. https://doi.org/10.1016/j.future.2015.10.017.

11. Haque, I. T., & Abu-Ghazaleh, N. (2016). Wireless software defined networking: A survey and taxonomy. *IEEE Communications Surveys & Tutorials, 18*(4), 2731–2737. https://doi.org/10.1109/COMST.2016.2571118.
12. Hsu, T. H., & Wu, J. S. (2008). An application-specific duty cycle adjustment MAC protocol for energy conserving over wireless sensor networks. *Computer Communications, 31*(18), 4081–4088. https://doi.org/10.1016/j.comcom.2008.08.010.
13. Hu, F., Hao, Q., & Bao, K. (2014). A survey on software-defined network and OpenFlow: From concept to implementation. *IEEE Communications Surveys & Tutorials, 16*(3), 2181–2206. https://doi.org/10.1109/COMST.2014.2326417.
14. Jararweh, Y., Al-Ayyoub, M., Darabseh, A., Benkhelifa, E., Vouk, M., & Rindos, A. (2016). Software defined cloud: Survey, system and evaluation. *Future Generation Computer Systems, 58*, 56–74. https://doi.org/10.1016/j.future.2015.10.015.
15. Khan, J. A., Qureshi, H. K., & Iqbal, A. (2015). Energy management in wireless sensor networks: A survey. *Computers & Electrical Engineering, 41*, 159–176. https://doi.org/10.1016/j.compeleceng.2014.06.009.
16. Kim, H., & Feamster, N. (2013). Improving network management with software defined networking. *IEEE Communications Magazine, 51*(2), 114–119. https://doi.org/10.1109/MCOM.2013.6461195.
17. Kobo, H. I., Abu-Mahfouz, A. M., & Hancke, G. P. (2017). A survey on software-defined wireless sensor networks: Challenges and design requirements. *IEEE Access, 5*, 1872–1899. https://doi.org/10.1109/ACCESS.2017.2666200.
18. Kruger, C. P., Abu-Mahfouz, A. M., & Hancke, G. P. (2015). Rapid prototyping of a wireless sensor network gateway for the internet of things using off-the-shelf components. In *Proceedings of the 2015 IEEE International Conference on Industrial Technology (ICIT)* (pp. 1926–1931). Seville, Spain.
19. Kumar, A., & Hancke, G. P. (2015). A Zigbee-based animal health monitoring system. *IEEE Sensors Journal, 15*(6), 610–617. https://doi.org/10.1109/JSEN.2014.2349073.
20. Lee, W. L., Datta, A., & Cardell-Oliver, R. (2006). Handbook of Mobile Ad Hoc and Pervasive Communications. American Scientific Publishers, Valencia, CA, USA. *Network Management in Wireless Sensor Networks.*
21. Lopez, M., Sabater, J. M., Daemitabalvandani, M., Gomez, J. M., Carmona, M., & Herms, A. (2013). Software management of power consumption in

WSN based on duty cycle algorithms. In *Proceedings of the 2013 IEEE EUROCON* (pp. 399–406). Zagreb, Croatia.

22. Louw, J., Niezen, G., Ramotsoela, T., & Abu-Mahfouz, A. (2016). A key distribution scheme using elliptic curve cryptography in wireless sensor networks. In *Proceedings of the 2016 IEEE 14th International Conference on Industrial Informatics (INDIN)* (pp. 1166–1170). Poitiers, France.
23. Luo, T., Tan, H. P., & Quek, T. Q. S. (2012). Sensor OpenFlow: Enabling software-defined wireless sensor networks. *IEEE Communications Letters, 16*(12), 1896–1899. https://doi.org/10.1109/LCOMM.2012.092812.121712.
24. Ma, Y. W., Chen, J. L., Huang, Y. M., & Lee, M. Y. (2010). An efficient management system for wireless sensor networks. *Sensors, 10*(12), 11400–11413. https://doi.org/10.3390/s101211400.
25. Mudumbe, M. J., & Abu-Mahfouz, A. M. (2015). Smart water meter system for user-centric consumption measurement. In *Proceedings of the 2015 IEEE 13th International Conference on Industrial Informatics (INDIN)* (pp. 993–998). Cambridge, UK.
26. Ntuli, N., & Abu-Mahfouz, A. (2016). A simple security architecture for smart water management system. *Procedia Computer Science, 83*, 1164–1169. https://doi.org/10.1016/j.procs.2016.04.239.
27. Orfanidis, C. (2016). Ph.D. Forum Abstract: Increasing robustness in WSN using software defined network architecture. In *Proceedings of the 2016 15th ACM/IEEE International Conference on Information Processing in Sensor Networks (IPSN)* (pp. 1–2). Vienna, Austria.
28. Phala, K. S. E., Kumar, A., & Hancke, G. P. (2016). Air quality monitoring system based on ISO/IEC/IEEE 21451 standards. *IEEE Sensors Journal, 16*(17), 5037–5045. https://doi.org/10.1109/JSEN.2016.2555935.
29. Reegan, A. S., & Baburaj, E. (2013). Key management schemes in wireless sensor networks: A survey. In *Proceedings of the 2013 International Conference on Circuits, Power and Computing Technologies (ICCPCT)* (pp. 813–820). Nagercoil, India.
30. Ruiz, L. B., Nogueira, J. M., & Loureiro, A. A. (2003). Manna: A management architecture for wireless sensor networks. *IEEE Communications Magazine, 41*(4), 116–125. https://doi.org/10.1109/MCOM.2003.1179560.
31. Schurgers, C., Tsiatsis, V., & Srivastava, M. B. (2002). STEM: Topology management for energy efficient sensor networks. In *Proceedings of the 2002 IEEE Aerospace Conference* (pp. 1099–1108). Big Sky, MT, USA.

32. Silva, B., Fisher, R. M., Kumar, A., & Hancke, G. P. (2015). Experimental link quality characterization of wireless sensor networks for underground monitoring. *IEEE Transactions on Industrial Informatics, 11*(4), 1099–1110. https://doi.org/10.1109/TII.2015.2471263.
33. Song, H., Kim, D., Lee, K., & Sung, J. (2005). UPnP-based sensor network management architecture. In *Proceedings of the International Conference on Mobile Computing and Ubiquitous Networking* (pp. 1–6). Osaka, Japan.
34. Srbinovski, B., Magno, M., Edwards-Murphy, F., Pakrashi, V., & Popovici, E. (2016). An energy aware adaptive sampling algorithm for energy harvesting WSN with energy hungry sensors. *Sensors, 16*(4), 448. https://doi.org/10.3390/s16040448.
35. Wang, X., Ma, J. J., Wang, S., & Bi, D. W. (2007). Prediction-based dynamic energy management in wireless sensor networks. *Sensors, 7*(3), 251–266. https://doi.org/10.3390/s7030251.
36. Yu, Z., & Guan, Y. (2008). A key management scheme using deployment knowledge for wireless sensor networks. *IEEE Transactions on Parallel and Distributed Systems, 19*(10), 1411–1425.
37. Zhang, B., & Li, G. (2009). Survey of network management protocols in wireless sensor network. In *Proceedings of the 2009 International Conference on E-Business and Information System Security* (pp. 1–5). Wuhan, China.
38. Zhang, Y., Liang, J., Zheng, B., & Chen, W. (2016). A hybrid key management scheme for WSNs based on PPBR and a tree-based path key establishment method. *Sensors, 16*(4), 509. https://doi.org/10.3390/s16040509.
39. Zhang, Y., Liang, J., Zheng, B., Jiang, S., & Chen, W. (2016). Key management scheme based on route planning of mobile sink in wireless sensor networks. *Sensors, 16*(2), 170. https://doi.org/10.3390/s16020170.
40. Zhao, Y., Anjum, M. N., Song, M., Xu, X., & Wang, G. (2015). Optimal resource allocation for delay constrained users in self-coexistence WRAN. In *Proceedings of the 2015 IEEE Global Communications Conference (GLOBECOM)* (pp. 1–6). San Diego, CA, USA.

CHAPTER 9

SCHEDULING MECHANISMS IN SERVERLESS COMPUTING

Contents

INTRODUCTION

In serverless computing, scheduling techniques are essential for effectively allocating resources and maximizing task completion in dynamic, scalable environments. In contrast to conventional computing paradigms, serverless computing focuses on executing functions in response to events or triggers without the need to provision or manage servers. It does this by abstracting infrastructure management. Workload-aware algorithms, which dynamically allocate resources based on real-time workload characteristics like CPU usage, memory requirements, and latency sensitivity, are important scheduling mechanisms.

These algorithms guarantee effective load balancing across the available computing resources and efficient resource utilization. They make it possible for serverless platforms to elastically scale resources in response to fluctuating demand, preserving performance and fulfilling service level goals. Deadline-aware scheduling algorithms make sure that functions are completed within set deadlines by prioritizing tasks according to their time constraints.

This is essential for real-time applications like financial transactions or IoT data processing, where processing events in a timely manner is vital. These algorithms increase the responsiveness and dependability of the system by allocating resources optimally based on task priorities and deadline proximity. The goal of cost-optimized scheduling algorithms is to keep performance levels constant while reducing operating expenses. Based on workload trends and cloud service pricing, they employ dynamic pricing models, spot instances, or predictive analytics to allocate resources in an economical manner. By intelligently managing resource provisioning and utilization, this approach helps organizations optimize their cloud spending, especially in scenarios where workloads fluctuate.

All things considered, efficient scheduling techniques for serverless computing lead to increased scalability, better performance, and lower costs. In an ever-changing digital landscape, they are essential in helping businesses to meet strict budgetary and performance requirements while leveraging cloud resources in a dynamic manner.

9.1. RESOURCE ALLOCATION AND MANAGEMENT

In serverless computing, resource allocation and management are essential components of scheduling mechanisms that are critical to maximizing scalability, cost effectiveness, and performance. Efficient resource management maximizes task processing while lowering operating costs in serverless architectures, where functions are performed in response to events without permanent infrastructure.

9.1.1. Dynamic Resource Allocation Strategies

Dynamic resource allocation in serverless computing involves provisioning computing resources (CPU, memory, storage) based on real-time demand. Key aspects include:

- **Elastic Scaling:** Serverless platforms automatically scale resources up or down based on workload fluctuations. This ensures that functions receive adequate resources during peak periods while reducing costs during idle times.
- **Event-Driven Provisioning:** Resources are allocated dynamically in response to incoming events or triggers. This event-driven approach allows serverless functions to scale instantly to handle varying workloads without manual intervention.
- **Fine-Grained Resource Management:** Serverless platforms allocate resources at a granular level, matching specific requirements of individual functions based on their computational needs and performance constraints.

9.1.1.1. Efficiency and Optimization

Efficient resource allocation in serverless computing involves:

- **Load Balancing:** Distributing workload evenly across available resources to prevent overloading and ensure optimal performance. Load balancing algorithms consider factors like function runtime, memory usage, and current system capacity.
- **Cost Optimization:** Algorithms and strategies are employed to minimize operational costs by intelligently managing resource utilization. This includes leveraging spot instances or preemptible VMs to capitalize on cost savings during low-demand periods.
- **Performance Monitoring:** Continuous monitoring of resource usage and function performance metrics allows for proactive adjustments in resource allocation. This ensures that functions meet their performance targets while optimizing resource utilization.

9.1.1.2. Challenges and Considerations

Managing resource allocation in serverless computing poses several challenges:

- **Cold Start Mitigation:** Minimizing cold start delays by pre-warming function instances or optimizing initialization processes. This is crucial for applications requiring low latency and immediate responsiveness.

- **State Management:** Handling stateful computations in stateless serverless environments requires efficient data management strategies, such as leveraging external storage services or serverless databases.
- **Predictive Scaling:** Using predictive analytics or machine learning models to anticipate workload patterns and adjust resource allocation preemptively. This approach enhances responsiveness and reduces the impact of sudden workload spikes.

Optimizing performance, scalability, and cost-effectiveness in serverless computing requires efficient resource allocation and management. Organizations can effectively meet the demands of modern, event-driven applications while capitalizing on the advantages of serverless architectures through the implementation of cost optimization strategies, load balancing mechanisms, and dynamic provisioning. Improvements in resource management will have a significant impact on how serverless computing is adopted and used in various application scenarios as it develops.

9.1.2. Elastic Scaling and auto-Scaling Mechanisms in Serverless Environments

In serverless computing environments, elasticity and auto-scaling play a key role by providing dynamic resource allocation to effectively manage changing workloads. In contrast to conventional computing models, which usually require provisioning fixed-capacity servers for scalability, serverless platforms dynamically modify resources in real-time according to demand. This feature guarantees that resources are only allocated when necessary, which improves cost-effectiveness while simultaneously optimizing performance.

9.1.2.1. Elastic Scaling

In serverless computing, elastic scaling describes the platform's capacity to smoothly modify resources in accordance with workload demands. It functions according to the idea of scaling up (adding more resources) or down (reducing resources) in response to various inputs, including event triggers, incoming requests, and processing demands. Because of their agility, serverless apps can grow during times of high usage, guaranteeing responsiveness and keeping up performance without the need for human intervention.

Elastic scaling is achieved through:

- **Event-Driven Architecture:** Serverless functions are triggered by events (e.g., HTTP requests, database updates), prompting the platform to allocate resources dynamically. This event-driven approach ensures that resources are provisioned in direct response to workload demands.

- **Automatic Provisioning:** Serverless platforms automatically provision and de-provision resources in near real-time, eliminating the need for capacity planning or manual scaling operations. This scalability feature is particularly beneficial for applications with unpredictable or fluctuating workloads.

9.1.2.2. Auto-Scaling Mechanisms

Auto-scaling mechanisms complement elastic scaling by continuously monitoring application metrics and adjusting resource allocations accordingly. These mechanisms ensure that serverless functions have access to sufficient resources while optimizing cost efficiency. Key aspects include:

- **Performance Metrics Monitoring:** Metrics such as CPU utilization, memory usage, and request latency are monitored in real-time. Thresholds are set based on these metrics to trigger scaling actions when predefined thresholds are exceeded.
- **Horizontal Scaling:** Auto-scaling horizontally by adding more function instances in response to increased demand. This approach distributes workload across multiple instances, enhancing overall system performance and resilience.
- **Scaling Policies:** Defined scaling policies specify how and when to scale resources based on application-specific requirements. Policies may include rules for scaling based on traffic patterns, time of day, or other performance indicators.

9.1.2.3. Benefits and Challenges

The benefits of elastic scaling and auto-scaling mechanisms in serverless environments are substantial:

- **Improved Performance:** Applications maintain consistent performance levels by dynamically adjusting resources to match workload fluctuations.
- **Cost Efficiency:** Resources are provisioned only when needed, optimizing cost by eliminating idle capacity and leveraging cost-effective pricing models (e.g., pay-per-use).
- **Scalability:** Serverless architectures inherently support scalability without the limitations of traditional infrastructure, accommodating sudden spikes in demand seamlessly.

Careful thought must be given to issues like handling cold starts, guaranteeing seamless transitions during scaling events, and adjusting scaling policies to strike a balance between performance and cost effectiveness. However, auto-scaling and elastic scaling are crucial features of contemporary serverless computing, allowing businesses to create scalable, responsive, and reasonably priced applications that can successfully adjust to changing business requirements.

9.1.3. Strategies for Efficient Resource Utilization and Cost Management

In order to ensure optimal performance while controlling operational expenses, serverless computing scheduling mechanisms must take cost management and efficient resource utilization into account. These tactics are necessary because serverless architectures are dynamic, meaning that functions run in response to events without requiring permanent infrastructure.

9.1.3.1. Strategies for Efficient Resource Utilization

1. **Granular Resource Allocation:** Serverless platforms allocate resources on-demand at a granular level, matching specific requirements of individual functions. This ensures that resources (CPU, memory, storage) are provisioned precisely as needed for each task, minimizing waste and maximizing efficiency.
2. **Concurrency Management:** Efficiently managing concurrency allows serverless applications to handle multiple simultaneous requests without over-provisioning resources. Techniques such as connection pooling, thread management, and task batching optimize resource usage, reducing latency and improving throughput.
3. **Parallel Execution:** Leveraging parallel execution of tasks enables serverless functions to process workloads faster and more efficiently. By distributing work across multiple instances or containers, applications can achieve better scalability and utilize resources more effectively during peak demand periods.
4. **Optimized Cold Start Handling:** Mitigating the impact of cold starts, where functions experience initialization delays, is crucial for maintaining responsiveness. Strategies include pre-warming function instances, optimizing initialization scripts, and leveraging warm-up mechanisms provided by serverless platforms to reduce latency and improve user experience.

9.1.3.2. Strategies for Cost Management

1. **Usage-Based Pricing Models:** Taking advantage of pay-per-use pricing models offered by serverless providers ensures that organizations only pay for actual resource consumption. This flexibility allows cost to align closely with application demand, minimizing expenditures during periods of low activity.
2. **Spot Instances and Preemptible Resources:** Utilizing spot instances or preemptible VMs, if supported by the serverless platform, can significantly reduce costs compared to standard on-demand pricing. These resources are available at discounted rates but may be reclaimed by the provider with short notice, requiring resilient application design.
3. **Resource Scheduling and Auto-Scaling Policies:** Implementing intelligent resource scheduling and auto-scaling policies helps optimize cost-efficiency. By scaling resources based on workload patterns, time of day, or other performance metrics, organizations can ensure adequate capacity during peak periods while reducing costs during off-peak times.
4. **Monitoring and Optimization Tools:** Leveraging monitoring tools and analytics dashboards provided by serverless platforms enables continuous optimization of resource usage and cost management. Real-time visibility into performance metrics allows for proactive adjustments to scaling policies and resource allocations based on changing application requirements.

In order for enterprises to fully benefit from scalability, performance, and cost-effectiveness, scheduling mechanisms in serverless computing must include effective resource utilization and cost management.

Businesses can efficiently meet the demands of fluctuating workloads by optimizing their serverless applications through the use of usage-based pricing models, concurrency management, granular resource allocation, and optimized cold start handling.

Additionally, in the dynamic and ever-changing world of serverless computing, integrating cost management techniques like using spot instances, putting in place efficient auto-scaling policies, and utilizing monitoring tools guarantees that organizations can attain optimal resource allocation while keeping control over operational expenses.

9.2. TYPES OF TASK SCHEDULING ALGORITHMS IN CLOUD COMPUTING ENVIRONMENT

One of the most significant technologies of the modern era is cloud computing, which enables users—individuals as well as organizations—to remotely access computing resources—hardware, software, and platforms—as services via the Internet. Cloud computing's scalability, adjustable costs, accessibility, dependability, and pay-as-you-go on-demand services set it apart from more conventional computing paradigms. With millions of users being served concurrently, cloud computing needs to be able to respond to all user requests with high performance and a quality of service (QoS) guarantee. Therefore, in order to fairly and effectively fulfill these requests, we must implement an appropriate task scheduling algorithm. One of the most important problems in the cloud computing environment is task scheduling because it has a major impact on cloud performance. There are many different kinds of scheduling algorithms. Static scheduling algorithms are good for small- to medium-sized cloud computing environments, while dynamic scheduling algorithms are better suited for larger cloud computing settings. Cloud computing is a new technology that is based on distributed and grid computing. It is the use of computing resources (platforms, software, and hardware) as a service that is made available to users over the Internet whenever they need them. It is the first technological application of the idea of commercial computer science implementation for general public use. It depends on the virtualization technique being used to share resources among users. Cloud computing can deliver high performance by equitably and efficiently allocating workloads across all resources to minimize waiting times, maximize throughput, and effectively utilize resources. Although cloud computing still faces many difficulties, task scheduling and load balancing remain the most significant since they are thought to be the primary determinants of other performance parameters like availability, scalability, and power consumption.

9.2.1. Tasks Scheduling Algorithms overview

Tasks scheduling algorithms are defined as the mechanism used to select the resources to execute tasks to get less waiting and execution time.

9.2.1.1. Workload-Aware Scheduling Algorithms

In serverless computing environments, workload-aware scheduling algorithms are essential for maximizing performance and resource utilization. The goal of these algorithms is to dynamically assign resources according to the demands and characteristics of incoming workloads.

Here's an overview of workload-aware scheduling algorithms:

1. *Definition and Purpose*

   Workload-aware scheduling algorithms are designed to make intelligent decisions about how and when to allocate resources to serverless functions or tasks based on real-time workload characteristics. The main objectives include:

- **Resource Efficiency:** Maximizing resource utilization to minimize costs and improve performance.
- **Load Balancing:** Distributing workloads evenly across available resources to avoid bottlenecks and optimize throughput.
- **Response Time Optimization:** Ensuring tasks are executed within acceptable response time limits by allocating adequate resources.

2. *Types of Workload Characteristics*

   Workload-aware algorithms typically consider various characteristics of incoming workloads, such as:

- **CPU and Memory Requirements:** Tasks may have different resource demands based on their computational intensity.
- **I/O Intensity:** Some tasks may require significant input/output operations, affecting their performance characteristics.
- **Latency Sensitivity:** Certain tasks may have strict latency requirements, necessitating faster resource allocation.
- **Temporal Patterns:** Workloads may exhibit periodic or bursty patterns, influencing resource allocation strategies.

3. *Common Workload-aware Scheduling Algorithms*

a. Threshold-based Scheduling

- **Description:** Assigns resources to tasks based on predefined thresholds of workload characteristics (e.g., CPU utilization, queue length).
- **Advantages:** Simple implementation, effective for predictable workloads.
- **Challenges:** May not adapt well to sudden workload changes or complex patterns.

b. Predictive Scheduling

- **Description:** Uses historical data or machine learning models to predict future workload patterns.
- **Advantages:** Can anticipate workload spikes and adjust resource allocations proactively.

- **Challenges:** Requires accurate predictions and continuous model refinement.

c. **Feedback Control Scheduling**

- **Description:** Monitors system performance metrics (e.g., response time, queue length) and adjusts resource allocations based on feedback loops.
- **Advantages:** Responsive to real-time changes in workload and system conditions.
- **Challenges:** Overhead of monitoring and decision-making processes.

d. **Queue-based Scheduling**

- **Description:** Prioritizes tasks in a queue based on their characteristics (e.g., FIFO, priority queues).
- **Advantages:** Fairly simple implementation, suitable for handling different task priorities.
- **Challenges:** May lead to resource contention if not managed carefully.

4. *Implementation Considerations*

- **Scalability:** Algorithms should scale efficiently with increasing workload and system size.
- **Adaptability:** Ability to adjust resource allocations dynamically in response to changing workload patterns.
- **Overhead:** Minimizing overhead associated with monitoring, decision-making, and resource allocation processes.
- **Integration:** Compatibility with existing serverless platforms and frameworks (e.g., AWS Lambda, Azure Functions).

5. *Evaluation Metrics*

- **Resource Utilization:** Measure of how effectively resources are utilized across tasks.
- **Response Time:** Average time taken to execute tasks from submission to completion.
- **Fairness:** Even distribution of resources among concurrent tasks or users.
- **Cost Efficiency:** Optimization of resource usage to minimize operational costs.

As serverless computing gains traction, workload-aware scheduling algorithms keep developing with the goal of balancing resource efficiency, performance optimization, and cost-effectiveness in dynamic and unpredictable environments.

9.2.1.2. Deadline-Aware Scheduling Algorithms

In serverless computing, deadline-aware scheduling algorithms are essential for meeting task or function deadlines while maximizing resource utilization. These algorithms are primarily concerned with scheduling tasks according to deadline requirements and dynamically allocating resources.

Here's an overview of deadline-aware scheduling algorithms:

1. Definition and Purpose

   Deadline-aware scheduling algorithms prioritize tasks based on their deadlines, aiming to meet or optimize their completion within specified time constraints. The primary objectives include:

- **Deadline Compliance:** Ensuring tasks are completed within their defined deadlines to meet application requirements.
- **Resource Efficiency:** Optimizing resource allocation to maximize utilization while meeting deadlines.
- **Performance Guarantees:** Providing predictable and reliable performance for time-sensitive tasks.

2. Types of Deadline Requirements

   Tasks in serverless computing can have various deadline requirements, influencing scheduling decisions:

- **Hard Deadlines:** Tasks must complete by a specific time to avoid significant consequences (e.g., financial transactions, real-time processing).
- **Soft Deadlines:** Desired completion times that, if missed, result in degraded performance or user experience.

3. Common Deadline-aware Scheduling Algorithms

a. Earliest Deadline First (EDF)

- **Description:** Prioritizes tasks based on their earliest absolute deadline.
- **Advantages:** Simple and effective for real-time tasks with strict deadlines.
- **Challenges:** May lead to resource contention if not all tasks can be accommodated within their deadlines.

b. **Latest Deadline First (LDF)**

- **Description:** Prioritizes tasks based on their latest absolute deadline.
- **Advantages:** Ensures that tasks with later deadlines are not starved of resources.
- **Challenges:** Risk of missing earlier deadlines if not managed carefully.

c. **Deadline Monotonic (DM)**

- **Description:** Assigns priorities based on deadlines, where shorter deadlines receive higher priority.
- **Advantages:** Prevents higher-priority tasks from missing their deadlines.
- **Challenges:** Requires accurate estimation and prediction of task deadlines.

d. **Utility-based Scheduling**

- **Description:** Considers task utility functions that combine deadline proximity and resource usage to optimize scheduling decisions.
- **Advantages:** Flexible approach that can balance deadline compliance and resource efficiency.
- **Challenges:** Complexity in defining and implementing utility functions.

4. Implementation Considerations

- **Dynamic Adjustment:** Algorithms should dynamically adjust resource allocations based on real-time workload and deadline changes.
- **Predictive Capabilities:** Utilizing historical data or predictive models to anticipate future workload patterns and deadline requirements.
- **Scalability:** Ensuring scalability to handle increasing numbers of tasks and varying workload intensities.

5. **Evaluation Metrics**

- **Deadline Compliance Rate:** Percentage of tasks completed within their specified deadlines.
- **Resource Utilization:** Efficiency of resource usage across tasks while meeting deadlines.
- **Response Time:** Average time taken to complete tasks relative to their deadlines.

- **Fairness:** Equitable distribution of resources among concurrent tasks to avoid starvation.

Algorithms for scheduling that consider deadlines are essential for applications that demand predictable performance guarantees and real-time responsiveness. These algorithms will be essential for efficiently allocating resources and satisfying demanding application requirements as serverless computing develops.

9.2.1.3. Cost-Optimized Scheduling Algorithms

In serverless computing, cost-optimized scheduling algorithms seek to reduce running costs while preserving or improving resource efficiency and performance. These algorithms concentrate on using cost considerations to make wise decisions regarding task scheduling and resource allocation.

Here's an overview of cost-optimized scheduling algorithms:

1. Definition and Purpose

   Cost-optimized scheduling algorithms prioritize resource allocation and task scheduling to minimize the overall operational costs associated with executing functions or tasks in serverless environments.

The primary objectives include:

- **Cost Efficiency:** Optimizing resource usage to reduce cloud service costs, including computation, storage, and data transfer expenses.
- **Performance Optimization:** Ensuring tasks are completed within acceptable time frames while minimizing resource wastage.
- **Scalability:** Handling variable workloads and efficiently scaling resources to meet demand without incurring unnecessary costs.

2. Factors Influencing Cost Optimization

   Cost-optimized scheduling algorithms consider several factors to make informed decisions:

- **Resource Pricing Models:** Understanding the cost structures (e.g., pay-per-use, reserved instances) of cloud services and resource types (e.g., CPU, memory).
- **Workload Characteristics:** Analyzing workload patterns, peak times, and resource demands to allocate resources efficiently.
- **Performance Metrics:** Balancing cost considerations with performance metrics such as response time, throughput, and latency.

3. Common Cost-optimized Scheduling Algorithms

a. **Threshold-based Cost Optimization**

- **Description:** Sets thresholds or limits on resource usage based on cost considerations (e.g., maximum budget allocation).
- **Advantages:** Simple implementation, effective for controlling costs under predictable workloads.
- **Challenges:** May not adapt well to sudden workload changes or complex cost structures.

b. **Predictive Cost Optimization**

- **Description:** Uses historical data or predictive models to forecast future workload patterns and cost implications.
- **Advantages:** Proactively adjusts resource allocations to optimize costs based on anticipated demand.
- **Challenges:** Requires accurate prediction models and continuous refinement based on changing workload behaviors.

c. **Spot Instance Utilization**

- **Description:** Utilizes spot instances or preemptible VMs (if supported by the serverless platform) to leverage cost savings during periods of low demand.
- **Advantages:** Significant cost savings compared to on-demand instances.
- **Challenges:** Instances may be reclaimed by the cloud provider with short notice, impacting task execution reliability.

d. **Dynamic Pricing and Auction-based Algorithms**

- **Description:** Incorporates auction mechanisms or dynamic pricing strategies to allocate resources based on real-time supply and demand.
- **Advantages:** Maximizes cost savings by responding to fluctuations in cloud resource availability and pricing.
- **Challenges:** Complexity in implementation and potential variability in cost predictability.

4. Implementation Considerations

- **Cost Visibility:** Ensuring visibility into cost structures and utilization patterns to make informed scheduling decisions.
- **Integration with Cloud Providers:** Leveraging APIs and integrations provided by cloud service providers for real-time cost monitoring and management.

- **Adaptive Resource Allocation:** Dynamically adjusting resource allocations based on real-time cost fluctuations and workload changes.

5. **Evaluation Metrics**

- **Cost Savings:** Percentage reduction in operational costs achieved through the use of cost-optimized scheduling algorithms.
- **Resource Utilization Efficiency:** Measure of how effectively resources are utilized relative to cost optimization goals.
- **Performance Metrics:** Impact on task completion times and system responsiveness while optimizing costs.
- **Risk Management:** Mitigation strategies for handling unexpected cost spikes or resource shortages.

Cost-optimized scheduling algorithms are crucial for organizations aiming to maximize the efficiency and cost-effectiveness of their serverless computing deployments. By balancing performance requirements with cost considerations, these algorithms enable businesses to achieve optimal resource utilization and operational efficiency in cloud environments

9.2.2. Tasks Scheduling Algorithms Definition and Advantages

Tasks scheduling algorithms are defined as a set of rules and policies used to assign tasks to the suitable resources (CPU, memory, and bandwidth) to get the highest level possible of performance and resources utilization.

9.2.2.1. Task scheduling algorithms advantages

- Manage cloud computing performance and QoS.
- Manage the memory and CPU.
- The good scheduling algorithms maximizing resources utilization while minimizing the total task execution time.
- Improving fairness for all tasks.
- Increasing the number of successfully completed tasks.
- Scheduling tasks on a real-time system.
- Achieving a high system throughput.
- Improving load balance.

9.2.2.2. Tasks scheduling algorithms classifications

Tasks scheduling algorithms classified as in Figure 9.1.

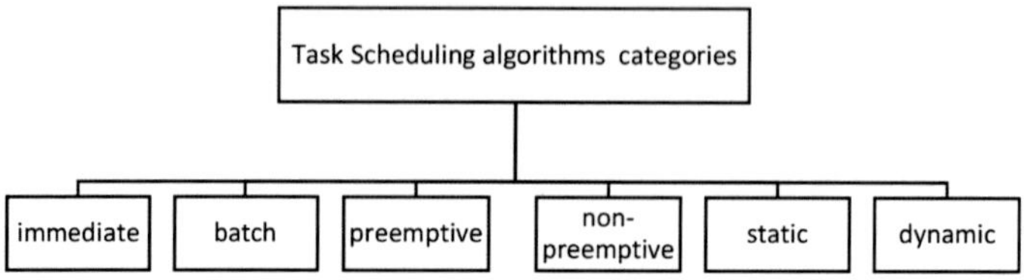

Figure 9.1. *Tasks scheduling classes.*

Source: https://cdnintech.com/media/chapter/71902/1512345123/media/F1.png.

9.2.2.3. Tasks scheduling algorithms can be classified as follows

- **Immediate scheduling:** when new tasks arrive, they are scheduled to VMs directly.
- **Batch scheduling:** tasks are grouped into a batch before being sent; this type is also called mapping events.
- **Static scheduling:** is considered very simple compared to dynamic scheduling; it is based on prior information of the global state of the system. It does not take into account the current state of VMs and then divides all traffic equivalently among all VMs in a similar manner such as round robin (RR) and random scheduling algorithms.
- **Dynamic scheduling:** takes into account the current state of VMs and does not require prior information of the global state of the system and distribute the tasks according to the capacity of all available VMs.
- **Preemptive scheduling:** each task is interrupted during execution and can be moved to another resource to complete execution.
- **Non-preemptive scheduling:** VMs are not re-allocated to new tasks until finishing execution of the scheduled task.

First service (FCFS), shortest job first (SJF), and MAX-MAX scheduling algorithms in complexity and cost within a small or medium scale.

9.2.2.4. Task Scheduling System in Cloud Computing

The task scheduling system in cloud computing passes through three levels.

- The first task level: is a set of tasks (Cloudlets) that is sent by cloud users, which are required for execution.
- The second scheduling level: is responsible for mapping tasks to suitable resources to get highest resource utilization with minimum makespan. The makespan is the overall completion time for all tasks from the beginning to the end.

- The third VMs level: is a set of (VMs) which are used to execute the tasks as in Figure 9.2.

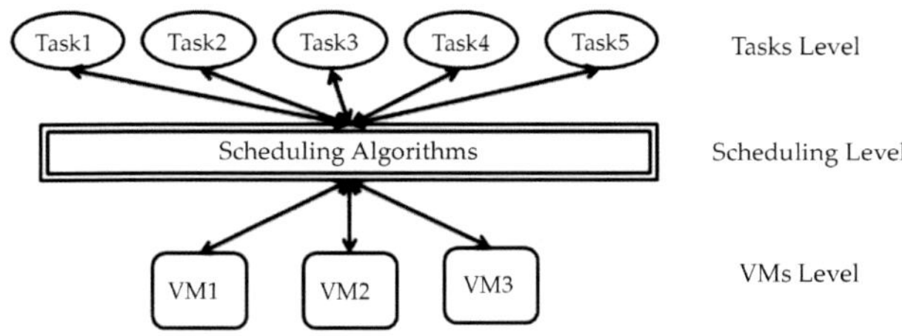

Figure 9.2. *Task scheduling system.*

Source: https://cdnintech.com/media/chapter/71902/1512345123/media/F1.png.

9.3. PERFORMANCE OPTIMIZATION

In order to ensure that applications meet desired service level objectives (SLOs) and take advantage of the scalability and cost-efficiency inherent in serverless architectures, it is imperative that scheduling mechanisms in serverless computing be optimized for performance.

Here's an exploration of strategies and considerations for optimizing performance in serverless computing environments:

- ***Understanding Performance in Serverless Computing***

Performance in serverless computing is measured by factors such as:

- **Latency:** The time taken for a function to start executing in response to an event or request.
- **Throughput:** The rate at which functions can be processed simultaneously or within a specific timeframe.
- **Reliability:** Ensuring functions execute consistently and predictably, meeting availability requirements.
- ***Strategies for Performance Optimization***

1. **Function Design and Architecture:**

- **Statelessness:** Design functions to be stateless whenever possible. State management can introduce complexity and impact performance in serverless environments.
- **Granularity:** Decompose applications into smaller, more focused functions. This promotes better scalability and allows for more efficient resource utilization.

2. **Cold Start Optimization:**

- **Warm-up Strategies:** Utilize techniques like function pre-warming to reduce the impact of cold starts. Keeping functions warm or initializing them proactively can minimize latency when handling sudden spikes in workload.

3. **Concurrency Management:**

- **Adjusting Limits:** Configure concurrency limits ased on workload characteristics and expected traffic patterns. Optimizing these limits ensures that functions can handle concurrent requests efficiently without resource contention.

4. **Memory and Resource Allocation:**

- **Right-sizing:** Allocate appropriate amounts of memory and CPU resources to functions based on their requirements. Over-provisioning or under-provisioning can affect performance and cost-efficiency.

5. **Parallel Execution and Asynchronous Patterns:**

- **Event-driven Design:** Leverage asynchronous processing and event-driven architectures. This allows functions to execute in parallel, maximizing throughput and responsiveness to incoming events.

6. **Performance Monitoring and Optimization:**

- **Real-time Metrics:** Implement monitoring tools to track performance metrics such as latency, error rates, and throughput. Use these metrics to identify bottlenecks and optimize resource allocation and function design.
- **Auto-scaling:** Configure auto-scaling policies based on performance metrics to dynamically adjust resources in response to workload changes. This ensures that applications can maintain performance under varying traffic conditions.
- ***Challenges and Considerations***
- **Vendor-specific Limitations:** Serverless platforms may impose constraints on execution duration, memory allocation, and concurrency, which can impact performance optimization strategies.
- **Network and I/O Bound Tasks:** Functions with high I/O or network dependency may experience latency issues. Optimizing data access patterns and leveraging caching can mitigate these challenges.
- **Security and Compliance:** Implementing performance optimizations while adhering to security best practices and regulatory requirements is crucial to maintaining application integrity and user trust.

Serverless computing performance optimization necessitates a comprehensive strategy that combines proactive monitoring, efficient function design, and effective resource management. Through the implementation of these strategies, enterprises can attain high-performance applications that exhibit dynamic scalability, uphold dependability, and optimize operational expenses within the rapidly changing cloud computing landscape. Performance optimization strategies must be continuously assessed and modified in order to accommodate shifting workload requirements and technology developments in serverless platforms.

9.3.1. Mitigating Cold Starts and Optimizing Warm Start Performance

Key challenges in serverless computing, where functions are instantiated dynamically in response to events or requests, are mitigating cold starts and optimizing warm start performance. Cold starts, which result in latency that may affect an application's responsiveness, happen when a function instance is initialized for the first time or following a spell of inactivity.

Here's an exploration of strategies to mitigate cold starts and optimize warm start performance:

9.3.1.1. Strategies to Mitigate Cold Starts

1. **Pre-warming Function Instances:**

- **Scheduled Invocations:** Trigger function invocations periodically to keep instances warm. This approach ensures that function instances are ready to handle requests instantly, reducing cold start latency.
- **Predictive Scaling:** Anticipate workload spikes or known peak times to preemptively warm up function instances. Predictive analytics or historical data analysis can inform scheduling decisions for pre-warming.

2. **Optimizing Initialization Time:**

- **Minimize Dependencies:** Reduce the number and complexity of dependencies required during function initialization. Lightweight dependencies and efficient initialization scripts can help minimize startup time.
- **Lazy Loading:** Load dependencies or resources on-demand rather than pre-loading everything at startup. Lazy loading techniques can expedite the initialization process by deferring resource allocation until needed.

3. **Optimizing Platform-specific Settings:**

- **Platform Configuration:** Adjust platform-specific settings such as memory allocation, instance size, and concurrency limits. Fine-tuning these configurations can affect cold start latency by optimizing resource availability and allocation.
- **Use of Warm-Up APIs:** Some serverless platforms provide warm-up APIs or capabilities to initialize function instances in advance of actual requests. Leveraging these APIs can preemptively reduce cold start latency.

9.3.1.2. Strategies to Optimize Warm Start Performance

1. **Efficient Resource Utilization:**

- **Memory Allocation:** Right-size memory allocation based on function requirements and workload characteristics. Adequate memory allocation can improve execution speed and responsiveness during warm starts.
- **Concurrency Settings:** Configure concurrency limits and adjust scaling policies to ensure sufficient resources are available for handling concurrent requests efficiently.

2. **State Management Strategies:**

- **Stateless Architectures:** Design functions to be stateless wherever possible to avoid carrying over state between invocations. Stateless architectures simplify warm start performance by reducing the overhead of managing and restoring state.

3. **Caching and Optimization Techniques:**

- **Result Caching:** Cache frequently accessed data or computation results to expedite subsequent warm starts. Caching can significantly reduce latency by eliminating the need to recompute or fetch data repeatedly.
- **Code Optimization:** Optimize function code for performance by identifying and eliminating inefficiencies. Techniques such as code profiling and performance testing help identify bottlenecks and areas for improvement.

9.3.1.3. Continuous Monitoring and Improvement

- **Performance Monitoring:** Implement robust monitoring and logging mechanisms to track cold start times, warm start performance metrics, and overall function execution times. Real-time visibility into performance indicators enables proactive adjustments and optimizations.

- **Iterative Optimization:** Continuously iterate on optimization strategies based on performance data and feedback. Regularly review and refine warm-up policies, resource allocations, and architectural decisions to align with evolving application requirements and platform capabilities

Proactive planning, platform-specific optimizations, and ongoing monitoring are needed to minimize cold starts and maximize warm start performance. Through the implementation of these strategies, organizations can optimize serverless computing benefits in dynamic and scalable environments, improve user experience, and increase application responsiveness.

9.3.2. Managing and reusing execution environments (containers or VMs)

In serverless computing, managing and reusing execution environments—whether they be virtual machines (VMs) or containers—is essential to maximizing resource utilization and reducing startup latency. Serverless platforms can minimize the overhead of repeatedly initializing environments for each function call by reusing execution environments.

Strategies for Managing and Reusing Execution Environments:

1. **Persistent Execution Contexts:** Maintain persistent execution contexts for frequently invoked functions. By keeping containers or VMs warm and ready, platforms can minimize cold starts and improve overall performance.
2. **Resource Pooling:** Implement resource pooling techniques to efficiently manage and allocate execution environments based on workload demands. This approach allows platforms to dynamically assign resources as needed while maintaining responsiveness.
3. **Lifecycle Management:** Employ efficient lifecycle management policies to recycle or terminate idle execution environments. Automated policies can ensure that resources are released when not in use, optimizing cost-effectiveness and resource allocation.
4. **Platform-Specific Optimizations:** Leverage platform-specific features and optimizations, such as instance size adjustments, concurrency settings, and caching mechanisms, to further enhance performance and scalability.

Effective management and reuse of execution environments enable serverless platforms to deliver consistent performance, minimize operational overhead, and support applications with varying workload patterns efficiently.

9.3.3. Parallel Execution and Concurrency Management Strategies

In serverless computing, concurrency control and parallel execution are crucial techniques for maximizing throughput, maximizing resource usage, and improving application responsiveness.

These techniques take advantage of the distributed and scalable characteristics of serverless architectures to enable the execution of multiple functions at the same time.

Strategies for Parallel Execution and Concurrency Management:

1. **Concurrency Limits:** Set appropriate concurrency limits for functions to ensure efficient resource allocation and prevent overloading of execution environments. By adjusting concurrency settings based on workload characteristics, platforms can balance resource utilization and maintain performance.
2. **Asynchronous Processing:** Design applications to leverage asynchronous patterns, where tasks are processed independently and concurrently. This approach allows serverless functions to handle multiple requests simultaneously without waiting for each operation to complete sequentially.
3. **Event-driven Architecture:** Utilize event-driven design principles to trigger parallel execution of functions in response to events or triggers. Events can initiate multiple functions concurrently, distributing workload and optimizing response times.
4. **Parallelism in Workflows:** Break down complex workflows into smaller, independent tasks that can be executed in parallel. This approach improves overall workflow performance by minimizing latency and maximizing throughput.

In serverless computing, careful consideration of workload distribution, resource constraints, and platform capabilities are necessary for effective concurrency management and parallel execution.

By putting these tactics into practice, businesses can create responsive and scalable apps that fulfill performance demands and make effective use of cloud resources.

9.3.4. Fault Tolerance and Reliability

In serverless computing, fault tolerance and dependability are crucial for making sure apps continue to function and respond in the event of errors or disruptions. Because server management is abstracted, serverless architectures naturally reduce the risk of certain traditional infrastructure-related failures. However, because serverless environments are distributed and event-driven, specific strategies are needed to ensure fault tolerance and reliability.

Strategies for Fault Tolerance and Reliability:

1. **Redundancy and Replication:** Implement redundant architectures and data replication across multiple availability zones or regions. This approach ensures that applications can withstand failures of individual components or infrastructure failures without disruption.
2. **Retry Mechanisms:** Incorporate retry logic into functions to handle transient errors or timeouts gracefully. Retry strategies can include exponential backoff to mitigate overload during transient spikes.
3. **Circuit Breaker Patterns:** Use circuit breaker patterns to prevent cascading failures by temporarily stopping requests to a failed service or function. This allows time for recovery and reduces the impact of failures on overall application performance.
4. **Monitoring and Alerting:** Implement robust monitoring and alerting mechanisms to detect and respond to failures in real-time. Monitoring metrics such as function invocation errors, latency spikes, and resource utilization provide visibility into system health and enable proactive mitigation of issues.
5. **State Management and Recovery:** Design stateless functions where possible and implement mechanisms for recovering stateful data in case of failures. Utilize serverless-compatible storage solutions for persistent data and ensure data integrity through backups and replication.

Organizations can improve serverless computing environments' fault tolerance and reliability by putting these strategies into practice. This will guarantee continuous operation, maintain service availability, and provide seamless user experiences even in the face of unforeseen difficulties or failures.

9.3.5. Security and Isolation

In serverless computing, security and isolation are essential components of scheduling mechanisms that guarantee the safety of resources, data, and applications in shared cloud environments. In order to achieve runtime isolation and security, serverless architectures abstract infrastructure management and rely on cloud providers. Nonetheless, extra care must be taken to minimize potential weaknesses and guarantee a strong security posture.

Key Strategies for Security and Isolation in Serverless Computing:

1. **Containerization and Sandbox Environments:** Serverless platforms use containerization or sandboxing techniques to isolate functions from each other and from the underlying infrastructure. This ensures that each function operates within its designated environment without impacting others.
2. **Access Control and Authentication:** Implement strong access control policies and authentication mechanisms to restrict access to functions, APIs, and resources based on least privilege principles. Use identity and access management (IAM) tools to manage permissions effectively.
3. **Encryption:** Encrypt data both at rest and in transit to protect sensitive information from unauthorized access or interception. Utilize encryption standards and protocols recommended by cloud providers to ensure data confidentiality.
4. **Vulnerability Management:** Regularly scan and assess serverless functions and dependencies for vulnerabilities. Apply patches and updates promptly to mitigate security risks and maintain a secure environment.
5. **Logging and Monitoring:** Implement comprehensive logging and monitoring solutions to detect anomalous behavior, unauthorized access attempts, or potential security incidents in real-time. Use these insights to respond swiftly and effectively to security events.

Organizations can improve the security and isolation of their serverless apps by incorporating these techniques into scheduling mechanisms. In addition to guarding against dangers, proactive security measures also foster trust in the dependability and integrity of serverless computing environments, which are vital for hosting sensitive data and important workloads.

9.3.6. Integration with Ecosystems

The enhancement of scheduling mechanisms' flexibility and functionality through integration with ecosystems in serverless computing facilitates smooth interaction with a variety of services and tools available within the cloud ecosystem. Serverless platforms enable robust application development and deployment workflows by supporting integration through APIs, event-driven architectures, and compatibility with third-party services.

Key Aspects of Integration with Ecosystems:

1. **API Gateway Integration:** Serverless functions can integrate directly with API gateways to expose endpoints for external access. This enables interoperability with external systems, web services, and microservices architectures.
2. **Event-Driven Architecture:** Leveraging event-driven patterns allows serverless functions to respond to events from various sources within the ecosystem, such as message queues, databases, and IoT devices. This enhances scalability and responsiveness by decoupling components and reducing dependencies.
3. **Service Composition:** Composing serverless functions with other cloud services, such as storage, databases, and machine learning tools, supports complex workflows and enhances application capabilities without managing underlying infrastructure.
4. **DevOps Toolchain Integration:** Integration with DevOps tools and continuous integration/continuous deployment (CI/CD) pipelines streamlines deployment processes. Automation tools enable seamless updates, version control, and testing of serverless applications across environments.
5. **Monitoring and Analytics:** Integrating with monitoring and analytics platforms provides visibility into performance metrics, resource utilization, and application health. This facilitates proactive management, troubleshooting, and optimization of serverless functions within the ecosystem.

Organizations can extend functionality through seamless interaction with a wide range of cloud services and tools, while also taking advantage of the scalability, agility, and cost-efficiency benefits of serverless computing, by embracing integration with ecosystems. In contemporary cloud environments, this promotes innovation, quickens development cycles, and supports a range of application requirements.

9.3.7. Real-time and Batch Processing

Because serverless architectures are inherently scalable and event-driven, scheduling mechanisms are essential to the efficient execution of both real-time and batch processing tasks in serverless computing.

- **Real-time Processing:** In serverless computing, real-time processing refers to managing events or data streams as quickly as possible. When events happen, like user interactions, sensor data updates, or system notifications, functions are immediately triggered. By ensuring that resources are distributed dynamically to handle these events quickly, scheduling mechanisms preserve high responsiveness and low latency. Applications that need to process data instantly, perform real-time analytics, or react quickly to user input should use this method.

- **Batch Processing:** Batch processing is the practice of carrying out operations on sizable datasets that can be triggered by accumulating data volumes or scheduled to run at predetermined intervals. Serverless platforms use scheduling mechanisms to coordinate batch jobs in order to maximize resource utilization and control task dependencies. Functions scale dynamically in response to workload demands, handling batches in an economical and efficient manner. This method works well for tasks involving a lot of data, such as data warehousing, ETL (Extract, Transform, Load) procedures, or recurring data analysis projects.
- **Integration:** Organizations can efficiently handle a wide range of application requirements thanks to the serverless computing environments' integration of batch and real-time processing capabilities. Businesses can achieve cost-effectiveness, scalability, and agility in managing data processing workflows by utilizing serverless functions for both scheduled batch operations and immediate event-driven tasks. Because of its adaptability, businesses can swiftly adjust to shifting operational and data requirements, allowing serverless computing to fully realize its potential for contemporary cloud-based applications.

REFERENCES

1. Al-Ali, Z., Goodarzy, S., Hunter, E., Ha, S., Han, R., Keller, E., & Rozner, E. (2018). Making serverless computing more serverless. In *IEEE 11th International Conference on Cloud Computing (CLOUD)* (pp. 456–459). IEEE.
2. Al-Maamari, A., & Omara, F. (2015). Task scheduling using PSO algorithm in cloud computing environments. *International Journal of Grid and Distributed Computing, 8*(5), 245–256.
3. Alqaryouti, O., & Siyam, N. (2018). Serverless computing and scheduling tasks on cloud: A review. *American Academy of Sciences Research Journal on Engineering and Technology Science, 40*(1), 235–247.
4. Aslanpour, M. S., Toosi, A. N., Cheema, M. A., & Gaire, R. (2022). Energy-aware resource scheduling for serverless edge computing. In *22nd IEEE International Symposium on Cluster, Cloud and Internet Computing (CCGrid)* (pp. 190–199). IEEE.
5. Aslanpour, M. S., Toosi, A. N., Cicconetti, C., Javadi, B., Sbarski, P., Taibi, D., Assuncao, M., Gill, S. S., Gaire, R., & Dustdar, S. (2021). Serverless edge computing: Vision and challenges. In *Australasian Computer Science Week Multiconference* (pp. 1–10).
6. Aytekin, A., & Johansson, M. (2019). Exploiting serverless runtimes for large-scale optimization. In *IEEE 12th International Conference on Cloud Computing (CLOUD)* (pp. 499–501). IEEE.
7. Bai, T., Nie, J. Y., Zhao, W. X., Zhu, Y., Du, P., & Wen, J. R. (2018). An attribute-aware neural attentive model for next basket recommendation. In *The 41st International ACM SIGIR Conference on Research and Development in Information Retrieval* (pp. 1201–1204).
8. Banaei, A., & Sharifi, M. (2022). ETAS: Predictive scheduling of functions on worker nodes of Apache OpenWhisk platform. *Journal of Supercomputing, 78*(4), 5358–5393.
9. Basu, S., Kannayaram, G., Ramasubbareddy, S., & Venkatasubbaiah, C. (2019). Improved genetic algorithm for monitoring of virtual machines in cloud environment. In *Smart Intelligent Computing and Applications* (pp. 319–326). Springer, Berlin.
10. Bi, J., Li, S., Yuan, H., & Zhou, M. (2021). Integrated deep learning method for workload and resource prediction in cloud systems. *Neurocomputing, 424*, 35–48.
11. Bisht, J., & Vampugani, V. S. (2022). Load and cost-aware min-min workflow scheduling algorithm for heterogeneous resources in fog, cloud,

and edge scenarios. *International Journal of Cloud Applications and Computing (IJCAC), 12*(1), 1–20.

12. Carver, B., Zhang, J., Wang, A., Anwar, A., Wu, P., & Cheng, Y. (2020). Wukong: A scalable and locality-enhanced framework for serverless parallel computing. In *Proceedings of the 11th ACM Symposium on Cloud Computing* (pp. 1–15).
13. Castro, P., Ishakian, V., Muthusamy, V., & Slominski, A. (2019). The server is dead, long live the server: Rise of serverless computing, overview of current state and future trends in research and industry. *arXiv preprint arXiv:1906.02888.*
14. Cheng, Y., & Zhou, Z. (2018). Autonomous resource scheduling for real-time and stream processing. In *IEEE Smart World, Ubiquitous Intelligence and Computing, Advanced and Trusted Computing, Scalable Computing and Communications, Cloud and Big Data Computing, Internet of People and Smart City Innovation (Smart World/SCALCOM/UIC/ATC/CBDCom/IOP/SCI)* (pp. 1181–1184). IEEE.
15. Choi, S., Shahbaz, M., Prabhakar, B., & Rosenblum, M. (2019). λ-NIC: Interactive serverless compute on SmartNICs. In *Proceedings of the ACM SIGCOMM Conference Posters and Demos* (pp. 151–152).
16. Das, S. (2021). Ant colony optimization for MapReduce application to optimize task scheduling in serverless platform. National College of Ireland, Dublin.
17. De Palma, G., Giallorenzo, S., Mauro, J., Trentin, M., & Zavattaro, G. (2022). A declarative approach to topology-aware serverless function-execution scheduling. In *2022 IEEE International Conference on Web Services (ICWS)* (pp. 337–342). IEEE.
18. Endo, P., Rodrigues, M., Gonçalves, G., Kelner, J., Sadok, D., & Curescu, C. (2016). High availability in clouds: Systematic review and research challenges. *Journal of Cloud Computing: Advances, Systems and Applications.*
19. Gadepalli, P. K., Peach, G., Cherkasova, L., Aitken, R., & Parmer, G. (2019). Challenges and opportunities for efficient serverless computing at the edge. In *38th Symposium on Reliable Distributed Systems (SRDS)* (pp. 261–2615). IEEE.
20. García-López, P., Sánchez-Artigas, M., Shillaker, S., Pietzuch, P., Breitgand, D., Vernik, G., Sutra, P., Tarrant, T., & Ferrer, A. J. (2019). ServerMix: Tradeoffs and challenges of serverless data analytics. *arXiv preprint arXiv:1907.11465.*

21. Gouda, K., Radhika, T., & Akshatha, M. (2013). Priority-based resource allocation model for cloud computing. *International Journal of Science Engineering and Technology Research (IJSETR), 2*(1), 215–219.
22. Gramaglia, M., Serrano, P., Banchs, A., Garcia-Aviles, G., Garcia-Saavedra, A., & Perez, R. (2020). The case for serverless mobile networking. In *IFIP Networking Conference (Networking)* (pp. 779–784). IEEE.
23. Gunasekaran, J. R., Thinakaran, P., Kandemir, M. T., Urgaonkar, B., Kesidis, G., & Das, C. (2019). Spock: Exploiting serverless functions for SLO and cost aware resource procurement in public cloud. In *IEEE 12th International Conference on Cloud Computing (CLOUD)* (pp. 199–208). IEEE.
24. Haber, M. J., Chappell, B., & Hills, C. (2022). Cloud computing. In *Cloud Attack Vectors* (pp. 9–25). Springer, Berlin.
25. Hellerstein, J. M., Faleiro, J., Gonzalez, J. E., Schleier-Smith, J., Sreekanti, V., Tumanov, A., & Wu, C. (2018). Serverless computing: One step forward, two steps back. *arXiv preprint arXiv:1812.03651.*
26. HoseinyFarahabady, M. R., Taheri, J., Zomaya, A. Y., & Tari, Z. (2021). Data-intensive workload consolidation in serverless (Lambda/FaaS) platforms. In *IEEE 20th International Symposium on Network Computing and Applications (NCA)* (pp. 1–8). IEEE.
27. Kaffes, K., Yadwadkar, N. J., & Kozyrakis, C. (2019). Centralized core-granular scheduling for serverless functions. In *Proceedings of the ACM Symposium on Cloud Computing* (pp. 158–164).
28. Kallam, S., Patan, R., Ramana, T. V., & Gandomi, A. H. (2021). Linear weighted regression and energy-aware greedy scheduling for heterogeneous big data. *Electronics, 10*(5), 554.
29. Khan, Y., & Varma, S. (2020). An efficient cloud forensic approach for IaaS, SaaS, and PaaS models. In *2nd International Conference on Data, Engineering, and Applications (IDEA)* (pp. 1–6). IEEE.
30. Kijak, J., Martyna, P., Pawlik, M., Balis, B., & Malawski, M. (2018). Challenges for scheduling scientific workflows on cloud functions. In *IEEE 11th International Conference on Cloud Computing (CLOUD)* (pp. 460–467). IEEE.
31. Kim, Y. K., HoseinyFarahabady, M. R., Lee, Y. C., & Zomaya, A. Y. (2020). Automated fine-grained CPU cap control in serverless computing platforms. *IEEE Transactions on Parallel and Distributed Systems, 31*(10), 2289–2301.

32. Krishna, S. R., Majji, S., Kishore, S. K., Jaiswal, S., Kostka, J. A. L., & Chouhan, A. S. (2021). Optimization of time-driven scheduling technique for serverless cloud computing. *Turkish Journal of Computer and Mathematics Education, 12*(10), 1–8.

33. Kritikos, K., & Skrzypek, P. (2018). A review of serverless frameworks. In *IEEE/ACM International Conference on Utility and Cloud Computing Companion (UCC Companion)* (pp. 161–168). IEEE.

34. Kumar Garg, S., & Buyya, R. (2012). Green cloud computing and environmental sustainability. Australia: Cloud Computing and Distributed Systems (CLOUDS) Laboratory, Department of Computer Science and Software Engineering, The University of Melbourne.

35. Lakhan, A., Mohammed, M. A., Rashid, A. N., Kadry, S., Panityakul, T., Abdulkareem, K. H., & Thinnukool, O. (2021). Smart-contract aware Ethereum and client-fog-cloud healthcare system. *Sensors, 21*(12), 4093.

36. Larrucea, X., Santamaria, I., Colomo-Palacios, R., & Ebert, C. (2018). Microservices. *IEEE Software, 35*(3), 96–100.

37. Li, Y., Lin, Y., Wang, Y., Ye, K., & Xu, C. Z. (2022). Serverless computing: State-of-the-art, challenges, and opportunities. *IEEE Transactions on Services Computing*. https://doi.org/10.1109/TSC.2022.3166553.

38. Lloyd, W., Vu, M., Zhang, B., David, O., & Leavesley, G. (2018). Improving application migration to serverless computing platforms: Latency mitigation with keep-alive workloads. In *IEEE/ACM International Conference on Utility and Cloud Computing Companion (UCC Companion)* (pp. 195–200). IEEE.

39. Lorido-Botran, T., Miguel-Alonso, J., & Lozano, J. A. (2014). A review of auto-scaling techniques for elastic applications in cloud environments. *Journal of Grid Computing, 12*(4), 559–592.

40. Mahmoudi, N., & Khazaei, H. (2020). Temporal performance modelling of serverless computing platforms. In *Proceedings of the Sixth International Workshop on Serverless Computing* (pp. 1–6).

41. Mampage, A., Karunasekera, S., & Buyya, R. (2021). Deadline-aware dynamic resource management in serverless computing environments. In *IEEE/ACM 21st International Symposium on Cluster, Cloud and Internet Computing (CCGrid)* (pp. 483–492). IEEE.

42. Martins, H. J. M. (2019). *Plataformas De Computação Serverless: Estudo E Benchmark*. Universidade de Coimbra.

43. McGrath, G., & Brenner, P. R. (2017). Serverless computing: Design, implementation, and performance. In *IEEE 37th International Conference*

on Distributed Computing Systems Workshops (ICDCSW) (pp. 405–410). IEEE.

44. Mustafa, S., Nazir, B., Hayat, A., & Madani, S. A. (2015). Resource management in cloud computing: Taxonomy, prospects, and challenges. *Computers & Electrical Engineering, 47*, 186–203.
45. Niu, X., Kumanov, D., Hung, L. H., Lloyd, W., & Yeung, K. Y. (2019). Leveraging serverless computing to improve performance for sequence comparison. In *Proceedings of the 10th ACM International Conference on Bioinformatics, Computational Biology, and Health Informatics* (pp. 683–687).
46. Oakes, E., Yang, L., Zhou, D., Houck, K., Harter, T., Arpaci-Dusseau, A., & Arpaci-Dusseau, R. (2018). {SOCK}: Rapid task provisioning with {serverless-optimized} containers. In *2018 USENIX Annual Technical Conference (USENIX ATC 18)* (pp. 57–70).
47. Pawlik, M., Banach, P., & Malawski, M. (2019). Adaptation of workflow application scheduling algorithm to serverless infrastructure. In *European Conference on Parallel Processing* (pp. 345–356). Springer, Berlin.
48. Pérez, A., Moltó, G., Caballer, M., & Calatrava, A. (2018). Serverless computing for container-based architectures. *Future Generation Computer Systems, 83*, 50–59.
49. Pu, Q., Venkataraman, S., & Stoica, I. (2019). Shuffling, fast and slow: Scalable analytics on serverless infrastructure. In *16th USENIX Symposium on Networked Systems Design and Implementation (NSDI 19)* (pp. 193–206).
50. Ramotra, A., & Bala, A. (2013). Task-aware priority-based scheduling in cloud computing [Master thesis]. Thapar University.
51. Rausch, T., Rashed, A., & Dustdar, S. (2021). Optimized container scheduling for data-intensive serverless edge computing. *Future Generation Computer Systems, 114*, 259–271.
52. Raza, A., Matta, I., Akhtar, N., Kalavri, V., & Isahagian, V. (2021). SoK: Function-as-a-Service: From an application developer's perspective. *Journal of Systems Research, 1*(1).
53. Sánchez-Artigas, M., & Sarroca, P. G. (2021). Experience paper: Towards enhancing cost efficiency in serverless machine learning training. In *Proceedings of the 22nd International Middleware Conference* (pp. 210–222).
54. Scheuner, J., & Leitner, P. (2020). Function-as-a-Service performance evaluation: A multifocal literature review. *Journal of Systems and Software, 170*, 110708.

55. Sewak, M., & Singh, S. (2018). Winning in the era of serverless computing and function as a Service. In *3rd International Conference for Convergence in Technology (I2CT)* (pp. 1–5). IEEE.

56. Shafiei, H., Khonsari, A., & Mousavi, P. (2022). Serverless computing: A survey of opportunities, challenges, and applications. *ACM Computing Surveys, 54*(11s), 1–32. Article No: 239. https://doi.org/10.1145/3510611

57. Shahrad, M., Balkind, J., & Wentzlaff, D. (2019). Architectural implications of function-as-a-Service computing. In *Proceedings of the 52nd Annual IEEE/ACM International Symposium on Microarchitecture* (pp. 1063–1075).

58. Silab, M. V., Hassanpour, S. B., Khonsari, A., & Dadlani, A. (2022). On skipping redundant computation via smart task deployment for faster serverless. In *ICC-IEEE International Conference on Communications* (pp. 5475–5480). IEEE.

59. Singh, S., Chana, I., & Singh, M. (2017). The journey of QoS-aware autonomic cloud computing. *IT Professional, 19*(2), 42–49.

60. Singhvi, A., Houck, K., Balasubramanian, A., Shaikh, M. D., Venkataraman, S., & Akella, A. (2019). Archipelago: A scalable low-latency serverless platform. *arXiv preprint arXiv:1911.09849.*

61. Solaiman, K., & Adnan, M. A. (2020). WLEC: A not so cold architecture to mitigate cold start problem in serverless computing. In *Proceedings of the IEEE International Conference on Cloud Engineering (IC2E)* (pp. 144–153). IEEE.

62. Suresh, A., & Gandhi, A. (2019). FNSCHED: An efficient scheduler for serverless functions. In *Proceedings of the 5th International Workshop on Serverless Computing* (pp. 19–24).

63. Suresh, A., & Gandhi, A. (2021). Server more: Opportunistic execution of serverless functions in the cloud. In *Proceedings of the ACM Symposium on Cloud Computing* (pp. 570–584).

64. Totoy, G., Boza, E. F., & Abad, C. L. (2018). An extensible scheduler for the OpenLambda FaaS platform. In *Min-Move'18.*

65. Van Eyk, E., Iosup, A., Seif, S., & Thömmes, M. (2017). The SPEC Cloud Group's research vision on FaaS and serverless architectures. In *Proceedings of the 2nd International Workshop on Serverless Computing* (pp. 1–4).

66. Wang, B., Ali-Eldin, A., & Shenoy, P. (2021). LASS: Running latency sensitive serverless computations at the edge. In *Proceedings of the 30th International Symposium on High-Performance Parallel and Distributed Computing* (pp. 239–251).

67. Wang, H., Liu, T., Kim, B., Lin, C. W., Shiraishi, S., Xie, J., & Han, Z. (2020). Architectural design alternatives based on cloud/edge/fog computing for connected vehicles. *IEEE Communications Surveys & Tutorials, 22*(4), 2349–2377.
68. Werner, S., Girke, R., & Kuhlenkamp, J. (2020). An evaluation of serverless data processing frameworks. In *Proceedings of the Sixth International Workshop on Serverless Computing* (pp. 19–24).
69. Wu, J., Wu, M., Li, H., Li, L., & Li, L. (2022). A serverless-based, on-the-fly computing framework for remote sensing image collection. *Remote Sensing, 14*(7), 1728.
70. Xu, B., Zhao, C., Hu, E., & Hu, B. (2011). Job scheduling algorithm based on Berger model in cloud environment. *Advances in Engineering Software, 42*(7), 419–425.
71. Yao, C., Liu, W., Tang, W., & Hu, S. (2022). EAIS: Energy-aware adaptive scheduling for CNN inference on high-performance GPUs. *Future Generation Computer Systems, 130*, 253–268.
72. Younge, A. J., Von Laszewski, G., Wang, L., Lopez-Alarcon, S., & Carithers, W. (2010). Efficient resource management for cloud computing environments. In *Proceedings of the International Conference on Green Computing* (pp. 357–364). IEEE.
73. Yuvaraj, N., Karthikeyan, T., & Praghash, K. (2021). An improved task allocation scheme in serverless computing using gray wolf optimization (GWO) based reinforcement learning (RIL) approach. *Wireless Personal Communications, 117*(3), 2403–2421.
74. Zhao, L., Yang, Y., Li, Y., Zhou, X., & Li, K. (2021). Understanding, predicting and scheduling serverless workloads under partial interference. In *Proceedings of the International Conference for High Performance Computing, Networking, Storage and Analysis* (pp. 1–15).
75. Zuk, P., & Rzadca, K. (2022). Reducing response latency of composite functions-as-a-service through scheduling. *Journal of Parallel and Distributed Computing, 167*, 18–30.

CHAPTER 10

SERVERLESS CLOUD COMPUTING: STATE OF THE ART AND CHALLENGES

Contents

INTRODUCTION

Serverless cloud computing represents a significant shift in the way applications are built and deployed, offering a more efficient, scalable, and cost-effective approach to infrastructure management. Serverless computing abstracts the underlying servers and infrastructure, allowing developers to focus solely on writing code and implementing business logic without worrying about provisioning, scaling, or maintaining servers. This paradigm shift is made possible through services like AWS Lambda, Azure Functions, and Google Cloud Functions, which automatically handle the execution and scaling of functions in response to events.

One of the primary advantages of serverless computing is its ability to automatically scale applications in response to demand. Traditional server-based applications require careful planning and provisioning of resources to handle varying levels of traffic, often leading to either underutilized or overwhelmed servers. In contrast, serverless platforms dynamically allocate resources based on real-time needs, ensuring optimal performance and cost-efficiency. This elasticity allows businesses to respond quickly to changes in traffic without the overhead of managing server capacity.

Cost efficiency is another key benefit of serverless computing. Traditional infrastructure models typically involve paying for pre-allocated server capacity, regardless of actual usage. Serverless computing, however, operates on a pay-as-you-go model, where charges are based on the actual execution time and resources consumed by the application. This means that businesses only pay for what they use, which can result in significant cost savings, especially for applications with variable workloads or intermittent usage patterns.

Serverless computing also enhances developer productivity by reducing the operational complexity associated with infrastructure management. Developers can focus on writing and deploying code while the cloud provider handles tasks such as server provisioning, patching, and monitoring. This streamlined approach accelerates the development process, enabling faster iteration and deployment of new features. Additionally, serverless architectures promote modularity and microservices, encouraging the development of smaller, reusable functions that can be independently deployed and scaled.

10.1. SERVERLESS CLOUD COMPUTING

John McCarthy envisioned in 1961 the possibility of selling computers' execution power as a service, similar to how electricity or water are sold, thanks to time-sharing. McCarthy's concept was put into practice in what is now known as cloud computing because of the democratization of high-speed

Internet access in the mid-2000s. By giving service providers responsibility for the infrastructure, businesses and individuals can significantly lower the costs associated with purchasing and maintaining the hardware required to run their applications. The term "Infrastructure as a Service" (IaaS) refers to this concept.

New trends that aimed to lessen the responsibilities of the customer have emerged over time. For instance, customers using the "Platform as a Service" (PaaS) model access the machines supporting their applications through specialized interfaces, rather than having direct control over them. These models charge the customer for resources that are not always in use. This is because in order to handle hardware failures and absorb sudden spikes in activity, reserved resources frequently need to be overprovisioned.

Serverless customers do not reserve hardware resources, which is a paradigm shift in the cloud compared to traditional models. Their code is executed based on events (HTTP requests, cron jobs, etc.).) and charging is determined by the real use of resources. In exchange, the provider is in charge of assigning resources and placing tasks. Although serverless is primarily promoted as a public cloud offering in the wild, solutions are being actively developed and supported by reliable industry players to enable the development of serverless platforms for private clouds.

"Function as a Service" (FaaS), the initial serverless offering, has serious drawbacks that could outweigh the advantages for clients and suppliers in terms of costs and dependability for clients and resource multiplexing for suppliers. Resolving these issues would enable significant financial and energy savings for suppliers and consumers alike. The objective of this chapter is to provide a thorough overview of these drawbacks and to present cutting-edge research to address the issues preventing serverless from taking the lead in cloud computing.

10.1.1. The Promises of Cloud Computing

The NIST definition of cloud computing gives five essential characteristics for the cloud computing model, as opposed to on-premises and/or bare metal deployments:

- **On-demand self-service**—Customers can book hardware resources through e.g., a web interface rather than by interacting with operators. In return, they usually have limited control over the geographic location for these resources;
- **Broad network access**—These resources are immediately made available over public broadband connections by the provider;
- **Resource pooling**—Compute time, storage capacity, network bandwidth are all shared between customers. Virtualization

techniques are used to ensure isolation between workloads;

- **Rapid elasticity**—Applications can benefit from increased or decreased computing power through scaling, as resources are dynamically provisioned and released to absorb variations in demand;
- **Measured service**—Cloud providers instrument their infrastructures so as to precisely monitor resource usage. Customers can then be charged in a fine way according to their needs.

These characteristics are found in three cloud service models, as shown in Figure 10.1:

- **Software as a Service (SaaS)**—Targets the end user by offering access to fully managed software (the application);
- **Platform as a Service (PaaS)**—Targets developers and DevOps teams who want to deploy their applications quickly without managing servers, generally through the use of containers. Customers deploy their applications on top of a runtime environment that is managed by the provider;
- **Infrastructure as a Service (IaaS)**—Targets architects and system administrators who want fine-grained control over their infrastructures. IaaS customers are in charge of their own servers, usually virtual.

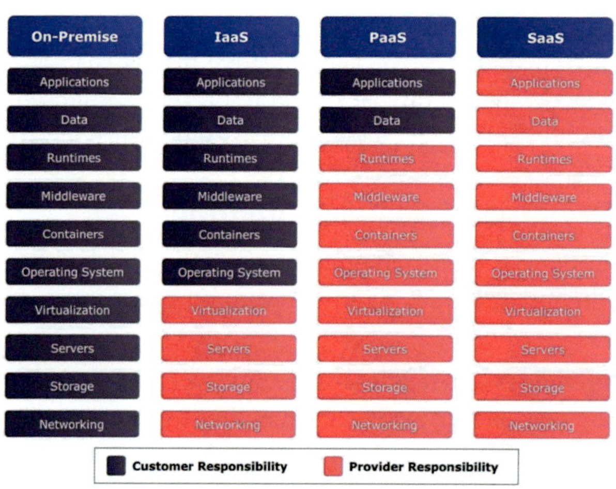

Figure 10.1. *Comparison of the different cloud service models in terms of customer responsibility.*

Source: https://dgtlinfra.com/wp-content/uploads/2023/02/Cloud-Service-Models-Responsibility-Comparison-Matrix-Customer-Provider-1024x768.jpg.

IaaS and PaaS deployments are inherently unable to provide elasticity, in the sense of "automatic scaling.." It is the responsibility of developers to plan ahead and specify their requirements, which entails reserving a sufficient number of resources. Cloud providers usually refer to these as "instances.." Cloud instances are generally classified based on the type and capacity of resources they offer. For instance, some instances may have multiple CPU cores, while others may have access to a GPU or other hardware accelerator. An application's selection of instance type(s) and number is determined by (a) the type of computations it performs, (b) the acceptable latency, and (c) the desired throughput. It is the customer's duty, nevertheless, to avoid providing more than is necessary. There are more implications to this offering design. First of all, it indicates that billing is done coarsely—that is, based on instances reserved rather than on resources really utilized. Additionally, because an application always needs at least one instance running to handle an incoming request, idle resources are always paid for, and scaling to zero is not possible in this configuration. Due to the large number of customer jobs that cloud computing platforms must support, there is a significant need for multitenancy, which calls for appropriate isolation and virtualization techniques.

10.2. VIRTUALIZATION TECHNOLOGIES

One feature that sets cloud computing apart is multitenancy. It is the capacity of a cloud provider to distribute resources among several clients in order to achieve financial savings. Direct channels between processes in the user space are created when resources are pooled and used by various applications. This means that multitenancy entails a provider's obligation to ensure privacy and security across the various workloads of its clients. Providers are forced to use security mechanisms that ensure airtightness between processes that aren't meant to know about one another in order to meet these guarantees. Isolation is the process of transparently presenting a different execution environment with a unique filesystem, address space, and set of permissions. Providers may use virtualization technologies for this purpose. Hardware virtualization is the process of building a virtual machine on top of an existing operating system and hardware. An environment that is rationally isolated from the underlying hardware is offered by virtual machines. The virtual machine is referred to as a guest machine, and the host machine is the one on which it is created. The hypervisor, which is either software or firmware, is in charge of managing this virtual machine.

10.2.1. Hypervisor

The hypervisor is a firmware or low-level program that acts as a Virtual Machine Manager. There are two types of hypervisor: Type 1 hypervisors run on unmodified systems. Examples of Type 1 hypervisors are VirtualLogic VLX, Oracle VM, Sun xVM Server, RTS Hypervisor, and LynxSecure. The Type 1 hypervisor can be seen in the following diagram (Figure 10.2).

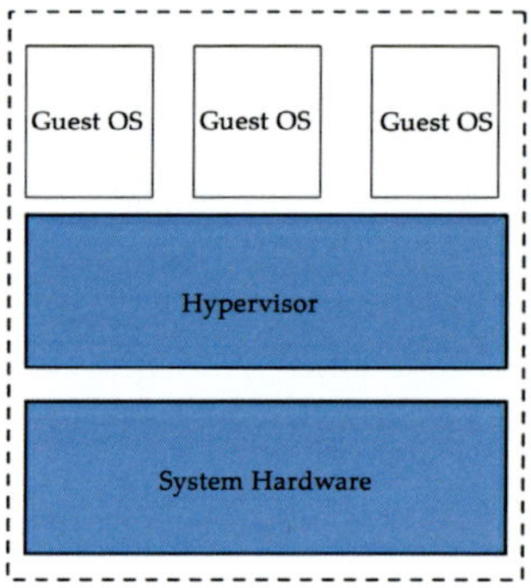

Figure 10.2. *Type 1 hypervisor.*

Source: https://www.gacbe.ac.in/pdf/ematerial/18MCS35E-U3.pdf.

The type1 hypervisor does not have any host operating system because they are installed on a bare system. A software interface known as a type 2 hypervisor simulates the devices that a system typically communicates with. Examples of Type 2 hypervisors are Containers, KVM, Microsoft Hyper V, VMware Fusion, Virtual Server 2005 R2, Windows Virtual PC, and VMware Workstation 6.0. The Type 2 hypervisor is depicted in the diagram below (Figure 10.3).

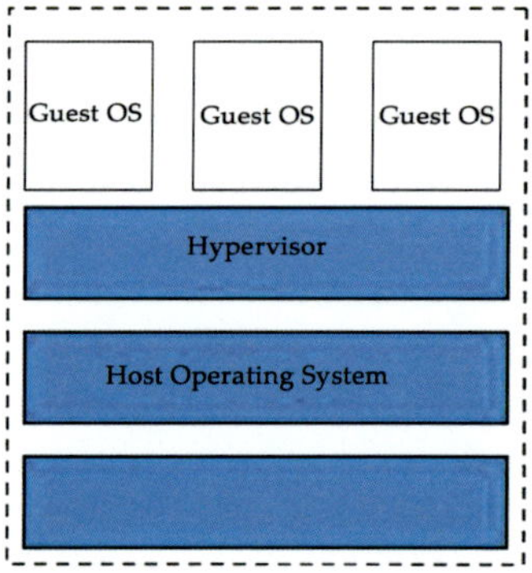

Figure 10.3. *Type 2 hypervisor.*

Source: https://www.gacbe.ac.in/pdf/ematerial/18MCS35E-U3.pdf.

10.2.2. Types of Hardware Virtualization

Here are the three types of hardware virtualization:

- Full Virtualization

- Emulation Virtualization
- Paravirtualization

10.2.2.1. Full Virtualization

The underlying hardware is fully simulated in full virtualization. Running guest software doesn't require any changes (Figure 10.4).

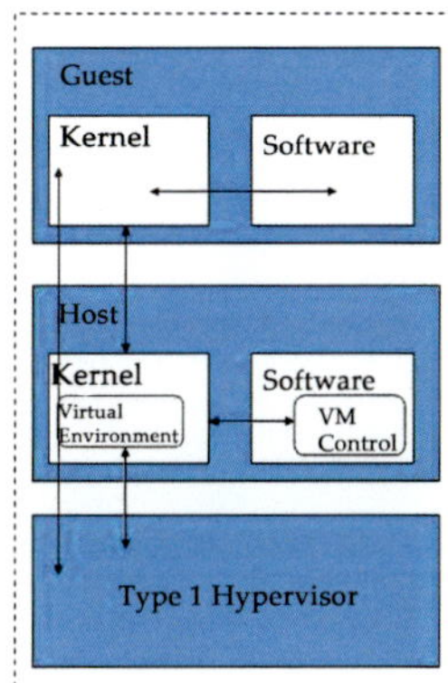

Figure 10.4. *Full virtualization.*

Source: https://www.gacbe.ac.in/pdf/ematerial/18MCS35E-U3.pdf.

10.2.2.2. Emulation Virtualization

The virtual machine emulates the hardware during emulation, becoming independent of it in the process. In this case, there is no need to modify the guest operating system (Figure 10.5).

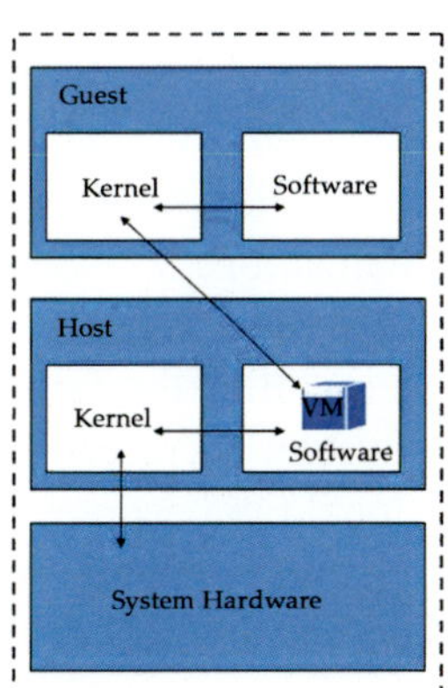

Figure 10.5. *Emulation virtualization.*

Source: https://www.gacbe.ac.in/pdf/ematerial/18MCS35E-U3.pdf.

10.2.2.3. Paravirtualization

In Paravirtualization, the hardware is not simulated. The guest software run their own isolated domains (Figure 10.6).

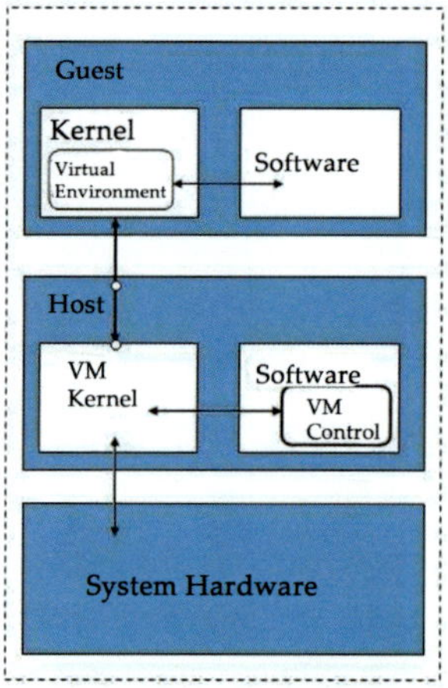

Figure 10.6. *Paravirtualization.*

Source: https://www.gacbe.ac.in/pdf/ematerial/18MCS35E-U3.pdf.

A highly developed infrastructure, VMware vSphere provides a virtualization management infrastructure framework. Hardware for networking, storage, and the system are all virtualized.

10.2.3. Tools for Virtualization

To put it simply, virtualization is the process of deploying an operating system, memory, or storage capacity instead of deploying the physical resource. Software for virtualization essentially has the ability to divide a single computer into several. The relationship between a virtualized operating system and the underlying hardware and the interaction between a virtual host and physical host are the two aspects of virtualization. Software for virtualization functions in the same manner as regular software. Installation discs or .iso files can be used to install an operating system after the virtualization software has been loaded. The installed operating system is currently operating on what is known as a virtual machine. Any additional OS becomes the "guest," and the primary OS becomes the "host.." Installed additional OS functions as if it were a brand-new device.

Hypervisors are virtualization programs that control the setup and operation of virtual machines. To improve VM performance, some virtualization solutions might also make use of the CPU technology virtualization extensions. We call this kind of virtualization hardware-assisted. Because virtualization requires less hardware to be deployed, its primary benefit is its lower cost. Other features include the ability to create a computing environment that is independent of hardware and the centralized management of multiple resources on a single machine.

10.2.3.1. Ganeti

Google created Ganeti, a cluster server management tool that is based on open-source software, KVM, and Xen, two popular virtualization technologies. Ganeti lacks a number of the features associated with larger open cloud projects because it was first developed as a VMware substitute for network, storage, and virtual machine management rather than as a cloud platform. It was intended to manage virtual server clusters and provide fast and simple recovery using commodity software in the event of physical failures. Virtualization software needs to be pre-installed on the servers in order for Ganeti to function. Once installed, Ganeti takes over the management of the virtual instances; it can be used to move a virtual machine (VM) away from a failing physical machine and manages disk creation, OS installation, shutdown, startup, and migration. Ganeti can be used for OpenStack-based large-scale computing as well as single-host management similar to Xen Tools or Libyirt.

10.2.3.2. KVM (Kernel-based Virtual Machine)

AMD-V and Intel VT virtualization extensions are included in KVM, an open-source virtualization tool for Linux. It can run in hardware mode or emulation, but the overall performance will be subpar without the CPU extensions. Although KVM was meant to be used with a command line, it has a good management interface that makes it easy for users to launch and stop virtual machines and take screenshots.

Xen virtual machines can also be controlled via the Virtual Machine Manger, or VMM, interface. Every KVM virtual machine has its own virtualized hardware, such as a network adapter, disk, graphics adapter, etc. KVM is your best option if you're looking for a free modern virtualization solution with an unlimited usage mode, no extra feature fees or licensing costs, and a strong command line interface.

10.2.3.3. oVirt

A virtualization tool called oVirt is used to build and manage virtual datacenters. oVirt uses an intuitive web-based administration and user portal to manage virtualized networks, virtual machines, and storage options. oVirt offers support for a number of cutting-edge virtualization features, including high availability, live storage migration, and controllable and programmable virtual machine deployment. This Red Hat-backed project consists of the oVirt engine in addition to other parts, such as oVirt Node, which is a trimmed-down Linux version with sufficient code to run virtual machines. The oVirt project also incorporates warehouse and data reporting components, built upon the work of open source software vendors Talend and Jaspersoft.

10.2.3.4. Packer

System administrators can use Packer to build virtual machine images and then manage their operations. You can create an image on Digital Ocean, AWS, vagrant, and VirtualBox using the same commands and files. This makes it possible for you to develop a system and use it in production. Packer runs on all major operating systems and is notably light and performant. It puts together and sets up every part of a virtual machine, then builds images that can be used on several different platforms. Packer is not a replacement for configuration management tools like Puppet or Chef; in fact, Packer can use these tools to install applications on images when creating them.

10.2.3.5. Vagrant

A framework and configuration format for building, administering, and sharing virtualized development environments are offered by the command-line tool Vagrant. These environments are cross-platform, running on Linux, Mac OS X, and Windows, and they can reside on your desktop or in the cloud. One unique feature of Vagrant is Vagrant Share, which allows users to share their active Vagrant environment online. This facilitates communication and sharing on development environments, resulting in standardized working environments for virtual machine-using software development teams. Additionally, Vagrant can be used with configuration management programs like Puppet and Chef.

10.2.3.6. VirtualBox

Currently under the care of Oracle, VirtualBox is an open source, cross-platform product. One of the veterans of the virtualization space, VirtualBox is still a simple-to-install, dependable, and lightweight virtualization tool. VirtualBox has added touchscreen support along with other easily identifiable features like Webcam pass-through, support for IPv6 with VRDP, and video capture support in its most recent release. The inability of VirtualBox to boot from pre-existing Boot Camp partitions is a significant limitation.

10.2.4. Containers

One method of OS-level virtualization is containerization. The resource allocation is handled by the kernel of the host operating system. Containers virtualize the operating system by giving the containerized process the appearance of having the entire machine at its disposal, but in reality, the host kernel places restrictions and limitations on how much resource it can use. The execution platform appears to the running application as if it were made of bare metal. But in reality, the resources it is allotted are a virtualized portion of the host's hardware resources.

Containers constitute a lightweight isolation mechanism that relies on the kernel isolation capabilities of the host system, as shown in Figure 10.7. Namely, under Linux:

- chroot changes the apparent root directory for a given process tree. It allows a container to operate on a virtual/directory that could be located anywhere on the host's filesystem;
- cgroups create hierarchical groups of processes and allocates, limits, and monitors hardware resources for these groups: I/O to and from block devices, accesses to the CPU, memory and network interfaces;
- namespaces are an abstraction layer around global system resources, such as networking or IPC. Processes within a namespace have their own isolated instances of these resources.

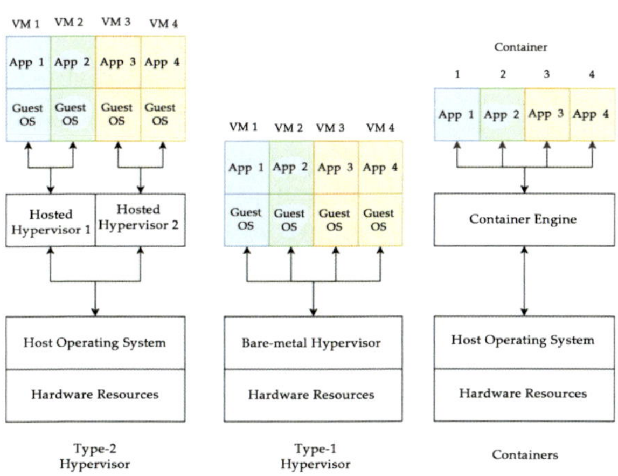

Figure 10.7. *Overview of different isolation models: virtualization and containerization.*

Source: Rajalakshmi Krishnamurthi, Adarsh Kumar, Sukhpal Singh Gill and Rajkumar Buyya. Serverless Computing: Principles and Paradigms. ISBN 978-3-031-26633-1.

The purpose of containers is to sandbox the running of an application in a process that is separate from the main system. An image containing all the dependencies required to either build or run the application is used to bootstrap that process. Since its launch in 2013, Docker has gained significant traction within the container ecosystem. Through the Open Container Initiative, Docker played a key role in defining industry standards for container runtimes and formats (OCI).

The Linux Foundation launched the OCI specification as an effort to create an open standard for containers. It defines runtime specifications that specify how to run application bundles as they are unpacked on the host OS, as well as container image specifications that provide instructions on how to create an OCI image with its manifest, filesystem layers, and configuration. This is how that specification translates in the case of Docker:

- dockerd is the daemon that provides both the Docker Engine application programming interface (API) and console line interface (CLI), capable of building distributable images representing the initial state of future containers. It is the highlevel interface through which the user can either programmatically or interactively manage networking, storage, images and containers lifecycle;
- contained, a Cloud Native Computing Foundation (CNCF) initiative, handles containers lifecycle (hypervision, execution) and manages images (push and pull to and from image registries), storage and networking by establishing links between containers namespaces;
- runc implements the Open Container Initiative specification and contains the actual code allowing a container's execution. It creates and starts containers, and stops their execution.

10.2.5. From Monoliths to Microservices

Cloud computing saw the birth of new development techniques. "Cloud-native development" means building applications for the cloud from the ground up, with scaling capacities in mind. When an application grows, there are two ways of making room for new requests by scaling:

- **Vertically:** attaching more hardware resources to the servers that support the application. It may mean moving data to new, more powerful servers, thus impacting application availability;
- **Horizontally:** increasing the server count for running the application. It may mean introducing a load balancing mechanism to route requests and responses between users and the multiple instances of an application, thus impacting complexity.

An application that is monolithic is created as a single unit. Since all of the services it exposes are included in the same codebase, there is no decoupling between them. Adding more resources (scaling vertically) to a monolithic application does not address the issue of competing priorities within the application: as a monolithic application becomes more popular, certain areas of the codebase will be strained more than others, but this strain will not be evenly distributed throughout the application. However, because not every component of an application experiences load spikes at the same time, spinning up more monolith instances (also known as horizontal scaling) may prove to be costly. This is seen in Figure 10.8, a rise in authentication requests necessitates scalability of the application's entire infrastructure.

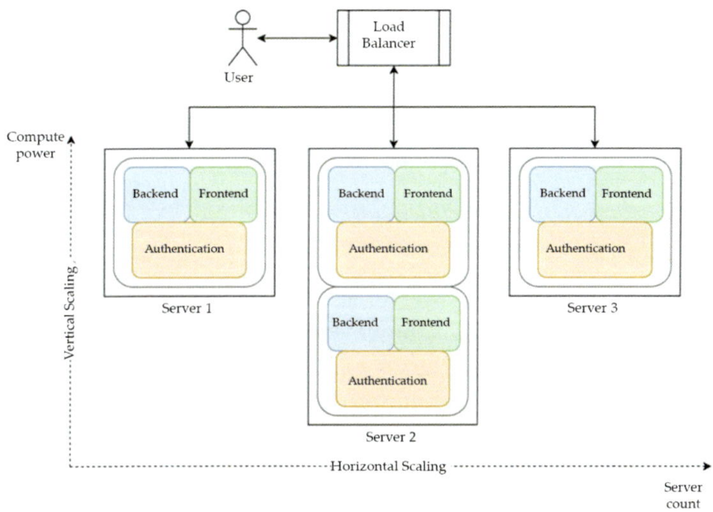

Figure 10.8. *Scaling out a monolith-architectured application requires replicating the monolith on multiple servers.*

Source: Rajalakshmi Krishnamurthi, Adarsh Kumar, Sukhpal Singh Gill and Rajkumar Buyya. Serverless Computing: Principles and Paradigms. ISBN 978-3-031-26633-1.

One recommended approach for developing cloud-native applications is to "[execute] the app as one or more stateless processes," according to the Twelve-Factor App methodology. A microservices architecture is one that organizes an application as a group of loosely connected services. To achieve service level objectives, each of these services can be deployed to scale independently on heterogeneous servers, runs in a separate process, and communicates with the others via message-passing: in Figure 10.9, merely expanding the infrastructure for the authentication microservice will be sufficient to handle a rise in authentication requests.

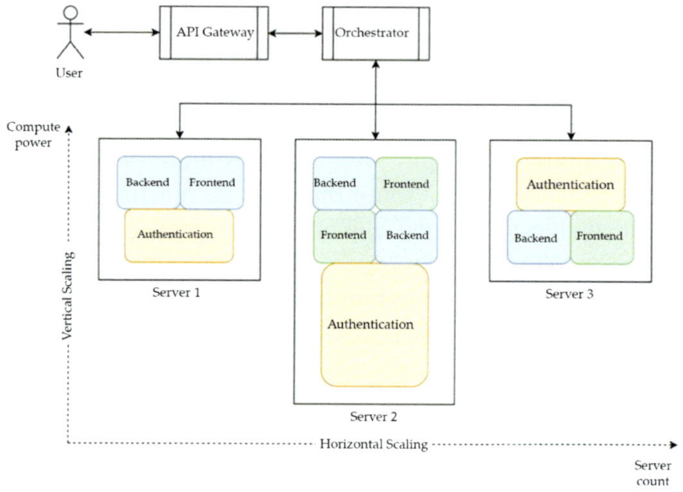

Figure 10.9. *Scaling out a microservices-architectured application allows distributing and replicating each microservice independently.*

Source: Rajalakshmi Krishnamurthi, Adarsh Kumar, Sukhpal Singh Gill and Rajkumar Buyya. Serverless Computing: Principles and Paradigms. ISBN 978-3-031-26633-1.

A microservices architecture, however, suggests a sophisticated level of centralized management, which raises expenses for DevOps teams as well as operations. It is dependent on enduring backend services (messaging buses, databases, etc.) that also need to be kept an eye on and controlled. Particularly in IaaS and PaaS environments, the developer experience is unsatisfactory because cloud deployment entails a systems administration burden. Writing container image recipes does not add value to the product because it relates to operational logic rather than business logic, which is why microservices alone cannot solve the deployment problem.

The fundamental concepts of the DevOps culture are Continuous Integration (CI) and Continuous Delivery or Deployment (CD), which hold that the codebase of an application is always in a functional state, regardless of the stage of its lifecycle. This can be accomplished by automating the execution of unit and integration test suites (CI), as well as by deploying the main code trunk in an automated manner, heavily relying on monitoring and reporting, to a staging or pre-production environment. It enables developers to make sure that adding new features won't result in regression. Continuous practices fit right in with the microservices architecture, which allows for the deployment of microservices updates—which are small, gradual changes to the application as a whole. The cloud environment has changed as a result of the widespread adoption of microservice architecture and DevOps methodologies. The Function as a Service model and cloud programming can be partially compared to the microservice architecture.

10.3. SERVERLESS, A NEW PARADIGM

We present the serverless paradigm for developing and implementing cloud applications. We will cover the key features of serverless platforms and draw attention to the trade-offs that application developers and service providers must take into account when aiming for serverless infrastructures.

10.3.1. Characteristics of Serverless Platforms

In cloud computing, serverless refers to both a programming language and a service model. Developers create their apps as a combination of stateless functions in a serverless architecture. Stateless computing, also referred to as "pure" or "side-effect free" computing, depends only on the inputs. These functions generate a result that is saved in a persistent storage tier, taking as inputs a payload and an invocation context.

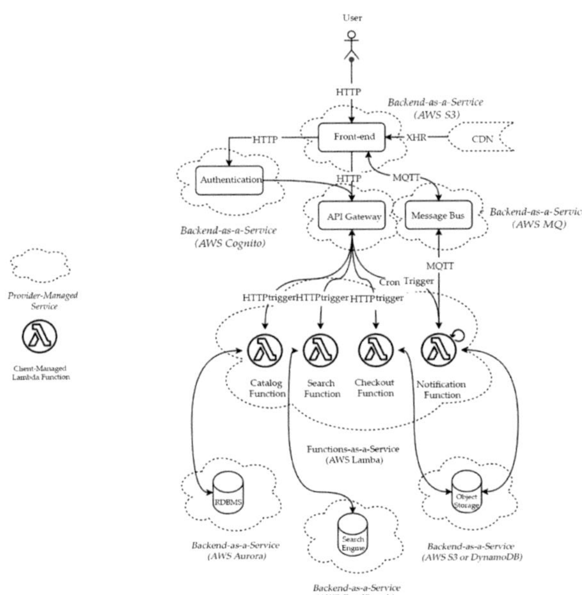

Figure 10.10. *Fictional reference architecture for a serverless e-commerce web application deployed in the Amazon web services ecosystem.*

Source: Rajalakshmi Krishnamurthi, Adarsh Kumar, Sukhpal Singh Gill and Rajkumar Buyya. Serverless Computing: Principles and Paradigms. ISBN 978-3-031-26633-1.

An event, such as an HTTP request, cron job, file upload, etc., that can be defined as the notification of an incoming message, starts their execution. Serverless computing is therefore an event- or demand-driven paradigm. An example serverless application is shown in Figure 10.10 to illustrate the aforementioned design.

Depending on the requested HTTP endpoint, the user's request triggers the execution of various functions when it reaches the serverless platform's API gateway; these functions are not daemons waiting for events (e.g., On demand, they are performed on an opened socket.

Serverless is typically referred to as Function as a Service (FaaS) in commercial offerings. Functions serving as an abstraction over cloud computing are thought to be a feature of serverless offerings in their initial generation and may vary in subsequent iterations. Similar to PaaS, serverless refers, from the standpoint of the customer, to an abstraction over computing resources that enables engineers to stop worrying about the actual servers supporting their applications.

This does not imply that servers are no longer used to host and run applications. They are spared from having to think about the ideal number of instances required to run their workloads in a capacity-planning manner, thanks to auto-scaling mechanisms.

Customers don't have to worry about having to define explicit scaling strategies because serverless platforms are made to handle demand fluctuations and scaling requirements. The SPEC Research Group presents a FaaS reference architecture in a layered vision of cloud deployments, demonstrating how serverless development brings developers as close to business logic as possible.

Developing for serverless platforms requires re-thinking an application's architecture.

Indeed, long-running backend servers are relegated to serverful solutions that provide always-on servers, such as IaaS offerings. As Shafiei et al. pointed out in their 2022 survey on serverless computing, there is no formal definition for the concept of serverless computing, although we can identify various essential differences between the serverful and serverless models (summed up in Table 10.1).

A major difference between PaaS and FaaS is that FaaS achieves scaling to zero: providers only bill customers when their application actually uses hardware resources, i.e., when functions are executed on the platform. That is made possible because, in the FaaS paradigm, applications are designed as a collection of short running microservices.

Table 10.1. *Comparison of Key Characteristics in Serverless and Serverful Service Models*

Characteristic	Serverful (IaaS, PaaS)	Serverless (FaaS)
Provisioning	Customer responsibility	Fully **managed** (i.e. by the provider)
Billing	Pay for **provisioned** resources	Pay for **consumed** resources
Scaling	Customer responsibility	**Auto-scaling** built in
Availability	Depends on **provisioned** resources	Code runs in multiple high availability zones
Fault tolerance	Depends on deployment strategy	Backend services are fully **managed** and retries are guaranteed
Concurrency	Depends on **provisioned** resources	Virtually **infinite**

Source: Rajalakshmi Krishnamurthi, Adarsh Kumar, Sukhpal Singh Gill and Rajkumar Buyya. Serverless Computing: Principles and Paradigms. ISBN 978-3-031-26633-1.

Business-oriented Backend as a Service (BaaS) solutions entail commercial, managed offerings of backend functionalities provided to developers through a unified API. Typically, backend services involve ongoing, stateful operations that cannot be diminished to no usage. To keep a consistent pricing approach, providers make these services accessible through a payment structure that mirrors the pay-as-you-go plan they use for serverless functions. These third party services constitute the backbone infrastructure of serverless applications by handling the state of the functions deployed by developers, through e.g., key-value stores or file storage; providing authentication to application endpoints; allowing communications between functions using message buses; etc. Figure 10.10 shows possible dependencies between serverless functions and BaaS software: the example application relies on provider-managed authentication, message bus, relational database, search engine and object storage, and is accessed by the user through the provider's API gateway. This situation introduces a high degree of coupling between the application and vendor-specific services, potentially tying developers to their initial choice of service provider.

By abstracting away server management, serverless technology reduces developer overhead while enabling providers to share physical resources at a very fine granularity, improving efficiency. The provider can offer perfect elasticity thanks to the fine level of granularity provided by the FaaS model: in a typical pay-as-you-go pricing model, scaling out and scaling in are event-driven. It is desirable for providers to deploy code across multiple geographic zones because of this abstraction. This fail-over mechanism reduces the possibility of a function failure cascading through the application and ensures availability in the event of an outage in one deployment zone.

10.3.2. Suitable Workloads

Serverless use cases can be identified by the following attributes, according to the Cloud Native Computing Foundation (CNCF), an initiative of the Linux Foundation backed by over 800 industrial members offering cloud services.

- "Embarrassingly parallel" workloads: asynchronous and concurrent, with little to no communication and no synchronization between processes;
- Infrequent with unpredictable variance in scaling requirements, i.e., event-driven or interactive jobs rather than batch jobs;
- Stateless and ephemeral processes, without a major need for instantaneous start time.

It can be argued that these requirements are excessively stringent for general computing, as they suggest that FaaS deployments are not suitable for jobs with extended lifespans. In order to implement serverless workflows, providers have introduced mechanisms like Step Functions or Durable Functions. To create stateful workflows, an orchestration function keeps track of state across all stateless functions in the application. Developers are already implementing serverless functions for some of the logic in their applications. Examples of such logic include data transformation pipelines, high-availability alerting platforms, ETL (Extract, Transform, Load, batch data manipulation) tools, media transcoding, etc., according to a 2018 survey conducted by the publisher of the Serverless framework among a panel of their users. These applications, which apply purely functional transformations to data, are a subset of computer programs that generate output that solely depends on the program's input.

Full-fledged applications can be designed with FaaS in mind because there are fundamental similarities between an application designed for FaaS deployment and an application with a microservices architecture. An example of an e-commerce web application's architecture is shown in Figure 10.10. The business logic of the application consists of one function (notification), which is scheduled to run on a regular basis, and three serverless functions (catalog, search, and checkout), which are activated by user navigation. Since the load of the application determines how these functions are spun up and down, state needs to be kept in persistent storage, i.e., an object store and a relational database under the provider's management. The application also depends on provider-managed services; a BaaS solution powers the search engine, notification system, and authentication process.

This type of application could scale to 150 TB of RAM and 90 000 vCPUs using AWS Lambda in less than two seconds in 2022, enabling prompt response to load variations.

10.3.3. Tradeoffs in Serverless Deployments

For teams relying on BaaS offerings, serverless programming offers the immediate benefit of lower development costs. Rather than building internal backend services like authentication or notifications, developers just need to add boilerplate to their codebase to connect frontend apps to the BaaS APIs of their cloud provider. But because of that level of coupling, developers run the risk of being forced to work in a setting that is vendor-specific and losing control over deployment expenses. Perfect scaling is achieved from the perspective of the customer when FaaS and managed BaaS are combined. Clients are billed precisely for the time that their requests are processed, only when resources are utilized. From the perspective of the provider, more tenancies open up the possibility of improving resource multiplexing, which leads to higher productivity and, ultimately, higher earnings. There is a latency cost associated with this auto-scaling mechanism: initialization times can cause cold starts, in which function execution times are dominated by sandbox spin-ups in response to incoming requests. Further throughput implications of serverless auto-scaling arise from the need to persist function state in disaggregated storage. Applications exhibiting extensive inter-function communication patterns may experience delays in data shipping to compute nodes. The rise in the number of jobs per customer is one of the side effects of the FaaS service model. Although the increase in concurrency, density, and resource consumption is a selling point for FaaS providers and clients, these transient tasks must be isolated from one another to avoid confidential information from being disclosed to clients or to the extent of an application that combines several distinct functions into one. In order to leverage the benefits of the model, providers and customers need to weigh the trade-offs involved in serverless deployments. Key lessons learned when deploying apps to the cloud with serverless computing are compiled in Table 10.2.

Table 10.2. *Considerations Regarding the FaaS Service Model*

Pros	Cons
Reduced **development costs** for teams leaning on BaaS offerings	Can we map **any application** to the FaaS architecture?
Reduced **costs in operations** thanks to fully managed infrastructure	Risks of **vendor lock-in** due to high degree of coupling with BaaS offerings
Perfect scaling allows billing granularity close to actual use of resources	Increase in **latency** due to cold starts, and decreased **throughput** from communications through slow storage to handle statefulness
Providers can achieve **better efficiency** in resources multiplexing leading to increased profits	Massive multitenancy might involve **security** threats

Source: Rajalakshmi Krishnamurthi, Adarsh Kumar, Sukhpal Singh Gill and Rajkumar Buyya. Serverless Computing: Principles and Paradigms. ISBN 978-3-031-26633-1.

10.4. PROBLEMS ADDRESSED IN CLOUD COMPUTING

To attain performance and flexibility on par with PaaS or IaaS offerings, FaaS providers must address significant issues impeding serverless computing's advancement towards becoming the standard in cloud computing. One major obstacle in fixing these flaws is avoiding "serverful" answers to the dynamic resource allocation issue, i.e., assigning extra stable resources that are deliberate non-zero scale resources.

10.4.1. Cold Start Delays and Frequency

Compared to PaaS containers or IaaS virtual machines, serverless containers are spun up and down more frequently because they have to spend a minimum amount of time in an idle state. The container or virtual machine hosting the function's code must go through its initialization phase each time a function is called and needs to be scaled from zero; this is known as a "cold start.." In complex applications, delays that accumulate during function composition can exacerbate cold starts' latency penalties.

Typically, functions are called in spurts. To optimize concurrency, the AWS Lambda execution model can instantiate a function in hundreds or thousands of sandboxes spread across various geographic locations. A function's sandbox is released from the execution node minutes after processing a request; however, there is no guarantee that subsequent new instances will be created on the same node. This causes circumstances where the environment of a function is not cached on the node. Cold start latency is caused by the need to retrieve and copy code and related libraries to the filesystem once more. Pre-allocating hardware resources to maintain a pool of function containers available for new requests would be the "naive" approach. Since it completely rules out the possibility of scaling to zero, this is unacceptable. Vahidinia et al. propose a comprehensive study of the position and strategies of various commercial FaaS offerings regarding cold start. While serverless computing suggests spinning up disposable instances of functions to handle each incoming request, the authors note that commercial actors such as AWS, Google and Microsoft all re-use execution sandboxes to some extent, keeping them running during a timeout period in order to circumvent latency costs incurred by cold starts.

10.4.2. Reducing Initialization Times

Cloud providers can use various strategies to reduce the function sandbox initialization time. Given that function invocations typically follow unpredictable patterns, this work is essential.

10.4.2.1. Sandbox Optimization Approach

In (Müller I, Marroquín R, Alonso G (2020)), In the context of distributed data analytics, the authors suggest using Lambada to solve the cold start issue by batching the invocation of workers in parallel. The evaluation reveals that there is a bottleneck in the process of calling new workers: 1000 AWS Lambda workers must be called in between 3.4 and 4.4s. Each worker's contribution consists of calling a subsequent generation of sandboxes, which must be called in turn by a subsequent generation of workers, and so on, until the scalability process is finished. With this method, thousands of workers can be created in less than 4 seconds.

In (Manco F, Lupu C, Schmidt F, 2017), to put virtual machine boot times closer to those of containers, the authors suggest using LightVM. The authors demonstrate that instantiation times increase linearly with image size, indicating that sandboxing an application's execution environment is an I/O-bound process. The Xen control plane is redesigned, and lightweight virtual machines (VMs) with the bare minimum of prerequisites for the sandboxed application are used to achieve boot times that are on par with the Linux fork/exec implementation. The authors suggest that while processes are sufficient to isolate functions at the granularity of a single application, full-blown isolation mechanisms such as containers are required to isolate workloads among customers. Within SAND, an isolation mechanism is implemented on top of Docker, allowing for low-latency, elastic, resource-efficient interactions between functions.

The authors (Agache A, Brooker M, Iordache A, 2020) introduce Firecracker, which at AWS Lambda has evolved into the de facto serverless virtualization technology. In order to address the trade-off between isolation and performance, they replace containers as a sandboxing mechanism for serverless workloads with lightweight virtual machines, or MicroVMs. By swapping out QEMU for a specially designed virtual machine monitor that operates on top of KVM and can create up to 150 MicroVMs per second and per host with a 3 percent memory overhead, Firecracker achieves boot times of less than 125 ms.

10.4.2.2. Snapshotting Approach

In [Xia Y, Zang B, Yu T, Du D, et al. 2020], the authors contend that the application-agnostic nature of virtualization-based sandboxes contributes to startup overhead. As they demonstrate, the primary factor influencing the overall startup latency is the application initialization latency. The authors of Catalyzer demonstrate how sandbox instances of the same function have remarkably similar initialization states. To circumvent the application's initialization phase when scaling from zero, they offer a snapshotting solution that enables the restoration of a function instance from a checkpoint image. They develop a system based on Google's gVisor that routinely performs an order of magnitude better than cutting-edge tools like Firecracker, HyperContainer, and Docker.

In [Ustiugov D, Petrov P, et al. 2021], the authors present vHive, a benchmarking framework for serverless experimentation that allows them to show that high latency can be attributed to frequent page faults during sandboxes initialization, with very similar patterns among executions of a same function—97% of the memory pages being identical across invocations of studied functions. They propose REAP to create images of a sandbox memory layout that enable prefetching pages from disk to memory, eagerly populating the guest memory before function execution and thus avoiding the majority of page faults at initialization time. This technique allows a cold start delay speedup of 3.7 times on average.

10.4.3. Caching Approach

In [Oakes E, Yang L, Zhou D, et al. 2018], The authors contend that long container initialization times impair the latency performances of deployed applications, even though serverless technology reduces costs through enhanced elasticity and developer velocity. They locate bottlenecks in the Linux primitives used to initialize containers; the main culprit in I/O operations during sandboxing is package dependencies. They present SOCK, a package-aware caching system-based container system built on OpenLambda and optimized for serverless tasks. They demonstrate that their solution outperforms Docker by up to 21 times. In [Fuerst A, Sharma P (2021)], the author demonstrates how object caching and function keep-alive are conceptually similar, enabling them to create strategies that shorten cold start delays. Expanding upon that comparison, they suggest a keep-alive policy, which is essentially an eviction or function termination policy. Maintaining warmth for as long as feasible (i.e., with its OpenWhisk-based implementation, FaasCache doubles the number of serviceable requests (as long as server resources permit it). One of the main distinctions between serverless platforms and traditional cloud service models is the latter's inability to scale a function to zero replicas, thereby avoiding billing customers for idle resources. It is crucial to conduct research on methods to reduce the effect of a cold start on function latency because lengthy initialization times make it more difficult for FaaS to compete with PaaS platforms.

10.4.4. Data Communications Overhead

Functions in FaaS offerings are not addressable; instead, composition is accomplished by storing results in a slow, stateful storage tier that is typically not connected to the computing tier. Because functions within the same application cannot share file descriptors or memory in order to achieve IPC, message-passing interfaces must be used to establish communication between them. This introduces overhead whenever data needs to move through the application. This issue is especially problematic when data-hungry applications need to process cold data, i.e., data kept on lower performing storage devices, like hard drives situated on distant nodes, that are infrequently accessed and hence not cached. In [. Jiang J, Gan S, Liu Y, Wang F, et al. 2021], the authors present LambdaML, a benchmarking platform that enables comparing performances of distributed machine learning model training across IaaS and FaaS offerings. They find out that using FaaS for ML training can be profitable as long as the models present reduced communication patterns.

In [Müller I, Marroquín R, Alonso G (2020)], The authors demonstrate that when performing intermittent, interactive queries on gigabytes to terabytes of cold data, FaaS can be financially advantageous. With Lambada, serverless-specific data operators can perform interactive queries on over 1 TB of data stored on Amazon S3 in about 15 seconds, which is comparable to paid Query-as-a-Service options. In [Chandhry GI, Romero F, et al.,2021]. The authors contend in that serverless solutions do not have an in-memory perapplication data caching layer, which would enable auto-scaling and transparent operation. When multiple instances of an application are spun up, Faa$T can form a strongly consistent distributed caching layer. The most recent caching node disappears as the application scales down to zero, thereby enabling billing based on efficient resource usage. According to the experiments, Faa$T can, on average, increase application performance by 57% while costing 99% less than serverful alternatives. An application's functionalities are always deployed on the same node in SAND. A node-local bus facilitates fast sequential execution by acting as a shortcut for inter-function communications. Reliability is ensured by fault tolerance in a global bus that is distributed among nodes. When it comes to message delivery, the local bus in SAND outperforms the global bus by nearly three times. Reduce the overhead of inter-function communication as serverless functions are inherently ephemeral and because of the isolation mechanisms implemented by providers to meet privacy and security objectives. This presents a twofold challenge: on the one hand, serverless platforms require domain-specific solutions that take into account the characteristics of the data that are fed to and returned by the functions; on the other hand, general advancements in the field of distributed caches are warranted.

10.4.5. Durable State and Statefulness

"State," also known as "local state," describes the data that a process typically reads and writes to and from variables or disk while it is running. Regarding the availability of such storage over several executions, FaaS makes no guarantees. The term "stateless" refers to this because functions that require persistence of data must be externally stored, and idempotence of functions is required to guard against state corruption. Moreover, arbitrary restrictions on a function's execution time, payload size, and memory allocation are presented by FaaS offerings. Designing "real world" applications with long-term tasks and/or functionalities that require synchronization or communication presents an issue to transmit intermediate findings based on a temporary condition.

Given the ephemeral nature of function instances, one must be aware of fault tolerance and data consistency in their application when they deploy to FaaS.

In (Wu C, Sreekanti V, Hellerstein JM (2020)), In serverless function composition, where an application is split up into multiple functions that can run concurrently on different nodes while accessing remote storage, the authors discuss I/O latency. Their concept of Multisite Transactional Causal Consistency—causal consistency within the context of a single transaction split across several nodes—is put forth in the form of the HydroCache system. They see performance gains of up to an order of magnitude while maintaining consistency. HydroCache works better than cutting-edge programs like ElastiCache and Anna.

In (Perron M, Fernandez RC, DeWitt DJ, Madden S (2020)), The authors contend that by attaining elasticity, serverless database analytics would enable data analysts to avoid upfront expenses. But because these workloads are inherently unpredictable, cloud providers frequently struggle to supply enough resources, which results in elastic solutions that occasionally experience minutes of latency during scaling phases. They introduce Starling, a query execution engine based on FaaS. Its three stages of functions—Producers, Combiners, and Consumers—can handle datasets kept in remote cold storage by scaling independently. According to their analysis, Starling can scale on a per-query basis, exhibit good latency results for ad-hoc analytics on cold data in Amazon S3, and be cost-effective on moderate query volumes (under 120 queries per hour on a 10 TB TPC-H dataset).

When activity resumes after an idle period in a serverless system, scaling from zero is typically event-driven. This causes high latency when there are no hardware resources available right away to resume workloads. In [Poppe O, Guo Q, Lang W, Arora P, Oslake M, Xu S, Kalhan A (2022)], The proactive auto-scaling feature for their serverless Azure SQL database offering is examined by the writers. In order to minimize resource reclamation when idle periods are brief and to prevent latency when resuming activity, the contribution focuses on predicting pause and resume patterns. They discovered that only 23% of production databases are unpredictable by using samples from thousands of databases. They then developed a prediction system by training machine learning models on three weeks' worth of historical data. At Azure, the strategy has been effectively implemented in production, resulting in up to 50% fewer pauses and 80% of proactive resumes.

In (Sreekanti V, Wu C, Lin XC, et al. 2020), the authors build on the Anna KVS (Wu C, Faleiro JM, Lin Y, Hellerstein JM (2018)) to propose a stateful FaaS platform. Cloudburst achieves low-latency mutable state and communication with minimal programming effort. Leveraging Anna's capabilities, they provide essential building blocks to allow statefulness in an FaaS context: direct communication between functions, low-latency access to shared mutable state with distributed session consistency, and programmability to transparently implement Cloudburst consistency protocols. In their evaluation against real-world applications, Cloudburst outperforms both commercial and state-of-the-art solutions by at least an order of magnitude while maintaining auto-scaling capabilities.

10.4.6. Distributed Data Stores

Event-driven invocation means that an application's functions might not always run on the same node, which means they can't use shared memory or interprocess communication. Functions are also not always in an execution state and, as a result, are not network addressable due to the nature of serverless offerings that permit scaling to zero. In order to handle statefulness within their applications, developers are forced to rely on increased communications via slow storage, like S3 buckets.

Scaling a database to zero involves difficult challenges; developing a database design that enables true serverless computing requires continuous engineering and research. Recently, Microsoft suggested adding auto-scaling features to their Azure SQL database. D1, which is based on SQLite, was introduced by Cloudflare in 2022. Since key-value stores (KVS) can be distributed across nodes and are essentially stateless, they scale much more naturally than databases and are therefore frequently used in conjunction with serverless applications. Since serverless statefulness relies on KVS systems, implementing consistent, effective, and elastic KVS is an active area of research. Nevertheless, serverless characteristics were not taken into consideration when designing industry-grade storage systems, which led to reduced elasticity, costs that increased more quickly than the infrastructure's size, and variable performance depending on the system's size.

In (Wu C, Faleiro JM, Lin Y, Hellerstein JM (2018)), the store has to be incredibly effective on a single node and able to scale up elastically to any cloud deployment, according to the authors' goal of creating a KVS for any scale. Their design specifications include wait-free execution to minimize latency, coordination-free consistency models to prevent bottlenecks during communications across cores and nodes, and partitioning the key space (beginning at the multi-core level to ensure performance) with multi-master replication to achieve concurrency. Anna can effectively combine state in an asynchronous (or wait-free) manner by using lattices, a cutting-edge data structure. According to the evaluation, when used in a distributed setting across four 32-core nodes located in different geographical locations, Anna performs 10× better than Cassandra.

The authors argue that existing store services have objectives orthogonal or contradictory to those of a serverless KVS: they sacrifice performance or cost for durability or high availability of data. In particular, they find that these systems are inherently not suitable for intermediate (or "ephemeral") data in the context of interfunctions communications, as they require a long-running agent to achieve communication among tasks. The authors present Pocket, a distributed data store designed for intermediate data sharing in the context of serverless analytics, with sub-second response times, automatic resource rightsizing and intelligent data placement across multiple storage tiers (DRAM, Flash, disk). This is achieved by dividing responsibilities between three planes that scale independently: a control plane that implements data placement policies, a metadata plane that allows distributing data across nodes, and the data storage plane. When evaluated against Redis for MapReduce operations on a 100 GB dataset, Pocket shows comparable performance while saving close to 60% in cost. It is also significantly faster than Amazon S3, with a 4.1× speedup on ephemeral I/O.

10.4.7. Ephemeral Storage

Cloud storage is designed as a tiered service where data is divided between a fast, expensive medium and a slow, inexpensive medium based on factors like size, age, and frequency of use (Table 10.3). Targeting a market midway between Flash SSDs and DRAM, Intel Optane persistent memory (PM) modules have marginally higher latency and bandwidth than DRAM, but they still provide SSD-caliber non-volatile memory capacities at a lower cost.

In (Chen Y, Lu Y, Yang F, Wang Q, Wang Y, Shu J (2020)), the authors aim at delivering a key-value storage engine that would take advantage of persistent memory (PM, or NVM for non-volatile memory) technology to achieve greater performance than on spinning disks or Flash memory. They focus on write-intensive, small-sized workloads: indeed, previous studies have shown that Memcached pools in the wild are mainly used to store small objects, e.g., 70% of them are smaller than 300 bytes at Facebook. Moreover, serverless analytics exchange short-lived data and thus are very write-intensive, while object stores have historically been used as a read-dominated caching layer. Building on these observations, and characteristics specific to PM devices, they present FlatStore, a KVS engine with minimal write overhead, low latency and multi-core scalability. As persistent memories present fine-grain addressability and show low latency as compared to HDDs and SSDs, the authors designed FlatStore for minimal batching of write operations so as to avoid contention. When benchmarked on Facebook data with tiny (1–13 bytes) to large (> 300 bytes) items, evaluation shows that FlatStore performs 2.5–6.3 times faster than state-of-the-art solutions.

Table 10.3. *A Simplified Overview of Media Choice in Tiered Infrastructures*

Capacity	TB			GB	
Addressability	Block			Byte	
Consideration	Cost			Data	
Latency	s	ms	μs	μs	ns
Data	Cold	Warm	Hot	Hot	Mission critical
Medium	Tape	HDD	SSD (Flash)	NVRAM	DRAM

Source: Rajalakshmi Krishnamurthi, Adarsh Kumar, Sukhpal Singh Gill and Rajkumar Buyya. Serverless Computing: Principles and Paradigms. ISBN 978-3-031-26633-1.

One of the main issues with serverless platforms is statefulness. In order to close the gap between traditional service models and FaaS, service providers are implementing a range of BaaS software, which enables developers to deploy their entire applications to their serverless offerings. Because serverless functions are deployed dynamically to multiple geographic zones on hardware resources that are dynamically allocated by the provider, they present intrinsically disaggregated compute and storage. They require a way to work with data that is sufficiently fast, provides consistency assurances, and expands coherently with the pay-as-you-go pricing structure. Research on distributed data stores and throughput acceleration with newly developed non-volatile memory is still warranted.

REFERENCES

1. Agache, A., Brooker, M., Iordache, A., Liguori, A., Neugebauer, R., Piwonka, P., & Popa, D. M. (2020). Firecracker: Lightweight virtualization for serverless applications. In *Proceedings of the 17th USENIX Symposium on Networked Systems Design and Implementation (NSDI 20)* (pp. 419–434). USENIX Association.
2. Akkus, I. E., Chen, R., Rimac, I., Stein, M., Satzke, K., Beck, A., Aditya, P., & Hilt, V. (2018). SAND: Towards high-performance serverless computing. In *Proceedings of the 2018 USENIX Conference on Usenix Annual Technical Conference (USENIX ATC '18)* (pp. 923–935). USENIX Association.
3. Almeida Morais, F. J., Vilar Brasileiro, F., Vigolvino Lopes, R., Araujo Santos, R., Satterfield, W., & Rosa, L. (2013). Autoflex: Service agnostic auto-scaling framework for IaaS deployment models. In *Proceedings of the 13th IEEE/ACM International Symposium on Cluster, Cloud, and Grid Computing* (pp. 42–49). IEEE.
4. Andrae, A., & Edler, T. (2015). On global electricity usage of communication technology: Trends to 2030. *Challenges, 6*(1), 117–157.
5. Anjali, Caraza-Harter, T., & Swift, M. M. (2020). Blending containers and virtual machines: A study of Firecracker and gVisor. In *Proceedings of the 16th ACM SIGPLAN/SIGOPS International Conference on Virtual Execution Environments*.
6. Atikoglu, B., Xu, Y., Frachtenberg, E., Jiang, S., & Paleczny, M. (2012). Workload analysis of a large-scale key-value store. *SIGMETRICS Performance Evaluation Review, 40*(1), 53–64.
7. Baarzi, A. F., Kesidis, G., Joe-Wong, C., & Shahrad, M. (2021). On merits and viability of multi-cloud serverless. In *Proceedings of the ACM Symposium on Cloud Computing* (pp. 600–608). ACM.
8. Bacis, M., Brondolin, R., & Santambrogio, M. D. (2020). BlastFunction: An FPGA-as-a-service system for accelerated serverless computing. In *Proceedings of the 2020 Design, Automation and Test in Europe Conference and Exhibition (DATE)* (pp. 852–857). IEEE.
9. Barbalace, A., & Do, J. (2021). Computational storage: Where are we today? In *Proceedings of the Conference on Innovative Data Systems Research (CIDR 2020)* (p. 6).
10. Bentaleb, O., Belloum, A. S. Z., Sebaa, A., & El-Maouhab, A. (2022). Containerization technologies: Taxonomies, applications and challenges. *Journal of Supercomputing, 78*(1), 1144–1181.

11. Boukhobza, J., Rubini, S., Chen, R., & Shao, Z. (2017). Emerging NVM: A survey on architectural integration and research challenges. *ACM Transactions on Design Automation of Electronic Systems, 23*(2).
12. Burckhardt, S., Chandramouli, B., Gillum, C., Justo, D., Kallas, K., McMahon, C., Meiklejohn, C. S., & Zhu, X. (2022). Netherite: Efficient execution of serverless workflows. *Proceedings of the VLDB Endowment, 15*(8), 1591–1604.
13. Buyya, R., Garg, S. K., & Calheiros, R. N. (2011). SLA-oriented resource provisioning for cloud computing: Challenges, architecture, and solutions. In *Proceedings of the International Conference on Cloud and Service Computing* (pp. 1–10). IEEE.
14. Cadden, J., Unger, T., Awad, Y., Dong, H., Krieger, O., & Appavoo, J. (2020). SEUSS: Skip redundant paths to make serverless fast. In *Proceedings of the Fifteenth European Conference on Computer Systems* (pp. 1–15). ACM.
15. Chahal, D., Palepu, S., Mishra, M., & Singhal, R. (2020). SLA-aware workload scheduling using hybrid cloud services. In *Proceedings of the 1st Workshop on High Performance Serverless Computing* (pp. 1–4). ACM.
16. Chaurasia, N., Kumar, M., Chaudhry, R., & Verma, O. P. (2021). Comprehensive survey on energy-aware server consolidation techniques in cloud computing. *Journal of Supercomputing, 77*(10), 11682–11737.
17. Chikhaoui, A., Lemarchand, L., Boukhalfa, K., & Boukhobza, J. (2021). Multi-objective optimization of data placement in a storage-as-a-service federated cloud. *ACM Transactions on Storage, 17*(3), 1–32.
18. Dartois, J. E., Ribeiro, H. B., Boukhobza, J., & Barais, O. (2019). Opportunistic MapReduce on ephemeral and heterogeneous cloud resources. In *Proceedings of the 12th IEEE International Conference on Cloud Computing (CLOUD)* (pp. 396–403). IEEE.
19. Diamantopoulos, D., Polig, R., Ringlein, B., Purandare, M., Weiss, B., Hagleitner, C., Lantz, M., & Abel, F. (2021). Acceleration-as-a-μ service: A cloud-native Monte-Carlo option pricing engine on CPUs, GPUs and disaggregated FPGAs. In *Proceedings of the 14th IEEE International Conference on Cloud Computing (CLOUD)* (pp. 726–729). IEEE.
20. Dragoni, N., Lanese, I., Larsen, S. T., Mazzara, M., Mustafin, R., & Safina, L. (2018). Microservices: How to make your application scale. In Petrenko, A. K., & Voronkov, A. (Eds.), *Perspectives of System Informatics* (Vol. 10742, pp. 95–104). Springer International Publishing.

21. Du, D., Yu, T., Xia, Y., Zang, B., Yan, G., Qin, C., Wu, Q., & Chen, H. (2020). Catalyzer: Sub-millisecond startup for serverless computing with initialization-less booting. In *Proceedings of the 25th International Conference on Architectural Support for Programming Languages and Operating Systems* (pp. 467–481). ACM.

22. Elsakhawy, M., & Bauer, M. (2020). FaaS2F: A framework for defining execution-SLA in serverless computing. In *Proceedings of the 2020 IEEE Cloud Summit* (pp. 58–65). IEEE.

23. Fuerst, A., & Sharma, P. (2021). FaasCache: Keeping serverless computing alive with greedy-dual caching. In *Proceedings of the 26th ACM International Conference on Architectural Support for Programming Languages and Operating Systems* (pp. 386–400). ACM.

24. Gill, S. S., Xu, M., Ottaviani, C., Patros, P., Bahsoon, R., Shaghaghi, A., Golec, M., Stankovski, V., Wu, H., Abraham, A., Singh, M., Mehta, H., Ghosh, S. K., Baker, T., Parlikad, A. K., Lutfiyya, H., Kanhere, S. S., Sakellariou, R., Dustdar, S., Rana, O., Brandic, I., & Uhlig, S. (2022). AI for next generation computing: Emerging trends and future directions. *Internet of Things, 19*, 100514.

25. Golec, M., Ozturac, R., Pooranian, Z., Gill, S. S., & Buyya, R. (2022). iFaaSBus: A security- and privacy-based lightweight framework for serverless computing using IoT and machine learning. *IEEE Transactions on Industrial Informatics, 18*(5), 3522–3529.

26. Greenberger, M. (1962). Management and the computer of the future (pp. 220–248). M.I.T. Press and Wiley.

27. Gujarati, A., Elnikety, S., He, Y., McKinley, K. S., & Brandenburg, B. B. (2017). Swayam: Distributed autoscaling to meet SLAs of machine learning inference services with resource efficiency. In *Proceedings of the 18th ACM/IFIP/USENIX Middleware Conference* (pp. 109–120). ACM.

28. Handaoui, M., Dartois, J. E., Boukhobza, J., Barais, O., & d'Orazio, L. (2020). ReLeaSER: A reinforcement learning strategy for optimizing utilization of ephemeral cloud resources. In *Proceedings of the 2020 IEEE International Conference on Cloud Computing Technology and Science (CloudCom)* (pp. 65–73). IEEE.

29. Hellerstein, J. M., Faleiro, J. M., Gonzalez, J., Schleier-Smith, J., Sreekanti, V., Tumanov, A., & Wu, C. (2019). Serverless computing: One step forward, two steps back. In *9th Biennial Conference on Innovative Data Systems Research (CIDR 2019)*. Online proceedings.

30. Horta, E., Chuang, H. R., VSathish, N. R., Philippidis, C., Barbalace, A., Olivier, P., & Ravindran, B. (2021). Xar-Trek: Run-time execution

migration among FPGAs and heterogeneous-ISA CPUs. In *Proceedings of the 22nd International Middleware Conference* (pp. 104–118). ACM.

31. Izraelevitz, J., Yang, J., Zhang, L., Kim, J., Liu, X., Memaripour, A., Soh, Y. J., Wang, Z., Xu, Y., Dulloor, S. R., Zhao, J., & Swanson, S. (2019). Basic performance measurements of the Intel Optane DC persistent memory module.
32. Jia, Z., & Witchel, E. (2021). Nightcore: Efficient and scalable serverless computing for latency-sensitive, interactive microservices. In *Proceedings of the 26th ACM International Conference on Architectural Support for Programming Languages and Operating Systems (ASPLOS '21)* (pp. 152–166). Association for Computing Machinery.
33. Jiang, J., Gan, S., Liu, Y., Wang, F., Alonso, G., Klimovic, A., Singla, A., Wu, W., & Zhang, C. (2021). Towards demystifying serverless machine learning training. In *Proceedings of the 2021 International Conference on Management of Data.*
34. Jonas, E., Schleier-Smith, J., Sreekanti, V., Tsai, C., Khandelwal, A., Pu, Q., Shankar, V., Carreira, J., Krauth, K., Yadwadkar, N. J., Gonzalez, J. E., Popa, R. A., Stoica, I., & Patterson, D. A. (2019). Cloud programming simplified: A Berkeley view on serverless computing.
35. Khandelwal, A., Kejariwal, A., & Ramasamy, K. (2020). Le Taureau: Deconstructing the serverless landscape and a look forward. In *Proceedings of the 2020 ACM SIGMOD International Conference on Management of Data* (pp. 2641–2650). ACM.
36. Kivity, A., Kamay, Y., & Laor, D. (2007). KVM: The Linux virtual machine monitor. In *Proceedings of the 2007 Ottawa Linux Symposium (OLS '07)* (p. 8).
37. Klimovic, A., Wen Wang, Y., Stuedi, P., Trivedi, A. K., Pfefferle, J., & Kozyrakis, C. E. (2018). Pocket: Elastic ephemeral storage for serverless analytics. *USENIX Magazine, 44*.
38. Kuenzer, S., Bădoiu, V. A., Lefeuvre, H., Santhanam, S., Jung, A., Gain, G., Soldani, C., Lupu, C., Teodorescu, S., Răducanu, C., Banu, C., Mathy, L., Deaconescu, R., Raiciu, C., & Huici, F. (2021). Unikraft: Fast, specialized unikernels the easy way. In *Proceedings of the Sixteenth European Conference on Computer Systems* (pp. 376–394). ACM.
39. Liu, N., Li, Z., Xu, J., Xu, Z., Lin, S., Qiu, Q., Tang, J., & Wang, Y. (2017). A hierarchical framework of cloud resource allocation and power management using deep reinforcement learning. In *Proceedings of the 37th IEEE International Conference on Distributed Computing Systems (ICDCS)* (pp. 372–382). IEEE.

40. Lloyd, W., Vu, M., Zhang, B., David, O., & Leavesley, G. (2018). Improving application migration to serverless computing platforms: Latency mitigation with keep-alive workloads. In *Proceedings of the 2018 IEEE/ACM International Conference on Utility and Cloud Computing Companion (UCC Companion)* (pp. 195–200). IEEE.
41. Lopes, R. V., & Menasce, D. (2016). A taxonomy of job scheduling on distributed computing systems. *IEEE Transactions on Parallel and Distributed Systems, 27*(12), 3412–3428.
42. Manco, F., Lupu, C., Schmidt, F., Mendes, J., Kuenzer, S., Sati, S., Yasukata, K., Raiciu, C., & Huici, F. (2017). My VM is lighter (and safer) than your container. In *Proceedings of the 26th Symposium on Operating Systems Principles (SOSP '17)* (pp. 218–233). Association for Computing Machinery.
43. Marshall, P., Keahey, K., & Freeman, T. (2010). Elastic site: Using clouds to elastically extend site resources. In *Proceedings of the 10th IEEE/ACM International Conference on Cluster, Cloud and Grid Computing* (pp. 43–52). IEEE.
44. Masanet, E., Shehabi, A., Lei, N., Smith, S., & Koomey, J. (2020). Recalibrating global data center energy-use estimates. *Science, 367*(6481), 984–986.
45. Matei, O., Skrzypek, P., Heb, R., & Moga, A. (2020). Transition from serverfull to serverless architecture in cloud-based software applications. In R. Silhavy, P. Silhavy, & Z. Prokopova (Eds.), *Software Engineering Perspectives in Intelligent Systems* (Vol. 1294, pp. 304–314). Springer International Publishing.
46. McGrath, G., & Brenner, P. R. (2017). Serverless computing: Design, implementation, and performance. In *Proceedings of the 37th IEEE International Conference on Distributed Computing Systems Workshops (ICDCSW)* (pp. 405–410). IEEE.
47. Mell, P., & Grance, T. (2011). The NIST definition of cloud computing. *National Institute of Standards and Technology Special Publication 800–145.*
48. Mohan, A., Sane, H., Doshi, K., Edupuganti, S., Nayak, N., & Sukhomlinov, V. (2019). Agile cold starts for scalable serverless. In *Proceedings of the 11th USENIX Workshop on Hot Topics in Cloud Computing (HotCloud 19)* (p. 6). USENIX Association.
49. Müller, I., Marroquín, R., & Alonso, G. (2020). Lambada: Interactive data analytics on cold data using serverless cloud infrastructure. In *Proceedings of the 2020 ACM SIGMOD International Conference on Management of*

Data (pp. 115–130). ACM.

50. Nishtala, R., Fugal, H., Grimm, S., Kwiatkowski, M., Lee, H., Li, H. C., McElroy, R., Paleczny, M., Peek, D., Saab, P., Stafford, D., Tung, T., & Venkataramani, V. (2013). Scaling memcache at Facebook. In *10th USENIX Symposium on Networked Systems Design and Implementation (NSDI 13)* (pp. 385–398). USENIX Association.
51. Oakes, E., Yang, L., Zhou, D., Houck, K., Harter, T., Arpaci-Dusseau, A., & Arpaci-Dusseau, R. (2018). SOCK: Rapid task provisioning with serverless-optimized containers. In *Proceedings of the 2018 USENIX Annual Technical Conference (USENIX ATC 18)* (pp. 57–70). USENIX Association.
52. Perron, M., Fernandez, R. C., DeWitt, D. J., & Madden, S. (2020). Starling: A scalable query engine on cloud functions. In *Proceedings of the 2020 ACM SIGMOD International Conference on Management of Data.*
53. Pons, D. B., Artigas, M. S., París, G., Sutra, P., & López, P. G. (2019). On the FaaS track: Building stateful distributed applications with serverless architectures. In *Proceedings of the 20th International Middleware Conference.*
54. Poppe, O., Guo, Q., Lang, W., Arora, P., Oslake, M., Xu, S., & Kalhan, A. (2022). Moneyball: Proactive auto-scaling in Microsoft Azure SQL database serverless. In *Proceedings of the VLDB Endowment* (pp. 1279–1287). ACM.
55. Schleier-Smith, J., Sreekanti, V., Khandelwal, A., Carreira, J., Yadwadkar, N. J., Popa, R. A., Gonzalez, J. E., Stoica, I., & Patterson, D. A. (2021). What serverless computing is and should become: The next phase of cloud computing. *Communications of the ACM, 64*(5), 76–84.
56. Schuler, L., Jamil, S., & Kuhl, N. (2021). AI-based resource allocation: Reinforcement learning for adaptive auto-scaling in serverless environments. In *2021 IEEE/ACM 21st International Symposium on Cluster, Cloud and Internet Computing (CCGrid)* (pp. 804–811). IEEE.
57. Shafiei, H., Khonsari, A., & Mousavi, P. (2022). Serverless computing: A survey of opportunities, challenges, and applications. *ACM Computing Surveys* (Just Accepted).
58. Shahin, M., Ali Babar, M., & Zhu, L. (2017). Continuous integration, delivery and deployment: A systematic review on approaches, tools, challenges, and practices. *IEEE Access, 5*, 3909–3943.
59. Shahrad, M., Fonseca, R., Goiri, Í., Chaudhry, G., Batum, P., Cooke, J., Laureano, E., Tresness, C., Russinovich, M., & Bianchini, R. (2020).

Serverless in the wild: Characterizing and optimizing the serverless workload at a large cloud provider. *arXiv preprint*.

60. Shaw, R., Howley, E., & Barrett, E. (2022). Applying reinforcement learning towards automating energy efficient virtual machine consolidation in cloud data centers. *Information Systems, 21*.
61. Singhvi, A., Balasubramanian, A., Houck, K., Shaikh, M. D., Venkataraman, S., & Akella, A. (2021). Atoll: A scalable low-latency serverless platform. In *Proceedings of the ACM Symposium on Cloud Computing* (pp. 138–152). ACM.
62. Soni, D., & Kumar, N. (2022). Machine learning techniques in emerging cloud computing integrated paradigms: A survey and taxonomy. *Journal of Network and Computer Applications, 205*, 103419.
63. Sreekanti, V., Wu, C., Lin, X. C., Schleier-Smith, J., Faleiro, J. M., Gonzalez, J. E., Hellerstein, J. M., & Tumanov, A. (2020). Cloudburst: Stateful functions-as-a-service. *Proceedings of the VLDB Endowment, 13*, 2438–2452.
64. Taibi, D., El Ioini, N., Pahl, C., & Niederkofler, J. (2020). Patterns for serverless functions (Function-as-a-Service): A multivocal literature review. In *Proceedings of the 10th International Conference on Cloud Computing and Services Science* (pp. 181–192). SCITEPRESS—Science and Technology Publications.
65. Tan, B., Liu, H., Rao, J., Liao, X., Jin, H., & Zhang, Y. (2020). Towards lightweight serverless computing via unikernel as a function. In *2020 IEEE/ACM 28th International Symposium on Quality of Service (IWQoS)* (pp. 1–10). IEEE.
66. Thalheim, J., Okelmann, P., Unnibhavi, H., Gouicem, R., & Bhatotia, P. (2022). VMSH: Hypervisor-agnostic guest overlays for VMs. In *Proceedings of the Seventeenth European Conference on Computer Systems* (pp. 678–696). ACM.
67. Ustiugov, D., Petrov, P., Kogias, M., Bugnion, E., & Grot, B. (2021). Benchmarking, analysis, and optimization of serverless function snapshots. In *Proceedings of the 26th ACM International Conference on Architectural Support for Programming Languages and Operating Systems* (pp. 559–572). ACM.
68. Vahidinia, P., Farahani, B., & Aliee, F. S. (2020). Cold start in serverless computing: Current trends and mitigation strategies. In *2020 International Conference on Omni-layer Intelligent Systems (COINS)* (pp. 1–7). IEEE.
69. van Eyk, E., Iosup, A., Abad, C. L., Grohmann, J., & Eismann, S. (2018). A SPEC RG cloud group's vision on the performance challenges of FaaS

cloud architectures. In *Companion of the 2018 ACM/SPEC International Conference on Performance Engineering* (pp. 21–24). ACM.

70. Vaquero, L. M., Rodero-Merino, L., & Morán, D. (2011). Locking the sky: A survey on IaaS cloud security. *Computing, 91*(1), 93–118.
71. Vilanova, L., Maudlej, L., Bergman, S., Miemietz, T., Hille, M., Asmussen, N., Roitzsch, M., Härtig, H., & Silberstein, M. (2022). Slashing the disaggregation tax in heterogeneous data centers with FractOS. In *Proceedings of the Seventeenth European Conference on Computer Systems* (pp. 352–367). ACM.
72. Villamizar, M., Garces, O., Castro, H., Verano, M., Salamanca, L., Casallas, R., & Gil, S. (2015). Evaluating the monolithic and the microservice architecture pattern to deploy web applications in the cloud. In *2015 10th Computing Colombian Conference (10CCC)* (pp. 583–590). IEEE.
73. Wanninger, N. C., Bowden, J. J., Shetty, K., Garg, A., & Hale, K. C. (2022). Isolating functions at the hardware limit with vitrines. In *Proceedings of the Seventeenth European Conference on Computer Systems* (pp. 644–662). ACM.
74. Weissman, C. D., & Bobrowski, S. (2009). The design of the Force.com multitenant internet application development platform. In *Proceedings of the 2009 ACM SIGMOD International Conference on Management of Data* (pp. 889–896). ACM.
75. Wu, C., Sreekanti, V., & Hellerstein, J. M. (2020). Transactional causal consistency for serverless computing. In *Proceedings of the 2020 ACM SIGMOD International Conference on Management of Data* (pp. 83–97). ACM.
76. Yalles, S., Handaoui, M., Dartois, J. E., Barais, O., d'Orazio, L., & Boukhobza, J. (2022). Riscless: A reinforcement learning strategy to guarantee SLA on cloud ephemeral and stable resources. In *2022 30th Euromicro International Conference on Parallel, Distributed and Network-Based Processing (PDP)* (pp. 83–87). IEEE.
77. Zhang, T., Xie, D., Li, F., & Stutsman, R. (2019). Narrowing the gap between serverless and its state with storage functions. In *Proceedings of the ACM Symposium on Cloud Computing* (pp. 1–12). ACM.
78. Zhang, W., Fang, V., Panda, A., & Shenker, S. (2020). Kappa: A programming framework for serverless computing. In *Proceedings of the 11th ACM Symposium on Cloud Computing (SoCC '20)* (pp. 328–343). Association for Computing Machinery.

CHAPTER 11

COMETCLOUD: AN AUTONOMIC CLOUD ENGINE

Contents

INTRODUCTION

With their highly diverse and dynamic workloads, clouds usually have extremely dynamic resource demands. For instance, the application's workloads can vary greatly in terms of the quantity of tasks processed and the amount of computation needed for each task. Furthermore, the requirements for different applications' quality of service (QoS) can vary greatly and be dynamic. For instance, one application might need a high throughput, another might be budget-constrained, and a third might need to balance both. These fluctuating loads, failures, network conditions, and other factors can also affect a cloud service's performance and change the "QoS" that an application receives.

On-demand scale-up, scale-down, and scale-out can be supported by combining public cloud platforms and integrating them with current grids and data centers. Before scaling out onto a public cloud, users might want to utilize resources in their private cloud (or data center, or grid). They might also have a preference for a specific cloud or want to combine multiple clouds. But at the moment, achieving such integration and interoperability is difficult. Additionally, integrating these public cloud platforms with currently operational computational grids opens up possibilities for cloudbursts, or on-demand scale-up and scale-down.

We introduce the CometCloud autonomic cloud engine in this chapter. CometCloud's main objective is to create a virtual computational cloud with resizable computing capacity. It does this by integrating on-demand public cloud services with local computational environments and by offering abstractions and mechanisms that accommodate various programming paradigms and application requirements. CometCloud specifically makes policy-based autonomous cloudbursting and cloudbridging possible. Autonomic cloudbursting allows dynamic application scale-out to handle dynamic workloads, demand spikes, and other extreme requirements, while autonomic cloudbridging allows instantaneous integration of local computational environments (data centers, grids) and public cloud services (such as Amazon EC2 and Eucalyptus).

CometCloud supports highly heterogeneous and dynamic cloud/grid infrastructures, integration of public/private clouds, and cloudbursts. It is based on a decentralized coordination substrate. A decentralized and scalable task space that arranges the scheduling of tasks submitted by a dynamic group of users onto groups of dynamically provisioned workers on available private and/or public cloud resources based on their quality of service (QoS) constraints—such as cost or performance—is also supported by the coordination substrate. The right amount and combination of public and private clouds to assign to a given application request depends on a number of factors, including policies, past performance, resource availability, and QoS limitations. (I. Stoica, R. Morris,

D. Karger, et al., 2001). Additionally, this chapter shows how CometCloud can accommodate the changing needs of actual applications—as well as those of multiple application groups—with a range of computational requirements and QoS limitations. This chapter specifically covers two CometCloud-enabled applications: a high-throughput medical image registration application and a computationally demanding value at risk (VaR) application. Senior managers and regulators use VaR, a market-standard risk measure, to determine how risky a firm's holdings are. The computational requirements for a VaR calculation can vary greatly, and it must be finished in the allotted time. Finding the linear or nonlinear mapping between two images of the same object, or something similar, is the process of image registration. Various research groups, located in different regions of the world, use various image registration techniques to process their locally stored data. The collection of photos will usually have been taken in various coordinate systems, at different times, or from different viewpoints. Therefore, before doing any image analysis, it is essential to align those images into the same coordinate system. (T. Vercauteren, X. Pennec, A. Perchant, and N. Ayache, 2008).

11.1. COMETCLOUD ARCHITECTURE

An autonomous computing engine for grid and cloud environments is called CometCloud. It supports highly heterogeneous and dynamic cloud/grid infrastructures, integration of public/private clouds, and autonomic cloudbursts. It is based on the Comet decentralized coordination substrate. CometCloud operates on a peer-to-peer substrate that can traverse clouds, grids, and enterprise data centers.

In order to provide services to applications, resources can be incorporated into its peer-to-peer overlay instantly and on demand. In order to deterministically map the information space onto the dynamic set of peer nodes, CometCloud (and Comet) modify the Squid information discovery scheme.

A locality-preserving semantic distributed hash table (DHT) atop a self-organizing structured overlay is the resultant structure. It ensures that content-based queries with bounded costs are provided while preserving content locality and utilizing flexible content descriptors like wildcards, partial keywords, and keywords. Using Squid, Comet creates an abstraction of a tuple-based coordination space that is associatively accessible to all system peers and does not require host identifiers or tuple location information. CometCloud additionally offers transient spaces, which let programs take advantage of context locality in an explicit way.

11.1.1. CometCloud Layered Abstractions

Figure 11.1. shows a schematic overview of the CometCloud architecture. The Squid information discovery and content-based routing substrate, which is built on top of Chord, and the Chord self-organizing overlay are utilized by the infrastructure layer. Flexible content-based routing and sophisticated querying with partial keywords, wildcards, or ranges are supported by the routing engine. Additionally, it ensures that every peer node that has data elements matching a message or query will be found. Because nodes supplying resources in the overlay play different roles, their access privileges vary as well, depending on their qualifications and skills. In addition to handling node failures and dynamic joins and leaves, this layer also offers replication and load balancing services. Every node maintains a copy of the state of its successor node, and it updates this copy whenever its successor updates it. It also informs the one before it of any modifications to its state. In the event that a node fails, the replica is merged into the parent node's state, and a new replica of the successor is then created. When a new node joins, the replica of the joining node is updated by its predecessor to reflect the joining node's state, and the joining node receives its state information from its successor. Every time a node joins or leaves, load needs to be redistributed among the nodes in order to maintain load balancing.

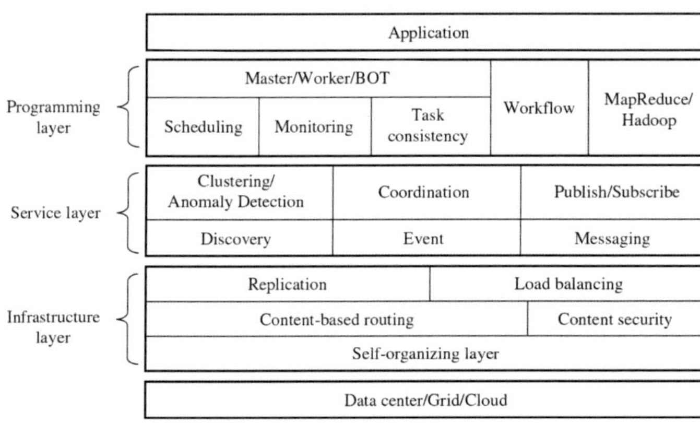

Figure 11.1. *The CometCloud architecture for autonomic cloudbursts.*

Source: Hyunjoo Kim and Manish Parashar, CometCloud: An Autonomic Cloud Engine, ISBN 978 0 470 88799 8.

A variety of services are offered by the service layer to support autonomics at the application and programming levels. This layer offers associative access primitives, a virtual shared-space abstraction, and support for the Linda-like tuple space coordination model. The basic coordination primitives are listed below:

- **out (ts, t):** a nonblocking operation that inserts tuple t into space ts.
- **in (ts, t'):** a blocking operation that removes a tuple t matching template t' from the space ts and returns it.
- **rd (ts, t'):** a blocking operation that returns a tuple t matching template
- **t' from the space ts.** The tuple is not removed from the space.

A tuple can be inserted into the space using the out function, and it can be read from the space using the in and rd functions. While rd only reads the tuple, in removes it after it has been read. Since we support range queries, you can search through all tuples by using "*." Since the aforementioned uniform operators do not discriminate between local and remote spaces, context-transparent applications are a natural fit for the Comet.

However, this abstraction may negatively impact the effectiveness of applications imposing context-awareness, such as mobile applications, and does not maintain geographic locality between peer nodes. These applications impose requirements for context-awareness, meaning that they demand that context locality be maintained in addition to content locality. CometCloud supports dynamically created transient spaces with a defined scope definition (e.g., within the same physical subnet or geographical region) in order to address this problem.

All peer nodes can access the global space, which serves as the standard platform for coordination. Access to the temporary spaces is restricted through the use of membership and authentication procedures. The global space and the transitory space have the exact same structure.

A program has the ability to use multiple spaces at once and to switch between them at runtime. Evening services and asynchronous (publish/subscribe) messaging are also offered by this layer. Lastly, online clustering services facilitate self-monitoring and control and assist autonomic management. Events that describe how system components are operating or behaving are grouped together, and this grouping is used to identify unusual behavior.

The fundamental framework for managing and developing applications is provided by the programming layer. A variety of paradigms are supported, such as the master/worker/BOT paradigm. Tasks are created by masters and completed by workers. Workers and masters can converse directly or through a virtual shared space.

The application framework supports task scheduling and monitoring. Lost tasks are managed by the task consistency service. Network congestion can cause a task to fail even though the infrastructure layer provides replication. In this instance, infrastructure level replication might not be able to handle it because there isn't a failure. The master could take care of this, for instance, by waiting a predetermined amount of time for each task's result and then regenerating the lost task if it doesn't receive it. When the master gets more than one result for a task, it chooses the first one and disregards the others. Along with Mapreduce and Hadoop, workflow-based applications are also supported paradigms.

11.1.2. Comet Space

A tuple in Comet is a straightforward XML string with an ordered list of elements containing the tuple's fields after the tuple's tag as the first element. Every field is named and then has a value. For a tuple, the tag, field names, and values must be real data; for a template tuple, wildcards (*) are permitted. This lightweight format can support rich matching relationships and is versatile enough to represent the data for a variety of applications. Additionally, XML's cross-platform compatibility makes it a good format for exchanging data in dispersed, heterogeneous environments.

If a tuple in Comet matches a template tuple exactly or fairly, it can be retrieved. As in Linda's case, exact matching requires the template tuple's tag and field names to be specified exactly, without the use of wildcards. However, since applications (like service discovery) might not be aware of precise tuple structures, this rigorous matching pattern needs to be loosened in extremely dynamic environments. Comet only needs the tag of the template tuple to be specified using a keyword or a partial keyword to support tuple retrievals with incomplete structure information via approximate matching. Examples are shown in Figure 11.2. In this figure, tuple (a) tagged "contact" has fields "name, phone, email, dep" with values "Smith, 7324451000, smith@gmail.com, ece" and can be retrieved using tuple template (b) or (c).

Comet maps tuples from a semantic information space to a linear node index by modifying the Squid information discovery scheme and using the Hilbert space-filling curve (SFC). Users of the application define the semantic information space, which is made up of English words and based-10 numbers. A computational storage resource, for instance, might be a part of the 3D storage space that has the coordinates "space," "bandwidth," and "cost." The tag and field names, which serve as a tuple's keys, are linked to k keywords for each tuple. For instance, in a 2D student information space, the keys of tuple (a) in Figure 11.2 could be "name, phone." If two tuples share a common keyword or are lexicographically close to one another, they are considered local in the information space. Applications have the ability to specify which keys to select.

```
<contact>
   <name> Smith </name>
   <phone> 7324451000 </phone>
   <email> smith@gmail.com </email>
   <dep> ece </dep>
</contact>
```

(a)

```
<contact>
   <name> Smith </name>
   <phone> 7324451000 </phone>
   <email> * </email>
   <dep> * </dep>
</contact>
```

(b)

```
<contact>
   <na*> Smith </na*>
   <*>
   <*>
   <dep> ece </dep>
</contact>
```

(c)

Figure 11.2. *Example of tuples in CometCloud.*

Source: Hyunjoo Kim and Manish Parashar, CometCloud: An Autonomic Cloud Engine, ISBN 978 0 470 88799 8.

A locality-preserving continuous mapping from a k-dimensional (kD) space to a 1D space is called a Hilbert SFC. Because nearby points on the curve are mapped from nearby points in the kD space, it preserves locality. It is easy to extend the Hilbert curve to any number of dimensions. The tuple space is able to preserve content locality in the index space because of its locality-preserving property. The peer nodes in Comet create a one-dimensional overlay that is indexed using a Hilbert SFC. The tuples are mapped from the multi-dimensional information space to the linear peer index space using the Hilbert mapping. Consequently, Comet builds the distribute hash table (DHT) for tuple distribution and lookup using the Hilbert SFC. A tuple is mapped as a point in the information space and found on at most one node if its keys only contain complete keywords. The tuple identifies a region in the information space if its keys are made up of ranges, wildcards, or partial keywords. This region corresponds to a set of points in the index space and is mapped to a group of segments on the SFC. The keys that correspond to the portion of the curve that separates each node from its predecessor are stored in each node. As an illustration, consider Figure 11.3, where five nodes (with the ID displayed in a solid circle) are indexed using SFC from 0 to 63. The region (23, 15) and the point (2, 1) tuples are mapped to two segments on the SFC and correspond to nodes 13 and 32, respectively.

11.2. AUTONOMIC BEHAVIOR OF COMETCLOUD

11.2.1. Autonomic Cloudbursting

Autonomic cloudbursts aim to provide the abstraction of resizable computing capacity by seamlessly and securely integrating data centers and private enterprise clouds with public utility clouds on-demand. It permits the dynamic deployment of application components onto a public cloud to handle dynamic workloads, demand spikes, and other extreme requirements. Normally, application components run on internal organizational compute resources. Furthermore, typical over-provisioning strategies are no longer practical due to the growing scales of applications and infrastructure, as well as the associated costs of cooling, operation, and management. Based on a variety of metrics, autonomous cloudbursts can use utility clouds to offer on-demand scale-out and scale-in capabilities.

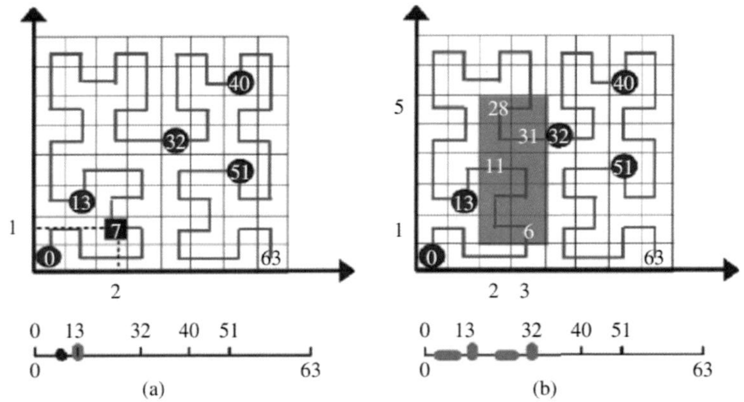

Figure 11.3. *Examples of mapping tuples from 2D information space to 1D index space. (Z. Li and M. Parashar, 2007).*

Source: https://studytm.wordpress.com/wp-content/uploads/2014/03/cloud-computing-principles-paradigms.pdf.

Figure 11.4. presents the overall strategy for CometCloud's autonomic cloudburst support. CometCloud assigns capabilities to three types of clouds based on perceived security and trust. The first is a highly reliable, strong, and secure cloud that is usually used to host masters and other important roles (such as management, scheduling, and monitoring). It is typically made up of trusted/secure nodes within an enterprise. States are also kept in storage by these nodes. Because most applications need to protect the confidentiality and integrity of sensitive data, only cloud nodes with the necessary credentials should be able to perform tasks involving sensitive data. The cloud of secure workers, or nodes made up of such credentials, is the second kind of cloud. These two clouds may be divided by a privileged Comet space that holds important information, tasks, and other parts of the application-logic/workflow. Casual workers make up the last category of cloud computing. These workers are not a part of the space, but if they provide the necessary credentials, they can access the space through the proxy and a request handler to obtain (possibly encrypted) work units. Any of these clouds allows for the intentional addition or deletion of nodes. Autonomic cloudbursts target secure worker to scale up if the space needs to be scaled up to store dynamically growing workload in addition to requiring more computing capability. However, unsecured workers are only added in cases where additional processing power is needed.

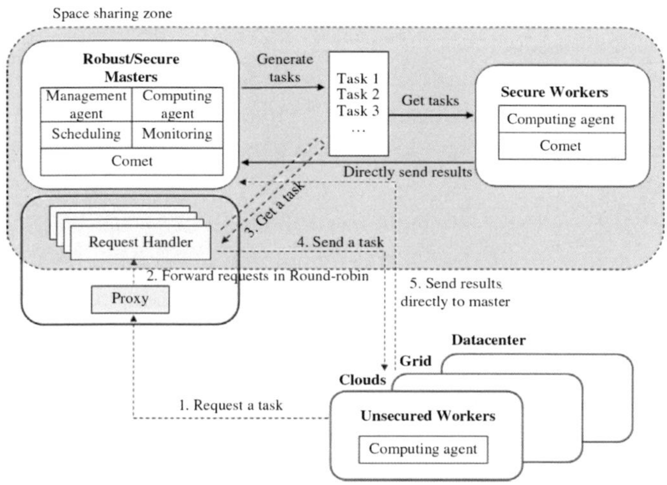

Figure 11.4. *Autonomic cloudbursts using CometCloud.*

Source: https://studytm.wordpress.com/wp-content/uploads/2014/03/cloud-computing-principles-paradigms.pdf.

Key motivations for autonomic cloudbursts include:

- ***Load Dynamics***: Workloads for different applications can differ greatly. This covers both the quantity of application tasks and the processing power needed for each task. In order to keep to tight deadlines, the computational environment must dynamically expand (or contract) in response to these dynamics.
- ***Accuracy of the Analytics***: The amount of highly dynamic market parameters that determine the required accuracy of risk analytics directly affect the computational demand, such as the number of scenarios in the Monte Carlo VaR formulation. To meet the accuracy requirements and adhere to tight deadlines, the computational environment must be able to dynamically adapt.
- ***Collaboration of Different Groups***: The same application can be used by various groups with various dataset policies. Policy refers here to the user's SLA constrained by their conditions, including timelines, financial constraints, and economic models. To meet their SLA, the computational environment must expand or contract as collaboration groups join or depart the project.

- ***Economics***: Application tasks need to be scheduled and resource-allocated based on their often-variable and dynamic priorities. Depending on the importance and urgency of the application task, computational resources can be dynamically provisioned using budgets and economic models. For instance, budgets and resource assignments for application tasks may be made in accordance with this budget. The computational environment needs to be capable of managing dynamic and heterogeneous scheduling and provisioning needs.
- ***Failures***: There are tight deadlines involved, so missing them can have disastrous results. The computation needs to be able to handle errors without compromising the timeliness and accuracy of the application's quality of service.

11.2.2. Autonomic Cloudbridging

The goal of autonomous cloudbridging is to link CometCloud with a virtual cloud that is made up of a grid, data center, and public cloud based on the application's changing requirements. The virtual cloud's clouds are heterogeneous, with varying resource types and pricing structures. In addition, each cloud's performance may fluctuate over time based on the quantity of active users. Therefore, it is important to consider how the cloud environment and application resource requirements change when choosing the types of clouds to use, the number of nodes in each cloud, and the types of resources for each node.

Figure 11.5. shows an overview of the operation of the CometCloud based autonomic cloudbridging. One or more scheduling agents may be present, and their role is to oversee autonomic cloudbursts via the virtual cloud. A strong, secure master site is home to a scheduling agent. A distinct scheduling agent can be used in the master site by each cooperating research group if they need to generate tasks using their own data and manage the virtual cloud according to their own policies. The CometCloud virtual shared space, spanning master nodes at each site, logs the requests for tasks generated by the various sites. Workers then use these tasks, and they can run on public cloud infrastructure, a shared data center, a grid, or local computational nodes at the site. A scheduling agent controls its site's autonomic cloudbursts and QoS limitations in accordance with the established policy. With the proper credentials, the employees can enter the area, access tasks that are permitted, and submit the completed work to the designated master as specified by the task itself.

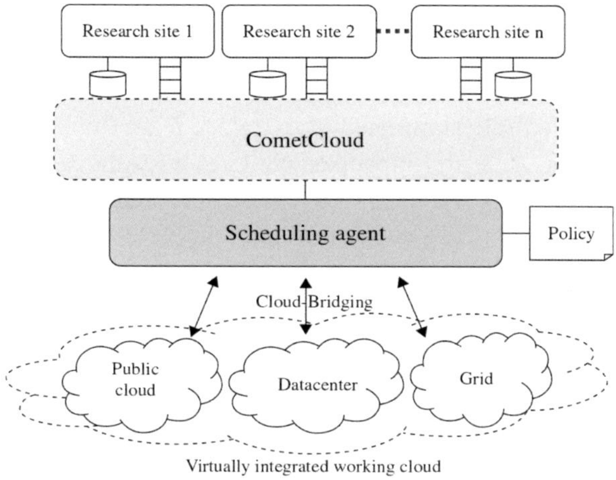

Figure 11.5. *Overview of the operation of autonomic cloud bridging.*

Source: Hyunjoo Kim and Manish Parashar, CometCloud: An Autonomic Cloud Engine, ISBN 978 0 470 88799 8.

Autonomous cloudbridging is controlled by a scheduling agent, which also ensures QoS according to user policies. An example of an autonomous cloudburst is when resource provisioning is altered so as to comply with established policy.

We define three types of policies.

- ***Deadline-Based.*** When an application needs to be completed as soon as possible, assuming an adequate budget, the maximum required workers are allocated for the job.
- ***Budget-Based.*** When a budget is enforced on the application, the number of workers allocated must ensure that the budget is not violated.
- ***Workload-Based.*** When the application workload changes, the number of workers explicitly defined by the application is allocated or released.

11.2.3. Other Autonomic Behaviors

11.2.3.1. Fault-Tolerance

Sustaining fault-tolerance during runtime is essential to meeting the deadline for the application. We provide two levels of fault-tolerance support: one at the programming layer and one at the infrastructure layer. In the infrastructure layer, the replication substrate offers a way to preserve coordination space and overlay information in a state identical to that of its successor. The overlay's overview of replication is displayed in Figure 11.6. In the infrastructure layer, each node has a replica space and a local space in the service layer. The node updates the replica space when a tuple is inserted or extracted from the local space, and the predecessor updates the replica space as well. As a result, each node maintains an identical copy of the local space of its successor. When a node malfunctions, the preceding node is notified by another node in the overlay that has detected the malfunction. All of the tuples from the failed node are then recovered when the predecessor of the failed node merges the replica space into the local space. Additionally, the predecessor node creates a fresh replica of its new successor for the local space. Fault-tolerance is also supported in the programming layer. Even though a replica of every node is kept up to date, network congestion or task generation during failure may cause some tasks to be lost during runtime. The master regenerates lost tasks and checks the area on a regular basis to solve this problem.

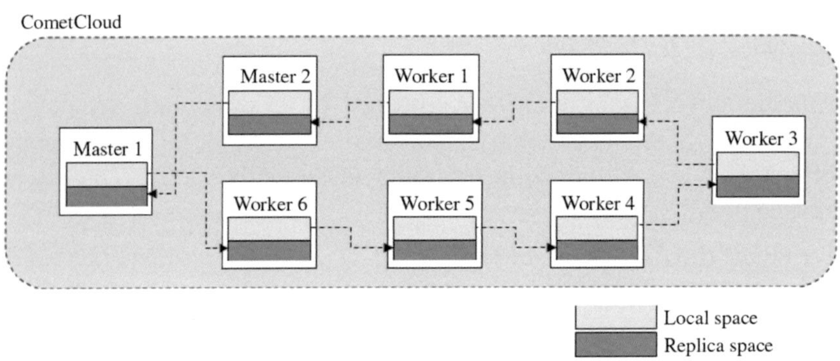

Figure 11.6. *Replication overview in the CometCloud overlay.*

Source: https://studytm.wordpress.com/wp-content/uploads/2014/03/cloud-computing-principles-paradigms.pdf.

11.2.3.2. Load Balancing

There are two essential steps involved in executing application requests on underlying grid resources in a cloud environment. The first, referred to as "VM Provisioning," is the process of building virtual machines (VMs) that are tailored to each application request's unique specifications and attributes. Mapping and scheduling these requests onto dispersed physical resources is the second step (Resource Provisioning). A range of general-purpose virtual machine classes with generic resource configurations are currently offered by the majority of virtualized data centers; however, these quickly run out of capacity to handle the extremely diverse and interleaved workloads. In addition, clients may underestimate or overestimate their needs due to application complexity and/or uncertainty, which makes it easy for them to misjudge the requirements. This tendency toward conservatism frequently leads to overprovisioning.

The distributed nature of enterprise grids and clouds is specifically addressed by the decentralized clustering technique. The strategy expands upon a decentralized messaging and data analysis framework that offers density-based clustering and monitoring features. Workload requests can be clustered across data center job queues to enable autonomic virtual machine provisioning through the characterization of various resource classes. The capacity to analyze jobs across a dynamic set of distributed queues, the lack of presumption regarding the number of clustering classes, the ease of online application, and the ability to promptly adjust to shifting workloads and resource availability are just a few benefits of this approach. Additionally, the robustness of the method enables it to maximize the quality and efficiency of the clustering while managing changes (joins/leaves) in the job queue servers as well as their failures.

11.3. OVERVIEW OF COMETCLOUD-BASED APPLICATIONS

Here, we discuss two application categories: image registration for medical informatics and VaR, which calculates the risk level of a firm's holdings. The computational requirements for a VaR calculation can vary greatly, and it must be finished in the allotted time. Furthermore, the need for extra computation arises sporadically.

Therefore, our focus for VaR will be on the operation of autonomic cloudbursts for workloads that change dynamically. Finding the linear or nonlinear mapping T between two images of the same object or one that is similar but taken from a different angle or at a different time is known as image registration.

Furthermore, jobs can be injected from multiple sites because different (geographically distributed) research groups process their locally stored data using a set of image registration methods.

Another notable distinction between the two applications is the size of the image registration data, which is significantly larger than the VaR data. A 3D image typically has a size of a few tens of megabytes. Because of this, image data should be kept apart from its task tuple. Instead, it should be stored on a different server, and the task tuple should specify where it is. Since image registration typically needs to be finished within a set budget, we will concentrate on CometCloud's budget-based policy approach.

11.3.1. Value at Risk (VaR)

The Monte Carlo Value at Risk (VaR) is a highly effective metric for assessing the risk of financial instrument portfolios. The VaR computation is complicated because it replicates portfolio returns. In order to achieve this, "guesses" about the possible future state of the world are made using Monte Carlo methods. The method can incorporate the complex distributions and correlations of various factors that influence portfolio returns into a discrete set of scenarios by making many guesses. We are able to compute the return on the portfolio under each of these Monte Carlo scenarios because each one includes a sufficiently detailed state of the world to value every instrument in the portfolio.

The first step in creating a Monte Carlo scenario is choosing the basic instruments, or invariants. Invariants are selected so that their returns exhibit a stationary normal probability distribution, thereby simplifying simulation modeling. In real life, these invariants include stock price returns, interest rate returns, foreign exchange rate returns, and so forth. It is necessary to choose the universe of invariants so that changes to the invariants are the only factors influencing portfolio returns.

We simulate multiple realizations of the invariants using Monte Carlo techniques in order to accurately capture the nonlinear pricing of option-containing portfolios. A scenario is used to describe each realization. The portfolio is valued and each option is priced using the invariants in each of these scenarios. As previously mentioned, a VaR number is computed and the portfolio returns for each scenario are ranked from worst loss to best gain.

11.3.2. Image Registration

The computationally costly process of figuring out the mapping T between two images of the same object or similar objects that were taken at different times, in different locations, or with various acquisition parameters or modalities is known as nonlinear image registration. It has been reported that intensity/area based and landmark based approaches work well for a variety of registration tasks.

For both 2D and 3D images, alternative landmark point detection and matching techniques are developed as part of the hybrid image registration algorithm. The algorithm begins by automatically identifying a set of landmarks in both stationary and moving images. Then, it uses the landmarks to estimate the nonlinear mapping from coarse to fine. To determine the point correspondence between landmarks in the stationary and moving images, intensity template matching is additionally utilized. The first landmark correspondence contains a significant amount of outliers, so a robust estimator called RANSAC is used to reject outliers. To finish the last nonlinear registration, a Thin Spline Transform (TPS) is robustly estimated using the final refined inliers. (H. Chui and A. Rangarajan, 2003).

11.4. IMPLEMENTATION AND EVALUATION

After explaining how the applications were implemented using CometCloud, we first assess fundamental CometCloud operations and then compare application runtime varying the number of nodes. Next, we use budget-based policy for image registration and workload-based policy for VaR evaluation. We assess CometCloud both with and without a scheduling agent. We only used deadline-based policies—which have no budget limits since they assign as many workers as possible—to compare the outcomes of budget-based policies with and without scheduling agents.

11.4.1. Evaluation of CometCloud

11.4.1.1. Basic CometCloud Operations

In this experiment, we assessed the Rutgers cloud's costs for simple tuple insertion and exact retrieval operations. In the CometCloud overlay, every machine was a peer node, and together, the machines made up a single CometCloud peer group. In the experiment, the tuple's size was fixed at 200 bytes. The experiment involved an application process that used the out operator to insert a tuple into the space, the rd operator to read the same tuple, and the in operator to delete it. This process was similar to ping-pong. The experiment used three-dimensional information space and exact matching in/rd operators.

11.4.1.2. Overlay Join Overhead

A node must join the CometCloud overlay in order to share the Comet space, and each node must maintain a finger table to keep track of its shifting neighbors. A node connects to a pre-established bootstrap node as soon as it joins the overlay and provides the bootstrap with its details, including its IP address. Subsequently, the bootstrap node creates a finger table and returns it to the node. Therefore, a greater join overhead occurs when more nodes join the overlay concurrently.

11.4.2. Application Runtime

Every task that the master creates is placed into the Comet space, and each one needs to have an XML tag that describes it uniquely for that application. The data to be computed may be found in the task itself or elsewhere, like on a file server. Since image data are typically larger than VaR data, we will use VaR tasks to show each case by including data inside the tuple and image registration tasks to show data outside of the tuple. A typical out task for VaR is described as shown below.

```
<VarAppTask>
  <TaskId>taskid</TaskId>
  <DataBlock>data blocks</DataBlock>
  <MasterNetName>master name</MasterNetName>
</VarAppTask>
```

Since each worker in image registration processes an entire image, the total number of tasks is equal to the number of images that need to be processed. Furthermore, when the master creates tasks, it only adds the task's data location as a tag because the image is too big to be displayed on a task. A worker connects to the data location and retrieves data after accepting a task from the Comet space.

A typical out task for image registration is described as shown below.

```
<ImageRegAppTask>
  <TaskId>taskid</TaskId>
  <ImageLocation>image location</ImageLocation>
  <MasterNetName>master name</MasterNetName>
</ImageRegAppTask>
```

11.4.3. Autonomic Cloudbursts Behaviors

11.4.3.1. VaR Using Workload-Based Policy

This experiment uses the number of workers who change to represent autonomic cloudburst. Based on the application workload, a predetermined number of workers are added (or released) when the workload increases or decreases. We specifically defined policies that are workload-specific and workload-bounded. A user can designate the workload that nodes are assigned or released under workload-specific. In a workload-bounded system, a predetermined number of workers is added whenever the workload rises above a given threshold. Similarly, the predetermined number of workers is released if the workload drops by more than the designated threshold.

11.4.3.2. Image Registration Using Budget-Based Policy

The virtual cloud environment utilized for the experiments comprised of two research sites situated at the University of Medicine and Dentistry of New Jersey and Rutgers University: a private data center at Rutgers (i.e., TW) and a public cloud (i.e., Amazon Web Service (AWS) EC2). Workers using EC2 or TW access these image servers to obtain the image specified in their assigned task.

The two research sites each maintained their own image servers and job queues. There are 250 images on each image server, which equals 500 tasks in total. Every image has a size of between 17 kB and 65 kB and is two-dimensional. The costing models provided in references 10 and 9, respectively, were used to calculate the costs related to executing tasks on EC2 and TW nodes. Our EC2 instances were standard small instances, costing $0.10/hour for computation, $0.10/GB for inbound data transfers, and $0.17/GB for outbound data transfers. Even if users only use the computer for a few minutes, they should still pay for the entire hour because the cost is based on an hourly basis. However, because the experiment's total runtime is less than an hour, we determined the cost in seconds.

REFERENCES

1. Chui, H., & Rangarajan, A. (2003). A new point matching algorithm for nonrigid registration. *Computer Vision and Image Understanding, 89*(2), 114–141.
2. Li, Z., & Parashar, M. (2007). A computational infrastructure for grid-based asynchronous parallel applications. In *Proceedings of the 16th International Symposium on High Performance Distributed Computing* (pp. 229–230). ACM.
3. Moon, B., Jagadish, H. V., Faloutsos, C., & Saltz, J. H. (2001). Analysis of the clustering properties of the Hilbert space-filling curve. *IEEE Transactions on Knowledge and Data Engineering, 13*(1), 124–141.
4. Schmidt, C., & Parashar, M. (2008). Squid: Enabling search in DHT-based systems. *Journal of Parallel and Distributed Computing, 68*(7), 962–975.
5. Stoica, I., Morris, R., Karger, D., Kaashoek, M. F., & Balakrishnan, H. (2001). Chord: A scalable peer-to-peer lookup service for internet applications. In *Proceedings of the 2001 Conference on Applications, Technologies, Architectures, and Protocols for Computer Communications* (pp. 149–160).
6. Vercauteren, T., Pennec, X., Perchant, A., & Ayache, N. (2008). Symmetric log-domain diffeomorphic registration: A demons-based approach. In *Proceedings of the International Conference on Medical Image Computing and Computer-Assisted Intervention* (Vol. 5241, pp. 754–761).
7. Yang, L., Gong, L., Zhang, H., Nosher, J. L., & Foran, D. J. (2009). A method for parallel platform-based acceleration of landmark-based image registration. In *Proceedings of the European Conference on Parallel Computing*. Netherlands.

INDEX

D

H

I

K

L

M

T

U

V

W

Y

FSC
www.fsc.org
MIX
Papier | Fördert
gute Waldnutzung
FSC® C083411

Kolibri 360 GmbH
Ferdinand-Jühlke-Straße 7
99095 Erfurt, Deutschland
produktsicherheit@kolibri360.de